# Theatre

## BRIEF VERSION

# Also by Robert Cohen

*Theatre*, Ninth Edition

## For the Acting Sequence:

*Acting One*, Fifth Edition

*Acting One, Acting Two*, Fifth Edition

*Acting Power*

*Acting Professionally: Raw Facts about Careers in Acting*, Seventh Edition (with James Calleri)

*Acting in Shakespeare*

## Anthologies:

*Eight Plays for Theatre*

*Twelve Plays for Theatre*

## Other:

*Giraudoux: Three Faces of Destiny*

*More Power to You*

*Creative Play Direction* (with John Harrop)

*The Prince (play)*

*The Misanthrope (play* translation)

*The Bourgeois Gentleman (play* translation)

# Theatre

## BRIEF VERSION | Ninth Edition

**Robert Cohen**

Claire Trevor Professor of Drama
University of California, Irvine

The McGraw-Hill Companies

Connect
Learn
Succeed™

Published by McGraw-Hill, an imprint of The McGraw-Hill Companies, Inc., 1221 Avenue of the Americas, New York, NY 10020. Copyright © 2011, 2008, 2006, 2003, 2000, 1997, 1994, 1988, 1981. All rights reserved. No part of this publication may be reproduced or distributed in any form or by any means, or stored in a database or retrieval system, without the prior written consent of The McGraw-Hill Companies, Inc., including, but not limited to, in any network or other electronic storage or transmission, or broadcast for distance learning.

This book is printed on acid-free paper.

1 2 3 4 5 6 7 8 9 0 DOW/DOW 9 8 7 6 5 4 3 2 1 0

ISBN: 978-0-07-733351-5
MHID: 0-07-733351-9

Vice President, Editorial: *Michael Ryan*
Publisher: *Chris Freitag*
Sponsoring Editor: *Betty Chen*
Editorial Coordinator: *Sarah Remington*
Marketing Manager: *Pamela Cooper*
Director of Development: *Nancy Crochiere*
Developmental Editor: *Nadia Bidwell*
Editorial Intern: *Emily DiPietro*
Production Editor: *Holly Rudelitsch*
Production Service: *The Left Coast Group, Inc.*
Manuscript Editor: *Patricia Herbst*
Text and Cover Designer: *Laurie Entringer*
Photo Research: *Inge King*
Production Supervisor: *Tandra Jorgensen*
Composition: *9/12 Stone Seri f by Laserwords Private Limited*
Printing: *#45 New Era Matte Plus by RR Donnelley & Sons*

Cover: Marcia Gay Harden, Hope Davis, Jeff Daniels, and james Gandolfini in the Tony Award-winning Broadway production of God of Carnage by Yasmina Reza, directed by Matthew Warchus; sets and costumes by Mark Thompson; lighting by Hugh Vanstone; music by Gary Yershon; sound by Simon Baker/Christopher Cronin.

Photo: © Joan Marcus.

Credits: The credits section for this book begins on page C-1 and is considered an extension of the copyright page.

**Library of Congress Cataloging-in-Publication Data**

Cohen, Robert.
Theatre: brief version/Robert Cohen. 9th ed.
    p. cm.
Includes bibliographical references and index.
ISBN-13: 978-0-07-733351-5 (alk. paper)
ISBN-10: 0-07-733351-9 (mhid : alk. paper)
1. Theatre. 1. Title.
PN2101.C632  2010
792–dc22                                                    2010017973

The Internet addresses listed in the text were accurate at the time of publication. The inclusion of a Web site does not indicate an endorsement by the authors or McGraw-Hill, and McGraw-Hill does not guarantee the accuracy of the information presented at these sites.

www.mhhe.com

# About Theatre : Brief Version

Cohen´s insider´s guide to the world of theatre
puts students in the front row

## INVITING STUDENTS INSIDE THE PROCESS

Coverage of design, acting, and directing, and photo essays, provide a behind-the-scenes look at professional theatre artists performing their craft.

**What's New**

- New photo essays: Theatre in the Borderlands; Putting the Play Together: *The School for Wives;* Don Holder (lighting designer); Catherine Zuber (costume designer); Scott Lehrer (sound designer); and James Called (casting director).

- New developments in LED technology, new section on projection design, and updated coverage of theatrical design and production in Chapter 6.

- Fuller examination of the craft of acting, with an expanded comparison of acting from the "inside" (emotion memory and the Stanislavsky legacy) and acting from the "outside."

- Explanation of the different roles and responsibilities of directors and producers.

## ILLUSTRATING LIVE THEATRE

Over 300 photographs from five continents, most of them showing recent stage productions, bring to life many exciting theatre companies and productions.

**What's New**

More than 150 new production photos from around the globe, personally selected by the author to help students visualize theatrical activities.

## INTRODUCING TODAY'S WORLD OF THEATRE

Coverage features current productions and contemporary forms and trends from around the world.

### What's New

- Expanded coverage of Latin theatre.

- Addition of Lynn Nottage to the "sampling" of current American playwrights in Chapter 3.

- Revised and updated sections on postmodern theatre and international theatre in Chapter 10, "Theatre Today."

## BRINGING PRACTITIONERS AND STAGING TO LIFE

### What's New

Spotlight and Stagecraft sidebars offer insights about acting, staging, and theatre history.

## DISTINGUISHING THE CRITIC AND THE DRAMATURG

Chapter 11, significantly revised, focuses not only on the drama critic but on the dramaturg, detailing what a dramaturg does within the theatre world and presenting a profile of Jerry Patch, a professional dramaturg.

# ONLINE LEARNING CENTER (www.mhhe.com/cohenbrief9e)

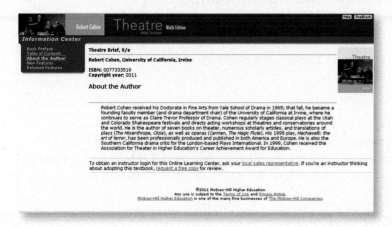

## Support for Instructors

- The **Instructor's Manual** includes learning objectives, an overview and outline, a list of significant names and terms, and suggested written works and videos that can serve as lecture launchers for each chapter.

- The **Test Bank,** organized by chapter, contains multiple-choice, true-false, and essay questions for in-class quizzes and testing. The Test Bank is also available in **EZ Test,** McGraw-Hill's flexible and easy-to-use electronic program that allows instructors to create tests keyed to the book's content.

- New **Lecture PowerPoints** highlight key points of each chapter.

## Support for Students

- *Enjoy the Play!* is a brief guide that leads students through the complete theater-going experience. It offers tips on everything from buying tickets to what to look for when watching a play. It also provides guidelines for writing a theatre report.

- **Quizzes** include multiple-choice, true-false, and essay questions to help students test their comprehension of the material, and **Internet Exercises** encourage students to explore theatre on the web.

- **Flashcards** help students review and learn important theatrical terms.

# REVIEWER ACKNOWLEDGMENTS

We would like to thank the following reviewers whose revision suggestions were uniformly thoughtful and helpful:

Claudia A. Beach, *Henderson State University*

John Patrick Bray, *Louisiana State University* Judy Cannady, *Ozarka College*

Lori Ann DeLappe, Sacramento City College

Judy Garey, *Ventura County Community College*

Richard Harmon, *Seminole Community College*

Candace M. Joice, *University of Colorado at Boulder*

Mark E. Lococo, *Loyola University Chicago*

William E. McCloskey, *Monroe County Community College*

Peter Savage, *Western Carolina University*

Robert Small, *Western Michigan University*

Michael Swanson, *Elizabethtown College*

Charlene Widener, *Hutchinson Community College*

Valerie Wilson, *University of Mississippi*

# To Whitney, Tod, and Nation Cohen

## AUTHOR ACKNOWLEDGMENTS

Every edition of this book has been in great measure dependent on the advice, knowledge, and information I have gleaned from conversations and correspondence with professional colleagues, friends, and helpful staff persons at theatres around the world, numbering well into the hundreds by now. For this ninth edition, I would particularly like to thank the following:

The superb professional theatre artists who permitted me to interview them in their workplaces and studios: Catherine Zuber, Don Holder, James Calleri, Jerry Patch, and Scott Lehrer.

The brilliant theatre photographers with whom I have had the pleasure working with personally while selecting the new photos for this edition: Geraint Lewis in England; Ken Reynolds in Scotland; Laurencine Lot in Paris; Luciano Romano in Italy; Thomas Aurin in Germany; Suzanne Barbezat in Mexico; Joan Marcus, Stephanie Berger, and Richard Termine in New York; and Craig Schwartz, Kevin Berne, and Tod Haddow in California.

My academic colleagues: Daphne Lei, Donovan Sherman, Lonnie Alcaraz, Stephen Barker, and Cameron Harvey on my own campus, and Charles Gore at the University of London, E. J. Westlake at the University of Michigan, Leonard Pronko at Pomona College, Robert Dunkerly at Clark Community College, William Sun at the Shangai Theatre Institute, and Anca Maniutiu at Babes-Bolyai University in Romania.

The many professional theatre artists and staff officers that have freely provided answers to my questions and immensely helpful responses to my requests: Bruce Lee at the Utah Shakespearean Festival; Catherine Beston at Cameron Mackintosh, Ltd.; Deb Styer at Steppenwolf Theatre in Chicago; Delphine Vasko at the Mark Taper Forum in Los' Angeles; Barclay Goldsmith and Emily Pratt at Borderlands Theatre in Tucson; Gabor Tompa and Noemi Krisztina Nagy at the Hungarian Theatre of Cluj in Romania; Joanna Klass and Marta Kubik at the Grotowski Institute in Wroclaw, Poland; Lisa England at Davidson and Choy Publicity in Los Angeles; Matthew Yeager at the Brooklyn Academy of Music; Michael McGoff at the New York Shakespeare Festival; Mihaela Ghenescu at the Sibiu International Theatre Festival in Romania; Mihai Maniutiu at the National Theatre of Cluj, Romania; Peter Meineck at the Aquila Theatre in New York; Phyllis Callazo at the *New York Times;* and Veress Ildiko at the Tamasi Aron Theatre in Sfântu Gheorghe, Romania.

And finally, the extraordinary team at McGraw-Hill and the entire production team which, while scattered all across the American continent, has evolved-through a handful of phone calls and 943 e-mails-as an ensemble of editors and production experts that has pulled this project together over the past fifteen months: Betty Chen, Sponsoring Editor; Nancy Crochiere, Director of Development; Nadia Bidwell, Developmental Editor; Holly Rudelitsch, Production Editor; Chris Schabow, Production Manager; Inge King, Photo Researcher; Pat Herbst, Copyeditor; and Sarah Remington, Editorial Coordinator.

# Letter from the Author

What's it like to be on the inside of a theatrical performance? Have you ever wondered? Well, to those of us who work in theatre, it's called "magic time."

I described such a phenomenon in the preface I wrote for the very first edition of this book, more than forty years ago.

Author Robert Cohen *(left)* sits with the executive director of the Utah Shakespearean Festival, Scott Phillips, as they study the scenic model for Cohen's production of *School for Wives* at the Tony Award—winning festival.

*At this moment, I am sitting in a darkened theatre during a technical rehearsal for a play I am directing. The action onstage has been put on hold for a few minutes while a pair of spotlights are being refocused, and I am trying to use the time to write this preface—but my eye is continually being pulled away from my pages by the dance of light now playing upon the stage. I am dazzled by its violet and amber hues, its sharp shafts of incandescence, and I gaze with admiration at the technicians who, above my head, are adjusting their instruments with precision. Looking around me, I see the sound designer carefully setting controls on her console, the scenery and costume designers seeing how their work appears in the lights and whispering to each other over their headsets, the stage managers recording lighting and sound cues in their promptbooks, and the actors standing patiently on the stage and going over their lines in their heads while they await the stage manager's cue for the rehearsal to resume.*

*Though all is relatively still and nothing but whispers can be heard, I am utterly hypnotized by these goings-on. The stage seems to be pulsing with torrents of passion and exhilaration just waiting to be unleashed. I am utterly alive with excitement and can only look back to these cold words I have written with dismay. How can I even think to express my love of theatre in these pages? How can I hope to share with you readers the awe and the thrill that course through my body when I engage in theatre's many mysteries?*

*For the theatre is not merely a body of plays, a collection of skills, or a collaborative art form. It is a life. It is people. It is people making art out of themselves. It has been the living reenactment of the human adventure for more than three thousand years, and never so alive as it is. today. Live theatre transcends by light-years anything that could be said or written about it, and I only hope I can do it justice.*

Well, I continue to feel every bit of this exhilaration today. By this time, I have staged more than a hundred productions as a director. But I have also worked as a producer, actor, stage manager, and lighting designer in both professional theatres and universities, and I have published over four hundred play reviews, articles, plays, and translations, as well as more than a dozen books on acting, directing, and dramatic literature—and just about everything in between. In the theatre, I am a throwback, a jack-of-all-trades in a field that is becoming increasingly specialized.

But my deepest connection to theatre is simply as a playgoer. Having been bitten by the drama bug when seeing my first professional play—Ray Bolger in the Broadway musical *Where's Charley?* in 1948—I have seen well over a thousand theatre productions, in almost every state in the nation and in thirty-some countries around the world. And in each of this book's nine editions, I have sought to express the exhilaration I have experienced when *seeing* theatre as much as when working to create it.

I am always asked how this book has changed over its three decades. This edition includes over one hundred new pages and two hundred new photos that I have personally taken or selected from stage productions during the three years since the previous (eighth) edition went to press. New theatre artists, new technologies, new plays and productions, and new movements and trends constitute the bulk of the revisions, but the most important overall change has been the extraordinary increase in theatre as a truly global art. For this edition, for example, I traveled to England, France, China, Romania, Poland, Spain, Mexico, and Italy over the past two years to see and report on new theatre companies and productions—and in this period I saw at least an equal number of stunning theatrical events on tours from Russia, Japan, Holland, Australia, Argentina, Canada, Italy, Poland, England, Ireland, Germany, Wales, Scotland, China, France, and Bulgaria. The "theatre world" is now a world of theatre, multicultural and accessible, coming to life right before our eyes.

Lights up! Curtain up! Enjoy the show!

—*Robert Cohen*

# Brief Contents

# Contents

## Chapter 11    The Critic and the Dramaturg   316

# Introduction

IT IS EVENING IN MANHATTAN, On Broadway and the streets that cross it-from 42nd to 54th-marquees light up, "Performance Tonight" signs materialize in front of double doors, and beneath a few box-office windows placards announce "This Performance Completely Sold Out." At Grand Central and Penn stations, trains disgorge suburbanites from Greenwich, Larchmont, and Trenton; students from New Haven and Philadelphia; day-trippers from Boston and Washington. Up from the Times Square subways troop denizens of the island city and the neighboring boroughs. At the Duffy Square "TKTS" booth, hundreds line up to buy the discount tickets that go on sale a few hours before curtain time for those shows` with seats yet to be filled. Now, converging on these few midtown blocks of America's largest city, come limousines, restaurant buses, private cars, and taxis, whose drivers search for a curbside slot to deposit their riders among the milling throng of pedestrian. Financiers and dowagers, bearded intellectuals, backpack-toting teenagers, sleek executives, hip Harlemites, arm-in-arm widows, out-of-town tourists and conventioneers, between-engagement actors, celebrities, honeymooners, and the precocious young-all commingle in this bizarre aggregation that is the New York Broadway audience. Even during (and perhaps especially during) troubled times in this vibrant city, it is as bright, bold, and varied a crowd as is likely to assemble at any single place in America.

It is eight o'clock. In close to forty theatres within two dozen blocks of each other, houselights dim, curtains rise, and spotlights pick out performers whose lives center on this moment. Here a hot new musical, here a star-studded revival of an American classic, here a contemporary English comedy from London's West End, here a new play fresh from its electrifying Seattle or Chicago premiere, here a one-woman show, here an offbeat off-Broadway musical moving to larger quarters, here a new avant-garde dance-drama, here a touring production from eastern Europe, and here the new play everyone expects will capture this year's coveted Pulitzer Prize. The hours pass.

It's 10:30. Pandemonium. All the double doors open simultaneously, as if on cue, and once again the thousands pour out into the night. At nearby restaurants, waiters stand by to receive the after-theatre onslaught. In Sardi's private upstairs room, an opening-night cast party gets under way; downstairs, the patrons rehash the evening's entertainment and sneak covert glances at the celebrities around them

The Broadway Theatre District centers on West 45th Street, which sports nine theatres within less than two blocks. Visible on the right side of the street are the Golden, Jacobs, Schoenfeld, Booth, and, with the *Lion King marquee,* the Minskoff. Directly across the street are the Imperial and the Music Box, and just across avenues on either side are the Hirschfeld and the Lyceum. This is the greatest concentration of professional theatres anywhere in the world.

and the actors heading for the upstairs sanctuary to await the reviews that will determine whether they will be employed next week or back on the street looking for new jobs.

Now let's turn back the clock. It is dawn in Athens, the thirteenth day of the month of Elaphebolion in the year 458 B.C. From thousands of low mud-brick homes in the city, from the central agora, from temples and agricultural outposts, streams of Athenians and visitors converge on the south slope of the Acropolis, Athens's great hill and home of its grandest temples. Bundled against the morning dampness, carrying breakfast figs and flagons of wine, they pay their tokens at the entrance to the great Theatre of Dionysus and take their places in the seating spaces allotted them. Each tribe occupies a separate area. They have gathered for the Great Dionysia festival, which celebrates the greening of the land, the rebirth of vegetation, and the long sunny days that stretch ahead. It is a time for revelry, for rejoicing at fertility and all its fruits. And it is above all a time for the ultimate form of Dionysian worship: the theatre.

The open stone seats carved into the hillside fill up quickly. The crowd of seventeen thousand here today comprises not only the majority of Athenian citizens but thousands of tradesmen, foreign visitors, slaves, and resident aliens as well. Even paupers are in attendance, thanks to the two obols apiece provided by a state fund to buy tickets for the poor they take their place with the latecomers on the extremities of the theatron, as this first of theatres is called. Now, as the eastern sky grows pale, a masked and costumed actor appears atop a squat building set in full view of every spectator. A hush falls over the crowd, and the actor, his voice magnified by the wooden mask he wears, booms out this text:

> I ask the gods some respite from the
>     weariness
> of this watchtime measured by years
>     I lie awake...

And the entranced spectators settle in, secure in the knowledge that today they are in good hands. Today they will hear and see a new version of a familiar story-the story of Agamemnon's homecoming and his murder, the revenge of that murder by his son, Orestes, and the final disposition of justice in the case of Orestes' act-as told in the three tragedies that constitute The Oresteia. This magnificent trilogy is by Aeschylus, Athens's leading dramatist for more than forty years. The spectators watch closely, admiring but critical. Tomorrow they or their representatives will decide by vote whether the festival's prize should go to this work, or whether the young Sophocles, whose

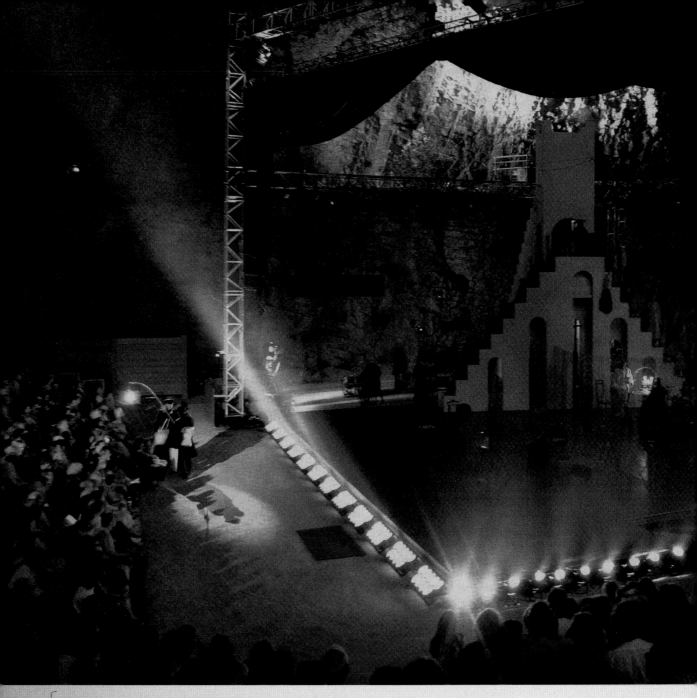

Theatre does not need a theatre building—just actors; a text, an audience, and a space to put them all together. Director Peter Brook once said "I can take any empty space and call it a bare stage," and proved it by staging his celebrated 1985 production of *Mahabharata* in the abandoned stone quarry Carrière Bouldon outside of Avignon, France. In 2006, Russian director Anatoli Vassiliev returned to this same quarry to mount a production of Alexander Pushkin's Mozart and Saiieri, with music by Vladimir Martynov and exceptional lighting—highlighting the quarry and audience as much as the dramatic action—by Ivan Danitchev.

So-called site-specific theatre may take place in a nontheatrical location such as a parking lot, a three-story home, or, in the case of *A Streetcar Named Popescu,* a chartered streetcar as it goes from Sibiu, Romania, to nearby Rasinari and back, with the audience as its passengers. The play-in-motion, adapted from the writings of a Romanian poet by Gavriil Pinte (who also directed), was presented as an experimental community project at the 2009 Sibiu (Romania) Theatre Festival.

plays were presented in this space yesterday, had better sensed the true pulse of the time. Even forty years later, the comic playwright Aristophanes will be arguing the merits and demerits of this day's work.

It is noon in London, and Queen Elizabeth I sits on the throne. Flags fly boldly atop three of the taller buildings in Bankside, across the Thames, announcing performance day at The Globe, The Rose, and The Swan. Boatmen have already begun ferrying theatergoers across the river, where The Globe will present a new tragedy by Shakespeare (something called *Hamlet,* supposedly after an old play by Thomas Kyd), and

The Rose promises a revival of Christopher Marlowe's popular *Dr. Faustus.*

Now, at The Globe, two thousand spectators have arrived for the premiere. A trumpet sounds, then sounds again, then builds into a full fanfare. Members of the audience, standing on the ground before the stage or seated in bleachers overlooking it, exchange a few final winks with their friends old and new—covert invitations to postperformance intimacies perhaps—and turn their attention to the platform stage. Through a giant door a guard bursts forth, lantern in hand, "Who's there?" he cries. In two thousand imaginations, the bright afternoon has turned to midnight, London's Bankside has given way to the battlements of Denmark's Elsinore, and a terrified shiver from the onstage actor has set up an answering chill among the audience. A great new tragedy has begun its course.

It is midnight in a basement in the East Village, or in a campus rehearsal room, or in a coffee shop in Pittsburgh, Seattle, Sioux Falls, or Berlin. Across one end of the room, a curtain has been drawn across a pole suspended by wires. It has been a long evening, but one play remains to be seen. The author is unknown, but rumor has it that this new work is brutal, shocking, poetic, strange. The members of the audience, by turns skeptics and enthusiasts, look for the tenth time at their programs. The lights dim. Performers, backed by crudely painted packing crates, begin to act.

What is the common denominator in all of these scenes? They are all theatre. There is no culture that has not had a theatre in some form, for theatre is the art of people acting out—and giving witness to—their most pressing, most illuminating, and most inspiring concerns. Theatre is at once a showcase and a forum, a medium through which a society displays its ideas, fashions, moralities, and entertainments, and debates its conflicts, dilemmas, yearnings, and struggles. Theatre has provided a stage for political revolution, for social propaganda, for civil debate, for artistic expression, for religious conversion, for mass education, and even for its own self-criticism. It has been a performance ground for priests, witch doctors, intellectuals, poets, painters, technologists, philosophers, reformers, evangelists, jugglers, peasants, children, and kings. It has taken place in caves, fields, and forests; in circus tents, inns, and castles; on street corners and in public buildings grand and squalid all over the world. And it goes on incessantly in the minds of its authors, its actors, its producers, its designers, and its audiences.

Theatre is, above all, a living art form. It does not simply consist of "plays" but also of "playing," and a play is not simply a series of "acts" but a collectivity of "acting." Just as *play* and act are both noun and verb, so theatre is both a thing and a happening, a result and a process: fluid in time, rich in feeling and human experience.

And above all, theatre is *live:* an art that continually forms before our eyes and is continually *present* to an audience even as it is *presented* by its actors. In fact, this very quality of "presentness" (or, in the actor's terminology, "stage presence") defines every great theatrical performance.

Unlike the more static arts, theatre presents us with a number of classic paradoxes:

It is spontaneous, yet it is rehearsed.
It is participatory, yet it is presented.
It is real, yet it is simulated.
It is understandable, yet it is obscure.
It is unique to the moment, yet it is repeatable.
The actors are themselves, yet they are characters.
The audience believes, yet it does not believe.
The audience is involved, yet it remains apart.

The theatre's actors "live in the moment" during performance yet carefully study, plan, and rehearse the details of their roles beforehand. And the audience responds to this performance by rooting for dramatic "characters" to achieve their goals, then applauding the "actors" who play those roles during the curtain call. Yet these paradoxes do not represent a flaw or weakness in the logic of theatrical construction; rather, they show the theatre's essential strength, which lies in its kinship and concern with the ambiguity and irony of human life. For it is we—the people of the real world—who are at the same time spontaneous yet premeditating, candid yet contriving, unique yet self-repeating, comprehensible yet fundamentally unknown and unknowable. The theatre shows us, and is us, in all of our living complexity.

Theorists of dramatic literature and of dramatic practice often ignore the theatre's paradoxes in their attempts to "explain" a play or the art of the stage. In this they do a disservice to art as well as to scholarship, for to "explain" the theatre without reference to its ambiguities is to remove its vital dynamic tension—in other words, to kill it. And although much valuable information can certainly be discovered at an autopsy table, it is information pertinent only to the appearance and behavior of a corpse.

In this book we shall not be concerned with corpses. Our task will be the harder one—to discover the theatre in being, alive and with all its paradoxes and ambiguities intact. From time to time it will be necessary for us to make some separations—between product and process, for example—but we must bear in mind at all times that these separations are conveniences, not representations or fact. In the end we shall be looking at the theatre as part of the human environment and at the ways in which we fit into that environment—as participants and observers, artists and art critics, role models and role players, actors and persons. As such, this book about the theatre is also about ourselves.

# Chapter 1

# What Is the Theatre?

WHAT IS THE THEATRE? The word *theatre* comes from the *Greek theatron,* or "seeing place." A theatre is a place where something is seen. The companion term *drama* comes from the Greek *dran,* "to do." Drama is something done, an action. Theatre: something is seen; something is done; an action is witnessed.

Today we use the word *theatre* in many ways. We use it to describe the building where plays are put on: the architecture, the structure, the space for dramatic performance—the place where "something is seen." We use the term to indicate where films are shown, as in "movie theatre." And we use it metaphorically to refer to a place where wars and surgeries occur: the "theatre of operations" and the "operating theatre." Those are "hardware" definitions of *theatre.*

The "software" definition—the activity involved in theatre—is far more important. For theatre also refers to the players (and owners, managers, and technicians) who perform in such a space and to the plays that such a company produces. This is the "something that is done." When we speak of "the Guthrie Theatre," we are referring not merely to a building in Minneapolis but also to the stage artists and administrators who work in that building and to the body of plays produced there. We also are referring to a body of ideas—a vision—that animates the Guthrie Theatre artists and integrates them with a body of plays.

A place to act and a place to watch: the basic requirements for theatre are exemplified by this 2006 open-air performance in front of the cathedral of Burgos, Spain, where three actors have erected a freestanding curtain in front of which the play will be acted, and through which the actors can "enter" as spectators sitting on the cathedral steps or standing on the surrounding sidelines watch. Theatres like this one have existed since the dawn of civilization and continue to be popular in European public gathering places.

*Theatre,* in this sense, is a combination of people, ideas, and the works of art that emanate from their collaboration.

We also use the word theatre to summon up an *occupation* that is the professional activity—and often the passion—of thousands of men and women all over the world. It is a vocation, and sometimes a lifetime devotion. *A Life in the Theatre* is the title of one theatre artist's autobiography (Tyrone Guthrie, in fact, for whom the Guthrie Theatre in Minneapolis is named), as well as the title of a play about actors by modern American dramatist David Mamet. But *A Life in the Theatre* is more universally known as the title for the unrecorded biographies of all theatre artists who have dedicated their professional lives to perfecting the special arts of acting, directing, designing,

managing, and writing for "the theatre" in all the senses described above.

Theatre as a building, a company, an occupation—let's look at all three of these usages more closely.

## THE THEATRE BUILDING

A theatre is not always an enclosed structure. The most ancient Greek theatron was probably no more than a circle of bare earth, where performers chanted and danced before a hillside of seated spectators. The requirements for building such a theatre were minimal: finding space to act and space to watch and hear. As theatre grew in popularity and importance, however, its simplicity required further elaboration. Attention had to be given to seating larger and larger numbers of people, so the hillside soon became an ascending bank of seats, each level providing a good view of the acting area. And as the theatron grew, attention had to be paid to *acoustics* (from the Greek *acoustos,* "heard"), so that the sounds coming from the stage would be protected from the wind and directed (or reflected) toward the *audience* (from the Latin *audientia,* "those who hear").

Often these spaces—for performing and for seeing and hearing—can be casually defined: the audience up there, the actors down there. Occasionally, the spaces are merged together, with the actors mingling with—and sometimes interacting with—the watchers and listeners. When the practice of selling tickets and paying actors began (more than twenty-five hundred years ago), rigid physical separation of these spaces began to be employed. Theatre buildings may be very elaborate structures. Greek theatres of the fourth century B.C.—the period immediately following the golden age of Greek playwrights—were gigantic stone edifices capable of holding upward of seventeen thousand spectators. Magnificent three-story Roman theatres, complete with gilded columns, canvas awnings, and intricate marble carvings, were often erected for dramatic festivals in the time of Nero and Caligula—only to be dismantled when the festivities ended. Grand freestanding Elizabethan theatres dominate the London skyline in illustrated sixteenth-century pictorial maps of the town. Opulent proscenium theatres were built throughout Europe and in the major cities of the United States in the eighteenth and nineteenth centuries. Many remain in full operation today, competing with splendid new stagehouses of every description and serving as the urban focus for metropolitan areas around the world. Theatres (the buildings) are central to modern urban architecture, just as theatre (the art) is central to contemporary life.

## THE COMPANY, OR TROUPE, OF PLAYERS

Theatre is a collaborative art, usually involving dozens, even hundreds, of people working closely together on a single performance. Historically, therefore, theatre practitioners of various specialties have teamed up in longstanding companies, or troupes. Since the third century B.C., such troupes of players (actors or, more literally, "playmakers") have toured the countrysides and settled in cities to present a repertory (or repertoire) of plays as

This watercolor depicts the opulent interior of Booth's Theatre in New York at its 1869 opening. This grand "temple of theatre" was built by America's finest actor of the time, Edwin Booth (the brother of Lincoln's assassin. Booth staged and performed in a classical repertory of Shakespearean plays at his theatre for four years. The side boxes, similar to those that still exist in older Broadway theatres, had poor sight lines: spectators electing to sit there were interested more in being seen than in seeing the play. The luxurious seating in the orchestra made this a particularly comfortable and elegant place to see classic theatre. Charles Witham, Booth's original stage designer, painted this watercolor; part of Witham's scenery (a street scene) is visible onstage.

a means of earning a livelihood. Generally such players have included actor-playwrights and actor-technicians, making the company a self-contained production unit capable of writing, preparing, and presenting whole theatrical works that tend to define the company itself.

Shakespeare's Globe has been meticulously reconstructed near its sixteenth-century location on the south bank of London's Thames River. The reconstruction was spearheaded by the late Sam Wanamaker, an American actor who labored many years to acquire the funding and necessary permits (the theatre has the first thatch roof laid in London since the Great Fire of 1666). This is scholarship's best guess as to the specific dimensions and features of The Globe in Shakespeare's time. Since its 1997 opening this Globe has produced a summer repertoire of the plays of Shakespeare's age, seen on a stage much like the stages they were written for.

Some of these troupes—and the works they produced—have become legendary: for example, the Lord Chamberlain's Men of London, which counted actor-playwright William Shakespeare as a member; and the Illustrious Theatre of Paris, founded and headed by the great actorwriter Moliere. These theatre companies have proven more long-lasting than the buildings that in some cases survived them. They represent the genius and creativity of theatre in a way that stone and steel alone cannot.

## THE OCCUPATION OF THEATRE

Theatre is a principal occupation of its practitioners. It is a vocation for professionals and an avocation for amateurs, yet in either case, theatre is work. Specifically,

it is that body of artistic work in which actors impersonate characters in a live performance of a play. Each aspect of theatre as occupation—work, art, impersonation, and performance—deserves individual attention.

### Work

The "work" of the theatre is indeed hard work. Rehearsals alone normally take a minimum of four to six weeks, which are preceded by at least an equal amount of time—and often months or years—of writing, researching, planning, casting, designing, and creating a production ensemble. The labors of theatre artists in the final weeks before an opening are legendary: the seven-day workweek becomes commonplace, expenditures of money and spirit are intense, and even the unions relax their regulations to allow for an almost unbridled invasion of the hours the ordinary world spends sleeping, eating, and unwinding. The theatre enterprise may involve hundreds of people: scores of different efforts—many more backstage the onstage—and the mobilization and coordination, these efforts is in itself a giant task. So when we think of the "work" embodied in the theatrical arts, we must think of work in the sense of physical toil as well as in the loftier sense of *oeuvre*, by which the French designate the sum of an artist's creative endeavor.

The work of the theatre is generally divisible into number of crafts:

*Producing*, which includes securing all necessary personnel, space, and financing; supervising all production and promotional efforts; fielding all legal matters; and distributing all proceeds derived from receipts

*Directing*, which includes controlling and developing the artistic product and providing it with a unified vision, coordinating all its components, and supervising all rehearsals

*Acting*, in which actors perform the roles of characters in a play

*Designing*, in which designers map out the visual and audio elements of a production, including the scenery, properties, costumes and wigs, makeup, lighting, sound, programs, advertising, and general ambience of the premises

*Building*, in which carpenters, costumers, wigmakers, electricians, makeup artists, recording and sound engineers, painters, and a host of other specially designated craftspeople translate the design into reality by constructing and finishing in detail the "hardware" of a show

*Crewing*, in which technicians execute in proper sequence and with carefully rehearsed timing the light and sound cues and the shifting of scenery, as well as oversee the placement and return of properties and the assignment, laundering, repair, and changes of costumes

*Stage managing*, which includes the responsibility for "running" a play production in all its complexity in performance after performance

*House managing*, which includes the responsibility for admitting, seating, and providing for the general comfort of the audience

And, above all, there is *playwriting*—and for musical theatre, *composing*—which are in a class by themselves. These are the crafts of theatre that are normally executed away from the theatre building and its associated shops. Indeed, they may take place continents and centuries away from tle productions they inspire.

Of course, the work of the theatre need not be divided exactly as the preceding list indicates. In any production, some people perform more than one kind of work; for example, many of the builders also crew. And it is not uncommon for playwrights to direct what they write, for directors to act in their own productions, and for designers to build at least some of what they design. On some celebrated occasions multitalented theatre artists have taken on multiple roles at the same time: Aeschylus, in ancient Greece, and Molière, in seventeenth-century Paris, each wrote, directed, and acted in their own plays, probably designing them as well; William Shakespeare was playwright, actor, and co-owner of the Lord Chamberlain's Men in Elizabethan times; Bertolt Brecht revolutionized both playwriting and acting when writing and directing his plays in Berlin after World War II; and Mel Brooks, in our own century, wrote the text and lyrics, composed the music, and produced his 2001 Broadway show, *The Producers*.

Theatre is also work in the sense that it is not "play." This distinction is more subtle than we might at once imagine. First, of course, recall that we ordinarily use the children's word play in describing the main product of theatre work: while children "play games," adults may "play roles" or "put on a play." This is not merely a peculiarity of the English language, for we find that the French *jeu*, the German *Spiel*, the Hungarian *játék*, the Chinese *xi*, and the Latin *ludi* all share the double meaning of the English *play*, referring both to children's games and to dramatic plays and playing. This association points to a relationship that is fundamental to our understanding of theatre: theatre *is* a kind of playing, and it is useful for us to see how and why this is so.

Theatre and games have a shared history. Both were developed to a high level of sophistication in Greek festivals: the Dionysian theatre festivals and the Olympian game—or sport—festivals were the two great cultural events of ancient Greece, each embodying the legendary Greek competition for excellence. Centuries later, the Romans merged sports and theatre in public circuses, where the two were performed side by side, often in competition with each other.

Games and serious theatre have always been related, and some plays combine these different "playing" motifs. Richard Greenberg's *Take Me Out* takes place in a baseball locker room in America, David Storey's *The Changing Room* in a rugby locker room in England. Pictured here, Andrew Lloyd Webber's musical *The Beautiful Game* takes place in Northern Ireland, on a soccer field, where it treats contemporary violence and religious intolerance rampant between English and Irish teenagers in recent decades.

And more than a millennium later, the Londoners of Shakespeare's time built "playhouses" that could accommodate dramatic productions on one day and bear-baiting spectacles (somewhat akin to more modern bullfights) on the next. The association—and popularity—of dramatic and sports entertainment continues today, where dramatizations (sitcoms, detective and courtroom dramas, even TV commercials) and games (spectator sports, quiz shows, "reality" contests) dominate television fare around the world. Meanwhile, professional athletes and stage entertainers are among the foremost (and most highly paid) celebrities of the modern age. Many a retired sports hero has even found a second career in the other type of play: acting.

This link between games and theatre is formed early in life, for "child's play" usually manifests both gamelike and dramalike aspects. Much child's play includes dressing-up and acting-out, where children create improvisations they may call "playing doctor" or "playing cops and robbers." Like drama, this play is also educational, as it helps children prepare for the necessary role-playing of adult life. Structured games are similarly instructional: hide-and-seek, for example, a playful and engrossing game, offers also an opportunity to act out one of childhood's greatest fears—the terror of separation from the parent, or "separation anxiety," as psychologists term it. Hide-and-seek affords the child a way of dealing with separation anxiety by confronting it "in play" until it loses much of its frightening power. Such "child's play" is often grounded in serious concerns, and through the act of playing the child gradually develops means of coping with life's challenges and uncertainties. The theatre's plays and playing often serve the same role for adults.

Drama and games are likewise linked in that they are among the very few occupations that also attract large numbers of wholly *amateur* "players," individuals who seek no compensation beyond sheer personal satisfaction. This is because both drama and games offer wonderful opportunities for intense physical involvement, friendly competition, personal self-expression, and emotional engagement—within limits set by precise and sensible rules. And both sport and drama also generate an audience for their activities, because the energies and passions expressed by each—common enough on children's playgrounds but rarely seen in daily adult life—can prove immensely engaging to nonparticipating spectators.

Nevertheless the theatre must be distinguished from child's play, and from sports as well, because theatre is by its nature a calculated act from beginning to end. Unlike adult games, which are open-ended, every theatre performance has a preordained conclusion. The Yankees may not win the World Series next year, but Hamlet definitely will die in the fifth act. The work of the theatre, indeed, consists in keeping Hamlet alive up to that point—brilliantly alive—to make of that foreordained end a profoundly moving, ennobling, even surprising climax.

We might say, finally, that *theatre is the art of making play into work*—specifically, into *a work of art*. It is exhilarating work, to be sure, and it usually inspires and invigorates the energies and imaginations of all who participate; it transcends more prosaic forms of labor just as song transcends grunts and groans. But it is work. That is its challenge.

## Art

The word art brings to mind a host of intangibles: creativity, imagination, elegance, power, aesthetic harmony, and fineness of form. We expect a work of art to capture something of the human spirit and to touch upon sensed but intellectually elusive meanings in life. Certainly great theatre never fails to bring together many of these intangibles. In great theatre we glimpse not only the physical and emotional exuberance of play but also the deep yearnings that propel humanity's search for purpose, meaning, and the life well lived.

Art, of course, is a supreme pursuit of humanity, integrating in a unique fashion our emotions with our intellects and our aesthetics with our revelations. Art is empowering both to those who make it and to those who appreciate it. Art sharpens thought and focuses feeling; it brings reality up against imagination

and presses creativity to the ever-expanding limits of human potential. Although life may be fragmented, inconclusive, and frustrating, a beautiful painting, choral hymn, jazz rendition, or dance video can provide us with near-instant fitegration, synthesis, and satisfaction. We might find similar values in religion as well, but art is accessible without subscribing to any particular set of beliefs; it is—for everyone—an open-ended response to life's unending puzzles. It is surely for this reason that all great religions—both Eastern and Western—have employed art and artworks (including dramatic art) in their liturgies and services from the earliest of times.

## Impersonation

The theatrical art involves actors impersonating characters. This feature is unique to the theatre and separates it from art forms such as poetry, painting, sculpture, music, performance art, cabaret acts, and like activities. Further, impersonation is the single most important aspect of the theatre; it is its very foundation.

Try to imagine what extreme conceptual difficulties the ancient creators of the theatre encountered in laying down ground rules for dramatic impersonation. How was the audience to distinguish the character being portrayed from the actor playing the character? Even today, daytime TV fans write letters to characters in their favorite soap operas, asking how they could possibly have fallen in love with some other character, and film buffs talk about what Leonardo DiCaprio said to Russell Crowe on his cell in *Body of Lies*. Given this confusion between the real actor and the fictional character he or she plays in what we like to think of as a sophisticated age, it is easy to see why the ancients had to resolve the problem of actor-character separation before the theatre could become a firmly established institution.

The solution the ancient world found was the mask. Western theatre had its true beginning that day in ancient Greece when an actor first stepped out of the chorus, placed an unpainted mask over his face, and thereby signaled that the lines he was about to speak were "in character." The mask provides both a physical and a symbolic separation between the impersonator (the actor) and the impersonated (the character), thus aiding literal-minded onlookers to temporarily suspend their awareness of the "real" world and to accept in its place the world of the stage. In a play, it must be the *characters* who have apparent life; the actors themselves are

Masks were fundamental to ancient theatre and often appear in contemporary productions, particularly in revivals of such classic works. Christina Uribe's masks, sculpted in the ancient Greek tradition, were employed in this Greek/French production of Sophocles' *Antigone* directed by Philippe Brunet for his Demodocos company, which since 1995 has been devoted to the pursuit of what Brunet calls "Dionysian mystery theatre." The production, with costumes by Florence Kukucka, was featured at the "off" schedule of France's 2008 Avignon Theatre Festival; shown here are two chorus members.

expected to disappear into the shadows, along with their personal preoccupations, anxieties, and career ambitions. This convention of the stage gives rise to what Denis Diderot, an eighteenth-century French dramatist (and author of the world's first encyclopedia), called the "paradox of the actor": when the actor has perfected his or her art, it is the *simulated* character, the mask, that seems to live before our eyes, while the real person has no apparent life at all. The strength of such an illusion still echoes in our use of the word *person,* which derives from the Latin word (*persona*) for mask.

But of course we know that the actor does not die behind the mask, and herein lies an even greater paradox: we *believe* in the character, but at the end of the play we *applaud* the actor. Not only that—as we watch good theatre we are always, somewhere in the back of our minds, applauding the actor. Our appreciation of theatre rests largely on our dual awareness of actor and character and on our understanding that they live inside the same skin.

Masks were used throughout the ancient Greek theatre period, and as we shall see in the pages that follow, they were also staples of many other theatres of the past, including the masquerade dramas of Nigeria, the *nō* and *kyōgen* drama of Japan, and the *commedia dell'arte* of Italy. They are still seen onstage today, not only in contemporary stagings of these historic forms but in expressionist and avant-garde productions. But beyond the mask's physical presence, the idea of masking—of hiding the performer while displaying the character—remains at the heart of impersonation. As such, the mask endures—often as the back-to-back masks of comedy and tragedy that adorn a theatre company letterhead—as the most fundamental symbol of theatre itself.

## Performance

Theatre is performance, but what, exactly, does *performance* mean? Performance is an action or series of actions taken for the ultimate benefit (attention, entertainment, enlightenment, or involvement) of someone else. We call that "someone else" the audience.

A strictly private conversation between two people is simply "communication." If, however, they engage in a conversation to impress or involve a third person who they know is in a position to overhear it, the "communication" becomes a "performance" and the third person becomes its "audience."

Obviously, performance is a part of everyday life; indeed, it has been analyzed as such in a number of psychological and sociological works. When two teenage boys wrestle on the schoolground, they may well be "performing" their physical prowess for the benefit of their peers. The student who asks a question in the lecture hall is frequently "performing" for the other students—and the professor "performs" for the same audience in providing a response. Trial lawyers examining witnesses invariably "perform"—often drawing on a considerable repertoire of grunts, snorts, shrugs, raised eyebrows, and disbelieving sighs—for the benefit of that ultimate courtroom audience, the jury. Politicians kiss babies for the benefit of parents (and others) in search of a kindly candidate. Even stony silence can be a performance—if, for example, it is the treatment a woman metes out to an offensive admirer. We are all performers, and the theatre only makes an art out of something we all do every day. The theatre expands our everyday performances into a formal mode of artistic expression.

The theatre makes use of two general modes of performance: presentational (or direct) and representational (or indirect). Presentational performance is the basic stand-up comedy or nightclub mode. Club performers directly and continuously acknowledge the presence of audience members by singing to them, dancing for them, joking with them, and responding openly to their applause, laughter, requests, and heckling. Dramatic forms of all ages have employed these techniques and a variety of other presentation methods as well, including asides to the audience, soliloquies, direct address, plays-within-plays, and curtain calls.

*Representational performance,* however, is the more fundamental mode of drama and is certainly the mode that makes drama "dramatic" as opposed to simply "theatrical." In representational performance, the audience watches behavior that seems to be staged as if no audience were present. As a result, the audience is encouraged to concentrate on the *events* that are being staged, not on the nature of their presentation. This allows members of the audience to "believe in" the play and forget that the characters are really actors and that the apparently spontaneous events are really a series of scripted scenes. This belief—or, to borrow Samuel Taylor Coleridge's famous double negative, this "willing suspension of disbelief"—attracts audience participation through empathy: our feeling of kinship with certain (or all) of the characters, which encourages us to identify with their aspirations, sympathize with their plights, exult in their victories, and care deeply about what happens to them. When empathy is present, the audience experiences what is often called the "magic" of theatre. Well-written and well-staged dramas make people *feel,* not just think; they draw in the spectators' emotions, leaving them feeling transported and even somewhat changed. This is as much magic as the modern world provides, and its effect is the same everywhere.

Occasionally, presentational and representational styles are taken to extremes. In the late nineteenth century, the representational movement known as *realism* sought to have actors behave onstage exactly as real people do in life, in settings made as lifelike as possible (on one occasion, a famous New York restaurant was completely disassembled and reconstructed on a stage, complete with its original moldings, wallpaper, furniture, silverware, and table linens). At times the representational ideal so dominated in certain theatres that actors spoke with their backs to audiences, directors encouraged lifelike pauses and inaudible mumblings, playwrights transcribed dialogue from fragments of randomly overheard conversations, and house managers timed intermissions to the presumed time elapsing in the play's story.

Rebelling against this extreme representationalism, the twentieth-century German playwright-director Bertolt Brecht created its opposite: a presentational style that, seeking to appeal directly to the audience

Presentational stymomake mu pretense of mimicking ordinary life. Here, director Susan Stroman creates a wonderful farcical moment in *The Producers* as "theatre queen" director Roger De Bris (played in drag by Gary Beach) desperately tries to keep his wig on.Facial expressions around the room focus the action and intensify the hilarity. Matthew Broderick and Nathan Lane (at left) are the producers of the musical's title. De Bris's hangers-on (with Roger Bart as his "common-law assistant, "Carmen Ghia) are perfectly arranged on the stairs by director Stroman to capture every possible droll expression. Scenic design is by Robin Wagner, costumes by William Ivey Long, and lighting by Peter Kaczorowski.

on a variety of social issues, featured lettered signs, songs, slide projections, chalk talks, political arguments directly addressed to the house, and an "alienated" style of acting intended to reduce empathy or theatrical "magic." Those extremes, however, exist more in theory than in practice. During naturalistic performances, we are always aware that we are watching actors perform for us, and the plays of Brecht and his followers, despite his theories, generate empathy when well performed. The fact is that theatrical performance is always both presentational and representational, though often iudifferent degrees.

Two other aspects of performance distinguish theatre from certain other forms of performance: theatre is live performance, and in most cases it is a scripted and rehearsed event.

**Live Performance** In contrast to video and cinema (although sometimes employing elements of both), the theatre is a living, real-time event in which performers and audience mutually interact, each fully aware of the other's immediate presence. This distinction turns out to be extremely important. Distinguished film stars, particularly those with theatre backgrounds (as most have), routinely return to the live dramatic stage despite the substantially greater financial rewards of film work, and they invariably prefer stage acting because of the immediate audience response that theatre provides, with its corresponding sensations of excitement and "presence." Beyond question, fundamental forces are at work in live theatre.

The first of these forces is the rapport existing between actor and audience. Both are breathing the same air; both are involved, at the same time and in the same space, with the stage life depicted by the play. Sometimes their mutual fascination is almost palpable: every actor's performance is affected by the way the audience yields or withholds its responses—its laughter, sighs, applause, gasps, and silences. Live theatrical performance is always—even in naturalistic theatre—a two-way communication between stage and house.

And second, live theatre creates a relationship among the audience members. Having arrived at the theatre as individuals or in groups of two or three, audience members quickly find themselves fused into a common experience with total strangers: laughing at the same jokes, empathizing with the same characters, experiencing the same revelations. This broad communal response is never developed by television drama, which is played chiefly to solitary or clustered viewers who (because of frequent commercials) are only intermittently engaged, nor is it likely to happen in movie houses, where audience members essentially assume a one-on-one relationship with the screen and rarely (except in private or group-oriented screenings) breaks out in a powerful collective response, much less applause. In contrast, live theatrical presentations generate audience activity that is broadly social: audience members arrive at the theatre at about the same time, they mingle and chat during intermissions, and they all depart together, often in spirited conversation about the play. Moreover, they communicate *during* the play: laughter and applause build upon themselves and gain strength from the recognition that others are laughing and applauding. The final ovation—unique to live performance—inevitably involves the audience applauding *itself,* as well as the performers, for understanding and appreciating the theatrical excellence they have all seen together. And plays with political themes can even generate collective political response. In a celebrated example, the Depression-era *Waiting for Lefty* was staged as if the audience were a group of union members; by the play's end the audience was yelling "Strike! Strike!" in response to the play's issues. Obviously, only a live performance could evoke such a response.

Finally, live performance inevitably has the quality of *immediacy*. The action of the play is taking place *right now,* as it is being watched, and anything can happen. Although in most professional productions the changes that occur in performance from one night to another are so subtle that only an expert would notice, the fact is that each night's presentation is unique and everyone present—in the audience, in the cast, and behind the scenes—knows it. This awareness lends an excitement that cannot be achieved by theatrical events that are wholly "in

Some actors prefer to act only on stage, and others only on camera, but most actors seek to do bath. The lure of the stage is hard for actors to resist, despite its significantly lower pay. Katie Holmes and John Lithgow, embracing joyously in this 2008 Broadway revival of Arthur Miller's World War II drama *All My Sons,* have extensive film and TV credentials—Holmes with more than 150 TV episodes and films, and Lithgow with more than 250, but they came with unequal stage experience. This was Lithgow's twenty-first Broadway role, and Holmes's first. Neverthess, "Holmes makes a fine Broadway debut," said the *New York Daily News* reviewer (as did your author, even playing opposite Lithgow and many distinguished veterans of the stage.

the can." One reason for the excitement, of course, is that mistakes can happen in live performance; this possibility occasions a certain abiding tension, perhaps even an edge of stage fright, which some people say creates the ultimate thrill of the theatre. But just as disaster can come without warning, so too can splendor. On any given night, each actor is trying to better her or his previous performance, and no

# Spotlight

## Film Stars on Stage Acting

The vast majority of film stars got their start acting onstage in high school or college or small theatres near their hometowns. Many of them—inducting: the most successful—return to live stage performing. Superstar Julia Roberts "felt passionate about" Richard Greenberg's *Three Days of Rain* and made her Broadway stage debut in a production of that play in 2006; in 2009 she announced herself still "stage struck" and was looking for a play to perform in on London's West End. Film and TV stars David Hyde Pierce, Katie Holmes, Jane Fonda, Matthew Broderick, Jeremy Irons, Frank Langella, James Gandolfini, Geoffrey Rush, and John Lithgow all found themselves acting on Broadway during its 2008-09 season, while *Star Trek*'s Captain Pícard Sir Patrick Stewart) and *Lord of the Rings* Gandalf (Sir Ian McKellen) trod the boards in London's sold-out production of *Waiting for Godot*. Why would these actors, plus the likes of Al Pacino, Christian Slater, Anthony Hopkins, Ethan Hawke, Meryl Streep, Denzel Washington, and Kevin Spacey in recent years, leave Hollywood for such vastly lower-paying stage work? Here are some of their replies:

Theater is about authenticity. It's in front of you; you feel it. It's so hard to feel stuff any more from film.... It can get very remote

-MERYL STREEP

If my movie career was totally terminated, I would be saddened and disappointed... but if that were to happen with the live theater, it would be devastating. [Theatre] is like a fountain that 1 have to return to

—PATRICK STEWART

One of the glorious things about the theatre is that it cannot be preserved. You can't look at it again; it's live.... Cinema's dead. You can laugh, you can cry, you can shout a the screen and the movie will carry on. But an audience in the theatre, whether it knows
it or not, is affecting the performance.... That's the stream of life at its best, isn't it?

—IAN MCKELLEN

In film, the challenge is to be able to shape a performance when the process is so piecemeal. And the
absolute joy of being onstage is you get to surf that wave. It's a much more muscular experience.

—CATE BLANCHETT

There is only so long you can go from film to film. Theatre is a more raw experience. For an actor a live audience is creative inspiration.

—JUDE LAW

My primary focus is theatre. It's the mostt satisfying place to be as an actor.

—KEVIN SPACEY

Acting on stage was the best life experience I've had.

—BEN AFFLECK

Nothing was going to stand in my way of doing that play.

—ASHLEY JUDD.
EXPLAINING WHY SHE TURNED DOWN THE TITLE ROLE IN HOLLYWOOD'S CATWOMAN TO BE ONSTAGE IN A NEW YORK REVIVAL OF CAT ON A *HOT TIN ROOF*

one knows when this collective effort will coalesce into something sublime. The actors' constant striving toward self-transcendence gives the live theatre a vitality altogether missing from performances permanently fixed and then played back, over and over, from their digitized or filmed originals. For the immediacy of live performance creates a "presentness," or "presence," that embodies the fundamental uncertainty of life itself. One prime function of theatre is to addresss the uncertainties of human existence, and the very format of live performance presents momentto-moment uncertainty right before our eyes. Ultimately, this "immediate theatre" helps us define the questions and confusions of our lives and lets us grapple, in the present, with their implications.

**Scripted and Rehearsed Performance** Theatre performances are largely prepared according to written and well-rehearsed texts, or play scripts. In this way they are often distinguished from several other forms of performance, such as improvisations, performance installations, and certain other performance art projects. Although improvisation and ad-libbing may play a role in the preparation process, and even in certain actual performances, most play productions are based on a script that was established before—and modified during—the play's rehearsal period, and most of the action is permanently set during these rehearsals as well. Mainstream professional play productions, therefore, appear nearly the same night after night: for the most part, the Broadway production of Wicked that you see on Thursday will be almost identical to the show your friend saw on Wednesday or your mother saw last fall. And if you were to read the published text, you would see on the page the same words you heard spoken or sung on the stage.

*But the text of a play is not, by any means, the play itself.* The play fully exists only in its performance—in its "playing." The script is merely the record the play leaves behind after the audience has gone home. The script, therefore, is to the play it represents only what a shadow painting is to the face it silhouettes: it outlines the principal features but conveys only the outer margins of the complexity, the color, the smell, and the spirit of the living person.

And published scripts are an imperfect record at that. Often they carry over material left out of the actual production, or they include new material the author thought of after the production was over. The published texts of Shakespeare's plays include differing versions of many of his plays, including two versions of *King Lear* now thought to have been written several years apart. When American dramatist Tennessee Williams published his *Cat on a Hot Tin Roof* after the play's premiere, he included both the third act that he originally wrote and the third act written at director Elia Kazan's request, which was actually used, and he invited readers to select their preferred version. Moreover, even a fixed script is often as notable for what it lacks as for what it contains. Plays published before the twentieth century rarely have more than rudimentary stage directions, and even now a published play tells us almost nothing about the play's nonverbal components. For how can a printed text capture the bead of sweat that forms on Hamlet's brow as he stabs Polonius, or Romeo's

nervous laugh as he tries to part dueling adversaries, or the throbbing anxiety in Beatrice's breast when she first admits to Benedick that she loves him? The published text gives us the printed but not the spoken words: it largely fails us in providing the sounds and inflections of those words, the tones and facial expressions of the actors, the color and sweep of costumes, the play of light and shadow, the movement of forms in space—and the audience response to all this—that come together in a living production.

What, then, is the chief value of play scripts? They generate theatrical productions and provide an invaluable, albeit imperfect, record of performances past. Two and a half millennia of play productions have left us a repository of thousands upon thousands of scripts, some awful, many ordinary, a few magnificent. This rich store puts us in touch with theatre history in the making and allows us a glimpse back at the nature of the originals in production. It also suggests ways in which the plays of yesterday can serve as blueprints for vital theatre today.

This, then, is the theatre: buildings, companies, and plays; work, art, impersonation, and performance; living performers and written, rehearsed scripts. It is a production; an assemblage of actions, sights, sounds, ideas, feelings, words, light; and, above all, people. It consists of playing and, of course, plays.

What is a play? That question deserves a separate chapter.

# Chapter 2

# What Is a Play?

A PLAY IS, ESSENTIALLY, WHAT HAPPENS in theatre. A play is not a thing but an event. Other theatrical events may be created onstage—performance art, rock concerts, stand-up comedy, poetry readings, storytelling, and cabaret performances—and we discuss some of these later in this chapter and later in the book as alternate theatrical presentations. But the theatre's basic unit, from the distant past to the present day, has been the play. It is the theatre's *drama*, whose origin, we remember, is from the Greek *dran*, "something done." A play is *action*, not just words in a book.

Action, however, is not merely movement. It is argument, struggle, persuasion, threats, seduction, sound, music, dance, speech, and passion. It comprises all forms of living human energy, including language, spatial dynamics, light, color, sonic shocks, aesthetic harmonies, and "remarkable things happening" from moment to moment.

Yet a play does not merely produce (or reproduce) live action; drama frames and focuses that action around a particular conflict that lends the action meaning and significance. As Shakespeare's Macbeth says, life may be "a tale told by an idiot, full of sound and fury, signifying nothing," but drama, which is also full of sound and fury, signifies all sorts of things: if not exactly answers, then at least perspectives, vocabularies, illuminating arguments, and aesthetic illuminations. Conflict—generally between characters but also within them—shapes the action into purposeful, meaningful (and meaning-filled) human struggles, the composite of which become dramatic stories against which we can judge our own struggles. A play presents characters that can serve as role models, both positive and negative; it offers themes, ideas, and revelations that we can accept, scorn, or store for future contemplation. A play is a piece of life-animated, shaped, and framed to become a work of art. It provides a structured synthesis—sometimes a critique and sometimes a celebration—of life's glories and life's confusions.

A play is also a piece of literature. In the West there has been a reading audience for plays at least since the time of the ancient Greeks, and play collections, such as Shakespeare's works, have been published since the Renaissance. Today, plays are often printed in literary anthologies, intermixed with poems, short stories, and even novels. But drama should not be thought of as merely a "branch" or "genre" of literature; it is a live performance, some of whose repeatable aspects (chiefly, the words) may be captured in a written and published text.*

Finally, a play is "playing," and those who create plays are "players." The theatrical play contains root notions of "child's play" in its acting-out and adventurism, of dressing-up in its costumes and props, and of the thrill of sportive competition in its energy and abandon. Like all play, drama is an exhibition, and in a real sense its players are willingly exhibitionistic. These are not fundamentally literary characteristics.

# CLASSIFYING PLAYS

Plays may be volatile, but they are also contained. They are framed, with a beginning and an end, and no matter how original or unique, they can be classified in a variety of ways, such as by *duration* and by *genre*. Although those categories were emphasized more in the past than they are today, they still play a part in our understanding of drama.

---

*If the arboreal metaphor is insisted upon, drama would have to be considered the "trunk" of the literary tree, not merely a branch. Certainly no other literary form—novel, epic poem, lyric poem, short story—has the same sustained level of literary excellence over twenty-five centuries as does the written dramatic work of Aeschylus, Sophocles, Euripides, Aristophanes, Marlowe, Shakespeare, Jonson, Chikamatsu, Racine, Corneille, Lope de Vega, Calderón, Molière, Congreve, Goethe, Schiller, Ibsen, Wilde, Chekhov, Shaw, O'Neill, Pirandello, Giraudoux, Sartre, Brecht, Beckett, Williams, Wilson, and so on.

## Duration

*How long is a play?* American playwright Arthur Miller admitted that when he first thought of writing for the theatre, "How long should it be?" was his most pressing question. The answer is far from obvious. And the fact that Arthur Miller had to puzzle over a play's duration makes it clear that this is something that people have to think about.

Historically, in Western drama, a "full-length" play has usually lasted between two and three hours. This is not an entirely arbitrary period of time; it represents roughly the hours between lunch and dinner (for a matinee) or between dinner and bed-time. The Jacobean playwright John Webster wrote that the actor "entertains us in the best leisure of our life, that is between meals, the most unfit time either for study or bodily exercise." Webster was thinking of the afternoon performances in the outdoor theatres of his day (c. 1615). A few years earlier, speaking of candlelit evening performances at court, Shakespeare's Theseus, in *A Midsummer Night's Dream,* asks for a play "to wear away this long age of three hours between our after-supper and bed-time." Elsewhere, however, Shakespeare refers to "the two-hours traffic of our stage" (in and about *Romeo and Juliet*), and in fact the average running time for the thirty new plays appearing on Broadway and off-Broadway in mid-2009 was an hour and fifty-three minutes. Shakespeare's sense of an audience's patience was much like our own.

But plays can be much shorter or longer. One-act plays of an hour or less or, increasingly today, "ten-minute plays" are occasionally combined to make a full theatre program. Short plays, known from ancient times, can be presented in lunchtime theatres, dramatic festivals, school assemblies, social gatherings, street entertainments, cabaret performances, or other nontraditional settings. The shortest play on record is probably Samuel Beckett's *Breath,* which can be performed in one minute. There are exceptionally long plays as well, particularly in Asia, where traditional Chinese theatre lasted all day and Indian dance-dramas lasted all night. In recent decades, eight- or nine-hour productions have proven popular in the West: Tom Stoppard's *Coast of Utopia* in London and New York, Peter Brook's *Mahabharata* in Paris, Peter Stein's production of Aeschylus's Oresteia in Berlin, and Tony Kushner's *Angels in America* in New York. (It has been reported that Robert Wilson's *Ka Mountain* was once performed over 168 continuous hours.) In short, Arthur Miller's question does not have a precise answer.

Aristotle's exemplary model of catharsis in ancient Greek tragedy is the act of Oedipus blinding himself at the climax of Sophocles' *Oedipus Tyrannos,* during which, offstage, the Theban ruler stabs through his eyeballs with his dead wife's brooches. In this 2009 French production, Bruno Ouzeau, as Oedipus, returns to the stage appropriately bloodied after this brutal act, But since this is a dramatic tragedy and not a horror film, the blood is portrayed in a stylized rather than a realistic manner, as would have been the case with the original actor of Sophocles' play, who while offstage would have replaced his standard "tragic mask" with a special mask painted with bloody eye sockets.

## Genre

Genre is a more subjective basis of classification than is duration, and the term brings with it certain critical perspectives. *Genre* is directly derived from the Old French word meaning "kind" (it is also the root word for *gender*). So to classify a play by genre is to say what kind of play it is.

Why do we care? Why don't we simply call a play a play? Mainly because knowing what kind of play it is lets people know whether or not they want to see it or read it. Just as there are different kinds of movies—comedies, westerns, action films, horror films, documentaries—so are there different genres of plays.

Historically, the first defined dramatic genres were *tragedy* and *comedy.* We are familiar with comedy in films: screenplays that humor us, make us laugh, and tickle our funny bones when we just think about them or describe them to friends. Tragedy, though, is not common in films, and not common even in the modern theatre. But many of the great masterpieces of theatre are so labeled—from ancient Greek times through Shakespeare and Racine—and tragedy deserves serious discussion.

A *tragedy* is a profoundly serious play. A tragedy always ends in the death of one or more of its main characters and focuses on a universal theme about the nature of human life and society. Tragedy was described by the Greek philosopher Aristotle (384-322 B.C.) in his monumental work Poetics, where he uses Sophocles' *Oedipus Tyrannos (Oedipus the King)* as his main example. In Aristotle's construction, the central character of a tragedy, the *protagonist,* is a person of high rank or stature.

During the play, the protagonist undergoes a decline of fortune, which leads to his or her suffering and usually to death. Integral to tragedy, according to Aristotle, is the protagonist's *self-recognition* (*anagnorisis* in Greek) of a fundamental sin (or error or flaw; the Greek word is *hamartia*). Self-recognition makes the protagonist change course (*peripeteia*) and thus leads to the protagonist's demise or dismemberment. This dire outcome elicits pity and terror from the audience and then a purging of those emotions (*catharsis*) aroused by the play's events.

In Aristotle's prime example, Oedipus, king of Thebes, hears that his city has been suffering the plague because its former king was assassinated and the assassin has not been found. Oedipus vows to find and destroy the killer. He then realizes that he himself was the killer, during an episode with an apparent stranger who, unbeknownst to him at the time, was his own father. Oedipus's wife (the victim's widow as it turns out, and therefore Oedipus's mother) kills herself at this discovery. Wracked with shame, Oedipus plucks out his eyes with the brooches he pulls from her gown, thus precipitating a catharsis in the audience.

Struggle, self-recognition, and catharsis are central to tragic drama, which is not to be confused with a merely sad or sentimental play. Tragedy is neither pathetic nor maudlin; it describes a bold, aggressive, heroic attack against huge, perhaps insurmountable, odds. Tragic protagonists (Medea, Hamlet, Macbeth, King Lear) are always flawed in some way; indeed, Aristotelian tragic theory insists that they must be flawed or at least acting in ignorance. But they are heroes, not victims. Indeed, their instigation of the play's action and their discoveries during its course bring the audience to deep emotional and intellectual involvement at the play's climax—and then great relief at its final conclusion.

The notion of *protagonist* (Greek: "carrier of the action") is complemented by the notion of antagonist ("opposer of the action"), which gives tragedy its fundamental conflict and character struggle. Tragic protagonists go forth against superhuman antagonists—gods, ghosts, fate—and their struggle, though doomed, takes on larger-than-life proportions. Through the heat of such conflict, they assume superhuman force and offer the audience a link with divine mysteries—or at least with the unconscious mind. The goal of tragedy is therefore to ennoble, not sadden, us. The tragic heroes we admire will fall, but not before they heroically challenge the elements, the universe, and death. They carry us to the brink of disaster, but it is *their* disaster and not ours—not yet at

Shakespeare took Sophocles' blinding motif one step further in his tragedy *King Lear,* some two thousand years later. Lear's friend, the Duke of Gloucester, is brutally blinded onstage by Lear's daughter and her husband. Here, Japanese actor Kazunori Akitaya plays the blinded Gloucester in a stylized production by the Globe Theatre of Tokyo

least. Experiencing a tragedy allows us to contemplate and rehearse in our own minds the great conflicts that may await us.

Can a modern play be termed a tragedy? Playwright Arthur Miller's *Death of a Salesman* (1947)—whose protagonist, an ordinary American salesman, commits suicide after realizing he has failed to fulfill his family obligations—has often been considered an attempt at tragedy. Miller named his protagonist "Willy Loman" (i.e., *low man*) to challenge the classical idea that a protagonist must be of high rank.

Arthur Miller's *Death of a Salesman* is often considered the American theatre's finest tragedy, since its protagonist, the likeable but morally flawed Willy Loman, experiences a decline of fortune that eventually leads to his suicide. Here, in a dream sequence from the much-heralded 1999 Goodman Theatre production, Brian Dennehy as Willy (*center*) leans on the shoulders of his two sons (played by Kevin Anderson and Ted Koch), not as they are now but as he remembers them from better days.

The antagonists Willy faces in the play are not gods but faceless bureaucrats, insensitive children, and an impersonal capitalistic economic system. Is the play a tragedy? *You* must decide. The classification of plays into genres is not a science but a matter of opinion. Even Shakespeare made fun of scholars who treated genres as absolute categories to be applied to each and every work.

The fact is that genres are mainly important to play producers and publishers who want to let the public know what sort of drama they are being asked to attend or read. The editors of the first edition (the First Folio) of Shakespeare's complete dramatic works divided them into Tragedies, Comedies, and Histories. The last category refers to plays about England's kings, more or less based on historical accounts. But some of those "histories" could be construed as tragedies—and vice versa—and some of the comedies include scenes as tragic as anything in Shakespeare's (or the world's) dramatic repertoire.

*Comedy* is a very clear and very popular genre and has been a staple of the theatre since ancient times. Playwrights of all eras have written comedies— sometimes with serious themes, sometimes with particularly dark humor (whereupon they may be classed as *dark comedy*). At yet other times playwrights have no purpose other than to create continuous hilarity through common devices like full-stage chases, mistaken identities, lovers hiding in closets or under tables, sexual puns, switched potions, switched costumes (often transsexual), misheard instructions, and sheer physical buffoonery; such works are usually labeled *farce*. Comedies have been immensely popular in all ages, but because they are topical, about ordinary life rather than larger-than-life heroes, they usually go out-ofdate sooner. And because they rarely probe as deeply into human destiny as do tragedies, they offer less fertile ground for academic scholarship and are hence less frequently published in anthologies, less frequently examined in scholarly literature, and less

The history genre remains popular—as long as the issues are universal and the characters fascinating. Here, in Robert Bolt's *A Man for All Seasons*, King Henry VIII (played by Patrick Page) awards the chain of the office of chancellor to Sir Thomas More (Frank Langella). The year is 1529; as the play goes on, these two monumental figures in English history battle ferociously over issues of church versus state, law versus loyalty, and papal law versus Reformation—particularly when King Henry wants to annul his marriage. As with most history plays, the costumes and jewelry (in this production designed by Catherine Zuber—see more in the photo essay on her work in the chapter on design) are based on extensive historical research.

occasional play about a historical figure; examples include George Bernard Shaw's *Saint Joan,* Bertolt Brecht's *Galileo,* and Robert Bolt's *A Man for All Seasons* about Sir Thomas More. More common today is the *documentary drama,* which is a play that makes use of actual documents—court records, for example, or transcribed interviews, or in one case recordings taken from the black boxes retrieved from crashed airplanes. *Tragicomedy,* as the name implies, is a genre that attempts to blend the two original genres. Maintaining a serious theme but varying the approach from serious to humorous and leaving the hero alive at the end, tragicomedy relaxes tragedy's larger-than-life scale and is sometimes known as "tragedy that ends happily." *Melodrama,* whose heyday was the nineteenth century, is an outwardly serious drama embellished with spectacular stagings and flamboyant dialogue (e.g., "Curse their old families—a bilious, conceited, thin lot of dried up aristocracy. I hate 'em. It makes my blood so hot I feel my heart hiss!"),* along with highly suspenseful, contrived plotting. Presenting a simple and finite confrontation between good and evil, rather than a complex exposition of universal human aspirations and sufferings, melodramas cannot sustain unpleasant endings or generate catharsis. When performed today, they are almost always staged as parodies of their originals and are played for laughs. The *musical* of course is a major genre—the most commercially successful genre in the American theatre today—and is the subject of a later chapter in this book.

Potentially there are as many theatrical genres as the imaginative playwright (or the diligent critic) wishes to define. "An Anti-Play," "A Conversation in One Act," "A Grim Comedy," and "A Tragic Farce" are a few of the "genres" modern authors—generally with tongue in cheek—have invented and claimed for one or another of their dramatic works. Certainly, no system of classification should obscure the fact that every play is unique and the grouping of any two or more plays into a common genre is only a convenience for purposes of comparison and analysis. But applying genres can help us comprehend the broad spectrum of purposes to which plays may be put, and help us to perceive important similarities and differences between individual works. For the theatre artist, awareness of the possibilities inherent in each genre—together with knowledge of the achievements made in each— stimulates the imagination and aids in setting work standards and ambitions.

frequently placed into college course syllabi. Nevertheless, some comedies (particularly those of Shakespeare and Molière) are considered true masterpieces of human observation, and comedy's place in the theatre world is every bit as secure as tragedy's—and its impact on audiences is as strong now as it was in Aristophanes' day.

Other genres are defined from time to time, and playwrights often have fun creating genres of their own, but none have any truly definitive value. The *history play,* mentioned briefly above, did not die with Shakespeare. It has come into the modern era as the

---

*From Dion Boucicault's *The Octoroon* (1859).

(*Left*) Satire is a dramatic style as old as Aristophanes, who brazenly ridiculed Socrates, Euripides, and contemporary Athenian politicians in his Greek comedies. Comedian Will Ferrell wielded a satirical pen in writing and starring in *You're Welcome America: A Final Night with George W. Bush,* which opened on Broadway in 2009 weeks before the end of the president's final term. Ferrell's success was achieved by depicting what he considered the president's limitations with light-hearted comic banter rather than direct attacks.

(*Below*) French "vaudeville" was a popular theatrical genre combining bald-face farce with brief songs. To open their 2008-09 season, Southern California's South Coast Repertory adapted such a work, Eugène Labiche and Marc Michel's 1851 *An Italian StrawHat.* The physical humor—upper-class characters heading for a wedding with their pants down, figuratively and in one case literally—blended with playful songs and skirmishes, proved as popular in the twenty-first century as in the nineteenth. Erika Whalen is the bride, Alan Blumenfeld her trouser-less father; the delightful costumes were designed by Shigeru Yaji.

# DRAMATURGY- THE CONSTRUCTION OF DRAMA AND DRAMATIC PERFORMANCE

A play is action, but it is *patterned* action. Unlike the action of a street riot, say, dramatic action has clearly identifiable components and a specified beginning and ending. Even when improvised or radically experimental, a play's dramatic action tends to be crafted in well-understood compositional patterns. We call these patterns a play's *dramaturgy*.

Action provides a play's thrills and excitement; dramaturgy provides momentum and meaning—so that a play's action becomes increasingly compelling and significant as the play heads toward an eventual climax and resolution. Dramaturgical devices lead an audience to see the play's action as *consequential,* rather than as a random series of events. The most successful dramaturgy, though buried deep within a play's dialogue and appearance, can create a profound engagement with the audience's thoughts, fantasies, and feelings.

Students of drama often visualize two intersecting axes along which they can analyze a play's dramaturgical techniques: a "vertical" axis where the play's various components (what it's composed of) can be identified, and a "horizontal" axis where the temporal structure of the performance—the order and timing of what happens—can be examined. Both perspectives are immensely useful to students, appreciators, and creators of drama.

## Drama's Components: The Vertical Axis

The division of plays into components is an ancient analytical practice begun by Aristotle. He identified six components of a tragedy (by which he meant a generally serious drama): plot, characters, theme, diction, music, and spectacle—in that order. With some modification and elaboration, Aristotle's list still provides a breakdown of the major elements of most dramas, although the importance of each component is a matter of continuing controversy.

**Plot** Although we may think of *plot* as synonymous with *story,* the meanings of the two words are quite different. The story is simply the narrative of what happens in the play, as might be described by someone who has seen it. *Plot* refers to the mechanics of storytelling: the sequencing of the characters' comings and goings, the timetable of the play's events, and the specific ordering of the revelations, reversals, quarrels, discoveries, and actions that take place onstage. (In English theatres of the sixteenth century, a written "platte," or "plotte," was hung on the wall backstage to remind the actors of the play's order of major events, entrances, and exits.) Plot is therefore the *structure of actions:* both outer actions (such as Romeo stabbing Tybalt) and inner ones (such as Romeo falling in love with Juliet).

Perhaps Aristotle listed plot first among drama's six elements because plot is what makes drama dramatic. Creating a compelling plot is often the most demanding test of a playwright's skill, for plot normally keeps the audience involved (and *increasingly* involved) during the play's two-plus-hour duration.

The primary demands of plot are logic and suspense. To satisfy the demand for logic, the actions portrayed must be plausible, and events must follow one upon another in an organic rather than an arbitrary fashion. To create and sustain suspense, however, these actions must set up expectations for further actions, drawing the audience through a plot that seems to move inescapably toward an ending that may be sensed but is never wholly predictable. "Well-made plays," as farces and melodramas of the late nineteenth century were called, relied heavily on intricate and suspenseful plots, and elements of these forms (or in some cases the forms themselves) are evidenced in many stage plays today.

**Characters** Characters are the human figures—the impersonated presences—who undertake the actions of the plot. Their potency in the theatre is measured by our interest in them as *people.* The most brilliant plotting cannot redeem a play if the audience remains indifferent to its characters; therefore, the fundamental demand of a play's characters is that they make the audience *care.* Characters cannot be mere stick figures, no matter how elaborately detailed. The great dramatic characters of the past—Hamlet, Juliet, Stanley Kowalski, Blanche DuBois, to name a few—bring to an experienced theatergoer's or playreader's mind personalities as vivid and memorable as the personalities of good friends (and hated enemies). They are whole images, indelibly human, alive with the attributes, feelings, and expectations of real people. We can identify with them. We can sympathize with them.

Character depth is what gives a play its psychological complexity, its sensuality, and its warmth. Without character depth we cannot experience love, hate, fear, joy, hope, despair—any of the emotions we expect to derive from theatre. And a theatre devoid of those emotions that stem from the humanness of the characters portrayed would soon be a theatre without an audience.

**Theme** A play's theme is its abstracted intellectual content. The theme may be described as the play's overall statement: its topic, central idea, or message, as the case may be. Some plays have obvious themes, such as Euripides' *The Trojan Women* (the horrors of war) or Molière's *The Bourgeois Gentleman* (the foolishness of social pretense). Other plays have less clearly defined themes, and the most provocative of these plays have given rise to much scholarly controversy. *Hamlet, Oedipus Tyrannos,* and *Waiting for Godot* all suggest many themes, and each play has spawned fierce debates about which of its themes is central.

Nothing demands that a play have a single theme, however, or that a theme be reducible to any straightforward intellectual generalization. Indeed, plays that are too obviously theme-intensive are often considered too propagandistic or academic for theatrical success: "If you want to send a message," one Broadway saying goes, "use Western Union." (Today we would say, "Text me.") Moreover, although the themes of plays address the central questions of society and húmanity, a play's theatrical impact normally hinges—at least in the Aristotelian model—on the audience's engagement with its plot and characterization.

Nevertheless, a play must have *something* to say, and that something—its theme—must seem pertinent to the audience. Otherwise why would we leave the outside world—filled as it is with actions and "scenes"—to come to the theatre? Further, the play must be sufficiently focused and limited to give the audience at least some insight into that something within its framework. Plays that try to say nothing, or, conversely, plays that try to say everything, rarely have even a modest impact no matter how entertaining or well plotted they may be. Thus playwrights working in every genre, be it tragedy, comedy, melodrama, musical comedy, or farce, have from the beginning of theatrical history learned to narrow and focus their field of intellectual investigation when crafting a play.

**Diction** Aristotle's fourth component, diction, relates not merely to the pronunciation of spoken dialogue. More crucially it refers to the literary character of a play's text, including its tone, imagery, cadence, and articulation, and to the playwright's use of literary forms and figures of speech such as verse, rhyme, metaphor, apostrophe, jest, and epigram.

The value of poetry has been well established from the theatre's beginning; indeed, until fairly recent times, most serious plays were written largely in verse. Today, although the use of verse is relatively rare, all plays continue to demonstrate carefully crafted language. Many, such as those by Tom Stoppard and Richard Greenberg, feature brilliant repartee, stunning epigrams, witty arguments, and dazzling tirades. Other, quite different, sorts of plays may feature rough-textured slang, local dialects, and crude vulgarities, or a poetry of silences and nearly inarticulate mutterings—dictions that can be no less effective than Stoppard's flamboyantly crafted verbal pyrotechnics.

The diction of a play is by no means the creation of the playwright alone. It is very much the product of the actor as well, and for that reason throughout the history of Western theatre, an effective stage voice has been considered the prime asset of the actor. Even today, the study of voice is a primary course at most schools and conservatories of classical acting. The chief aim of such study is to create an acting voice capable of dealing in spectacular fashion with the broad palette of dramatic diction demanded by the works of the world's most noted playwrights.

**Music** Any discussion of music, Aristotle's fifth component, forces us to remember that plays in Aristotle's time were sung or chanted, not simply spoken. That mode of presentation has all but disappeared, yet the musical component remains directly present in most plays performed today and is indirectly present in the rest.

Aristotle's "music" can take many forms. Songs are common in the plays of Shakespeare, as well as in the works of many modern writers. Many naturalistic dramatists work familiar songs into their scripts, sometimes by having the characters sing, at other times by having them play recordings onstage. Anton Chekhov and Tennessee Williams both make extensive use of offstage music. For example, a military marching band can be heard in Chekhov's *The Three Sisters,* and offstage dance-hall music can be heard in Williams's *Streetcar Named Desire* and music from a nearby cantina in his *Night of the Iguana.* More subtly, the music of a play may include a live or an electronically prerecorded sound score, created and implemented by a sound designer who can provide anything from incidental music between scenes to a full soundscape that intensifies the play's emotional range, punctuates its action, intensifies its rising suspense and climaxes, and moves its audience to an ever-deepening engagement.

Spectacle can be simple but still profound. The image of the aged Nagg and Nell in their ashcans, trying to kiss, in Samuel Beckett's grimly absurdist *Endgame* is unforgettable. Shown here are Liz Smith and Geoffrey Hutchings in their 2004 performance at London's Albert Theatre.

Not all of this will be tuneful: vocal tones, footsteps, sighs, shouts, railroad whistles, gunshots, animal cries, the hubbub of crowds, the shrilling of a telephone, and amplified live or special effects (heartbeats, heavy breathing, otherworldly harmonies) may combine into a sonic orchestration of such dramatic force that it can thrill even persons wholly unacquainted with the language of the dialogue.

**Spectacle** Aristotle's sixth component, spectacle, encompasses the visual aspects of production: scenery, costumes, lighting, makeup, properties, and the overall *look* of the theatre and stage. It would be wrong to infer that *spectacle* is synonymous with *spectacular,* for some productions are quite restrained in their visual artistry. Rather, *spectacle* here refers to its etymological root, meaning "something seen." Although this point may seem obvious, it is crucial. Theatre is as much a visual experience as it is an aural, emotional, and intellectual experience: the ancient Greeks clearly had this in mind when they chose the name *theatron* ("seeing place") to designate the site of their performances.

Much as the cinema has been called the art of moving pictures, so the theatre might be called the art of fluid sculpture. This sculpture is fashioned in part from the human body in motion and in part from still or moving scenery and props—natural and manufactured items of both dramatic and decorative importance, all illuminated by natural or artificially modulated light. It is a sculpture that moves in time as well as in space. And although it is primarily a support for the plot, characters, and theme of a play, it has an artistic appeal and an artistic heritage all its own. Certainly some ardent patrons of the theatre pay more attention to settings and costumes than to any other aspect of a play, and dramatic visual effects— such as the chandelier that crashes to the ground at the end of the first act of *Phantom of the Opera*—have occasionally become the most noted highlight of a production.

Memorable visual elements can be both grand and prosaic, imposing and subtle. Nineteenth-century romanticism, which survives today primarily in the form of grand opera, tends to favor elaborate palaces, impressive crowd scenes, parades of circus animals, and lavish, overscale costumes. In contrast, twentieth-and twenty-first-century dramas are more likely to be dressed in domestic environments and archetypal images: Jimmy and Cliff reading newspapers while Alison irons a shirt in John Osborne's *Look Back in Anger;* Laura playing with her glass animals in Tennessee Williams's *The Glass Menagerie;* Mother Courage pulling her wagon in Brecht's *Mother Courage;* and Nagg and Nell living in the ashcans of Samuel Beckett's *Endgame*. In the long run, the conceptual richness and precision of a play's visual presentation are far more telling than grandeur for its own sake.

**Conventions** To those six Aristotelian components we shall add a seventh, discrete, item that Aristotle apparently never saw reason to consider: theatrical conventions. The agreement between audience and actor—by which the audience willingly suspends its disbelief and accepts the play as a new and temporary "reality"—entails our unthinkingly accepting a set of conventions such as "when the stage lights fade out, the play (or act) is over." Other common conventions of the Western stage over the centuries have included the following:

- When an actor turns directly away from the other actors and speaks to the audience, the other characters are presumed not to hear him. This is the convention of the *aside* (a line addressed directly to the audience, unheard by the other characters).

- When actors all leave the stage and then they or others reenter (particularly when the lights change), time has elapsed. And if one actor then says to another, "Welcome to Padua," we are now in Padua even if in the previous scene we were in Verona.

- When actors "freeze," we are seeing some sort of "dream state" (of one of the characters, presumably), and the words we hear are to be considered a character's thoughts, not audible speech.

We can recognize conventions most clearly in theatres unlike our own (that is probably why Aristotle, knowing no theatre but his own, never thought of defining them). In the *wayang kulit* shadow puppet theatre on Bali, for example, the play is over when the "tree of life" puppet, previously seen only in motion, comes to a standstill at the center of the stage. In the ancient *nō* drama of Japan, the audience realizes that words sung by chorus members are to be considered speeches spoken by the actors who are dancing, and the audience interprets gestures with a fan to indicate wind, rain, or the rising moon. In the Chinese *xiqu*, or traditional opera, a character entering the bare stage while holding a boat paddle is understood to be rowing across a river, and one entering with a whip is understood to be riding a horse.

Theatrical conventions permit shorthand communication with the audience without the encumbrance of extensive physical elaboration or acting-out. If a locale can effectively be changed by the convention of a simple light shift instead of by moving a ton of scenery, the theatre saves money and the audience saves time. Thus stage violence is usually executed conventionally (that is, with little physical mayhem)

According to one Chinese theatre convention, a man paddling with an oar signifies "boatman," "boat," and "water" alike. Here, famed Shanghai actor Liu Yilong portrays the boatman ferrying his passengers in *The Meeting by the Lake,* a classic work of the Chinese *xiqu* (traditional opera) form.

rather than with lifelike (or cinematic) verisimilitude. The impossibility of realistically portraying severed torsos, rupturing intestines, or bleeding limbs onstage ordinarily outweighs any dramatic advantage in doing so; and the theatrical convention ("stab, grab, scream, collapse, and die") can be accepted fully if performed with emotional and psychological (though not physical) authenticity.

Each theatrical era sets up its own system of conventions, which the audience will accept without the slightest reflection. In modern times, playwrights and directors have deliciously exploited the theatrical conventions of the past or invented new ones. Peter Shaffer's *Black Comedy,* which is set in a room during a complete blackout, employs a convention that Shaffer attributes to the Chinese: when the lights are on, they are "off," and when they are off, they are "on." Eugene O'Neill's *Strange Interlude* and Steven Berkoff's *Kvetch* give us to understand that when the actors "freeze" and speak, we in the audience—but not the other characters in the play—hear their unspoken thoughts. Jean Anouilh's *Antigone* uses a variation on the Greek device of the chorus: a single man speaks with the author's voice as the characters onstage freeze in silence. Arthur Miller's *After the Fall* places an imaginary psychiatrist in the midst of the audience, and the play's protagonist repeatedly interrupts the action of the drama to address his analyst in highly theatrical therapy sessions. And thus, there is no formal requirement for the establishment of theatrical conventions, except that audiences must "agree" to suspend disbelief and accept them. And they do.

The seven components of every play—Aristotle's six plus the conventions that frame them—are the raw material of drama. All are important. Indeed, the theatre could not afford to dispense with any of them. Some plays are intensive in one or more components; most great productions show artistry in all. The balancing of these components in theatrical presentation is one of the primary challenges facing the director, who on one or another occasion may be called upon mainly to clarify and elaborate a theme, to find the visual mode of presentation that best supports the action, to develop and flesh out the characterizations in order to give strength and meaning to the plot, to heighten a musical tone in order to enhance sensual effect, or to develop the precise convention—the relationship between play and audience—that will maximize the play's artistic impact. For as important as each of these components is to the theatrical experience, it is their combination and interaction, not their individual splendor, that is crucial to a production's success.

## Drama's Timeline: The Horizontal Axis

The action of a dramatic performance plays out over time. The horizontal axis of dramaturgy is where we focus on temporal *structure*. Here, this term refers to much more than the events contained within the play's published (or unpublished) script. It pertains to three major groupings of a performance: *preplay, play,* and *postplay.* The play itself, quite properly, receives the most attention from drama scholars and theorists, but the surrounding preplay and postplay have been part of the overall theatrical experience from the theatre's earliest days and also merit attention.

**Preplay** Preplay begins with the attraction of an audience. Theatre has had this responsibility in every era, for there can be no "seeing place" *(theatron)* without seers.

The procession is one of the oldest known ways of publicizing the theatre. The circus parade, which still takes place in some of the smaller towns of Europe and the United States, is a remnant of a once-universal form of advertisement for the performing arts that probably began well in advance of recorded history. The Greeks of ancient Athens opened their great dramatic festivals with a *proagon* (literally, "pre-action"), in which both playwrights and actors were introduced at a huge public meeting and given a chance to speak about the plays they were to present on subsequent days. The Elizabethans flew flags atop their playhouses on performance days, and the flags could be seen across the Thames in "downtown" London, enticing hundreds away from their commercial and religious activities. The lighted marquees of Broadway theatres around Times Square and of London theatres in the West End are a modern-day equivalent of the flags that waved over those first great English public theatres. Today, posters, illustrated programs, multicolor subscription brochures, full-page newspaper advertisements, staged media events, articulate press releases, and, in New York, flashy television commercials summon patrons out of the comfort of their homes and into the theatre. Far from being an inconsequential aspect of theatre, publicity today occupies a place of fundamental importance in the thinking of theatrical producers, and it commands a major share of the budget for commercial theatrical ventures.

Once gathered at the theatre's door, the audience remains a collection of individuals preoccupied with their daily concerns. Now the theatre must shift their focus to the lives of dramatic characters, and transform the spectators into a community devoted to the concerns of the play. Ushers may lead them into the audience area, showing them to their seats and providing them with written programs that will prepare them for the fiction they are about to see. Preshow music or perhaps an ominously pulsing sound effect may be used to set a mood or tone, while stage lights may "warm" a curtain or illuminate the revealed stage and scenery with a romantic or eerie glow, creating the anticipation of dramatic actions about to take place. There may be some visible stage activity, such as a ticking clock or flickering carnival lights or perhaps a few actors engaged in quiet preshow activity , as incoming audience members observe the scene. In

Posters—on theatre walls, in subway stations and shop windows, and on special billboards—around theatre towns are universal for advertising current theatre productions. Here, in Tokyo's downtown Ginza district, theatergoers study posters advertising the new production at the Kabuki-za theatre, the world's outstanding showcase for Japanese kabuki drama.

most cases there will be much to look at, but unike moviegoers, the audience for a live theatre production will be aware of *itself,* because the seating area is fully illuminated and audience members are free to greet and chat with each other. As a live art, theatre's liveliness in part results from the fact that audience members are always part of the action and share their responses— laughter, sighing, and applause—with the actors as well as with one another.

Finally, a swift conclusion to the transition begins, usually with an announcement for audience members to turn off their cell phones so that the outside world will remain sealed out for the show's duration. Then the houselights dim, and (if all goes well) the audience is transported into the world of the play. In the familiar theatrical saying, "It's magic time."

**Play** In contrast to staged events such as performance art and stand-up comedy, a play normally contains a structured sequence of identifiable elements.

Here again, Aristotle affords some help, telling us that drama has a beginning, a middle, and an end. In his *Poetics,* Aristotle even proffers some details about these elements, all in the context of his first dramatic component: plot. We can elaborate on Aristotle's beginning, middle, and end somewhat, for four fairly consistent features are routinely recognized in the orderly plot sequencing of a conventionally Aristotelian dramatic experience: exposition, conflict, climax, and denouement.

*The exposition* No important play has ever begun with a character dashing onstage and shouting, "The house is on fire!" At best such a beginning could only confuse members of the audience, and at worst it could cause them to flee in panic. At that point they would have no way of knowing what house or why they should even care about it. Most plays, whatever their style or genre, begin with dialogue or action calculated to ease us, not shock us, into the concerns of the characters with whom we are to spend the next two hours or so.

*Exposition* is a word not much in favor now, coming as it does from an age when play structure was considered more cut-and-dried than it is today. But it remains a useful term, referring to the background information the audience must have in order to understand what's going on in the action of a play.

In the rather mechanical plotting of "well-made plays," the exposition is handled with little fanfare. A few characters—often servants (minor figures in the action to follow)—discuss something that is about to happen and enlighten one another (and, of course, the audience) about certain details around which the plot will turn. Consider these lines from the opening scene of Henrik Ibsen's 1884 classic, *The Wild Duck:*

*PETTERSEN, in livery, and JENSEN, the hired waiter, in black, are putting the study in order. From the dining room, the hum of conversation and laughter is heard.*

**PETTERSEN:** Listen to them, Jensen; the old man's got to his feet—he's giving a toast to Mrs. Sorby.

**JENSEN:** (*pushing forward an armchair*) Do you think it's true, then, what they've been saying, that there's something going on between them?

**PETTERSEN:** God knows.

**JENSEN:** He used to be quite the lady's man, I understand.

**PETTERSEN:** I suppose.

**JENSEN:** And he's giving this party in honor of his son, they say.

**PETTERSEN:** That's right. His son came home yesterday.

**JENSEN:** I never even knew old Werle had a son.

**PETTERSEN:** Oh, he has a son all right. But he's completely tied up at the Hoidal works. In all the years I've been here he's never come into town.

**A WAITER:** (in the doorway of the other room) Pettersen, there's an old fellow here ...

**PETTERSEN:** (mutters) Damn. Who'd show up at this time of night?

After a few more lines, Pettersen, Jensen, and the waiter make their exits and are seen no more. Their function is purely expository—to pave the way for the principal characters. Their conversation is a contrivance intended simply to give us a framework for the action—and the information they impart is presented by means of a conversation only because a convention of realism decrees that words spoken in a play be addressed to characters, not to the audience.

In contrast, the exposition of nonrealistic plays can be handled more directly. It was the Greek custom to begin a play with a prologue preceding the entrance of the chorus and the major play episodes; the prologue was sometimes a scene and sometimes a simple speech to the audience. Shakespeare also used prologues in some of his plays. In one particularly interesting example, Shakespeare's *Romeo and Juliet,* the play begins with an actor identified as "Chorus" who comes onto the stage and addresses the audience directly, telling where the play is presumed to take place (the city of Verona), explaining what the theatre's stage doors are to represent (the "two households" of the leading characters), and previewing the characters and plot:

**CHORUS:** Two households, both alike in dignity,
In fair Verona, where we lay our scene,
From ancient grudge break to new mutiny,
Where civil blood makes civil hands unclean.
From forth the fatal loins of these two foes
A pair of star-crossed lovers take their life;
Whose misadventured piteous overthrows
Do with their death bury their parents' strife.
The fearful passage of their death-marked love,
And the continuance of their parents' rage,
Which, but their children's end, nought could remove,
Is now the two hours' traffic of our stage;
The which if you with patient ears attend,
What here shall miss, our toil shall strive to mend.

By saying "our toil," the Chorus presents himself not as a character but as a member of the acting company, reminding the audience that putting on a "play" requires "work" from the actors as well as "patient ears" from the audience. In today's theatre, of course, some of the exposition the Chorus shares with us (normally the setting, at least) will instead be in a printed program distributed as we enter.

**The conflict** Now is the time for the character to enter shouting, "The house is on fire!" It is a truism that drama requires conflict; in fact, the word *drama*, when used in daily life, implies a situation fraught with conflict. No one writes plays about characters who live every day in unimpaired serenity; no one would ever choose to watch such a play. Conflict and confrontation are the mechanisms by which a situation becomes dramatic.

Why is this so? Why is conflict so theatrically interesting? The reasons have to do with plot, theme, and character. Plot can hold suspense only when it involves alternatives and choices: Macbeth has strong reasons to murder King Duncan and strong reasons not to. If he had only the former or only the latter, he would project no real conflict and we would not consider him such an interesting character. We are fascinated

Drama requires conflict, and Shakespeare's tragedy *Othello* is filled with it: between father and daughter, soldiers and officers, and, fatally, husbands and wives. In the Royal Shakespeare Company's 2009 production directed by Kathryn Hunter, Patrice Naiambana as Othello furiously hurls Natalia Tena as Desdemona to the ground in a jealous rage as the conflict between them escalates.

by such a character's actions largely in light of the actions he rejects and the stresses he has to endure in making his decisions. In other words, plot entails not only the actions of a play but also the inactions—the things that are narrowly rejected and *do* not happen. A character's decision must proceed from powerfully conflicting alternatives if we are to watch this behavior with empathy instead of mere curiosity. In watching a character act, the audience must also watch the character think; a playwright gets the character to *think* by putting him or her into conflict.

Conflict may be set up between characters as well as within them; it may be reducible to one central situation, or it may evolve out of many. Whatever the case, conflict throws characters into relief and permits the audience to see deeply into the human personality. To see a character at war with herself or in confrontation with another is to see how that character *works,* and this is the key to our caring.

The theme of a play is ordinarily a simple abstraction of its central conflict. In Sophocles' *Antigone,* for example, the theme is the conflict between divine law and civil law; in *Death of a Salesman,* it is the conflict between Willy's reality and his dreams. Conflicts are plentiful in farces and comedies as well; the conflicts inherent in a "love triangle," for example, have provided comic material for dramatists for the past two millennia. Many of the more abstract philosophical conflicts—independence versus duty, individuality versus conformity, idealism versus pragmatism, integrity versus efficiency, pleasure versus propriety, progress versus tradition, to name a few-suggest inexhaustible thematic conflicts that appear in various guises in both ancient and contemporary plays.

The playwright introduces conflict early in a play, often by means of an "inciting incident," in which one character poses a conflict or confrontation either to another character or to himself. For example:

**FIRST WITCH:** All hail, Macbeth, hail to thee, Thane of Glamis!
**SECOND WITCH:** All hail, Macbeth, hail to thee, Thane of Cawdor!
**THIRD WITCH:** All hail, Macbeth, that shalt be King hereafter!
**BANQUO:** (to MACBETH) Good sir, why do you start, and seem to fear
Things that do sound so fair?

In this, the inciting incident of Shakespeare's Macbeth (which follows two brief expository scenes), a witch confronts Macbeth with the prediction that he will be king, thereby posing an alternative that Macbeth has apparently already considered, judging from the startled response that elicits Banquo's comment.

Once established, conflict is intensified to crisis, usually by a series of incidents, investigations, revelations, and confrontations. Sometimes even nonevents serve to intensify a conflict, as in the modern classic *Waiting for Godot,* in which two characters simply wait, through two hour-long acts, for the arrival of a third, who never comes. Indeed, with this play, Samuel Beckett practically rewrote the book on playwriting technique by showing how time alone, when properly managed, can do the job of heightening and developing conflict in a dramatic situation.

**The climax** Conflict cannot be intensified indefinitely. In a play, as in life, when conflict becomes insupportable, something has to give. Thus every play, be it comic, tragic, farcical, or melodramatic, culminates in some sort of dramatic explosion.

As we have seen, Aristotle described that dramatic explosion, in tragedy, as a *catharsis,* a cleansing or purification. Aristotle's conception is susceptible to various interpretations, but it has been widely accepted and broadly influential for centuries. The catharsis releases the audience's pity and thereby permits the fullest experience of tragic pleasure, washing away the terror that has been mounting steadily during the play's tragic course. Such catharsis as accompanies Oedipus's gouging out his own eyes as he recognizes his true self illustrates the extreme theatrical explosion of which the classical Greek tragic form is capable.

For any dramatic form, the climax is the conflict of a play taken to its most extreme; it is the moment of maximum tension. At the climax, a continuation of the conflict becomes unbearable, impossible: some sort of change is mandated. Climaxes in modern plays do not, as a rule, involve death or disfiguration (although there are exceptions: Peter Shaffer's celebrated *Equus* reaches its climax with the blinding of six horses, and Edward Albee's *The Zoo Story* climaxes with one character's impaling himself on a knife held by another). However, climaxes inevitably contain elements of recognition and reversal if not of catharsis, and usually the major conflicts of a play are resolved by one or more of these elements.

**The denouement** The climax is followed and the play is concluded by a denouement, or resolution, in which a final action or speech or even a single word or gesture indicates that the passions aroused by the play's action are now stilled and a new harmony or understanding has been reached. The tenor of the denouement tends to change with the times. In the American theatre of the 1950s and 1960s, for example, the sentimental and message-laden denouement was the rule: in Robert Anderson's *Tea and Sympathy,* a teacher's wife prepares to prove to a sensitive boy that he is not a homosexual; in Dore Schary's *Sunrise at Campobello,* a future American president makes his way on crippled legs to a convention platform. In the current theatre—in this existential age that looks with suspicion on tidy virtues and happy endings—more ironic and ambiguous denouements prevail. The current theatre also provides less in the way of purgation than do more classical modes, perhaps because the conflicts raised by the best of contemporary drama are not amenable to wholesale relief. But a denouement still must provide at least some lucidity concerning the problems raised by the play, some vision or metaphor of a deeper and more permanent understanding. Perhaps the final lines of *Waiting for Godot,* although premiering in 1953, best represent the denouement of the current age:

**ESTRAGON:** Well, shall we go?
**VLADIMIR:** Yes, let's go.
They do not move.

**Postplay** The last staged element of a theatrical presentation is the *curtain call,* in which the actors bow and the audience applauds. This convention—customary in the theatre at least since the time of the Romans—plays an important but often overlooked role in the overall scope of theatrical presentation.

The curtain call is *not* simply a time for the actors to receive congratulations from the audience, although many actors today seem to think it is. Indeed, the actor's deeply bowed head was originally an offer for his patron—the nobleman who had paid for the performance—to lop off that head with his sword if the actor had not provided satisfaction! The curtain call remains a time in which the actors show their respect for the audience that patronizes them. And aesthetically, it is a time in which the audience allows itself to see the other side of the "paradox of the actor." The curtain call liberates the audience from the world of the play. Indeed, when there is no curtain call, audiences are often disgruntled, for this convention fulfills the last provision, so to speak, in the mutual agreement that characterizes the theatre itself: the agreement by which the audience agrees to view the actors as the characters the actors have agreed to impersonate. It is at the curtain call that actors and audience can acknowledge their mutual belonging in the human society, can look each other in the eye and say, in effect, "We all know what it is to experience these things we've just seen performed. We must all try to understand life a little better. We are with you." In the best theatre, this communication is a powerful experience—and it becomes even more powerful when the entire audience leaps to its collective feet in a standing ovation. Such a response becomes a sort of audience participation for theatergoers, who physically express their enthusiasm not only to the performers but also to fellow audience members standing and cheering around them.

What follows the curtain call? The audience disperses, of course, but the individual audience members do not die. Through them the production enjoys an extended afterlife—both in talk and in print—in late-night postmortems at the theatre bar, in probing conversations and published reviews over the next few days, and sometimes in formal classroom discussions, television talk shows, letters to the editor in the local newspaper, and scholarly articles and books seen weeks, months, or years later. Indeed, in a theatre devoted to community interaction, such as Los Angeles's Cornerstone (see the chapter titled "Theatre Today"), the end of the play is the beginning of a hoped-for new life of political change. For the theatre is a place of public stimulation, both intellectual and emotional, and it should be expected that the stimulation provided by a provocative production would generate both animated discussions and illuminating commentaries.

Both of these we may call *dramatic criticism*, which is the audience's contribution to the theatre. Criticism is as ancient as Aristotle and as contemporary as the essays and lectures that are presented daily in newspapers, journals, books, and academies all over the world. But criticism is not solely an expert enterprise; criticism—which combines analysis and evaluation—is everybody's job. We look further at this key aspect of the theatre's art in the final chapter of the book.

## NON-ARISTOTELIAN THEATRE EVENTS

Aristotle's influence in developing a "science" of dramatic structure has been profound, but because his precepts focus only on fifth-century B.C. Greek tragedy, they have not proven all-inclusive. Aristotle's notion of structure does not even pertain to the major form of fifth-century Greek comedy known as *Old Comedy,* in which the dramatic action stops around the midpoint of the play so that a character representing the author can come forward and address the audience with a speech (a *parabasis*) about current politics. And the modern era has witnessed considerable rebellion against this classical model. Plays by Luigi Pirandello from the 1920s, Antonin Artaud and Bertolt Brecht from the 1930s, plus "happenings" from the 1960s and performance art from the 1980s (all discussed in later chapters), explicitly reject Aristotelian forms as their creators bring forth new and revolutionary dramatic structures. Indeed, most of today's playwrights seek to create variations on Aristotle's formula, by undermining the differentiation of the real and fictional worlds (Pirandello), by interrupting plotted actions with didactic songs and speeches (Brecht), by jumping from nonsensical dialogue to over-the-top sadistic imagery (the "exploding vaginas" of Artaud's theatre of cruelty), or simply by presenting scenes in reverse chronological order so that exposition concludes rather than initiates the play's action (Harold Pinter in Betrayal). Indeed, traditional Aristotelian structure is as much mocked as followed in the current theatre, as when a character in the Broadway musical *Urinetown,* while slyly winking at the audience, jests to another character: "Nothing can kill a show like too much exposition."

For the search for novelty—creating something fresh and, more important, unexpected—is a feature of

Director Deborah Warner's citywide installation *The Angel Project* is essentially a walking tour through selected buildings in New York City, staged by Warner and designed by Tom Pye in 2003. Audience-participants are first led in groups and then sent out on their own to follow instructions in a guidebook. There is no plot whatsoever, and only a few, mainly mute, characters; but various themes, developing angel motifs, and quotations from Milton's epic poem *Paradise Lost* make the installation a stylistically coherent (if not dramatic) theatre event.

all art and has led playwrights of nearly all periods to subvert or at least to reinvent the structures of drama. The ancient Greek tragedian Euripides, in his Electra, satirizes as simplistic the recognition scene in which *Electra* discovers her brother's identity as it had previously been depicted in plays by Euripides' rivals Aeschylus and Sophocles. Shakespeare mocks his audience's willing suspension of disbelief by having a character in *Twelfth Night* remark, concerning the situation he's in at the moment, "If this were played on the stage now, I would condemn it as an improbable fiction." And the devilishly clever contemporary British playwright Alan Ayckbourn, whose sixtyninth play is titled *Improbable Fiction,* has practically reinvented dramatic structure sixty-nine times in his long career, writing plays that run backward, forward, sideways, and sometimes with simultaneous and interconnecting plots.

Theatrical presentations in today's age, which we sometimes call "postmodern," may dispense with sequential plotting altogether. They may invite audience members to stroll as they wish among several activities taking place simultaneously, thus creating their own "play" from the actions they choose to observe in the order they choose to observe them. Or theatrical presentations may incorporate the audience into the action or invite the audience to provide the dialogue or to cast the performers. Or they may create an "anti-theatre" that parodies the very play that is being performed—taking Shakespeare's "improbable fiction" line as a historical justification. All these approaches bring excitement and hilarity—and indeed intriguing philosophical meditations—to the stage.

Still, we must acknowledge that Aristotelian-influenced drama continues to dominate the theatre.

For although novelty may be stimulating, the fact is that nothing remains novel very long.

Moreover, theatre exists in a time continuum. A contemporary painting or sculpture in an art museum may be absolutely astonishing—and in the contemporary art world, astonishment is almost everything. But the average period of time that museum visitors spend looking at any single work of art, no matter how admirable, is in the neighborhood of five to ten *seconds*. A play, in contrast, runs on average about two hours. Mere astonishment cannot sustain our interest for that period.

Likewise, a professional circus act, no matter how amazing or seemingly impossible, can run a maximum of seven minutes. This is the historic discovery of circus directors: after seven minutes of piling acrobats on top of a bicycle, it's time to bring on the dancing elephants. And seven minutes later, it's time for the clowns.

Without a plot to pull us along, and characters to engage us in a complexity of ideas, human relationships, and hopes attained or dashed, the theatre will always struggle to keep its audience involved for the duration. And here's where a play's duration, components, and structure—discussed in this chapter—come together. The problem with simply replacing the Aristotelian ingredients with novelty is that such novelty must *continue* to be novel—and, more important, to be *increasingly* astonishing—long after members of the audience have grown accustomed to what they saw onstage when they entered the theatre. The invention of drama—structured action with a plot that engages you, characters that you care about and feel for, and an increasing tension in the developing events—creates a theatrical compulsion that can keep an audience on the edge of its collective seats for two hours, or nine hours, at a time.

Remember, Aristotle did not invent classical dramatic structure; he was just the first person who described it. The structure was invented by playwrights: Greek tragedians who lived a hundred years before Aristotle, and Egyptian playwrights who lived thousands of years before that. The classical models have served well for many millennia and will not be wholly undone by the experiments of any era. It is little surprise that the finest contemporary plays—Tony Kushner's nine-hour *Angels in America* may be the best exemplar of this—create ravishing theatre by retaining the essential core of these ancient principles while at the same time making brilliantly original variations that augment but do not supplant their contribution to theatrical magic.

# 3

# The Playwright

AT HOME, AS I GAZE at my computer screen, I am the total master of my stage. Actions cascade through my head; whole characters pop into my imagination; great words, speeches, scenes, and visions flow directly from my brain to my fingers to the words leaping onto my screen. They are my ideas, *my* people, *my* language, and *my* play that will soon be resounding through theatre walls around the world; it will be *me* up there receiving the critics' raves, press interviews, and speaking invitations as a result of my play's success; it will be *me* mounting the stage to accept my `best play' award, perhaps even sitting one day in Stockholm, next to my fellow Nobel Prize winners—this year's Einstein and Marie Curie who, like me, have also rocked the modern world.

"But that's only at home. In the theatre, I am the loneliest of figures. I huddle inconspicuously in the back row, taking notes in the dark. I am unnoticed by the actors and, indeed, rarely allowed to speak directly to them. The designers look at me with condescension and suspicion. At the end of the rehearsal, when I politely offer to share my notes with the director, she glares at me. And when she finally listens, it's with a noncommittal face and a dismissive agreement that, yes, she'll think about all of this tomorrow.'

"I am totally convinced that the theatre is nothing more than an instrument for massacring my manuscript!"

This monologue is imaginary—and perhaps a bit extreme. Playwrights, by their creative natures, generally have vivid imaginations, which can and often do lead to both mania and paranoia. But this inner monologue expresses the great fear of every playwright, reflecting the great paradox of theatrical creation: the playwright is both the most central and the most peripheral figure in the theatrical event.

The playwright is central in the most obvious ways. She or he provides the point of origin for nearly every play production—the script, which is the rallying point around which the director or producer gathers the troops. Yet that point of origin is also a point of departure. The days when a Shakespeare or a Molière would gather actors around, read his text to them, and then coach them in its proper execution are long gone. What we have today is a more specialized theatrical hierarchy in which the director is interposed as the playwright's representative to the theatrical team: the actors and designers. More and more, the playwright's function is to write the play and then disappear, for once the script has been printed, duplicated, and distributed, the playwright's physical participation is relegated mainly to serving as the director's sounding board and rewrite person. Indeed, the playwright's mere physical presence in the rehearsal hall can become an embarrassment, more tolerated than welcomed—and sometimes not even tolerated.

Fundamentally, today's playwright is considered an independent artist whose work, like that of the novelist or poet, is executed primarily if not exclusively in isolation. There are exceptions, of course. Some playwrights work from actors' improvisations, and others participate quite fully in rehearsals, even to the point of serving as the initial director of their plays (as Edward Albee, Sam Shepard, and Neil LaBute often do) or, more extraordinarily, by acting in them (as Athol Fugard and August Wilson have done).

But the exceptions, in this case, do not disprove the rule; since the age of romanticism, the image of the playwright has turned increasingly from that of theatre coworker and mentor to that of isolated observer and social critic. In the long run, this change should occasion no lamentation, for if theatre production now demands collaboration and compromise, the art of the theatre still requires individuality, clarity of vision, sharpness of approach, original sensitivity, and devotion to personal truth if it is to challenge the artists who are called upon to fulfill it and the audiences who will pay money to experience it.

Therefore, the *independence* of the playwright is generally her or his most important characteristic. Playwrights must seek from life, from their own lives—and not from the theatrical establishment—the material that will translate into exciting and meaningful and entertaining theatre; and their views must be intensely personal, grounded in their own perceptions and philosophy, in order to ring true. We look to the theatre for a measure of leadership, for personal enlightenment derived from another's experience, for fresh perspectives, new vision. Simple mastery of certain conventional techniques will not suffice to enable a playwright to expand our lives.

## WE ARE ALL PLAYWRIGHTS

Playwriting is not just something we learn. It's something we already do. All of us. Every day—or night.

Every night, dreams come to us in our sleep. Or, rather, they *seem* to come to us: in fact, we create them, for each of us has our own "playwright-in-residence" somewhere in the back of our minds, churning out a nightly mixture of vivid, believable, and sometimes terrifying fantasies that create half-real, half-imagined characters, idealized settings, surprising plot complications, nostalgic visions, and often nightmarish climaxes and reversals. The situations and characters of our dreams are our own creations, drawn from our careful observations, colored by our unconscious phobias and fancies, stylized into associations of words, scenes, and "stagings" that ring with deep resonance of our innermost plans, fears, and secrets.

Of course there's more to playwriting than dreaming up characters and a story. As dreamers, we are only beginning playwrights. What happens next is the subject of this chapter.

## LITERARY AND NONLITERARY ASPECTS OF PLAYWRITING

Because drama is often thought of as a form of literature (and is taught in departments of literature) and because many dramatic authors begin (or double) as poets or novelists, it may seem as if playwriting is primarily a literary activity. It is not. Etymology helps here: *playwright* is not *playwrite*. Writing for the theatre entails considerations not common to other literary forms. Although by coincidence the words *write* and *wright* are homonyms, a "playwright" is a person who *makes* plays, just as a wheelwright is a person

Who makes wheels. This distinction is particularly important, because some plays, or portions of plays, are never written at all. Improvisational plays, rituals, scenes of comic business, subtextual behaviors, and documentary dramas may be created largely or entirely in performance or are learned simply through oral improvisation and repetition. Some are created with a tape recorder and the collaboration of multiple imaginations and may or may not be committed to writing after the performance is concluded. And others, though dramatic in structure, are entirely nonverbal—that is, they include no dialogue, no words, and very little that is written other than an outline of mimetic effects.

So while drama is one of the literary arts, it is much more than an arrangement of words. It is rather a structured assemblage of vocal and physical interactions, a compilation of the many elements of the theatrical medium: movement, speech, scenery, costume, staging, music, spectacle, and silence. It is a literature whose impact depends on a collective endeavor and whose appreciation must be, in large part, spontaneous and immediate.

A play attains its finished form only in performance upon the stage: the written script is not the final play but the *blueprint* for the play, the written foundation for the production that is the play's complete realization. Some of a play's most effective writing may look very clumsy as it appears in print. Take, for example, the following lines from Shakespeare:

| | |
|---|---|
| Oh! Oh! Oh! | **—Othello** |
| Howl, howl, howl, howl! | **—King Lear** |
| No, no, the drink, the drink. O my dear Hamlet, The drink, the drink! I am poisoned. | **—Hamlet** |

These apparently unsophisticated lines of dialogue in fact provide great dramatic climaxes in an impassioned performance; they are *pretexts for great acting*, the creation of which is far more crucial than literary eloquence to the art of playwriting.

Of course some formal literary values are as important to the theatre as they are to other branches of literature: allusional complexity, descriptive precision, poetic imagery, metaphoric implication, and a careful crafting of verbal rhythms, cadences, and textures all contribute powerfully to dramatic effect. But they are effective only insofar as they are fully integrated with the whole of the theatrical medium, as they stimulate action and behavior through stage space and stage time in a way that commands audience attention and

Pultizer Prize—winning playwright Suzan-Lori Parks is one of America's most provocative young dramatists, as seen in her *Fucking A,* which, from its title onward, provides in-your-face drama. Paralleling Nathaniel Hawthorne's *The Scarlet Letter* but set in an impoverished, dictator-ruled country, the play treats a young man, played by Mos Def, who has been incarcerated since childhood, and his mother (S. Epatha Merkerson, *seated*), who, hvaing provided abortions to earn money for his release, has been branded with a"Fucking A" on her skin. The 2003 New York Public Theatre production was directed by Michael Greif.

involvement. Mere literary brilliance is insufficient as theatre, as a great many successful novelists and poets have learned to their chagrin when they attempted to write plays.

# PLAYWRITING AS EVENT WRITI NG

The core of every play is action. Unlike with other literary forms, the inner structure of a play is never a series of abstract observations or a collage of descriptions and moralizings; it is an ordering of observable, dramatizable events. These events are the basic building blocks of the play, regardless of its style or genre or theme.

Sarah Buhl's *In the Next Room,* orthe *Vibrator Play* received great acclaim in its Broadway appearance in 2009-10. Its key action shows a late-nineteenth-century doctor treating female patients´ "hysteria" with the newly invented electric vibrator, which not only "cures" but delights his patients. Ruhl, whose *The Clean House* (2005) was nominated for a Pulitzer Prize, has been known for her witty dialogue and off-beat, semicomical characters, but this play—and its surprising central "prop"— wonderfully penetrate the miscommunications between men and women on matters of sexual intimacy, then and now. Les Waters directed this Lincoln Center production; Maria Dizzia is the patient and Michael Cerveris the doctor. The period costumes—petticoats and all—were designed by David Zinn.

Fundamentally, the playwright works with two tools, both representing the externals of human behavior: dialogue and physical action. The inner story and theme of a play—the psychology of the characters, the viewpoint of the author, the impact of the social environment—must be inferred by the audience from outward appearances, from the play's events as the audience sees them. Whatever the playwright's intended message and whatever the playwright's perspective on the function and process of playwriting itself, the play cannot be put together until the playwright has conceived of an event—and then a series of related events—designed to be enacted on a stage.

It is this series of related events that constitutes the play's scenario or, more formally, its *plot.*

The events of drama are, by their nature, compelling. Some are bold and unusual, such as the scene in which Prometheus is chained to his rock. Some are subdued, as when the military regiment in Chekhov's *The Three Sisters* leaves town at the play's end. Some are quite ordinary, as in the domestic sequences depicted in most modern realist plays. But they are always aimed at creating a memorable impression. To begin playwriting, one must first conceptualize events and envision them enacted in such a way as to hold the attention of an audience.

The events of a play can be connected to each other in a strict chronological, cause-effect continuity. This has been a goal of the realistic theatre, in which dramatic events are arranged to convey a lifelike progression of experiences in time. Such plays are said to be *continuous* in structure and *linear* in chronology, and they can be analyzed like sociological events: the audience simply watches them unfold as it might watch a family quarrel in progress in an apartment across the way.

Continuous linearity, however, is by no means a requirement for play construction. Many plays are discontinuous or nonlinear. The surviving plays of ancient Greece are highly discontinuous: choral odes alternate with character-driven episodes in the tragedies, and choral interjections and a direct speech to the audience (*parabasis*) interrupt the action of Old Comedies. Shakespeare's plays are structured in a highly complex arrangement of time shifts, place shifts, style shifts, songs, and subplots ingeniously integrated around a basic theme or investigation of character. And many contemporary plays break with chronological linearity altogether, flashing instantly backward and forward through time to incorporate character memories, character fantasies, direct expressions of the playwright's social manifesto, historical exposition, comic relief, or any other ingredient the playwright can successfully work in.

Linear, point-to-point storytelling has not disappeared from the theatre—indeed, it remains the basic architecture of most popular and serious plays. But modern (and postmodern) audiences have proven increasingly receptive to less-conventional structures: the exuberance of the music hall, for instance, inspired the structuring of Joan Littlewood's *Oh, What a Lovely War!;* the minstrel show served as a structure for George C. Wolfe's *The Colored Museum;* and the didacticism of the lecture hall underlay much of the theatre of Bertolt Brecht. Nonlinear, discontinuous, and even stream-of-consciousness structures can provide powerful and sustained dramatic impact in the theatre, provided they are based in the dramatization of events that the audience can put together in some sort of meaningful and satisfying fashion.

# THE QUALITIES OF A FINE PLAY

As with any art form, the qualities that make up a good play can be discussed individually. But only in their combination, only in their interaction—only in ways that cannot be dissected or measured—do these qualities have meaning.

## Credibility and Intrigue

To say that a play must be credible is not at all to say that it has to be lifelike, for fantasy, ritual, and absurdity have all proven to be enduringly popular theatrical modes. *Credibility* is the audience-imposed demand that requires a play's actions to appear to flow logically from its characters, its situation, and the theatrical context the playwright provides. In a credible play, what happens in act 2 appears to be a reasonable outgrowth of what happened in act 1.

Credibility requires that the characters in a play appear to act out of their own individual interests, instincts, and intentions rather than serving as mere pawns for the development of theatrical plot or effect, or as empty disseminators of propaganda. Credibility requires that characters maintain consistency within themselves: their thoughts, feelings, hopes, fears, and plans must appear to flow from human needs rather than purely theatrical ones. Credibility also requires that human characters appear to act and think like human beings (even in humanly impossible situations) and not purely as thematic automatons. Credibility, in essence, is a contract between author and audience, whereby the audience agrees to view the characters as "people" as long as the author agrees not to shatter that belief in order to accomplish other purposes.

Thus James Barrie's famous play *Peter Pan*, though undeniably fantastical, creates a cast of characters wholly appropriate to their highly imaginary situation and internally consistent in their actions within the context of their developing experience. All of their aspirations (including those of the dog!) are human ones, and their urgencies are so believable that when Tinkerbell steps out of the play's context to ask the audience to demonstrate its belief in fairies, the audience is willing to applaud its approval. At that moment, the world of the play becomes more credible, more "real," than that of the audience. So much for the power—and consequently the necessity—of dramatic credibility.

*Intrigue* is the quality of a play that makes us curious (sometimes fervently so) to see "what happens next." Sheer plot intrigue—which is sometimes called "suspense" in that it leaves us suspended (that is, "hanging")—is one of the most powerful dramatic approaches. Whole plays can be based on little more than artfully contrived plotting designed to keep the audience in a continual state of anticipation and wonder. Plot, however, is only one of the elements of a play that can support intrigue. Most plays that aspire to deeper insights than whodunits or farces develop intrigue in character as well and even in theme. Most of the great plays demand that we ask not so much "What will happen?" as "What does this mean?" Most great plays, in other words, make us care about the characters and invite us to probe the mysteries of the human condition.

Look, for example, at this dialogue from David Mamet's *Glengarry Glen Ross,* in which a disgruntled real-estate salesman proposes to a colleague that they rob their front office, stealing some real-estate "leads" (names of potential customers) that they can then sell to a competitor.

MOSS: I want to tell you something.

AARONOW: What?

MOSS: I want to tell you what somebody should do.

AARONOW: What?

MOSS: Someone should stand up and strike back.

AARONOW: What do you mean? Moss: Somebody ...

AARONOW: Yes... ?

MOSS: Should do something to *them.*

AARONOW: What?

MOSS: Something. To pay them back. *(Pause)* Someone, someone should hurt them. Murray and Mitch.

AARONOW: Somebody should hurt them.

MOSS: Yes.

AARONOW: *(Pause)* How?

MOSS: How? Do something to hurt them. Where they live.

AARONOW: What? *(Pause)*

MOSS: Someone should rob the office.

AARONOW: Huh.

MOSS: That's what I'm *saying.* We were, if we were that kind of guys, to knock it off, and *trash* the joint, it looks like a robbery, and take the fuckin' leads out of the files ... [... ] *(Pause)*

AARONOW: Are you actually *talking* about this or are we just...

MOSS: No, we're just ...

AARONOW: We're just *"talking"* about it.

MOSS: We're just *speaking* about it. (Pause) As an *idea.*

AARONOW: As an idea.

MOSS: Yes.

AARONOW: We're not actually *talking* about it.

MOSS: No.

AARONOW: Talking about it as a...

MOSS: No.

AARONOW: As a *robbery.*

MOSS: As a "robbery"?! No.

AARONOW: *Well.* Well ...

The basic action of this scene could be expressed in just two or three lines of dialogue; but since a conspiracy is being proposed, each character must proceed with extreme caution—as his colleague could turn him in at any time. As each of the thirty-two short lines, and each of the five indicated pauses, takes the conspiracy one tiny—but precise—step forward, the credibility is exacting while the intrigue builds to an increasingly higher level of tension.

Intrigue draws us into the world of a play; credibility keeps us there. In the best plays the two are sustained in a fine tension of opposites: intrigue demanding surprise, credibility demanding consistency. Combined, they generate a kind of "believable wonder," which is the fundamental state of drama. Credibility alone will not suffice to make a play interesting, and no level of intrigue can make a noncredible play palatable. The integration of the two must be created by the playwright in order to establish that shared ground that transcends our expectations but not our credulity.

## Speakability, Stageability, and Flow

The dialogue of drama is written upon the page, but it must be spoken by actors and staged by directors. Thus the goal of the dramatist is to fabricate dialogue that is actable and stageable and that flows in a progression leading to theatrical impact.

One of the most common faults of beginning playwrights is that their lines lack *speakability.* This is not to say that dramatic dialogue must resemble ordinary speech. No one imagines people in life speaking like characters out of the works of Aeschylus, Shakespeare, or Shaw, or even modern writers like Tom Stoppard or Edward Albee. Brilliantly styled language is a feature of most of the great plays in theatre history, and lifelikeness, by itself, is not a dramatic virtue—nor is its absence a dramatic fault.

Rather, speakability means that a line of dialogue should be so written that it achieves its maximum impact when spoken. In order to accomplish this, the playwright must be closely attuned to the *audial shape* of dialogue: the rhythm of sound that creates emphasis, meaning, focus, and power. Verbal lullabies and climaxes, fast punch lines, sonorous lamentations, sparkling epigrams, devastating expletives, significant pauses, and electrifying whispers—these are some of the devices of dialogue that impart audial shape to great plays written by master dramatists. Look, for example, at Andrew Undershaft's chiding of his pretentious son, Stephen, in George Bernard Shaw's *Major Barbara*, where Stephen has just said that he knows "the difference between right and wrong."

> **UNDERSHAFT:** You don't say so! What! no capacity for business, no knowledge of law, no sympathy with art, no pretension to philosophy; only a simple knowledge of the secret that has puzzled all the philosophers, baffled all the lawyers, muddled all the men of business, and ruined most of the artists: the secret of right and wrong. Why, man, you're a genius, a master of masters, a god! At twenty-four, too!

No one would call this "everyday speech" as in the David Mamet dialogue quoted earlier. But it is immensely speakable and its cascading sarcasm develops a fiercely intimidating momentum, leaving Stephen speechless and, with a great actor playing it, the audience breathless.

Speakability also requires that the spoken line appear to realistically emanate from the character who utters it and that it contain—in its syntax, vocabulary, and mode of expression—the marks of that character's milieu and his or her personality. The spoken line is not merely an expression of thé author's perspective; it is the basis from which the actor develops characterization and the acting ensemble creates a play's style. Thus the mastery of dramatic dialogue writing demands more than mere semantic skills; it requires a constant awareness of the purposes and tactics underlying human communication, as well as of the multiple psychological and aesthetic properties of language.

*Stageability*, of course, requires that dialogue be written so that it can be spoken effectively upon a stage, but it requires something more: dialogue must be conceived as an integral element of a particular staged situation, in which setting, physical acting, and spoken dialogue are inextricably combined. A stageable script is one in which staging and stage

# Spotlight

## Two English Playwrights

The two leading English playwrights of the past fifty years exhibit radically different styles. The plays of Harold Pinter, which are filled with abrupt, almost inexplicable transitions, intense pauses and glances, and elliptical dialogue that seems to contain innuendos we don't fully comprehend, create an almost palpable sense: of foreboding and spookiness that plunges the audience deeper and deeper into Pinteresque moods and reveries. The plays of Tom Stoppard, in contrast, race glibly through brilliant rhetorical flights of language that always manage to stay one step ahead of the audience's capability to follow, keeping the audience breathless while forcing them to remain intellectually alert.

**BATES:** *(moves to ELLEN)* Will we meet tonight?
**ELLEN:** I don't know. *(Pause)*
**BATES:** Come with me tonight.
**ELLEN:** Where?
**BATES:** Anywhere. For a walk. *(Pause)*
**ELLEN:** I don't want to walk.
**BATES:** Why not? *(Pause)*

**ELLEN:** I want to go somewhere else. *(Pause)*
**BATES:** Where?
**ELLEN:** I don't know. *(Pause)*
**BATES:** What's wrong with a walk?
**ELLEN:** I don't want to walk. *(Pause)*
**BATES:** What do you want to do?
**ELLEN:** I don't know. *(Pause)*
**BATES:** Do you want to go somewhere else?
**ELLEN:** Yes.
**BATES:** Where?
**ELLEN:** I don't know. *(Pause)*

-FROM PINTER'S SILENCE (1969)

**COCKLEBURY-SMYTHE:** May I be the first to welcome you to
Room 3B. You will find the working conditions primitive, the hours antisocial, the amenities nonexistent and the catering beneath contempt. On top of that the people are for the most part very boring, with interests either so generalized as to mimic wholesale ignorance or so particular as to be lunatic obsessions. Their level of conversation would pass without comment in the lavatory of a mixed comprehensive and the lavatories, by the way, are few and far between.

-FROM STOPPARD'S *DIRTY LINEN* (1976)

business—as well as design and the acting demands—are neither adornments for the dialogue nor sugarcoating for the writer's opinions but are intrinsic to the very nature of the play.

Both speakability and stageability are contingent upon human limitations—those of the actors and directors as well as those of the audience. Speakability must take into account that the actor must breathe from time to time, for example, and that the audience can take in only so many metaphors in a single spoken sentence. Stageability must reckon with the forces of gravity and inertia, which both the poet and the novelist may conveniently ignore. The playwright need not simply succumb to the common denominator—all the great playwrights strive to extend the capacities of actors and audience alike—but still must not forget that the theatre is fundamentally a human event that cannot transcend human capabilities.

A speakable and stageable script flows rather than stumbles; this is true for nonlinear plays as well as for more straightforwardly structured ones. Flow requires a continual stream of information, and a play that flows is one that is continually saying something, doing something, and meaning something to the audience. To serve this end, the playwright should address such technical problems as scene-shifting, entrances and exits, and act breaks (intermissions) as early as possible in the scriptwriting process. Furthermore, in drafting scenes, the writer should be aware that needless waits, arid expositions (no matter how "necessary" to the plot), and incomprehensible plot developments can sink the sturdiest script in a sea of audience apathy.

## Richness

*Depth, subtlety, fineness, quality, wholeness,* and *inevitability*—these words are often used in reference to plays that we like. They are fundamentally subjective terms, easier to apply than to define or defend, for the fact is that when a play pleases us, when it "works," the feelings of pleasure and stimulation it affords are beyond the verbal level. Certainly *richness* is one of the qualities common to plays that leave us with this sense of satisfaction—richness of *detail* and *richness* of dimension.

A play that is rich with detail is not necessarily one that is rife with detail; it is simply one whose every detail fortifies our insight into the world of the play. For going to a play is in part a matter of paying a visit to the playwright's world, and the more vividly created that world, the greater the play's final impact. In Margaret Edson's *Wit,* for example, Vivian, a terminally ill English professor, addresses the audience from her hospital bed. Her tone is professorial, and her vocabulary is filled with medical terminology, little of which the average audience member will understand, but in the context of an intellectual woman struggling against a fatal disease, Edson's dialogue creates an immensely compelling and affectingly detailed portrait:

VIVIAN: I don't mean to complain, but I am becoming very sick. Very, very sick. Ultimately sick, as it were.

In everything I have done, I have been steadfast, resolute—some would say in the extreme. Now, as you can see, I am distinguishing myself in illness.

I have survived eight treatments of Hexamethophosphacil and Vinplatin at the *full* dose, ladies and gentlemen. I have broken the record. I have become something of a celebrity. Kelekian and Jason [*her* doctors] are simply delighted. I think they foresee celebrity status for themselves upon the appearance of the journal article they will no doubt write about me.

But I flatter myself. The article will not be about *me,* it will be about my ovaries. It will be about my peritoneal cavity, which, despite their best intentions, is now crawling with cancer. What we have come to think of as *me* is, in fact, just the specimen jar, just the dust jacket, just the white piece of paper that bears the little black marks.

Vivian's free use of seven-syllable words, her refining of words on the spot (from "very sick" to "very, very sick" to "ultimately sick"; from "steadfast" to "resolute"), her public style of presentation ("ladies and gentlemen"), her parallel phrases ("I have . . . I have ... I have . . . ," "just the ... just the ... just the . . ."), her alliteration of consonants ("just ... jar ... just ... jacket, just"), and her use of antithesis ("white piece of paper ... little black marks") tell us volumes about her character and how she is "distinguishing" herself in illness. Richness of linguistic detail lends a play authority, an aura of sureness. It surrounds the play's characters as a city surrounds homes and gives them a cultural context in which to exist. It lends a play specificity: specific people are engaged in specific tasks in a specific place. Going to (or even reading) a play rich with texture is like taking a trip to another world—it is an adventure no travel agent could possibly book.

Richness is not an easy quality to develop in writing. It demands of its author a gift for close observation, an uninhibited imagination, a consummate vocabulary, and an astute sense of what to leave out as well as what to include. A person who can recollect

Edward Albea, whose had century of playwriting extends from The Zoo Story in 1959 to *Me, Myself and I* in 2008, is a master at developing characters through dialogue—so much so that they seem to develop lives of their own. There are only two characters in his one-act *Zoo Story*—Peter, a middle-aged businessman, and Jerry, a slightly younger vagrant who accosts him in New York's Central Park—but they have become so vivid in theatergoers' memories that forty-five years later Albee brought them back into a new play, *Peter and Jerry,* in which *Zoo Story* has a prequel called *Homelife.* Pictured in its 2004 world premiere production, directed at the Hartford Stage by Pam MacKinnon, are Frank Wood (*seated*) as Peter and Frederick Weller as Jerry.

personal experiences in great detail, who can conjure up convincing situations, peoples, locales, and conversations, and who is closely attuned to nuance can perhaps work these talents into the writing of plays.

## Depth of Characterization

Depth of characterization presents perhaps the greatest single stumbling block for novice playwrights, who tend either to write all characters "in the same voice" (normally the author's own) or to divide them into two camps: good characters and bad. Capturing the depth, complexities, and uniqueness of real human beings, even seemingly ordinary human beings, is a difficult task.

Depth of characterization requires that every character possess an independence of intention, expression, and motivation; moreover, these characteristics must appear sensible in the light of our general knowledge of psychology and human behavior. In plays as in life, all characters must act from motives that appear reasonable to *them* (if not to those watching them or to those affected by them). Moreover, the writer should bear in mind that every character is, *to himself or herself* an important and worthwhile person, regardless of what other people think. Thus even the great villains of drama—Shakespeare's Richard III, Claudius, and Iago, for example—must be seen to believe in themselves and in the fundamental "rightness" of their causes. Even if we never completely understand their deepest motivations (as we can't fully understand the motives of real villains such as Hitler, Caligula, or John Wilkes Booth), we should be able to sense at the bottom of any character's behavior a validity of purpose, however twisted or perverse we may find it.

The realistic theatre—Chekhov, Williams, Miller, and the like—has provided many works in which the psychological dimensions of the characters dominate all other aspects of the theatrical experience. Look, for example, at this speech of Big Mama in Tennessee Williams's *Cat on a Hot Tin Roof*:

BIG MAMA [*outraged that her son-in-law, Gooper, is offering her a written trusteeship plan which would give him and his wife control over the estate of Big Daddy, Mama's ailing husband*]: Now you listen to me, all of you, you listen here! They's not goin' to be any more catty talk in my house! And Gooper, you put that away before I grab it out of your hand and tear it right up! I don't know what the hell's in it, and I don't want to know what the hell's in it. I'm talkin' in Big Daddy's language now; I'm his *wife*, not his *widow*, I'm still his *wife*! And I'm talkin' to you in his language an'—

Williams has brilliantly crafted Big Mama's rage with aggressive verbs ("grab," "tear"), local vernacular ("they's"), clause repetitions ("I'm his wife ... I'm still his wife"), loaded adjectives ("catty"), profanities rare for a southern woman ("hell"), dialectical contractions ("goin'," "talkin'"), and individual word emphases as marked by italics. But he has also undermined her rage by having her admit to assuming her husband's vocabulary—so that while she states that she's not Big Daddy's widow, her language indicates that she knows, even if only unconsciously, that it will soon be otherwise.

Modern dramatists have even made psychotherapy part of their dramatic scheme in many cases. Psychiatrist characters appear (or are addressed) in plays such as Williams's *Suddenly, Last Summer,* Miller's *After the Fall,* Peter Shaffer's *Equus,* and the 1941 American musical *Lady in the Dark,* each of which portrays a principal character undergoing psychotherapy and discussing what he or she learns. Certainly the psychological sophistication of modern theatre audiences has afforded playwrights expanded opportunities to explore and dramatize characters' psyches, and it has helped to make the "case study" drama a major genre of the current theatre.

## Gravity and Pertinence

*Gravity* and *pertinence* are terms used to describe the importance of a play's theme and its overall relevance to the concerns of the intended audience. To say that a play has gravity is to say simply that its central theme is one of serious and lasting significance in humanity's spiritual, moral, or intellectual life. The greatest dramas—comedies as well as tragedies—are always somehow concerned with what is sometimes called the human predicament: those universal problems—aging, discord, love, insecurity, ambition, loss—for which we continually seek greater lucidity. Gravity does not mean somberness, however; it requires only a confrontation with the most elemental tasks of living. When an audience truly understands and identifies with a play's experiences, even the darkest tragedy radiates power and illumination.

Look, for example, at Bynum's speech in August Wilson's *Joe Turner's Come and Gone.* Bynum is what Wilson calls a rootworker (conjuror). A younger man, Jeremy, has just praised a woman as knowing "how to treat a fellow," and Bynum chastises him for his shallowness:

You just can't look at it like that. You got to look at the whole thing. Now, you take a fellow go out there, grab hold to a woman and think he got something 'cause she sweet and soft to the touch. It's in the world like everything else. Touching's nice. It feels good. But you can lay your hand upside a horse or a cat, and that feels good too. What's the difference? When you grab hold to a woman, you got something there. You got a whole world there. You got a way of life kicking up under your hand. That woman can take and make you feel like something. I ain't just talking about in the way of jumping off into bed together and rolling around with each other. Anybody can do that. When you grab hold to that woman and look at the whole thing and see what you got ... why she can take and make something of you. Your mother was a woman. That's enough right there to show you what a woman is. Enough to show you what she can do. She made something out of you.

Using only simple words (see, for instance, Vivian's speech in *Wit*), Wilson's Bynum probes at the heart of a profound subject: the most meaningful relationship between a man and a woman. When these lines are well acted, their impact stays with us long after we leave the theatre.

*Pertinence* refers to the play's touching on current audience concerns, both of-the-moment and timeless. Plays about current political situations or personalities are clearly pertinent; they may, however, quickly become outdated. Plays whose concerns are both ephemeral and universal, however, such as Miller's *The Crucible*—which, in treating the Salem witch trials of 1692, pertains as well to the McCarthy trials of the 1950s and to corrupt investigations in all eras—will have a more enduring relevance. The greatest plays are not merely pertinent to a given moment but also serve as archetypes for all time.

## Compression, Economy, and Intensity

Compression, economy, and intensity are also aspects of the finest plays. *Compression* refers to the playwright's skill in condensing a story (which may span many days, even years, of chronological time) into a theatrical time frame. *Economy* relates to an author's skill in eliminating or consolidating characters, events, locales, and words in the service of

compression. Unlike other literary or visual art forms that can be examined in private and at the leisure of the observer, a play must be structured to unfold in a public setting and at a predetermined pace.

Many beginning playwrights attempt to convert a story to a play in the most obvious way: by writing a separate scene for every event described in the story (and sometimes including a different setting and supporting cast for each scene). Economy and compression, however, require that most stories be restructured in order to be dramatically viable. If the play is to be basically realistic, the playwright has traditionally reworked the story so as to have all the

Although better known now as a film actor with numerous Oscar, Emmy, and Golden Globe nominations, Sam Shepard has been one of America's leading playwrights since the early 1960s, having written forty-five plays—most of them set in the American West and all provocative and experimental—and receiving the Pulitzer Prize for Drama for *Buried Child* in 1979. Shepard's *Kicking a Dead Horse,* shown here in its 2008 world premiere at the National Theatre of Ireland with Stephen Rea as "Hobart "—a New York art dealer who heads out to the desert to find his true self when his horse keels over and dies. The play represents a favorite and probably autobiographical dialectic of the author: the contrast between "authentic" small-town America and the country's postmodern urbanism.

events occur in one location, or perhaps in two locations with an act break between to allow for scenery changes. Events that are integral to the story but cannot be shown within the devised settings can simply be reported (as in Shaw's *Misalliance,* for example, in which an airplane crash occurs offstage as the onstage characters gawk and exclaim). More common today is the use of theatricalist techniques that permit an integration of settings so that events occurring in various places can be presented on the same set without intermission, or an integration of characters by which an actor, by a sudden change in voice or posture or mannerism, switches from playing one character to another.

The effects of economy and compression are both financial and aesthetic. Obviously, when scenery changes and the number of actors are held to a minimum, the costs of production are minimized as well. But beyond that, compression and economy in playwriting serve to stimulate intrigue and focus audience expectation: a tightly written play gives us the feeling that we are on the trail of something important and that our quarry is right around the next bend. Thus, economy and compression actually lead to *intensity,* which is one of the theatre's most powerful attributes.

Dramatic intensity can take many forms. It can be harsh, abrasive, explosive, eminently physical, or overtly calm. It can be ruminative, tender, or comic. But whenever intensity occurs and in whatever mood or context, it conveys to the audience an ineradicable feeling that this moment in theatre is unique and its revelations are profound. Intensity does not come about by happy accident, obviously, but neither can it be simply injected at the whim of the playwright. It must evolve out of a careful development of issues, through the increasing urgency of character goals and intentions and the focused actions and interactions of the plot that draw characters and their conflicts ever closer to some sort of climactic confrontation. A play must spiral inward toward its core—that is, its compression must increase and its mood must intensify as it circles toward its climax and denouement. Too many tangential diversions can deflect a play from this course, rendering it formless and devoid of apparent purpose.

## Celebration

Finally, a great play celebrates life; it does not merely depict or analyze or criticize it. The first plays were presented at festivals that—though perhaps haunted by angry or capricious gods—were essentially joyful celebrations. Even the darkest of the ancient Greek tragedies sought to transcend the more negative aspects of existence and to exalt the human spirit, for the whole of Greek theatre was informed by the positive (and therapeutic) elements of the Dionysian festival: spring, fertility, and the gaiety and solidarity of public communion.

The theatre can never successfully venture too far from this source. A purely didactic theatre has never satisfied either critics or the public, and a merely grim depiction of ordinary life has little to offer this art form. Although the word *theatrical* usually suggests something like "glittery" or "showy," it better accords with the theatre's most fundamental aspirations: to extend our known experience, to illuminate life, and to raise existence to the level of art—the art of theatre. This celebration can easily be perverted. Dramas intended to be merely "uplifting"—with a reliance on happy endings and strictly noble sentiments—or written in self-consciously "elevated" tones do not celebrate life; they merely whitewash it. The truest and most exciting theatre has always been created out of a passionate, personal vision of reality and deep devotion to expressing life's struggles and splendors, for the theatre is fundamentally an affirmation. Writing, producing, and attending plays are also acts of affirmation: attesting to the desire to share and communicate, and celebrating human existence, participation, and communion. Purely bitter plays, no matter how justly based or how well grounded in history or experience, remain incomplete and unsatisfying as theatre, which simply is not an effective medium for nihilistic conveyance. Even the bleakest of modern plays radiates a persistent hopefulness—even joyousness—as archetypally represented by Samuel Beckett's two old men who sing, joke, and entertain each other, and us as well, in the forlorn shadow of a mostly leafless tree while waiting for a probably nonexistent Godot.

## THE PLAYWRIGHT'S PROCESS

How does one go about writing a play? It is important to know the elements of a play (as discussed in the chapter titled "What Is a Play?") and the character istics of the best plays—credibility, intrigue, speakability, stageability, flow, richness, depth of characterization, gravity, pertinence, compression, economy, intensity, and celebration—as discussed in the preceding sections. But that is not enough; one must still confront the practical task of writing.

The blank sheet of paper is the writer's nemesis. It is the accuser, the goad and critic that coldly commands action even as it threatens humiliation. There is no consensus among writers as to where to begin. Some prefer to begin with a story line or a plot outline. Some begin with a real event and write the play to explain why that event occurred. Some begin with a real character or set of characters and develop a plot around them. Some begin with a setting and try to animate it with characters and actions. Some begin with a theatrical effect or an idea for a new form of theatrical expression. Some write entirely from personal experience. Some adapt a story or a legend, others a biography of a famous person, others a play by an earlier playwright; others simply expand upon a remembered dream.

A documentary might begin with a transcript of a trial or a committee hearing. Other documentary forms might begin with a tape recorder and a situation contrived by the playwright. Some plays are created out of actors' improvisations or acting-class exercises. Some are compilations of material written over the course of many years or collected from many sources.

The fact is, writers tend to begin with whatever works for *them* and accords with their immediate aims. On the one hand, because playwrights usually work alone, at least in the initial stages, they can do as they please whenever they want: there is no norm. On the other hand, certain steps can be followed as introductory exercises to playwriting, and these may in fact lead to the creation of an entire play.

## Dialogue

Transcription of dialogue from previous observation and experience—in other words, the writing down of *remembered dialogue* from overheard conversations or from conversations in which the author has participated—is step one of a fundamental playwriting exercise; probably most finished plays contain such scenes. Because we remember conversations only selectively and subjectively, a certain amount of fictionalizing and shading inevitably creeps into these transcriptions; and often without even meaning to do so, authors also transform people in their memory into characters in their scenes.

Writing scenes of *imagined dialogue* is the logical next step, for all the author need do now is to extend the situation beyond its remembered reality into the area of "what might have happened." The dialogue then constructed will be essentially original yet in keeping with the personalized "characters" developed in the earlier transcription. The characters now react and respond as dramatic figures, interacting with each other freshly and under the control of the author. Many fine plays have resulted from the author's working out, in plot and dialogue, hypothetical relations between real people who never confronted each other in life; indeed, many plays are inspired by the author's notion of what *should* have happened among people who never met. In this way, the theatre has often been used as a form of psychotherapy, with the patient-playwright simply acting out—in imagination or with words on paper—certain obligatory scenes in life that never occurred.

## Conflict

Writing scenes of *forced conflict* accelerates the exercise and becomes a third step in the exercise and the first step toward the creation of a play. Events such as discovery, victory, rejection, revelation, separation, or death become climactic scenes in a play and define its structure. If a writer can create a convincing scene of high conflict that gets inside *each* of the characters involved and not merely one of them, then there is a good chance of making that scene the core of an exciting play—especially if it incorporates some subtlety and is not dependent entirely on shouting and denunciation. What is more, such a scene will be highly actable in its own right and thus can serve as a valuable tool for demonstrating the writer's potential.

Exercises that result in scripted scenes—even if only a page or two in length—have the advantage of allowing the writer to test her or his work as it progresses, for a short scene is easily producible: all it requires is a group of actors and a modest investment of time, and the playwright can quickly assess its impact. Moreover, the performance of such a scene can sometimes generate enthusiasm for the theatrical collaboration needed for a fuller theatrical experience.

## Structure

Developing a complete play demands more than stringing together a number of scenes, of course, and at some point in the scene-writing process the playwright inevitably confronts the need for structure. Many playwrights develop outlines for their plays after writing a scene or two; some have an outline ready before any scenes are written or even thought of. Other playwrights never write down anything theatre that most playwriting is in fact *rewriting*—rewriting aimed principally at organizing and reorganizing the play's staged actions and events.

A strong dramatic structure compels interest and attention. It creates intrigue by establishing certain expectations—both in the characters and in the audience—and then by creating new and bigger expectations out of the fulfillment of the first ones. A good dramatic structure keeps us always wanting more until the final curtain, and at the end it leaves us with a sense of the inevitability of the play's conclusion, a sense that what happened onstage was precisely as it had to be. A great structure makes us comfortable and receptive; we feel in good hands, expertly led wherever the play may take us. And we are willing, therefore, to abandon ourselves to a celebration of vital and ineffable matters.

## THE PLAYWRIGHT'S REWARDS

There will always be a need for playwrights, for the theatre never mutes its clamor for new and better dramatic works. Hundreds of producers today are so anxious to discover new authors and new scripts that they will read (or instruct an associate to read) everything that comes their way; so a truly fine play need not go unnoticed for long. Moreover, playwrights are the only artists in the theatre who can bring their work to the first stage of completion without any outside professional help at all; they do not need to be auditioned, interviewed, hired, cast, or contracted to an agent in order to come up with the world's greatest dramatic manuscript.

The rewards that await successful playwrights can be very fulfilling. Playwrights receive remuneration commensurate with their commercial success; and they may acquire influence and prestige on the basis of their personal vision, for while the public may adore an actor or admire a director or designer, it *listens* to the playwright who truly has something to say. The impact of playwrights such as Arthur Miller, Tennessee Williams, Tony Kushner, August Wilson, and Lynn Nottage on American social thought and cultural mores, for example, is easily measurable. At its best, playwriting is more than a profession and more than just another component of the theatrical machine. It is a creative political act that enlarges human experience and enriches our awe, understanding, and appreciation of life.

Some plays, particularly in the contemporary postmodern era, dispense altogether with conventional structure in favor of a collage of events, images, and poetic perceptions. Sarah Kane's last play, *4.48 Psychosis*, treats disorientation, death, and despair in an entirely nonlinear way—with no attempt to convey a coherent plotline or even an identification of who the characters are or who speaks which lines. Even the first half of the title is meaningless: Kane says 4:48 is simply the time she usually wakes up in the morning. Nonetheless, and although the playwright died before it was performed, the play is now produced all over the world, usually drawing high praise for its poetic beauty and intensely portrayed psychological complexities. Illustrated is a moment of extreme anguish from Poland's TR Warsawa company's production, performed at the Edinburgh International Theatre Festival in 2007. Magdalena Cielecka is the suffering central (but unnamed) character.

except dialogue and stage directions yet find an overall structure asserting itself almost unconsciously as the writing progresses. But the beginning playwright should bear in mind that intrigue, thematic development, compression, and even credibility depend on a carefully built structure and that it is an axiom of

# A SAMPLING OF CURRENT AMERICAN PLAYWRIGHTS

Literally hundreds of American playwrights are producing works on professional American stages today, and several have international reputations. In this section, we focus on five contemporary writers who have made major impacts on the national theatre scene and from whom we may eagerly expect to see new and important works in the decades ahead. These are, in the order of their birth dates, David Mamet, Tony Kushner, David Henry Hwang, Neil LaBute, and Lynn Nottage.

## David Mamet

David Mamet (born 1947) is called a Chicago playwright because Chicago is his birthplace, his home, the setting of most of his plays, and the city where his plays have most often been premiered; moreover, Mamet served for some time as an associate artistic director of Chicago's Goodman Theatre. He is, however, a truly national figure. Mamet's plays employ at least fragments of intensely realistic writing and feature rhythmic language patterns that, though brutal, seem almost musical. Indeed, Mamet's dialogue is often strung out of mere language fragments: the tortured syntax of everyday speech rather than the turned phrases of eloquent discourse, often consisting of a series of frustrated stammerings, grunts, curses, repetitions, trail-offs, and the hemmings and hawings of nervous conversation. In all, there might not be but one or two complete sentences in an entire Mamet play.

*Sexual Perversity in Chicago* brought Mamet broad attention in 1974, and *American Buffalo* (1977), *A Life in the Theatre* (1977), and the Pulitzer Prize-winning *Glengarry Glen Ross* (a scathing depiction of greed, deceit, and crime in an all-male real-estate office, premiering in 1984) solidified it. All four of these plays were written to be performed with all-male casts, however, confronting Mamet with questions as to whether he could write women's roles as well— questions to which he responded with a new play, *Speed-the-Plow*, which featured the actress Madonna in its 1988 Broadway premiere.

In the 1990s, Mamet turned some of his attention to the cinema, with screenplays such as *Hannibal, Heist,* and *The Spanish Prisoner.* But in 1992 he strongly returned to the theatre with the scorching play *Oleanna,* a masterful and intense drama about a charge of sexual (and academic) harassment brought by a college student (female) against her professor (male).

Mamet's latest work shows the author experimenting in a surprising variety of theatrical styles. *Boston Marriage* (2001) is an elegant and epigrammatic drama about a long-term relationship between two unmarried women; *Dr. Faustus* (2004) is a classically based disquisition on morality after the classic by Christopher Marlowe; the hilarious *Romance* (2005) is an out-and-out farce occurring in a courtroom; and *November* (2008) proved a savagely funny political comedy, which, starring Nathan Lane, was Mamet's first play to open directly on Broadway. From 2008 through 2010, a spate of Mamet revivals played on Broadway, including *American Buffalo, Speed-the-Plow, Oleanna,* and *A Life in the Theatre;* and in 2009-10, his latest Broadway premiere, *Race,* portraying a wealthy white man accused of raping a black woman, garnered strong reactions. These new and revived works, together with Mamet's two intriguing books on theatre theory and practice—*True and False: Heresy and Common Sense for the Actor* (1997) and *Three Uses of the Knife: On the Nature and Purpose of Drama* (1998)— reveal that Mamet has not merely returned boldly to the theatre but is eager to play a revolutionary role in both dramaturgy and styles of production.

## Tony Kushner

Surely no play has burst upon the contemporary American theatre scene with such thrilling panache as the seven-hour, two-part *Angels in America* by Tony Kushner (born 1956). Initially commissioned by the Eureka Theatre in San Francisco, *Angels* was subsequently developed at the Mark Taper Forum in Los Angeles and (part one only) at the National Theatre in London. The two parts had separate openings on Broadway in 1993 (under the direction of George C. Wolfe) and received rapturous critical acclaim. Part one, *Millennium Approaches,* took the Tony Award and Pulitzer Prize in 1993, and part two, *Perestroika,* took the Tony in 1994—an unprecedented achievement. By 1995 the play had fully entered the inter national repertoire and was featured in major productions in theatre capitals and drama festivals throughout the world.

*Angels* fully merits this extraordinary attention: it is a masterpiece of modern drama; many critics consider it the finest American play of the present generation. Dealing unstintingly with the AIDS crisis, Kushner has laid bare still-unsettled issues in American culture that touch upon race, religion, gender,

David Mamet's most recent play, *Race,* exposes the roots of hidden racism that continue to permeate contemporary American society. Here, in its author-directed 2009 Broadway premiere, James Spader and Kerry Washington play white and black attorneys arguing how—and even if—their law firm should defend a white celebrity client who has been accused of raping a black woman.

politics, economics, and sexual orientation. Pairing a heterosexual couple (Joe and Harper Pitt, Mormons from Utah) with a homosexual couple (Louis Ironson, a New York Jew, and Prior Walter, afflicted with both AIDS and a lineage that goes back to the *Mayflower*), Kushner interweaves their stories and shakes up their lives within a vast medical-political "America," which is run in Kushner's imagination by Roy Cohn—the (real) self-hating, self-baiting, sometime gay Jewish lawyer in raging self-denial right up to his awful AIDS-ravished demise. A black nurse (male) and a white angel (female) also play sustained roles in this adventure, which is additionally peopled with another twenty-five characters, real and imagined and all played by the eight actors in the cast: a rabbi, an Eskimo, a travel agent, a real-estate saleswoman, the ghost of Ethel Rosenberg, various doctors, nurses, angels, and a man we are told is "the world's oldest Bolshevik." What is astonishing about Kushner's

work is its explosive humor; this is one of the funniest American plays of the twentieth century. But it's also one of the saddest. Though not meant for all audiences (rejected by many theatre producers in conservative cities, the play includes frontal nudity, grisly depictions of AIDS suffering, savage religious satire, the blatant miming of homosexual acts, and a good deal of in-your-face hurling of loathing invectives), *Angels* has a transporting and transforming effect on spectators who are attuned to its rhythms and subject. Most claim to come out of the seven-hour performance ennobled. Many more experienced the same feelings when a cable-television version of the play, directed by Mike Nichols, premiered on HBO in 2003.

Born in New York City and raised in Louisiana, Kushner was known, pre-*Angels,* mainly for his clever adaptation of Pierre Corneille's French classic *The Illusion,* and for his sadly wistful *A Bright Room Called Day,* about a family trying to respond to the Nazi takeover

Tony Kushner's brilliant, two-part *Angels in America* is thought by many critics to be the finest American play in years or even decades. A complex work of comedy, sagacity, and fantasy, it casts a wicked eye on American politics, religion, economics, medicine, and racial and sexual bigotry—but it is also a moving story of human affection and alienation. In this 1993 Broadway production, an angel visits Prior Walter, who is dying of AIDS.

Kushner scored three more times following *Kabul,* and the variety of his topics, settings, and styles continues to be extraordinary. His 2003-04 *Caroline, or Change* is a full-on Broadway musical: it concerns a black maid in a 1960s Jewish Louisiana family much like Kushner's own. *Caroline* digs deeply but without polemic into America's complex race relations, finding, amid the misery, nuances of grace, humor, and hope. On Broadway it received six Tony nominations and afterward enjoyed a good run at London's National Theatre. His subsequent adaptation of Bertolt Brecht's classic of epic theatre, *Mother Courage,* premiered at the New York Shakespeare Festival with Meryl Streep in the title role and became the must-see event of the 2006 summer season in New York. And his *Intelligent Homosexual's Guide to Capitalism and Socialism with a Key to the Scriptures* opened in Minneapolis at the Guthrie Theater in 2009. Despite its exotic title and multiracial, ambisexual cast of characters, it is a straightforward dysfunctional family drama, so realistic in its writing that it often seems an homage to Anton Chekhov and George Bernard Shaw—who are referenced in the text, which also has covert allusions to the playwright's American realistic forebears: Williams, Miller, O'Neil, and Albee. A giant among American playwrights since *Angels in America,* Kushner seems dedicated to build upon that stature for decades to come.

## David Henry Hwang

Growing up in San Gabriel, California, David Henry Hwang (born 1957) began writing—"on a lark," he says—while an undergraduate at Stanford University. His first play, *FOB* (for "Fresh Off the Boat"), is a biting, honest, angry reaction to hidden (and not-so-hidden) American racism; it was first produced at Stanford and subsequently at the Eugene O'Neill Theatre Center in Connecticut and at the New York Public Theatre, for which it received the Obie Award.

Hwang's subsequent *M. Butterfly* (1988), his most celebrated work, explores the bizarre (and apparently true) relationship between a French diplomat and his Chinese mistress: bizarre because the mistress is revealed during the play to be—unbeknownst to the diplomat—a male in disguise. Hwang's main subject is "Orientalism," the ingrained sense of deprecation with which Western culture views the East. In *Butterfly,* Hwang, of Chinese heritage, brilliantly interweaves gritty Western romanticism (including portions of the Puccini opera that gives the play its name) with

of their homeland. After *Angels,* Kushner's interests again went overseas, with *Slavs! Thinking About the Longstanding Problems of Virtue and Happiness* (1995), a satirical comedy about Russian communism, and *Homebody/Kabul* (2001), a three-act, sixteen-actor, three-and-a-half hour intellectual extravaganza written in English, French, Pashto, Dari, Arabic, Esperanto, and international computerese. Set in London, Kabul, and the Afghan desert, *Homebody/Kabul* spans a global, mythic history that covers the history of central Asia, from Cain's burial to the present day. Astonishingly prescient ("You love the Taliban so much? ... don't worry, they're coming to New York!" cries a Pashtun woman in lines written months before the devastating 9/11 attack), *Kabul* also exemplifies its author's genius for combining the foreign with the familiar, the ancient with the contemporary, and dope-laden ecstasy with passionate intellectuality. Has there ever before been a play in which the word *dichlorodiphenyltrichloroethane* came trippingly off a character's tongue? or the verbal compound *synchitic expegeses*?

David Henry Hwang's *Yellow Face* is a semi-autobiographical work in which the author is represented by a character known only as DHH, the author's own initials, while the author's father is likewise known only by his initials, HYH. Francis Joe (*left*), and Pun Bandhu play the two roles in this 2009 production of the play at TheatreWorks in Palo Alto, California, directed by the company's artistic director, Robert Kelly.

Asian theatre and xiqu (Chinese opera) technique, lending it current-political and timeless-mythic proportions. *Butterfly* won Hwang the Tony Award in 1988 and international fame. His subsequent *Golden Child* (1998), a play about a traditional Chinese family assimilating to Westernizing influences after World War I, was also a Broadway critical success, earning its author another Tony nomination for best play.

Hwang's prominence continues in the twenty-first century. His latest play, the fascinating, semiautobiographical *Yellow Face*, treats his own efforts, since *M. Butterfly*, to increase the profile of Asian theatre artists in the American theatre (and the many paradoxes inherent in seeking to define what is truly "Asian" in America's increasingly multiethnic culture). *Yellow Face*

had its successful world premiere at the Mark Taper Forum in Los Angeles in 2007 and received an Obie when it was presented at New York's Public Theatre the following year. Hwang is even more widely known for his recent work as a librettist—as the author of "books" (spoken texts) for operas and musicals. Opera fans know his librettos for Unsuk Chin's *Alice in Wonderland*, Howard Shore's *The Fly,* and Philip Glass's *The Sound of a Voice*, which have premiered in Munich, Paris, and Cambridge (Massachusetts), respectively, since 2007. Broadway-goers know his libretti for the Disney productions of *Aida* and *Tarzan,* and his own adaptation of Rodgers and *Hammerstein's Flower Drum Song,* which played on Broadway after a Los Angeles premiere. Like Kushner and Mamet, Hwang moves gracefully and effectively from spoken to musical drama and is eager to create theatre within a great variety of styles.

## Neil LaBute

Neil LaBute (born 1963) burst into the public eye in his early thirties, when his eerily violent film *In the Company of Men,* first written as a stage play, took the Filmmakers Trophy at the 1997 Sundance Film Festival. LaBute followed *Company* with other films, but his greater success has come with a rapid series of highly successful plays—Bash (1999), *The Shape of Things* (2001), *The Distance from Here* (2002), *The Mercy Seat* (2002), and *Autobahn* (2004). All of them explore, in ways both shocking and revelatory, the hidden violence that can lie beneath seemingly stable human relationships.

*Bash* consists of three self-contained but thematically linked one-acts, all set within the context of the Church of Jesus Christ of Latter-day Saints, to which LaBute himself once belonged. Although the word bash occurs only in the sense of "party" during the play, it also suggests murder, and indeed each of the three separate acts reports a savage killing—monstrous, certainly, but also a bit giddy.

The first two plays, each a monologue for a single actor, have classic roots. In *Medea Redux,* a young Mormon woman sits at a bare steel table speaking to a presumed interrogator in the back of the house; by play's end she has confessed the details of a truly Medean infanticide: she electrocuted her child in a motel bathtub. LaBute's unnamed young woman lays out her horrifically ordinary story with seductive appeal, drawing upon the Greek notions—once taught to her by her predator-teacher—of fate and "atoxia," or world disorder. As played by a willowy-armed and bloody-eyed Calista Flockhart at its premiere, the woman's performance is momentous, making the banal significant, the inelegant profound. In the second act, titled *Iphigenia in Orem,* a hard-drinking corporate middle manager,

Neil LaBute has had well over a dozen of his plays produced in London and New York, but *reasons to be pretty,* which opened at the off-Broadway Lucille Lortel Theater in 2008, was, after some revisions and recasting, his first to make it to Broadway, where it was highly praised and nominated for a 2009 Tony Award. The play treats contemporary romantic relationships and the seemingly simple words that can propel—or destroy—them, such as this moment from the Lortel premiere when Steph (Alison Pill) is upset that Greg (Thomas Sadoski) has called her face "ordinary."

fooled into thinking he is facing job termination and depressed because of company downsizing and reciprocally escalating feminism, conspires in the fatal suffocation of his baby daughter—hoping for a sympathy response from his bosses. His odd chuckles as he relates his story—to a boozy stranger in his hotel room—make his incapacitating guilt both resonant and palpable. In the concluding act, *A Gaggle of Saints,* a young, newly engaged Mormon couple cheerfully recount an event of the previous night's bash (in both senses) at a New York hotel, where the groom-to-be beat a gay man to death in a public restroom while his future bride slept blithely in their suite. Each of *Bash's* three murders is appalling, but with brilliant dramaturgical finesse, LaBute has increased the charm of each narrator in parallel with our disgust at his or her criminal behavior, so that at play's end we walk out in an absolutely perplexed tension of horror and dizziness.

LaBute's subsequent plays, coming at more than one a year, are equally grim treatments of contemporary America but lack *Bash's* Mormon underpinnings. *The Shape of Things* portrays a young female art student in a midwestern university who cunningly charms and flatters a young male museum guard until he falls hopelessly in love with her—whereupon she dumps him. *"Watching The Shape of Things,* you think you're watching an episode of 'Friends,' comfortable with your popcorn—and then the chair gets pulled away from you," said Rachel Weisz, who played the young girl in the premiere (and the subsequent film).

*The Distance from Here* depicts three teenagers and their assorted parents and stepparents and the empty relationships among them all. The play is situated in various suburban haunts—the monkey cage at a zoo, a bus stop at a mall, a school parking lot and detention hall—and in front of a living-room TV. The dialogue consists mainly of conversations about food, car problems, and allowance cutbacks—spiced up with frequent "faggot" and "slut" insults. But when a girl makes the mistake of getting pregnant, her "boyfriend" smashes his fist into her stomach until she miscarries. And when a baby cries too much, he gets hurled over the fence of the zoo's penguin enclosure, to drown in the freezing pool. "Whatever!" is the principal explanation for all of this macabre behavior.

In LaBute's 2002 *The Mercy Seat,* a married man in his early thirties and a woman in her mid-forties, coworkers in a downtown Manhattan office, are engaged in a secret liaison in the woman's loft—on September 11, 2001. Because their office was in the World Trade Center, no one—certainly not the man's wife and children—knows that either of them is still alive. In the course of the play's single act, which takes place the following day, the couple confront the possibilities of running away and creating new lives, versus acknowledging and thus ending their adulterous relationship. The situation gives rise to a varied and intense spiral of guilt, sadness, lust, and recrimination—a virtual road map of middle-age angst in the affluent urban jungle.

LaBute's great contribution to the stage is his coruscating dialogue—vivid, penetrating, desperate, and palpably *real* in the mouths of his characters. The high-velocity flow of his dialogue seems as lifelike (and as "nonliterary") as normal speech (normal, at least, within the imagined world of his characters), including startling profanity, pauses, sentence trailoffs, nongrammatical syntax, and rapidly overlapping speeches—which he sometimes denotes by a slash within the lines. All of these techniques can be seen in this sample from *Mercy Seat:*

BEN: We've been given something here. A chance to ... I don't know what, to wash away a lot of the, just, rotten crap we've done. More than anything else, that's what this is. A chance. I know it is.

ABBY: Yeah, but it's tainted .../... it's a fluke.

BEN: What? / No, it's not that, no, it's ...

ABBY: We got lucky. Or, more specifically ... you did. But you didn't earn it.

BEN: What are you talking about?

ABBY: I'm just saying that it was a happy coincidence that you managed to be over here at my place yesterday morning, getting your proverbial cock sucked, when it happened ... that's all. (Beat.) Right?

BEN: I guess. Yes.

ABBY: The one day out of the year you're supposed to be down there for us and you decide to skip out, come over, get some head ... that's not bad.

BEN: So?

ABBY: So ... there's probably a lot of spouses out there right now who wish their dearly departed would've stopped to pick up a nice Frappuccino or dropped off that roll of film they were carrying around in their pocket ... hell, maybe paid for a blowjob, even. Whatever it takes to stay alive. (Beat.) I'm saying you really dodged a bullet there.

BEN: Plane. I dodged a plane.

ABBY: Ooooohhh. Careful with the humor thing, remember?

BEN: Yeah ...(Beat.) That's a shitty thing to say.

LaBute is certainly a prolific playwright—maybe the most prolific playwright in American history. His alternately affecting and dismaying *Fat Pig,* about a young man who falls in love with an overweight woman in

# PHOTO ESSAY: Playwright Neil LaBute

In November 2006, in his Los Angeles-area home, Neil LaBute chatted with the author about his life as a working writer of films and plays. Excerpts from the conversation follow (RC indicates Robert Cohen; NL, Neil LaBute).

**RC:** Where do you do your writing?
**NL:** Anywhere the feeling seizes me. I do a lot of writing on airplanes. I usually fly at night, and most of the time I stay up and write. But I find that I can write in most places: I'll perch on any windowsill or sit down in the grass or wherever. I don't feel I have to write from eight in the morning 'til noon, or anything like that; I write only when I feel compelled to. Usually I circle around my computer like a shark, closing in until I say "I have to do this" and then sit down and begin.

**RC:** What are your usual starting points?
Do you get captured by a story or...?
**NL:** Sometimes it's a story, but it could be as simple as a line of dialogue you have in your head. It may come to you in bed, like "Let's hurt somebody!" I thought of that line and said, "That's a provocative notion. What does that mean? What are we going to do with that?" And so one script [*In the Company of Men*, LaBute's first film] sprang from that. By the time I made the film, I ended up putting it at the end of the first scene rather than the beginning, but that line was the catalyst for the whole script. Maybe then comes a character. Or an idea. In one case it was: "I want to say something about art." So who's going to do this? "It's going to be an artist and a girl." So who does she need to work with? And then characters come to me: The Shape of Things grew out of that kind of

1. Neil LaBute is working on the Wrecks script in his Los Angeles-area office, with his extensive DVD collection shelved above him. The painting on the wall is a color rendition of W. Eugene Smith's well-known photograph "Walk to Paradise Garden," which LaBute bought at a flea market. "i thought it was the perfect thing for my office," the playwright says, "because the characters are turned away from us, and I always felt that was how I write, that you can never know a person completely, and they always have their back turned to you in a way."

2. Writing is rewriting. LaBute's Wrecks script looks at first like something of a wreck itself, but it shows the extraordinary amount of revision most writers do to perfect their scripts. Wrecks, at the time this photo was taken, had already had its world premiere in Ireland and a run in New York, both directed by the author. Even so, LaBute continues to work on it—deleting, adding, and revising individual lines and making notes on each page of the manuscript.

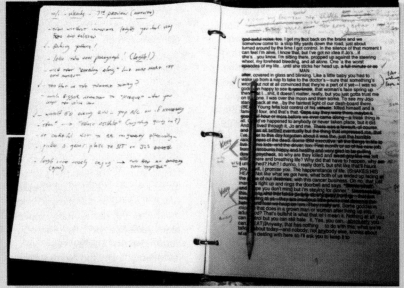

1.

2.

**3.** A one-time professor of drama, LaBute often returns to the classroom. Here he is working with students from the University of California—Irvine, on a writing/acting exercise of his own invention.

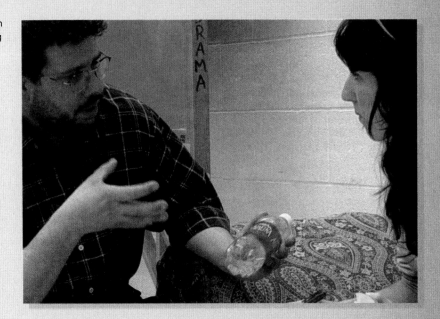

dialogue with myself. Sometimes it's simply a title. I admired the title of the Amy Mann song "This Is How It Goes." But what does that title mean? I ask myself these kinds of questions, and very often something grows out of it: in that case it was something about (*pause*) the flexibility of truth.

Places I tend not to look for material are those right in front of me. I don't look at "me" to give me inspiration. I don't say, "Oh, this is a great story from my youth" or about my parents, or how they got together, and I don't look in the newspaper for stories—which are usually more amazing than the ones I come up with, actually. What's in the newspaper is breathtaking stuff, it's real. For me it always seems to come just from my imagination, but I never know where it's going to take me next.

**RC:** One thing I always see in your writing is peer pressure: how groups of people transform us and affect what we do. Does this come from personal experience or … ?

**NL:** Well, I suppose it does, I mean, it can't help but start there but I've still never written from personal

experience. My interest is in the two selves that we have, the public and private self, the worlds that people juggle a lot of time just from being out there in the world: being one kind of person while trying to be another person. Or being "this" person and knowing this group over here won't like me if they know "this" about me, so trying to keep "this" person from them. The fact that this often leads to us becoming a smoldering wreck because of trying to maintain this deception is fascinating stuff.

**RC:** Betrayal and deception also seem common themes.

**NL:** Yes, a lot of what I write is about people being betrayed, or people who have a confession—one-person monologues which are a kind of confession: "I can't tell anybody else what I've done, so I'm telling you …" In fact, that's what's going on in [my 2006 play] *Wrecks*, which is a kind of moral exploration that [actor Ed] Harris nightly makes to an audience. He talks glowingly about love and I believe the

day you met them? And I don't know the answer to that. That's the beauty of being a writer: I don't have to know things. Fuck, I don't know! (*Laughter*) But I do love the investigation.

I don't write from a place of knowledge. I'm not saying, "I'm going to raise this question just so I can shove an answer down your throat." It's not like I already have this figured out; it's going to take a lot of writing for me to finally say, "This is what I think." Most times I think to myself, if an audience wonders why I've written something, "Why are you asking me? I only thought of the question. I wouldn't have written it if I had an answer!" For me, it's all about "what if?" And "why?" And sometimes by . the end I'm even farther away from the answer than when I began.

**RC:** One thing I love about your work is the sense of deferral. We're pulled into the play and then certain surprises come to us and we've discovered the play isn't what we thought it was. How much of that do you discover as you're writing the play—and how much of the ending have you prepared?

**4.** LaBute's play *Wrecks,* which the playwright was revising at the time of this
interview, is a solo performance about a
man who, grieving at his wife's funeral,
gradually lets us into his secrets.
The play's tragic dimension
(its title—like LaBute's *Medea Redux*—
echoes Greek tragedy, in this case *Oedipus Rex*) is not obscured by its contemporary dialogue. LaBute himself directed
the play, first in Cork, Ireland, in 2006 and
later that year at the Public Theatre in
New York. The fine actor Ed Harris played
the solo role on both occasions.

**NL:** Well, hopefully there's a place where [the ending] reveals itself to me. Sometimes I'm clear in knowing where I want to go, but I still don't know how the journey's going to happen. Like I knew where I was heading with Wrecks because of the kind of story that it was—I had the Greek model so the process was different—but exactly when that moment was going to drop, and where he's going to allow us to go, and how that reversal will work I didn't know until I'd written it. To answer the question: sometimes an ending is present as I begin writing, sometimes not. It's always an adventure.

You know, I'm not always working toward clarity. Sometimes I'm working toward the grayest area possible, because that's what I find attractive. Why do we always have to know everything? That's what is fascinating to me about people, and art. I love that a play could be shit to one person and art to somebody else and that they can both be right. It's when somebody tries to tell me their opinion is more valid than mine is when I get upset. I like to believe that just about everything can be more than one thing; I'm a big believer in "subjectivity."

**RC:** Like you said earlier, the flexibility of truth.

**NL:** Mm-hmm.

**RC:** Last question: Any thoughts to say to an emerging, young playwright, somebody who wants to try to write a play?

**NL:** There was a great quote and I often, as a teacher, would give it to students. It was [Russian dramatist Anton] Chekhov writing to [Maksim] Gorky around the turn of the [twentieth] century and all he said was "Write, write, write." There's just no way around it, other than sitting down and writing. I know a lot of people talk about being writers, but I know far fewer who actually give me a manuscript to read. And to me, that's the only mark of being a writer. Not that they worked at the Geffen [Theatre] or the Public [Theatre] or in London or if they've been published—it's just that they have *written* something, you know? That's the springboard for everything else, that you actually have something on paper. So, don't fear it, but wrestle your thoughts to the ground, do your best. That's the only thing that I've ever really done, is to sit down and write.

Ruined is Lynn Nottage's masterwork to date; in addition to the Pulitzer Prize, it received the Lucille Lortel Award, the Outer Critics Circle Award, and the increasingly important Independent Theatre Bloggers Award. Pictured are Condola Phyleia Rashad (*left*) as the "ruined" bar singer Sophie, and Cherise Booth (*standing*) and Quincy Tyler Bernstine as, respectively, Josephine and Salima, two of Mama Naid's "girls" who have been forced into prostitution to survive.

flippantly seduces and then abandons four girls, opened in London's West End with David Schwimmer in the unpleasant role of the male heel, just as LaBute's new film, *The Wicker Man,* was opening in both Europe and America. And his most recent play at time of writing, *reasons to be pretty,* also became his first Broadway production in 2009, earning excellent reviews and a Tony nomination for best play—as well as nominations for two of the play's actors.

## Lynn Nottage

When she received the 2009 Pulitzer Prize for Drama with *Ruined,* Lynn Nottage reached an important milestone not only in her career but also in her life. Born in Brooklyn in 1964, Nottage began writing plays and stories when she was eight years old. She first studied playwriting as an English concentrator (major) with Pulitzer-winner Paula Vogel at Brown University, then went to Yale, receiving her M.F.A. in playwriting in 1989. But rather than heading straight into theatre, Nottage spent her next four years at Amnesty International, soon becoming the national press officer of this preeminent worldwide organization dedicated to human rights. Thus *Ruined,* the capstone of her dramatic work so far, sprang not only from her playwriting experience but also from her deep commitment to social justice.

Ruined was conceived, Nottage says, as a contemporary adaptation of Brecht's Mother Courage but written from a woman's point of view and omitting Brecht's notion of emotional estrangement. Set in the Democratic Republic of Congo during that central African nation's seemingly eternal civil war—ongoing since 1998 and globally known for its extreme sexual violence against women—the play's action takes place in a small-town bar and brothel run by "Mama Nadi," the "Mother Courage" of the play, who doggedly seeks to create a survivable wartime environment for herself and those around her. Mama Nadi profits by prostituting women who have come to her establishment for shelter, but she also creates for them, as best she can, a haven of respect and security. "My girls [would] rather be here, any day, than back out there in their villages where they are taken without regard. They're safer with me," Mama Nadi insists to her would-be critics. And the stories we hear from these women are indeed horrifying, particularly from the beautiful but now semicrippled young Sophie, who, having been raped by soldiers' bayonets in her native village, has been deemed "ruined" for life. Sophie's is

a cafeteria but is then shamed by his office mates into abandoning her at a company beach-volleyball party, played to encouraging reviews at its 2004 New York premiere. His much darker *This Is How It Goes* premiered at New York's Public Theatre in 2005, with Ben Stiller playing an acknowledged racist who runs into an old high school flame who married a black man. Wrecks, a monologue by a guilt-ridden businessman (played by Ed Harris) at his wife's funeral—the title puns on *Oedipus Rex*—was performed at the Public in 2006 after its opening in Cork, Ireland, earlier that year. Also in 2006, *Some Girl(s),* about a guy who only one of the many stories that Nottage—and the director Kate Whoriskey—heard when they went to Africa and interviewed raped and mutilated Congolese refugees while researching this play. "Their husbands had rejected them," Nottage explained. "Their communities had rejected them. Friends didn't want to take them in, because they had leakage and smelled of urine. They needed money for medical expenses and operations, and the only thing they could do was turn to prostitution." Yet the grimness of the play's situations are transcended in Nottage's beautifully executed script (and in Whoriskey's finely tuned direction of its world premiere), for *Ruined* is also suffused with the warmth, beauty, music, and even humor of contemporary African life. "I also wanted to show the beauty, how gorgeous [Africa] is," Nottage has said. "I believe in engaging people emotionally, because I think they react more out of emotion ...[than by being] preached to." Nottage succeeded: *Ruined* elicits tears and joy as well as ideas and social engagement as it captivates its audience. When the play opened—first at Chicago's Goodman Theatre in 2008 and then at New York's Manhattan Theatre Club in 2009—it received rave press reviews and its powerful impact led to the formation of social-action groups in both cities and soon around the country, each group seeking new ways of remedying the human tragedies that have become endemic in parts of central Africa. Obviously, Nottage's four years with Amnesty International was no mere intermission in her playwriting career but rather its booster rocket.

Nottage's earlier works show the trajectory of her progress. *Crumbs from the Table of Joy,* premiering at off-Broadway's Second Stage in 1995, is a family drama set in her own Brooklyn hometown in 1950. There, a divorced African American father of two teenage girls has fallen under the influence of the era's most extreme radio evangelist, Father Divine—an ultra-puritan who claimed he was God himself—and has fled from the sexual overtures of his deceased wife's sister and into the arms of a white German immigrant lady whom he met in a subway car. The play, which is mainly a coming-of-age narrative of the older sister, Ernestine, is perhaps more accomplished in its well-drawn white and black characters than in its overall dramatic impact. It had strong runs at major theatres around the country (South Coast Repertory, Steppenwolf Theatre Company, Baltimore's Centerstage), and it put Nottage squarely on America's cultural map.

*Intimate Apparel,* which premiered at Baltimore's Centerstage in 2003, is another period play; set in 1905, it centers on Esther, a thirty-five-year-old unmarried black seamstress who lives and works in New York. Esther's specialty is designing and sewing women's intimate apparel, including wedding garments, which by the time the play opens have graced most of her friends at the boardinghouse where she lives. The time has come, Esther now feels, to find a husband of her own. And so she does, or thinks she does, through a chance correspondence with a man from Barbados who is now in Panama working on the construction of the Panama Canal. The core story is from the playwright's own family history: Nottage's great-grandmother was a seamstress who arrived in New York in 1902 and eventually corresponded with—and married—just such a Barbadan. Nottage departs from her family history early on, however, bringing in a panoply of diverse characters, black and white, including Esther's landlady, two of her customers (a prostitute and a society lady), and an Orthodox Jew who supplies her fabrics. "I am drawn to the interplay of voices on a stage," Nottage said in an interview in the program for *Intimate Apparel's* premiere, and the interplay here is not only between individuals but among races, creeds, countries, and social mores. With seventeen productions mounted in 2006, *Apparel* became the most-produced play in America's theatres that year, and its New York premiere received a best-play award from the New York Drama Critics Circle and the Outer Critics Circle and led to a 2007 MacArthur "genius" fellowship in recognition of her "original voice in American theatre." With a Pulitzer Prize now heading her résumé, Nottage is clearly a playwright who will be a force in the American theatre for decades to come.

# The Actor

# Chapter 4

S HE STANDS ALONE IN THE darkness, waiting in the wings, listening with one ear to the insistent rhythms of the dialogue played out upon the stage immediately beyond. Her heart races, and she bounces lightly on the balls of her feet, fighting the welling tension, exhilarated by the sense of something about to engulf her.

The stage ahead of her e is ablaze with light; dazzling colors pour on from all possible directions. The energy onstage is almost tangible: it is there in the eyes of the actors, the pace of the dialogue, the smell of the makeup, ' the sparkle of perspiration glittering in the lights, the bursts of audience laughter and applause, the sudden silence punctuated by a wild cry or a thundering retort.

She glances backward impatiently. Other actors wait in the backstage gloom. Some perform knee bends and roll their necks against the tension. Some gaze thoughtfully at the action of the play. Some stare at the walls. In one corner a stage manager, his head encased in electronic paraphernalia, his body hunched over a dimly lighted copy of the script, whispers commands into an intercom. The backstage shadows pulse with anticipation.

Suddenly the onstage pace quickens; the lines, all at once, take on a greater urgency and familiarity. It is the cue ... if only there were time to go to the bathroom... it is the cue... she takes a deep breath, a deeper breath, a gasp ... *it is the cue.* She bounds from the dimness into the dazzle: she is onstage, she is an actor!

Acting is perhaps the world's most bewildering profession. At the top, it can be extraordinarily rewarding. The thrill of delivering a great performance, the roar of validation from an enraptured audience, the glory of getting inside the skin of the likes of Hamlet, Harpagon, and Hecuba—these are excitements and satisfactions few careers can duplicate. Nor are the rewards purely artistic and intellectual; audience appreciation and the producer's eye for profit can catapult some actors to the highest income levels in the world, with salaries in the millions of dollars for actors achieving "star" status in films. And the celebrity that can follow is legendary. The private lives of the most universally admired actors become public property, their innermost thoughts the daily fare of television talk shows and fan magazines.

And yet, for all the splendor and glamor, the actor's life is more often than not an anxious one, beset by demands for sacrifice from every direction: psychological, financial, and even moral. Stage fright—the actor's nemesis—is an ever-present nightmare that often increases with experience and renown. Fear of failure, fear of competition, fear of forgetting lines, fear of losing emotional control, fear of losing one's looks, fear of losing one's audience—this list of concerns is endemic to acting as to no other profession.

Nor are the economic rewards in general particularly enticing. The six- and seven-figure salaries of the stars bear little relation to the scale pay for which most actors work: theirs is the lowest union-negotiated wage in the free-market economy, and actors often realize less income than the janitors who clean the theatres they perform in. And although the stars billed "above the title" may be treated like celebrities or royalty, the common run of actors are freely bullied by directors, bossed about by stage managers, capriciously hired and fired by producers, dangled and deceived by agents, squeezed and corseted by costumers, pinched by wig dressers, poked and powdered by makeup artists, and traduced by press agents. Certainly no profession entails more numbing uncertainties than acting, none demands more sacrifices, and none measures its rewards in such extreme and contradictory dimensions.

Belfast-born Kenneth Branagh is best known in the United States for his Shakespearean films (*Hamlet, Henry V, Much Ado About Nothing, Love's Labor's Lost, Othello*). He is deeply admired on the British stage for his dramatic passion, clearly apparent here in his 2008 performance in the title role of Chekhov's *Ivanov*, directed by Michael Grandage for London's Wyndham's Theatre.

## WHAT IS ACTING?

Since the first published discussions of acting, more than two thousand years ago, theatre theorists and practitioners have recognized two different and seemingly contradictory notions of what acting really is. The first notion is that an actor creates a performance from the "outside," first by imagining how the character should walk, talk, and behave, and then by performing, through mimicry (*mimesis* in Greek), the actions of this imagined "character." The second notion is that acting is created from the "inside" and the actor should concentrate not on imitating the behavior of an imagined character but by actually

No American actress in the past thirty-five years—indeed, probably no actress anywhere—has come close to equaling the achievement, both artistic and commercial, of Meryl Streep. Quickly moving from her Yale Drama School acting M.FA. degree into five Broadway shows between 1975 and 1977, Streep crossed into films and by 2010 had received more Academy Award nominations than any other actress. But Streep remains closely connected to the stage through the New York Shakespeare Festival, where, in 2001, she played Madame Arkadina in *Chekhov's The Seagull*. She is shown here in 2006 in one of the most demanding roles in modern theatre: the seventeenth-century war-profiteer Anna Fielding (Mother Courage) in Brecht's Mother Courage and *Her Children*. Audiences lined up from the early morning hours, rain or shine, to see Streep's three-and-a-half-hour outdoor performance in Cental Park's Delacorte Theatre. She received nearly unanimous praise for fully capturing Anna's hardbitten cynicism, raucous exuberance, and capitalist fervor—as well as for belting out Brecht's audacious songs with tremendous élan. The script was adapted by Tony Kushner, and the direction of this New York Shakespeare Festival production was by George C. Wolfe.

"experiencing" the actions and feelings that the character experiences.

These different modes have been described in various terms. The "outside" method has on occasion been designated "presentational," because the actor studiously "presents" the role to the audience. It has also been called "technical," because the finest of such actors have spent years mastering various performing techniques: vocal skills (articulation, resonance, and projection), rhetorical skills (phrasing, persuasive argumentation, building crescendos, and fiery

perorations), verse speaking and metrical scansion, the ability to speak flawlessly in a variety of regional dialects and foreign accents, and physical dexterity, agility, and elegant movement. A presentational actor will also seek to master a wide variety of individual performance modes, such as singing, dancing, juggling, fencing, and comic improvisation, and will study human behaviors from a broad range of historical periods, countries, and social classes, so as to apply them when creating characters from a variety of dramatic styles.

"There is no definitive *Hamlet*," says Jude Law, "because you don't play Hamlet, Hamlet plays you. You come out in him." Law played the title role of the play in London and on New York's Broadway in 2009, explaining to an interviewer that he let his emotions in each scene drive the next one, "almost as if he were improvising." Here he gives Hamlet's "To be or not to be" soliloquy in a winter snowfall; the production was directed by Michael Grandage.

The "inside" method, by contrast, asks the actor to enter into the mind of the character being played: to think the character's thoughts, feel the character's feelings, try to win the character's goals, and, when called for, cry the character's (real) tears. The inside method is therefore often referred to as "representational," since the actor is asked to represent the character's body and soul, his or her thoughts and emotions, rather than simply to present a made-up imitation of an imagined individual. The representational actor seeks not to "act" the character as much as to "be" the character during the course of the play, and to "act from the heart," not from the head.

Which is the "best" method? Twenty-five hundred years of debate has not completely resolved this, but most actors and directors and their teachers today insist that *both* of these notions—when integrated—are vital to great acting. Great acting is therefore both presentational and representational, both external and internal, emanating both from the actor's head and from the actor's heart. The relationship of inside and outside, therefore, should not be thought of as a debate as much as a paradox. And the paradox has been known since the beginning.

## The Paradox of Acting—from Socrates to Stanislavsky

It is often thought that ancient drama was performed in an entirely technical manner—mainly because Greek and Roman actors wore masks, elevated shoes, and flowing gowns. But one ancient Roman actor named Aesop became so overwrought when performing the revenge of Orestes that he ran his sword through a stagehand who unhappily strayed into his line of sight. Another, named Polus, brought the ashes of his own dead son onstage with him so that, as the character of Electra, he could cry real tears lamenting the "death" of his fictional brother. The Roman poet Horace (65-8 B.C.) once wrote that

"In order to move the audience, you must first be moved yourself," and this adage was repeated by commentators on acting right up through the Renaissance. So it is clear that ancient actors acted from the inside as well as the outside, feeling the emotions of their characters, and even, in the case of Polus, developing a technique (bringing a deeply moving memento of real life onstage) to do so.

The paradox of acting was itself described in this famous ancient dialogue, in which the philosopher Socrates inquired of the rhapsodist (poetic reciter) Ion, as to what role real emotion played in his recitations:

SOCRATES: Tell me, Ion, when you produce the greatest effect upon the audience ... are you in your right mind? Or are you not carried out of yourself [and] ... seem to be among the persons or the places of which you are speaking?

ION: Socrates, I must frankly confess that at the tale of pity my eyes are filled with tears, and when I speak of horrors, my hair stands on end and my heart throbs.

So Ion was not only feeling the emotions of his roles, he was imagining himself in the presence of the fictional characters he was speaking of. But he was also aware, during the very moments his eyes were filled with tears, of the effects his performance was having on the audience:

SOCRATES: ... and are you aware that you produce similar effects on most of the spectators?

ION: Only too well; for I look down upon them from the stage, and behold the various emotions of pity, wonder, sternness, stamped upon their countenances when I am speaking.

Thus Ion considered his acting both from the inside (his whole body experienced the story he was describing) and from the outside (he was, at the same time, checking out the audience's reaction). This inside *and* outside nature of acting, Socrates realized, is a paradox: when reciting, Ion is, at one and the same time, both inside and outside the fiction of his performance.

Much of the study of acting since Ion, and Horace, therefore, has not been whether the actor should get inside the role (or, we might say, cry real tears), but how to do it. The Roman orator Quintilian (c. 35 to c. 100 A.D.) described envisioning his wife's and children's imaginary deaths with such "extreme vividness" as to become "so moved" during his oration that he would be brought to tears, turn pale, and exhibit "all the symptoms of genuine grief." Quintilian's treatise on performance—and its privileging of these inside techniques—was widely cited up through the Renaissance; an eighteenth-century French critic even proposed that only actors who were truly in love should play lovers onstage.

Yet true to acting's paradox, Quintilian also acknowledged that he created his performances with a "regularity and discipline promised by calculation," and he cautioned fellow performers that "it is never correct to employ the left hand alone in gesture" and that "the hand [must not] be raised above the level of the eyes." And this notion of regularity and discipline became championed in the eighteenth century by the French essayist Denis Diderot, whose 1773 "Paradox of Acting" proclaimed the radical thesis that "a great actor . . . must [only be] an unmoved and disinterested onlooker." Diderot argued fiercely that it is better for an actor to imitate anger than to actually be angry, and that actors should therefore play from the head, not from the heart. "Actors impress the public not when they are furious, but when they play fury well," he declared, explaining that "actors who play from the heart . . . are alternately strong and feeble, fiery and cold. . . . Tomorrow they will miss the point they have excelled in today. ... But the actor who plays from thought ... will be always at his best; for he has considered, combined, learned and arranged the whole thing in his head." Diderot beautifully represents the rationalist view of the European Enlightenment, which sought to demystify both medieval superstition and Renaissance idealism, and his viewpoints circulated widely in Europe and America through the nineteenth century and remain influential in some measure in classical theatre training in the modern era, particularly in France and England.

In the American theatre, however, the inside method has increasingly held sway since the visits to the United States of Russian actor-director Konstantin Stanislavsky (1863-1938) and his Moscow Art Theatre in 1924 and 1925. Astounding American audiences with an intensely realistic and convincing acting style in New York and thirteen other cities, Stanislavsky's system of acting—described as the actor "living the life of his or her character on stage"—turned many American actors into Stanislavsky disciples. When taken up by various American acting teachers, particularly Lee Strasberg in New York, Stanislavsky's system became "the Method"— with a capital M. As taught by Strasberg at the Group Theatre in the 1930s and at the Actors Studio from 1951 until his death in 1982, variations of the Method became core beliefs of actors such as Paul Newman, Ann Bancroft, Al Pacino, James Dean, Dustin Hoffman, and Marilyn Monroe, and the Method became world renowned through the success of these actors on the stage and, more notably worldwide, in American films.

## Acting Today

In the current era, most of the fire has gone out of the inside/outside debate, and the distinction between European and American actors has largely diminished. Today's French and British actors study Stanislavsky's inner methods as well as external classical techniques, while American actors are trained in voice, speech, movement, and period styles along with their focus on "being real," "living the part," "being in the moment," "owning the role," and "personalizing their roles"—all colloquial references to inner or Method approaches. So we will follow this history with expanded discussions of inner and outer techniques and how they have come together in the current era.

## ACTING FROM THE INSIDE: THE STANISLAVSKY LEGACY

Stanislavsky's major pronouncements on living the life of the character were first conveyed to a wide public audience not in Russian but in English, as translated by Elizabeth Hapgood and published as *An Actor Prepares* in New York in 1936. This slender text presented a valuable though incomplete version of Stanislavsky's basic system of realistic acting, and it had a profound and immediate impact, becoming the core textbook of the American acting style for decades to come. Since 2008, however, it has been superseded by a more accurate and more complete translation by Jean Benedetti entitled *An Actor's Work,** which also includes Stanislavsky's following text, called *Building a Character,* in its initial (1949) English appearance. All quotations of Stanislavsky in the following pages are from the Benedetti translation.

In the beginning of *An Actor's Work,* Stanislavsky writes, "Our prime task is... to create the inner life of the character." We can do this, he says, by "bringing our own individual feelings to it, endowing it with all the features of our own personality."

---

*Konstantin Stanislavsky, *An Actor's Work,* trans. Jean Benedetti (London: Routledge, 2008). The literal translation of Stanislavsy's original title, published in Russian in 1938, is *The Actor's Work on Himself in the Creative Process of Experiencing.*

By "inner life" Stanislavsky meant the ambiguity of emotion, the mystery of love and death, and the confusion of experience. To create this life onstage, Stanislavsky sought to identify the separate steps of the actor's preparation. Primary to his vision was that the actor must base the performance in pursuing his or her character's task (in Russian, *zadacha,* which can also be translated as "problem" or, as by Hapgood, "objective"). The character's task is different from the actor's task. The actor's task may be to get a standing ovation from the audience, or a good review in the local press; but the character's task for, let's say, Juliet is to win Romeo's love or, at other times, to win her father's respect, the friar's blessing, or the nurse's assistance. By concentrating on *winning these tasks* (instead of on "being a great actress") during the performance, Stanislavsky discovered, the actress can lose her stage fright, throw herself into her character, and convincingly represent Juliet as a real and whole person rather than simply presenting her as a fictional—though admirable—Renaissance teenager. Identifying the character's tasks is Stanislavsky's key to this process.

Stanislavsky was not the first person to propose this strategy, but he was the first to systematically investigate how to carry it out. He spoke of a character's *motivations* for acting, and he advanced the notion that every move onstage must be seen to correspond to what the *character* (and not just the playwright or director or even the actor) is striving to achieve. "Everything that happens onstage must occur for *some reason or other.* When you sit there, you must also sit for a reason, not merely to show yourself off to the audience," he wrote.

Stanislavsky therefore believed actors must enter a circle of "solitude" to avoid shamelessly playing to the audience, and he urged actors to maintain a deep concentration on the other actors onstage: Your "tasks are ... directed toward the other actors, not to the audience," he proposed. He also established the concept that the play's text was accompanied by a profound "subtext" of meanings hidden beneath the lines, a subtext revealed *unconsciously* by actors when they were concentrating solely on their tasks and the characters around them. He despised empty theatricality, whereby the actor simply relies on showing off theatrical gimmicks and brazenly seeks to generate audience approval.

Stanislavsky was deeply, almost obsessively, concerned with the actor's emotion. In the writings of nineteenth-century French psychologist Théodule Armand Ribot, he had read that "all memories of

Although he had no lines to speak and few moves to make and was the only actor on the stage, Liam Neeson faced quite a challenge in "acting from the inside" when he played the title role in Samuel Beckett's *Eh Joe* in Dublin's Gate Theatre production seen in New York in 2008. Almost every action of his character is strictly internal: mental reactions to the words of an unseen actress whose amplified words, she tells him, are merely "the whisper in your head." Moreover, Neeson's face— as the author's directions specified—was hugely enlarged on a projection screen behind him. It was what his director Atom Egoyan called "the longest reaction shot that an actor can imagine." Neeson clearly proved up to the task, though he later admitted being bewildered by his success: "I got a review in the *New York Times*," he told a friend, "and, God, it's the best review I've ever got in thirty-three years!"

past experiences are recorded by the nervous system and ... may be evoked by an appropriate stimulus." So in his earlier years he experimented with recalling his own past emotional states, and he developed an acting technique known as *emotion memory* (or "emotional recall" or "affective memory") whereby mentally substituting remembered situations from his own life into the action of the play could allow him to reach the emotional levels the play required. By this method, Stanislavsky sought to make his own acting natural, truthful, and emotionally vivid for the performer and audience alike.

No country—not even Russia—has been as influenced by Stanislavsky's teaching as the United States.

Even before his 1924 tour, two of Stanislavsky's disciples, Richard Boleslavski and Maria Ouspenskaya, had moved to New York and founded the American Laboratory Theatre, bringing Stanislavsky's system to the attention of hundreds of young New York actors. One of these was Strasberg, an Austrian immigrant who, along with other Stanislavsky devotees including Harold Clurman, Clifford Odets, Elia Kazan, Morris Carnovsky, Stella Adler, and Sanford Meisner, formed the Group Theatre in 1931 to revolutionize not only American theatre but American acting.

The Group did not outlive its decade, but by the 1950s, all the first believers had developed major theatre careers (Odets as a playwright, Kazan and

# Stagecraft

## Basic Acting Exercises

Acting is easier to understand by doing it than by reading about it. Even if you have never acted before, the following four acting exercises can help you understand what acting is, from the inside and the outside.*

### REACH

Stand on your right foot; reach as high as you can with your left hand. Imagine there is something you greatly desire above your head: a beautiful jewel, a wad of thousand-dollar bills, or "the key to your true love's heart." Now reach again, and *really try to get it!*

This is the simplest acting exercise there is, and it illus- trates the difference between presentational (outside) and representational (internal) acting methods. When you're only asked to reach as high as you can, you respond by acting from the outside, since you reach only because you were told to. This is not even acting—it's simply calisthenics. But when you *really try* to get something—even though it is imaginary—you are acting from the inside because you are trying to achieve the goals of some imaginary character. And the goals come from your imagination: What kind of a jewel was it? How many thousand-dollar bills? And what (or who) was the key to your true love's heart? Rapunzel in her tower prison? Leonardo diCaprio in chains? By making this command ("reach again") your own, by using your imagination to create the target you were reaching for, you put yourself into the role of a character, and, in Stanislavsky's phrase, you "live the life of your character" for a few seconds. This is what acting is, and if you committed fully to it, you probably stretched your arm a bit farther, breathed a bit harder, found your pulse beating a bit faster, and felt just a touch exhausted—and/or exhilarated—when you stopped.

### SHADOWBOX

Make two fists; then, bouncing from foot to foot, with one fist held up to protect your chin, jab at an imaginary opponent with the other fist, extending your arm fully each time. As you do this, shout "BAM!" with every jab.

Continue to bounce from foot to foot, dodging your imaginary opponent's imaginary blows ("Rope-a-dope, Muhammad Ali called this). When you see an (imaginary)' ? opening, hit your opponent with your other fist—a potentially knockout punch known as a cross (a "right cross" if done with your right fist).

With every cross, shout "POW!" Use "BAM!" and "POW!" to cheer yourself on, to frighten an (imaginary) opponent into submission, and to encourage any witnesses to cheer for you (which will frighten your opponent even more).

### DANCE

Balancing on the balls of your feet, step forward on one foot while extending the same-side arm, wrist forward, in the same direction, letting your fingers follow after the wrist has eached its maximum extension. The movement is identical to your throwing a Frisbee. At the moment when the fingers, follow (or the imaginary Frisbee is released), cry "Dance!" Repeat with the other leg and arm, and keep repeating, in alternation, crying "Dance!" with each move.

Continue, switching to the word "Ballet!" As you step on your right foot, go up on your toes on your left foot, and vice versa. Say "Ballet!" in a way that encourages others to appreciate the beauty of ballet (whether or not you find it beautiful). Continue, switching to the word "Lamour!" (French for "love," pronounced "la-MOOR!") and imagining that you are casting beautiful flower petals—as love tokens—at the feet of beautiful persons. Say "L'amour!" in a way that encourages others to think you a wonderful and imaginative lover (whether or not you think you are). Exult in your magnificent ballet moves and your beautiful tossing of flower petals.

Did those last two exercises make you feel a bit foolish? Good—for that means you are learning what it means to perform behaviors beyond what you do in your everyday life. Actors do things all the time that would appear ridiculous if they did them in daily life—such as behave like an ass in A Midsummer Night's Dream or cry like a witch in Macbeth—yet these actors must believe in what they're doing, and believe that they want to do those things. The "shadowbox" and "dance" exercises involve outside acting—doing something you're told and finding a reason to make it seem

---

*Adapted from Robert Cohen, Acting One/Acting Two, 5th ed. (New York: McGraw-Hill, 2008).

---

Clurman as directors, the others as actors and acting teachers). The Actors Studio, created by Kazan and others in 1947 and headed by Strasberg from 1951, became the temple of American theatre—with the Method as its Bible and emotion memory as its First Commandment. The Actors Studio dominated the New York acting scene and quickly spread to Hollywood to become the gold standard of American acting both on the stage and in film. Perhaps because

Strasberg's Method privileged actors over the script—making their own feelings as much the "subject" of the play as their characters' actions—American actors and not a few celebrities (such as Marilyn Monroe) flocked to his school. Other American acting teachers who had been with the Group, notably Adler, Meisner, and Carnovsky, while notably deviating from Strasberg's commitment to emotion memory, perpetuated Stanislavsky's ideal in their classes as well.

like something you want to do, no matter how foolish you might have thought it when you were first asked to do it.

## CONTENTLESS SCENE
## WHAT DID YOU DO LAST NIGHT?

Here is a short dialogue exchange written for two actors. It has no fixed content: it takes on meaning only when it becomes part of a context, which, in this exercise, can be any of the seven situations listed below. To perform this exercise, one person memorizes the lines of role A and the other of role B. Then the players choose any of the seven situations and "perform" the scene accordingly. This exercise is best experienced in a classroom where half of the participants learn one role and half the other and each participant tries the scene several times, changing both situations and partners on each occasion.

### The Dialogue
**A:** Hi!
**B:** Hello.
**A:** How's everything?
**B:** Fine. I guess.
**A:** Do you know what time it is?
**B:** No. Not exactly.
**A:** Don't you have a watch?
**B:** Not on me.
**A:** Well?
**B:** Well what?
**A:** What did you do last night?
**B:** What do you mean?
**A:** What did you do last night?
**B:** Nothing.
**A:** Nothing?
**B:** I said, nothing!
**A:** I'm sorry I asked.
**B:** That's all right.

### The Seven Situations

1. A is a parent; B is a teenager. The scene takes place at the breakfast table. B is eating a bowl of cereal, and A is entering the room.

2. A and B (different sexes) are a young married couple. Last night, after an argument, B left the apartment. It is now the following morning. A is washing dishes. B returns.

3. A and B (same sex) are roommates. Both have been involved with the same boy (or girl) during the past few weeks, both are still interested in pursuing the relationship, and both are somewhat suspicious of the other's secrecy. They meet while returning to their room after a night's absence.

4. A and B are classmates who have been romantically interested in each other for some time. They meet in a cafeteria by accident, and A sits down next to B.

5. A and B (same sex) are auditioning for an important role. It is rumored that the director plays sexual favorites in casting. A and B meet at the bulletin board to await the announcement of callbacks.

6. A and B are siblings. B has recently been released from a psychiatric unit after a suicide attempt. After B has stayed out all night, A finds B in the waiting room of a bus depot.

7. A and B are friends. B has recently been released from a psychiatric unit after maniacally attacking a friend with a butcher knife. A, aware of this, comes upon B in an isolated spot.

When variations on contentless scenes are performed, with the actors switching partners each time, several things become evident.

In this exercise, the content is created entirely by the situation and what the actors bring to it from their own imaginations. It is happening in real time, therefore, and being experienced at the same time it is being performed. The words are instruments of the action, not the dictator of plot, character, or behavior. Thus the acting becomes a way of creating a spontaneously changing relationship, and the plot develops entirely out of what happens between you and your acting partner.

These exercises should teach you a little bit about acting, and they should be fun: they should allow you to move outside your own environment and into the lives of others who are both you and not-you at the same time. This is the paradox of acting.

## ACTING FROM THE OUTSIDE

Although Stanislavsky was committed to his primary principles of developing the inner life of the character, he himself never excluded the need to also create characters through external or technical means. He began his theatrical career, in fact, as a highly technical performer. Born to an aristocratic family, he had performed in plays, operettas, and operas from the age of six, often in large, fully equipped theatres that his family had built in their Moscow home and their country estate. As a singer, he had studied with a major Bolshoi Opera star; indeed, he was so good that Tchaikovsky had proposed writing an opera for him. Like Quintilian, he prized true emotion but also recognized the necessity for rational control in performance, and the second half of his *An Actor's Work* mainly concerns outside acting techniques.

Actress Ann Hathaway (*left*) had the task of playing the young woman Viola in Shakespeare's *Twelfth Night*—who spends all but the first and last moments of the play pretending to be a young man named Cesario, even after falling in love with the handsome Count Orsino (Raúl Esparza, *right*). How did Hathaway prepare for the Cesario scenes? From the outside, at least in part—by putting a rolled-up pair of socks down her trousers and getting used to thinking of it as part of her anatomy. "I'd be lying if I said that I haven't walked around my apartment with a sock shoved down the front!" she explained. "All of a sudden, you just understand. You stand differently and it's just like, yeah!" The highly successful 2009 New York production was directed by Daniel Sullivan.

"Feeling. . . does not replace an immense amount of work on the part of our intellects," Stanislavsky wrote in this section (which was unknown in the West until 1949 and received little attention there until Benedetti's translation), after which he went on to examine elocution, resonance, and rhetorical phrasing, even describing them with operatic terms. "Begin the speech quietly," he advises at one point. "Speak slightly louder after the first line, the next line louder still, until you reach *forte*. If you increase power step by step, you will ultimately reach *forte-fortissimo*." Elsewhere he explains that "upward inflections can be of definite shapes and heights: in intervals of a third, a fifth, or an octave." It is hard to imagine acting instructions more "technical" than these.

Indeed, by the middle of his career, Stanislavsky had even discarded emotion memory from his system, replacing it by a focus on *physical actions* as the key to truthful acting. He began to reproach his actors for excessive wallowing in their own emotion: "What's false here? You're playing feelings, your own suffering, that's what's false. I need to see the event and how you react to that event, how you fight people—how you react, not suffer. . . . To take that line ... is to be passive and sentimental. See everything in terms of action!" Even Stanislavsky understood that there is no question but that technical mastery is at least one critical part of career success in acting. For it is obvious that actors must be heard in the back row, generally understood in what they are saying, and fulfill the basic expectations that the text seems to promise and the production's director seeks to establish (that, for example, Prometheus be seen as fiery, Juliet as romantic, and Monsieur Jourdain as comical). And beyond that, professional actors must be able, at times, to amuse, electrify, delight, seduce, or thrill a paying audience—not just be heard by them. And that requires the level of trained and perfected skills sometimes called "virtuosity."

# THE ACTOR AS VIRTUOSO

The characters of drama are rarely mundane. They are exemplary, and so must be the actors who portray them. To deliver the genius of Hamlet, for example, an actor must embody that brilliance of mind. Similar resources are required to create the fury of Lear, the lyricism of Juliet, the fervor of Saint Joan, the pride of Prometheus, the bravura of Mercutio, the heroic charisma of Hecuba. The despair of Willy Loman in *Death of a Salesman* must be conveyed in his body, worn out by carrying display cases every day for forty years; in his voice, made desperate from trying daily to cover up his obvious, increasing failures; and in his gestures, riddled with the uncertainties of a man who can no longer distinguish between real-time events and his memories of the past. Outsized characters, whether in classical dramas or modern realism, demand outsized abilities and the capacity to project them throughout a crowded auditorium. Such characters draw the audience into the play's world: they not only "entertain" the audience but become archetypes of the play's themes and ideas. We are not only depressed by Willy's pain, we are fascinated by it, and we therefore become determined not to suffer his fate ourselves—if we can help it!

These demands require true virtuosity in dramatic technique. And the training of actors has concentrated on such technique at least since Roman times, not only through lessons in voice, speech, and stage movement but in skills such as singing, dancing, juggling, versifying, declaiming, clowning, miming, stage combat, acrobatics, and sleight of hand. Before the twentieth century, no actor had any chance of success without several of those skills, and today few actors reach the top of their profession without fully mastering at least some of them.

Whatever the individual abilities required of an actor over time, the sought-after dramatic technique common to history and our own times can be summed up in two features: a magnificently expressive voice and a splendidly supple body. These are the tools every actor strives to attain, and when brilliantly honed they are valuable beyond measure.

Throughout history, the actor's voice has received the greatest attention. Greek tragic actors were awarded prizes for their vocal abilities alone, and many modern actors, such as Liev Schreiber, Patrick Stewart, Rachel Weisz, and Meryl Streep, are celebrated for their stunning voices, which may be, by turns, resonant, mellow, sharp, musical, stinging, poetic, seductive, compelling, lulling, and dominating. A voice that can articulate complex ideas rapidly and explain subtleties clearly and convincingly, that can rivet attention and convey nuances, that can exult, dazzle, thunder with rage, and flow with compassion, can hold audiences spellbound.

The actor's use of her or his body—the capacity for movement—is the other fundamental element of virtuoso technique. Most of the best actors are strong and supple; all are capable of great physical self-mastery and are artists of body language. The effects that can be achieved through precise and subtle stage movement are as numerous as those that can be achieved through voice: the gifted and well-trained actor's arched eyebrow, toss of the head, flick of the wrist, whirl of the hem, or shuffle of the feet can command electric attention. But bold movements, too, produce indelible stage moments: Helene Weigel's powerful chest-pounding when, as Mother Courage, she loses her son; Laurence Olivier's breathtaking fall from the tower as Coriolanus; Paul Scofield's audacious upheaval of the laden dinner table, crashing pewter plates and beer mugs to the floor in Peter Brook's production of *King Lear*—these are sublime theatricalizations that are remembered long after the deaths of those who performed them.

And so theatrical virtuosity has made somewhat of a comeback in the American theatre since the mid-twentieth century, when Stanislavsky's *An Actor Prepares* went on sale, the Actors Studio had its heyday, and Hollywood's East of *Eden* (James Dean) and *On the Waterfront* (Marlon Brando)—along with European cinéma vérité (cinema of truth)— held sway in the film world. Why? In part because audiences continued to demand, on the live stage at least, clarity of speech, elegance of movement, and role models instead of just roles. Also in part because drama itself was changing. The theatre of distancing that Bertolt Brecht propounded, which prioritized the dialectic of social and political ideologies over the search for inner truth of individual characters, and the nonlinear structures, multidisciplinary styles, and metatheatrical techniques of our postmodern age, have occasioned a comeback for singing, dancing, circus techniques, direct address, and a generally "distanced" style of acting in many modern dramatic stagings. Multiskilled, multitalented, and multifaceted

The greatest actors succeed in a wide variety of dramatic styles. Mark Rylance is one of England's great contemporary classical actors (he was the initial artistic director of the reconstructed Globe Theatre in London); here, with Tamzin Outhwaite on top of him, he shows himself an admirable farceur as well in the French play *Boeing, Boeing* by Marc Camoletti, which won him the 2009 best actor Tony Award upon its Broadway transfer.

performers—men and women who can play multiple roles of both sexes and all ages, in plays with no costume or makeup changes deemed necessary—are in demand as never before. The actor is now as often seen as a versatile "performer" as he or she is viewed as a fixed "character"—and thus must be rich in talent and performing skills, capable not merely of depicting everyday life but of fashioning an artful and exciting theatrical expression of it.

It seems clear, then, that great acting today demands *both* creating a convincing inner life for the character *and* employing virtuoso skills that can deliver that character with some or all of these theatrical ideals:

clarity, excitement, vivacity, charm, sex appeal, a sense of danger, and a sense of exhilaration—along with a profound engagement with the dramatic text, its issues and ideas, and its production. Virtuosity for its own sake, possibly appealing in the cabaret or lecture hall, can only create performances of depth, complexity, and theatrical power when coupled with the convincing impersonation of a character's inner life.

## MAGIC

Are conviction and virtuosity all there is to great acting? Probably not.

Almost all theatergoers, directors, and critics find a final acting ingredient, often called "presence," "magnetism," "charisma," or even "magic," that has been felt by audiences throughout the centuries. It is a quality that, though impossible to precisely define, is universally felt—a quality we cannot explain except to say we know when we are under its spell.

What is it? We must always remember that the earliest actor was not a technician of the theatre but a priest—and that he (and in those days it was almost certainly a "he") embodied not ordinary men but gods. We may witness this apparent transcendence directly today in certain tribal dramas, in which a shaman or witch doctor is accepted by cocelebrants as the possessor of divine attributes or as one possessed by them. The greatest actors convey a hint of the divine. Elevated upon a stage and bathed in light, charged with creating an intensity of feeling, a vivid characterization, and a well-articulated eloquence of verbal and physical mastery, the actor at his or her finest becomes what we metaphorically consider an extraterrestrial being, a "star," or, in the French expression, a *monstre sacré* ("sacred monster").

This quality of "presence"—the ability not merely to "be present" but to project an aura of magic, of the divine—does not come about as a direct result of studying realistic impersonation or technical virtuosity. It is more surely a factor of the actor's inner confidence, which, though usually bred from the actor's mastery of his or her craft, cannot be taught as part of craft training. It is perhaps frustrating to find that this final measure of acting depends so heavily on an elusive, largely inexplicable goal, but it is also true that every art incorporates elements that must remain as mysteries. The best acting, like any art, ultimately transcends the reach of pure descriptive analysis; it cannot be acquired mechanically. The best acting strikes chords in the deepest, most inaccessible reaches of our brains; there it rings with a resonance we do not fully understand, and evokes an ancient reality we no longer consciously remember. We should extol, not lament, this fact.

# BECOMING AN ACTOR

How does one become an actor? Many thousands ask this question every year; many thousands, indeed, *act* in one or more theatrical productions every year. The training of actors is a major activity in hundreds of colleges, universities, conservatories, and private and commercial schools across the United States today; and theories of actor-training constitute a major branch of artistic pedagogy.

Essentially, actor-training entails two distinct phases: development of the actor's approach to a role (largely creating the character's inner life) and developing the actor's vocal and physical instrument (largely concerning virtuosity). There is no general agreement—indeed, there is substantial debate—on the order in which these phases should occur, but there is now widespread understanding that both are necessary and that the two are interrelated.

## The Approach

As the dust clears from the last phases of the debate over internal and external acting methods, an integrated, or fusion, technique has become nearly universal in actor-training in the West. The first element of this approach to acting is Stanislavsky's primary principle: the actor creates her or his performance through the pursuit of the character's *zadacha,* or task to be accomplished. Whether zadacha is translated as "objective," "intention," "problem," "victory," "want," or (this author's choice), "goal," the basic point—that the actor fully embodies (enters into) a role by pursuing the character's goal (to marry, to revenge), rather than by pursuing the actor's own goal (to get a standing ovation, to get a better part in the next production)—is widely accepted. This goal focuses the actor's energy, displaces her stage fright, aligns her with the character, and allows her to use all her technical skills to win the struggle that propels her words and actions.

Most contemporary teachers, including this author, also insist that these goals be achievable only through *other characters* in the play, so that acting is, in almost all cases, *interacting* with other people. Juliet does not simply want "to marry" but "to marry Romeo"; Hamlet wants not just "to revenge" but to "revenge his father's death by killing Claudius." The acting thus becomes *enlivened;* it occurs in real time onstage, with moment-to-moment *live* interplay between all the actors involved.*

The second element of the actor's approach is the identification of the *tactics* necessary to achieve goals

---

*Books that treat this subject in detail include Robert Cohen's *Acting Power* (1974), David Mamet's *True and False* (1999), and Declan Donnellan's *The Actor and His Target* (2002).

Today most acting teachers consider acting as fundamentally *interacting,* or really "getting into the heads" of the persons with whom you're acting. Here, in Italian director Roberto Bacchi's 2009 production of *Hamlet: Silence from the Body,* the prince (Italian film star Tazio Torrini, *center*) is trying to pry information from his former schoolmates, Rosencrantz and Guildenstern, who he feels (correctly) have been ordered to spy on him. The anguish and terror of Hamlet's former friends are fully evidenced in their faces but are provoked by Torrini's deeply felt anger and determination rather than by any directions by Bacchi to "make grimaces."

Actors Kristin Scott Thomas and Peter Sarsgaard create emotionally intense interactions between the famous but distant actress (Arkadina) and her adoring but psychologically damaged son (Constantine) in Anton Chekhov's *The Seagull,* a performance *New York Times* senior critic Ben Brantley called "the finest and most fully involving production of Chekhov that I have ever known." The 2008 Broadway production was directed by Ian Rickson.

and avoid defeats. Romeo woos Juliet by composing love poems to her and reciting them fetchingly; he silences Mercutio's jibes by wittily humoring him. Hamlet secures Horatio's aid in killing Claudius by speaking warmly to Horatio; he disorients Claudius's chamberlain, Polonius, by confusing him; and he steers his former girlfriend Ophelia out of harm's way (he believes) by frightening her. By means of these tactics Romeo and Hamlet try to make their goals come to fruition, and the voices and bodies of the actors who play them with committed vigor should pulse with anticipation, excitement, and alarm. Actors who play tactics boldly and with enthusiasm, and who allow themselves to believe that they will win their goals (even if the play dictates that they will not), convey the theatre's greatest intangible: hope. Hope achieved—as when the young deaf and blind Helen Keller finally utters the word "wawa" as her teacher splashes water on her hands in the final moments of William Gibson's *The Miracle Worker*—can be overwhelmingly thrilling. Hope dashed—as when Jim O'Connor tells Laura that he won't be able to invite her on a date in Tennessee Williams's *The Glass Menagerie*—can be unbearably poignant. It is in the alternation of these sorts of climaxes that great theatrical impact is achieved.

The third and most complicated element of the actor's approach requires research into the *style* of the play and the *mode* of performance that will govern the production, in which each role is but a single integer. Some plays, and some productions, invite—indeed, require—direct confrontation with the live audience. Others assume an environment in which the entire cast of characters expects and rewards elegantly refined speech, while still others assume an environment in which such speech is ridiculed as pretentious. Some plays contain several "worlds" of characters—the aristocrats, the "mechanicals" (common laborers), and the fairies in Shakespeare's *A Midsummer Night's Dream,* for example—and the actor's approach must lead to a deep and clear understanding of the nature of each of the play's separate or inclusive worlds.

## The Actor's Instrument

The actor's instrument is the actor's self—mind, mettle, and metabolism are the materials of an acting performance. The actor's voice is the Stradivarius to be played; the actor's body is the sculpting clay to be molded. An actor is a portrait artist working from inside the subject's self, creating characters with her or his own organs, hormones, and neurons. It is obvious that a great artist requires first-rate equipment. For the actor this means a responsive *self*: disciplined yet uninhibited and capable of rising to the enormous challenges of great roles.

The training of the actor's instrument is then both physiological and psychological; for that reason it must be accomplished under the personal supervision of qualified instructors. In the past, acting instructors were invariably master actors who took on younger apprentices; even today, students of classical French and Japanese acting styles learn their art by relentless imitation of the actors they hope to succeed. In America and many parts of Europe, however, acting instruction has expanded to include a great many educational specialists who may or may not have had extensive professional acting experience themselves; indeed, some of the most celebrated and effective acting teachers today are play directors, theatrical innovators, and academicians.

No one, however, has yet discovered the art of training an actor's instrument simply by reading books or thinking about problems of craft!

**Voice and Speech** Voice and speech, quite naturally, are the first elements of the actor's physiological instrument to be considered: "Voice, voice, and more voice" was the answer Tommaso Salvini, the famed nineteenth-century Italian tragedian, gave to the question "What are the three most important attributes of acting?" We already have discussed the importance of vocal skills in the acting profession. Voice- and speech-training programs are aimed at acquainting the actor with a variety of means to achieve and enhance these skills.

The basic elements of voice (breathing, phonation, resonance) and of speech (articulation, pronunciation, phrasing)—as well as their final combination (projection)—are all separate aspects of an integrated voice-training program. Such a program ordinarily takes three years or longer, and many actors continue working on voice and speech all their lives.

As devoted as teachers and scientists have been to the problems of perfecting voice and speech, however, a certain mystery still surrounds much of their work. Even the fundamental question of how the voice actually works is a subject of fierce dispute among specialists in anatomy and physiology. Moreover, the processes involved in breathing and speaking have acquired a certain mystique. For example, the dual meaning of *inspiration* as both "inhalation" and "spirit stimulus" has given rise to a number of exotic theoretical dictums that border on religiosity.

**Movement** Movement is the second element of the actor's physiological instrument. Movement training typically involves exercises and instruction designed to create physical relaxation, muscular control, economy of action, and expressive rhythms and movement patterns. Dance, mime, fencing, and acrobatics are traditional training courses for actors; in addition, circus techniques and masked pantomime have become common courses.

Most actors work out regularly. Longtime British stage and film star Laurence Olivier, for example, contended into his senior years that only sheer physical strength could provide the actor with the stamina needed to "hold stage" without strain or fatigue. In America, leading actress Jane Fonda became such a

# PHOTO ESSAY: Actor Patrick Stewart

**1.** In his dressing room, Stewart is making out a chart (in green) specifying where he is to make his entrances in the many different scenes of *Antony and Cleopatra*. During each performance he must leave the stage many times, going to his dressing room to change costume before reentering somewhere else each time. He feels safer with this "cheat sheet" on his dressing-room table to remind him of the location of each new entrance.

Sitting in all those thrones of England on the stage at Stratford-upon-Avon was nothing less than a preparation for sitting in the captain's chair of the *Enterprise*," said actor Patrick Stewart in an interview in early 2007. "This is an exaggeration, of course, but there are parallels," he insists, referring to his two long-standing artistic "homes"—with England's Royal Shakespeare Company and America's film and television franchise *Star Trek*.

"*Star Trek* isn't written in naturalistic dialogue," Stewart continues. "It has a certain heightened quality, a tonality which is not like *CSI* or any of those contemporary shows. It has a five-act structure, which very much follows classical principles. And the bridge set is like an Elizabethan stage: it had a huge opening; the 'view screen' where the audience is; entrances, down left and right and up left and right; and a raised area at the back with its own entrances. It is a very theatrical set, basically a stage format that hasn't changed much since the sixteenth century. And it is costume drama: no jeans or T-shirts, and, as with Elizabethan costumes, we have no pockets! No place to put our hands! And finally, the nature of the relationships of the principal cast very much conforms to what you might find in a Shakespearean history play. So there are many parallels!"

Certainly no living actor has performed more often or more expertly across all dramatic media (classical stage, modern stage, film, television), and on both sides of the Atlantic (in the United States and the United Kingdom), than Stewart. A principal actor with England's Royal Shakespeare Company (RSC) since 1966, and with major roles at London's National Theatre and on its West End stages, Stewart also has starred on New York's Broadway and America's regional stages, including Minneapolis's Guthrie, Los Angeles' Ahmanson and Huntington, Washington's Shakespeare Theatre Company, and the New York Shakespeare Festival. He is known worldwide for his 100-plus films and television appearances, particularly

2.

3.

2. From his dressing room, Stewart checks with the wig room—92 steps up—to see if his wig is ready. London's Novello Theatre, where the performance takes place, has dozens of individual dressing rooms scattered throughout the building's five backstage floors. The telephone is essential for communications with stage management before and during the show.

3. Onstage, the actors prepare with a physical and vocal warm-up, led by voice coach Lyn Darnley (*standing*). Lying on the floor with the rest of the cast, Stewart is sounding his vowels as Darnley directs.

4. In the makeup and wig room, Fiona Matthews applies Antony's graying hairpiece with tiny dabs of spirit gum adhesive. Becoming bald at age nineteen, Stewart, at first embarrassed, soon discovered it could be a theatrical asset. "Most of my hair went within a year," he told the London *Independent*, "and I was very depressed. But it was possibly one of the best things that could have happened. And of course it means I've got a head that's the perfect block for wearing hairpieces. I'm a wigmaker's dream." For Antony, Stewart felt the wig a necessity, in particular to justify the line "the curled Antony."

his 176 episodes as Captain Jean-Luc Picard on television's *Star Trek* and as Professor Charles Xavier in the *X-Men* films. In 2007-08 alone, Stewart played five of Shakespeare's greatest roles—Mark Antony, Prospero, Malvolio, Claudius, and Macbeth—and in 2009 he costarred with Ian McKellen in Samuel Beckett's *Waiting for Godot*, all to great acclaim on both sides of the Atlantic.

Yet Stewart is also deeply involved in theatre education, currently serving as chancellor at the University of Huddersfield and as the Cameron Mackintosh Visiting Professor of Theatre at Oxford. And he is widely known to U.S. theatre students through his many visits to American campuses, first through the RSC's "theatre-go-round," which visited the University of California at Irvine in 1968, and for a dozen years thereafter as the joint founding director of the ACTER group of British performers (now called Actors from the London Stage) who have toured American colleges annually since 1976.

One of the remarkable aspects of Patrick Stewart's career is his easy crossover between English drama (by Shakespeare, Pinter, and Stoppard, among others) and American drama (such as by Miller, Albee, and Mamet). Born in the north of England, he had to lose his Yorkshire accent before acting even in classic English plays, so finding

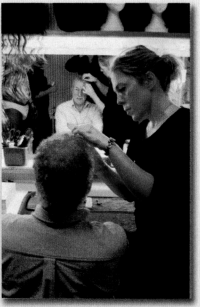

4.

the proper dialect was always part of his actor's preparation. Even today, forty-plus years into his professional acting career, Stewart joins the cast in preperformance warm-ups that tone not only his voice but the particular diction of the play he is in.

For his first American plays, Stewart admits, "the biggest handicap was the accent. I was very aware of this in an early movie where I played an American and they wrote in a line about me

saying, 'Oh, he was born in England.' Whenever you hear a line like that, you know it's about the accent!" Stewart attributes his now-polished American accent to vocal coach (and New York University faculty member) Deborah Hecht, "who completely transformed my experience and confidence in speaking American. That was for [Arthur Miller's] *Ride down Mount Morgan* on Broadway. We were aiming at sort of a cultivated, cultured, New York Jewish accent, and she brought me to a point where I felt so good with it that I felt physically like a different person. The accent changed the way I moved, the way I behaved; certainly the rhythms of speech changed. And she was very, very precise with me, very exact. I worked with her again on [Edward Albee's] *Who's Afraid of Virginia Woolf?* and I went to her again for a film role. Once I had 'slipped sideways' into feeling like an American, everything became much easier. Indeed, a year ago, when we started to rehearse *Antony and Cleopatra* (in England), I was perpetually teased by stage management for my American vowels!"

*Antony and Cleopatra* marked Stewart's return to the RSC for the first time in twenty-five years. The play, performed in repertory with *The Tempest,* in which he played Prospero, opened at Stratford in 2006 and reopened in London in 2007, with a tour to Ann Arbor, Michigan (as Prospero), in

between. Always an athlete (an expert squash player and scuba diver), Stewart, sixty-six at the time, worked out daily for seven months prior to tackling the role of the aging Roman general and politician. By all accounts (including this author's), he was superb.

Stewart obviously loves acting. "It's the liberty of total freedom, where I can be not myself—yet also purely myself. It is a kind of possession, where something takes over and I become everything I would like to be, and find a liberty to 'play' while knowing at the same time that there will be no consequences. Nobody's going to say, 'Oh, stop being a child! Stop being so selfish, so self-obsessed! Pull yourself together!' "

"I thank God that I am an actor," Stewart concludes. "And that I spend my days in the company of people who behave with such dignity, honesty, and openness. That's what's truly meant by 'theatrical'-not something merely flashy, but doing what actors must do to help people understand what is really going on."

5. Wig on, Stewart applies the "pathetic little makeup that I use" to play Mark Antony. He uses no base makeup, only a few very simple lines accented with an eyebrow pencil. Forty-five minutes before curtain, Stewart makes his final preparation, with light exercise and meditation, all intended to lead him to the ideal state of readiness for his first entrance,

6. Stewart as Mark Antony and Harriet Walker as Cleopatra in the 2006-07 production of Shakespeare's *Antony and Cleopatra*, produced by the Royal Shakespeare Company and directed by Gregory Doran at London's Novello Theatre. The costumes were designed by Kandis Cook.

7. Stewart is also highly accomplished in comedy, and this versatility brought him rave reviews at England's 2007 Chichester Festival, where he alternated between two classic roles: the hilariously officious steward Malvolio in Shakespeare's *Twelfth Night*, shown here, and the title role in Shakespeare's tragedy *Macbeth*.

Tadashi Suzuki, the founder/director of the Suzuki Company of Toga (Japan), is widely admired around the world for his intense, nō- and kabuki-inspired productions of ancient Greek tragedies, which showcase the supreme vocal and physical control acting methods he has pioneered in developing among his actors. Suzuki's most noted trademark is seen in his actors' feet, which are most often stamping rather than walking, shuffling, or tiptoeing. This production of his *Electra* (adapted from the opera libretto by Hugo von Hofmannsthal) placed the barefoot and bare-chested male chorus in wheelchairs; it was seen on tour in Poland in 2009.

fitness buff as to create a series of training videos to share her discoveries.

Control of the body permits an actor to stand, sit, and move on the stage with alertness, energy, and seeming ease. Standing tall, walking boldly, turning on a dime at precisely the right moment, extending the limbs joyously, sobbing violently, springing about uproariously, and occupying a major share of stage space (metaphorically becoming "larger than life") are among the capacities of the actor who has mastered body control through training and confidence.

Economy of movement, often taught through the selectivity of mime, permits the conveyance of subtle detail by seemingly inconspicuous movement. The waggle of a finger, the flare of a nostril, the quiver of a lip can communicate volumes in a performance of controlled movement. The beginning actor is often recognized by uncontrolled behaviors—fidgeting, shuffling, aimless pacing, and nervous hand gestures—that draw unwanted audience attention. The professional understands the importance of physical self-control and the explosive potential of a simple movement that follows a carefully prepared stillness. Surprise, one of the actor's greatest weapons, can be achieved only through the actor's mastery of the body. Collective movement, involving continuous physical contact between two or more people, is often taught through dance, contact improvisation, and even theatre games, all ways to release actors from their individual isolation and make them part of a creative and physically interactive ensemble. And specialty movements, as with period dance

Annette Bening plays the title role—a woman who murders her children-in Euripides' *Medea* in this 2009 production of the Greek tragedy staged by the distinguished Croatian director Lenka Udovicki for UCLA-Live in Los Angeles. Backed by a chorus largely composed of UCLA and Cal Arts students and alumni, Bening draws upon extensive stage training and experience to blend her decidedly contemporary fire and intelligence with the play's ancient Greek text-and its horrific context. "Annette has something inside of her that is very noble and yet warm," says Udovicki about her chosen actor for the title role. "She has the inner and outer beauty. Things are not black and white, or shallow. There is a depth. She really defends her characters." Costumes were designed by Bjanka Adzic Ursulov; the setting, with its sand floor, was by Richard Hoover.

and various forms of combat (hand-to-hand, fencing with a variety of weapons, gun battles) are also standard parts of actor training for today's theatre—and film.

All of these are components of an actor's physiological training, and the basic instructional technique for all of them is nearly identical to athletic training: demonstration, memorization, repetition, and constant drilling. This is where the actor learns that to be part of a "play" requires a tremendous amount of what can only be called "work."

**The Psychological Instrument** The psychological gift of *imagination,* and a willingness and ability to use it in the service of art, is an even more important component of the actor's instrument. At the first level, an actress must use her imagination to make the artifice of the theatre real enough to herself to convey a sense of reality to the audience: painted canvas flats—even in a Brechtian "distanced" production—must be imagined as brick walls, an offstage jangle must be imagined as a ringing onstage telephone, and a young actress must be imagined as a mother or grandmother.

At the second, far more important, level, the actor must imagine himself in an interpersonal situation created by the play: in love with Juliet, in awe of Zeus, in despair of his life. This imagination must be broad and all-encompassing: the successful actor is able to imagine himself performing and even relishing the often unspeakable acts of his characters, who may be murderers, despots, or monsters; insane or incestuous lovers; racial bigots, atheists, devils, perverts, or prudes. To the actor, nothing must be unimaginable; the actor's imagination must be a playground for expressive fantasy and darkly compelling motivations.

At the third, deepest, level, the actor's imagination must go beyond the mere accommodation of an accepted role pattern to become a creative force that makes characterization a high art, for each actor creates his or her role uniquely—each Romeo and Juliet are like no others before them, and each role can be uniquely fashioned with the aid of the actor's imaginative power. The final goal of creating a character is to make it fresh by filling it with the pulse of real blood and the animation of real, on-the-spot thinking and doing. The actor's imagination, liberated from stage fright and mechanical worries, is the crucial ingredient in allowing the actor to transcend the pedestrian and soar toward the genuinely unique and original.

The liberation of imagination is a continuing process in actor-training. Exercises and theatre games designed for that purpose are part of most beginning classes in acting, and many directors use the same exercises and games at the beginning of play rehearsal periods. Because the human imagination tends to rigidify in the course of maturation—the child's imagination is usually much richer than that of the adult—veteran professional actors often profit from periodic mindexpanding or imagination-freeing exercises and games.

**Discipline** The fourth and final aspect of an actor's instrument, and to a certain extent the one that rules them all, is simply discipline. As starring actress Maureen Stapleton once put it, "Actors are the only people, good or bad, hot or cold, who show up on time."

Artistic discipline keeps an actor within the established bounds and at the same time ensures artistic agility. The actor is not an independent artist, like a playwright or a composer or an oil painter. The actor works in an ensemble and is but one employee (paid or unpaid) in a large enterprise that can succeed only as a collaboration of many persons. Although actors are sometimes considered by the public to be egotistical or "divas" (temperamental), the truth is almost always the opposite: professional actors are among the most disciplined of artists, and the more professional they are, the more disciplined they are.

The actor, after all, leads a vigorous and demanding life. Makeup calls at 5:30 A.M. for film actors and both nightly and back-to-back weekend performances for stage actors make for schedules that are exceedingly challenging. Further, the physical and emotional demands of the acting process—the need for extreme concentration in rehearsal and performance, for physical health and psychological composure, the need to be both the instrument and the initiator of her or his performance, and the extraordinary demands of interacting with fellow performers at a profound level of mutual emotional and intellectual involvement—do not permit casual or capricious behavior among the members of a professional cast or company. So the discipline of professional actors is always at a very high level (despite what you might read in the celebrity-gossip magazines); and making calls (for rehearsals, costume fittings, photographs, makeup, auditions, and performances) at required times and learning lines and memorizing stage movements well before stipulated deadlines are absolute requirements for anyone hoping to have a career in this field.

# THE ACTOR'S ROUTINE

In essence, the actor's professional routine consists of three stages: audition, rehearsal, and performance. In the first, the actor gets a role; in the second, the actor learns the role; and in the last, the actor produces the role, either night after night on a stage or one time for filming or taping. Each stage imposes certain special demands on the actor's instrument and on his or her approach.

## Audition

Auditioning is the primary process by which acting roles are awarded to all but the most established professionals. A young actor may audition hundreds of times a year. In the film world, celebrated performers may be required to audition only if their careers are perceived to be declining: two of the more famous (and successful) auditions in American film history were undertaken by Frank Sinatra for *From Here to Eternity* and by Marlon Brando for *The Godfather*. Stage actors are customarily asked to audition no matter how experienced or famous they are.

In an audition the actor has an opportunity to demonstrate to the director (or producer or casting director) how well he or she can fulfill the role sought. To show this, the actor presents either a prepared reading or a "cold reading" from the script whose production is planned. Every actor who is seriously planning for a career in the theatre will prepare several audition pieces to have at the ready in case an audition opportunity presents itself. For the most part these pieces will be one- or two-minute monologues from plays, although sometimes short narrative cuttings from novels, short stories, and poems are used. Each audition piece must be carefully edited for timing and content (some alteration of the text, so as to make a continuous speech out of two or three shorter speeches, is generally permissible); the piece is then memorized and staged. The staging requirements should be flexible to permit adjustments to the size of the audition place (which might be a stage but could just as well be an agent's office) and should not rely on costuming or the use of particular pieces of furniture. Most actors prepare a variety of these pieces, for although auditions generally specify two contrasting selections (one verse and one prose, one serious and one comic, or one classical and one modern), an extra piece that fits a particular casting situation can often come in handy. An actor's audition pieces are as essential as calling cards in the professional theatre world and in many academies as well. They should be carefully developed, coached, and rehearsed, and they should be performed with assurance and poise.

The qualities a director looks for at an audition vary from one situation to another, but generally they include the actor's ease at handling the role; naturalness of delivery; physical, vocal, and emotional suitability for the part; and spontaneity, power, and charm. Most directors also look for an actor who is well trained and disciplined and capable of mastering the technical demands of the part, who will complement the company ensemble, and who can convey that intangible presence that makes for "theatre magic." In short, the audition can show the director that the actor not only knows her or his craft but also will lend the production a special excitement.

## Rehearsal

Plays are ordinarily rehearsed in a matter of weeks: a normal period of rehearsal ranges from ten weeks for complex or experimental productions to just one week for many summer stock operations. Much longer rehearsal periods, however, are not unheard of; indeed, the productions of Stanislavsky and Brecht were frequently rehearsed for a year or more. Three to five weeks, however, is the customary rehearsal period for American professional productions—but these are forty-hour weeks, and they usually are followed by several days (or weeks) of previews or out-of-town tryouts, with additional rehearsals between performances.

During the rehearsal period the actor learns the role and investigates, among other things, the character's biography; the subtext (the unspoken communications) of the play; the character's thoughts, fears, and fantasies; the character's objectives; and the world envisioned by the play and the playwright. The director will lead discussions, offer opinions, and issue directives with respect to some or all of these matters; the director may also provide reading materials, pictures, and music to aid in the actor's research.

The actor must memorize lines, stage movements ("blocking"), and directed stage actions ("business"—scripted or seemingly unconscious physical behaviors) during the rehearsal period. He or she must also be prepared to rememorize these if they are changed, as they frequently are: in the rehearsal of new plays it is not unusual for entire acts to be rewritten between rehearsals and for large segments to be changed, added, or written out overnight.

Memorization usually presents no great problem for young actors, to whom it tends to come naturally (children in plays frequently memorize not only their own lines but everyone else's, without even meaning to); however, it seems to become more difficult as one gets older. But at whatever age, memorization of lines remains one of the actor's easier problems to solve, contrary to what many naive audience members think. Adequate memorization merely provides the basis from which the actor learns a part; the actor's goal is not simply to get the lines down but to do it *fast* so that most of the rehearsal time can be devoted to other things.

The rehearsal period is a time for experimentation and discovery. It is a time for the actor to get close to the character's beliefs and intentions, to steep in the internal aspects of characterization that lead to fully engaged physical, intellectual, and emotional performance. It is a time to search the play's text and the director's mind for clues as to how the character behaves and what results the character aims for in the play's situation. And it is a time to experiment, both alone and in rehearsal with other actors, with the possibilities of subtle interactions that these investigations develop.

Externally, rehearsal is a time for the actor to experiment with timing and delivery of both lines and business—to integrate the staged movements (given by the director) with the text (given by the playwright) and to meld these into a fluid series of actions that build and illuminate by the admixture of the actor's own personally initiated behavior. It is a time to suggest movement and business possibilities to the director (assuming the director is the sort who accepts suggestions, as most do nowadays) and to work out details of complicated sequences with the other actors. It is also a time to "get secure" in both lines and business by constant repetition—in fact, the French word for rehearsal is *répétition*. And it affords an opportunity to explore all the possibilities of the role—to look for ways to improve the actor's original plan for its realization and to test various possibilities with the director.

Thus the rehearsal of a play is an extremely creative time for an actor; it is by no means a routine or boring work assignment—and for this reason some actors enjoy the rehearsal process even more than the performance phase of production. At its best, a rehearsal is both spontaneous and disciplined, a combination of repetition and change, of trying and "setting," of making patterns and breaking them and then making them anew. It is an exciting time, no less so because it invariably includes many moments of distress, frustration, and despair; it is a time, above all, when the actor learns a great deal about acting and, ideally, about human interaction on many levels.

## Performance

Performing, finally, is what the theatre is about, and it is before an audience in a live performance that the actor's mettle is put to the ultimate test. Sometimes the results are quite startling. The actor who has been brilliant in rehearsal can crumble before an audience and completely lose the "edge" of his or her performance in the face of stage fright and apprehension. Or—and this is more likely—an actor who seemed fairly unexciting in rehearsal can suddenly take fire in performance and dazzle the audience with unexpected energy, subtlety, and depth: one celebrated example of this phenomenon was achieved by Lee J. Cobb in the original production of Arthur Miller's *Death of a Salesman,* in which Cobb had the title role. Roles rehearsed in all solemnity can suddenly turn comical in performance; conversely, roles developed for comic potential in rehearsal may be received soberly by an audience and lose their comedic aspect entirely.

Sudden and dramatic change, however, is not the norm as the performance phase replaces rehearsal. Most actors cross over from final dress rehearsal to opening night with only the slightest shift; indeed, this is generally thought to be the goal of a disciplined and professional rehearsal schedule. "Holding back until opening night," an acting practice

occasionally employed over the past century, is universally disavowed today, and opening-night recklessness is viewed as a sure sign of the amateur, who relies primarily on guts and adrenaline to get through the evening. Deliberate revision of a role in performance, in response to the first waves of laughter or applause, is similarly frowned upon in all but the most inartistic of theatres today.

Nevertheless, a fundamental shift does occur in the actor's awareness between rehearsal and performance, and this cannot and should not be denied; indeed, it is essential to the creation of theatre art. The shift is set up by elemental feedback: the actor is inevitably aware, with at least a portion of her mind, of the audience's reactions to her own performance and that of the other players; there is always, in any acting performance, a subtle adjustment to the audience that sees it. The outward manifestations of this adjustment are usually all but imperceptible: the split-second hold for a laugh to die down, the slight special projection of a certain line to ensure that it reaches the back row, the quick turn of a head to make a characterization or plot transition extra clear.

In addition, the best actors consistently radiate a quality known to the theatre world as "presence." It is a difficult quality to describe, but it has the effect of making both the character whom the actor portrays and the "self" of the actor who represents that character especially vibrant and "in the present" for the audience. It is the quality of an actor who takes the stage and acknowledges, in some inexplicable yet indelible manner, that he or she is there *to be seen.* Performance is not a one-way statement given from the stage to the house; it is a two-way, participatory communication between the actors and the audience members in which the former employ text and movement and the latter employ applause, laughter, silence, and attention.

Even when the audience is silent and invisible—and, owing to the brightness of stage lights, the audience is frequently invisible to the actor—the performer feels its presence. There is nothing extrasensory about this: the absence of sound is itself a signal, for when several hundred people sit without shuffling, coughing, or muttering, their silence betokens a level of attention for which the actor customarily strives. Laughter, gasps, sighs, and applause similarly feed back into the actor's consciousness—and unconsciousness—and spur (or sometimes, alas, distract) his efforts. The veteran actor can determine quickly how to ride the crest of audience laughter and

No one can say that sex appeal is not a vital part of theatre, which almost always centers on themes of erotic passion. Nicole Kidman is here the star, opposite Iain Glen, in English playwright David Hare's steamy *The Blue Room,* in its London premiere in 1998.

their finances, awkwardly for their art—of performing the same part eight times a week, fifty-two weeks a year, with no end in sight. Of course the routine can vary with vacations and cast substitutions; and in fact very few actors ever play a role continuously for more than a year or two, but the problem becomes intense even after only a few weeks. How, as they say in the trade, does the actor "keep it fresh"?

Each actor has her or his own way of addressing this problem. Some rely on their total immersion in the role and contend that by "living the life of the character" they can keep themselves equally alert from first performance to last. Others turn to technical experiments—reworking their delivery and trying constantly to find better ways of saying their lines, expressing their characters, and achieving their objectives. Still others concentrate on the relationships within the play and try with every performance to "find something new" in each relationship as it unfolds onstage. Some actors, it must be admitted, resort to childish measures, rewriting dialogue as they go or trying to break the concentration of the other actors. This sort of behavior is abhorrent, but it is indicative of the seriousness of the actor's problems of combating boredom in a long-running production and the lengths to which some actors will go to solve them.

The actor's performance does not end with the play, for it certainly extends into the postplay moments of the curtain call—in which the actor—audience communion is direct and unmistakable—and it can even be said to extend to the dressing-room postmortem, in which the actor reflects on what was done today and how it might be done better tomorrow. Sometimes the postmortem of a play is handled quite specifically by the director, who may give notes to the cast. More typically, in professional situations, the actor simply relies on self-criticism, often measured against comments from friends and fellow cast members, from the stage manager, and from reviews in the press. There is no performer who leaves the stage in the spirit of a factory worker leaving the plant. If there has been a shift up from the rehearsal phase to the performance phase, there is now a shift down (or a letdown) that follows the curtain call—a reentry into a world in which actions and reactions are likely to be a little calmer. There would be no stage fright if there were nothing to be frightened *about,* and the conquering of one's own anxiety—sometimes translated as conquering of the audience: "I really killed them tonight"—fills the actor at the final curtain with a sense of awe, elation … and emptiness. It is perhaps this feeling that draws

how to hold the next line just long enough that it will pierce the lingering chuckles but not be overridden by them; he also knows how to vary his pace or redouble his energy when he senses restlessness or boredom on the other side of the curtain line. "Performance technique," or the art of "reading an audience," is more instinctual than learned. It is not dissimilar to the technique achieved by the effective classroom lecturer or TV talk-show host or even by the accomplished conversationalist. The timing it requires is of such complexity that no actor could master it rationally; he or she can develop it only through experience—both on the stage and off.

Professional stage actors face a special problem unknown to their film counterparts and seldom experienced by amateurs in the theatre: the problem of maintaining a high level of spontaneity through many, many performances. Some professional play productions perform continuously for years, and actors may find themselves in the position—fortunately for

England's most acclaimed actress, Judi Dench, playing the role of an acclaimed actress, here applies makeup in the 1999 Broadway production of David Hare's *Amy's View,* a story of broken relationships against a background of theatrical culture and an entertainment industry. Making up and making up are both the literal and the figurative topics. Design is by Bob Crowley.

the actor ever more deeply into the profession, for it is a feeling known to the rankest amateur in a high school pageant as well as to the most experienced professional in a Broadway or West End run. It is the theatre's "high," and because it is a high that accompanies an inexpressible void, it leads to addiction.

## THE ACTOR IN LIFE

Acting is an art. It can also be a disease. Actors are privileged people. They get to live the lives of some of the world's greatest and best-known characters: Romeo, Juliet, Phèdre, Cyrano, Saint Joan, and Willy Loman. They get to fight for honor, hunger for salvation, battle for justice, die for love, kill for passion. They get to die many times before their deaths, to duel fabulous enemies, to love magnificent lovers, and to live through an infinite variety of human experiences that, though imaginary, are publicly engaged. They get to reenter the innocence of childhood without

suffering its consequences and to participate in every sort of adult villainy without reckoning its responsibility. They get to fantasize freely and be seen doing so—and they get paid for it.

Millions of people want to be actors. It looks easy, and, at least for some people, it is easy. It looks exciting, and there can be no question that it is exciting, very exciting; in fact, amateurs act in theatres all over the world without any hope of getting paid merely to experience that excitement. Acting addicts, as a consequence, are common. People who will not wait ten minutes at a supermarket checkout stand will wait ten years to get a role in a Hollywood film or a Broadway play. The acting unions are the only unions in the world that have ever negotiated a *lower wage* for some of their members in order to allow them to perform at substandard salaries. To the true acting addict there is nothing else; acting becomes the sole preoccupation.

The addicted actor—the actor obsessed with acting for its own sake—is probably not a very good actor, for fine acting demands an open mind, a mind capable of taking in stimuli from all sorts of directions, not merely from the theatrical environment. An actor who knows nothing but acting has no range. First and foremost, actors must represent human beings, and to do that they must know something about humankind. Thus the proper study of acting is life, abetted but not supplanted by the craft of the trade. Common sense, acute powers of observation and perception, tolerance and understanding for all human beings, and a sound general knowledge of one's own society and culture are prime requisites for the actor—as well as training, business acumen, and a realistic vision of one's own potential.

A lifetime professional career in acting is the goal of many but the accomplishment of very few. Statistically, one's chances of developing a long-standing acting career are quite small. Only those individuals possessed of great talent, skill, persistence, and personal fortitude stand any chance of succeeding—and even then it is only a chance. But the excitement of acting is not the exclusive preserve of those who attain lifetime professional careers; on the contrary, it may be argued that the happiest and most artistically fulfilled actors are those for whom performance is only an avocation. The excitement of acting, finally, is dependent not on monetary reward, a billing above the title, or the size of one's roles but on the actor's deepest engagement with dramatic action and theatrical expression—which comprise the very heart of the theatre experience.

# Chapter 5

# The Director

THE ROOM IS ALREADY FILLED with people when she enters, a bit fussily, with a bundle of books and papers under her arm. Expectation, tension, and even a hint of panic can be sensed behind the muffled greetings, loose laughter, and choked conversation that greet her arrival,

She sits, and an assistant arranges chairs. Gradually, starting at the other end of what has suddenly become "her" table, the others seat themselves. An edgy silence descends. Where are they going? What experiences lie ahead? What risks, what challenges are to be demanded? What feelings, in the coming weeks and months, are going to be stirred to poignant reality?

Only she knows—and if she doesn't, no one does. It is in this silence, tender with hope and fear, that the director breaks ground for the production. It is here that plan begins to become work and idea begins to become art. It is the peak moment of directing and of the director.

That is an idealized scenario, to be sure. There are many directors who deliberately avoid invoking an impression of "mystique" and whose primary efforts are directed toward dispelling awe, dread, or any form of personall tension among their associates. Nonetheless, the picture holds a measure of truth for every theatrical production, for the art of directing is an exercise in leadership, imagination, and control;

in the director's hands, finally, rest the aspirations, neuroses, skills, and ideas of the entire theatrical company.

Directing is an art whose product is the most ambiguous, perhaps the most mysterious, in the theatre. The direction of a play is not visible like scenery or costumes; and unlike the actor's voice or the sound designer's score, it cannot be directly heard or sensed. Yet direction underlies everything we see and hear in the theatre. Utterly absorbed by the final theatrical experience, direction animates and defines that experience. A whole class of theatrical artists in our time has reached international eminence in this particular art. But what, exactly, is involved?

At the *technical* level, the director is the person who organizes the production. He or she schedules the work process and supervises the acting, designing, staging, and technical operation of the play. This is usually the easiest part of the director's job.

At the more fundamental, *artistic,* level, the director inspires a creation of theatre with each production. He or she conceptualizes the play, gives it vision and purpose—both social and aesthetic—and inspires the company of artists to join together in collaboration. This is the hard part, the part by which directors earn their reputations.

It is in the conjunction of the technical and the artistic that each director defines the directorial function anew. And it is with one foot in each that the director creates—through an adroit synthesis of text, materials, and available talent—a unique and vivid theatrical experience.

# A HISTORICAL OVERVIEW

Play productions have been directed ever since theatre began, but the emergence of a "director"—a person who guides the actors and designers in orchestrating the play's dramatic actions (and who takes credit for doing so)—has been relatively recent. Although playwrights from Aeschylus to Molière are known to have directed their own plays, the idea of an independent "director" did not even exist until the nineteenth century and did not become universal until just before the twentieth. Yet today the role of the director has become so significant that many critics and theatergoers speak of the current stage as a "director's theatre." And many directors, particularly in Europe and in film, have become world celebrities—more famous than the actors they direct.

The director's evolution, however, is not simply the rise of one member of the theatrical production ensemble. The director's new prominence has coincided with the broadening of the theatre's perspective during the past two centuries: expanding from a local or national art to a global one, and from a limited repertoire of one or two stylistic forms to a nearly unlimited palette of creative possibilities. For today's playwright, actor, and designer may draw from a vast world of resources, spanning three millennia, six continents, and an ever-increasing host of new technologies. And the role of director has risen accordingly, becoming a vital force in channeling individual play productions into unique, tightly focused, and wellshaped paths.

## Teacher-Directors

In the earliest days of the theatre and for some time thereafter, directing was considered a form of teaching. The Greeks called the director the *didaskalos,* which means "teacher," and in medieval times the director's designation, in all the various European languages, was "master." The underlying assumption of teaching, of course, is that the teacher already knows and understands the subject; the teacher's task is simply to transmit that knowledge to others. The earliest directors, therefore, were simply asked to pass along the accumulated wisdom and techniques of "correct" performance within a "given" convention. Often the playwrights themselves served as directors, for who would be better qualified to "teach" a play than the person who wrote it? In one famous dramatic scene, Molière delightfully depicts himself directing one of his own plays; this is surely an effective model of the author-teacher-director for the seventeenth century and indeed for much of the theatre's history.

The teacher-director reached a pinnacle of influence, albeit anonymously, during the late Enlightenment and the Victorian era—during the eighteenth and nineteenth centuries—partly in response to the remarkable fascination of those times with science, scientific method, and humanistic research: the same dedication to rationalism that fostered a profusion of libraries, museums, and historic preservation also emphasized accuracy, consistency, and precision in the arts. The temper of the times led to major directorial changes in the theatre, for on the one hand audiences were demanding revivals of classic plays—whose authors were no longer around to direct them—and on the other hand they were demanding that these revivals be historically edifying, that they have a museum-like authenticity. All of this required research, organization, and comprehensive coordination; in other words, it demanded an independent director.

Most of the directors of this time—nearly all of them until the latter part of the nineteenth century—received no more recognition for their efforts than the museum director who creates historical dioramas. Sometimes the directing was attributed to a famous acting star, such as the Englishman Charles Kean or the American Edwin Booth, when in fact the work was done by a lesser functionary. In Booth's case, for example, one D. W. Waller was the true director, but his name was all but buried in the program and never appeared in the reviews or publicity. Nevertheless, these teacher-directors who labored largely in the shadows began the art of directing as we know it today. They organized their productions around specific concepts—independently arrived at—and they dedicated themselves to creating unified and coherent theatrical works by "directing" an ensemble of actors, designers, and technicians toward established ends.

## Realistic Directors

The second stage in the development of modern-day directing began toward the end of the nineteenth century and brought to the fore a group of directors who restudied the conventions of theatrical presentation and strove in various ways to make them more lifelike. George II, Duke of Saxe-Meiningen, was the first of this breed and is generally regarded as the first modern director. The duke, who headed a provincial troupe of actors in his rural duchy, presented a series of premieres and classical revivals throughout Europe during the late 1870s and 1880s that were dazzling in their harmonized acting, staging, and scenery. Though still historically "correct," the duke's productions featured an ensemble of performances rather than a hierarchy of "star, support, and supernumerary." All of his performers were vigorously rehearsed toward the development of individual, realistically conceived roles—which were then played out in highly organic, even volatile, patterns of dramatic action. The stodgy lineup of spear carriers that had traditionally looked on while the star recited center stage was conspicuously absent from the Meiningen productions; so was the "super" who was customarily hired on the afternoon of performance, squeezed into a costume, and set upon the stage like so much living scenery. The totality of the Meiningen theatre aesthetic, embracing acting, interpretation, and design, was acclaimed throughout Europe: when the

Meiningen troupe ceased touring in 1890, the position of a director who would organize and rehearse an entire company toward a complexly and comprehensively fashioned theatrical presentation was firmly established.

In 1887 André Antoine began a movement of greater realism in Paris with his Théâtre Libre, and Konstantin Stanislavsky initiated his even-more-celebrated Moscow Art Theatre in 1898. Both of these directors, amateurs like Meiningen at the start of their careers, went on to develop wholly innovative techniques in acting and actor-coaching based on the staging concepts of the duke; both also theorized and worked pragmatically at the organizing of theatre companies, the development of a dramatic repertory, the reeducation of theatergoing audiences, and the re-creation of an overall aesthetic of the theatre. Although both Antoine and Stanislavsky were known primarily as naturalists—somewhat to their disadvantage, perhaps, for they had many other interests as well—they were above all idealists who sought to make the theatre a powerful social and artistic instrument for the expression of truth. Their ideals and their commitment practically forced them to expand the directorial function into an all-encompassing and inspirational art.

The importance of these directors—and of certain other pioneers of the same spirit, including Harley Granville—Barker in England, David Belasco in America, and Otto Brahm in Germany—was not merely that they fostered the developing realist and naturalist drama but also that they opened up the theatre to the almost infinite possibilities of psychological interpretation. Once the psychology of the human individual became crucial to the analysis and acting of plays, directors became more than teachers: they became part analyst, part therapist, and even part mystic; their *creative* function in play production increased substantially. The rise of realism in the theatre of the late nineteenth and early twentieth centuries and the rise of directors capable of bringing out realistic nuances and patterning them into highly theatrical productions brought about an irreversible theatrical renovation that in turn irrevocably established the importance of the director.

## Stylizing Directors

Right on the heels of the realist phase of direction came a third phase—one that brought the director to the present position of power and recognition. This

Katie Mitchell is arguably the most controversial director in London today. Her astonishing stagings anger purists because of their modern settings (*Iphigenia in Aulis* in World War II), texts cut in half (Chekhov's *The Seagull*), and, in this 2007 cut-down production of Euripides' *Women of Troy* at England's Royal National Theatre, full frontal nudity, pyromania, ballroom dancing, and women climbing tall ladders in long dresses and high heels. Here Sinead Matthews as a fire-happy Cassandra stares into the future—which is us.

phase arrived with the directors who joined forces with nonrealist playwrights to create the modern antirealistic theatre. Their forces are still growing. They are the ones who demand of directing that it aim primarily at the creation of originality, theatricality, and style. The stylizing directors are unrestrained by rigid formulas with respect to verisimilitude or realistic behavior; their goal is to create sheer theatrical brilliance, beauty, and excitement and to lead their collaborators in explorations of pure theatre and pure theatrical imagination.

Paul Fort, one of the first of these third-phase directors, launched his Théâtre d'Art in Paris in 1890 as a direct assault upon the realist principles espoused by Antoine. Similarly, Vsevolod Meyerhold, a one-time disciple of Stanislavsky, began his theatre of "biomechanical constructivism" (an acting method characterized by bold gestures and rapid, near-acrobatic movement) in Moscow to combat the master's realism. The movement toward stylized directing occasioned by these innovators and others like them introduced a lyricism and symbolism, an expressive and abstract use of design, an explosive theatricality, and certain intentionally contrived methods of acting that continue to have a profound effect on today's theatre and its drama.

Perhaps the most influential proponent of this third-phase position of the director, however, was not himself a director at all but an eminent designer and theorist: Gordon Craig. In a seminal essay titled "The Art of the Theatre" (1905), Craig compared the director of a play to the captain of a ship: an absolutely indispensable leader whose rule, maintained by strict discipline, extends over every last facet of the enterprise. "Until discipline is understood in a theatre to be willing and reliant obedience to the manager [director] or captain," wrote Craig, "no supreme achievement can be accomplished." Craig's essay was aimed at a full-scale "Renaissance of the Art of the Theatre," in which a "systematic progression" of reform would overtake all the theatre arts—"acting, scenery, costuming, lighting, carpentering, singing, dancing, etc."—under the complete control and organizing genius of this newcomer to the ranks of theatrical artistry, the independent director.

## The Contemporary Director

Craig's renaissance has arrived: this indeed is the "age of the director," an age in which the directorial function is fully established as the art of synthesizing script, design, and performance into a unique and splendid theatrical event that creates its own harmony and its own ineffable yet memorable distinction. If, as performance theorist J. L. Styan says, "the theatre persists in communicating by a simultaneity of sensory impressions,"* it is above all the director who is charged with inspiring these impressions and ensuring their simultaneity.

Today, in a world of mass travel and mass communications, the exotic quickly becomes familiar and the familiar just as quickly becomes trite. Nothing is binding; the directorial function has shifted from teaching what is "proper" to creating what is stimulating and wondrous. At the beginning of a production, the director faces a blank canvas but has at hand a generous palette. At his or her disposal are not only the underlying conventions of the time but also all those of the past, which can be revived for novel effects and stunning juxtapositions: our conglomerate theatre of today allows Shakespeare in modern dress, Greek tragedy à la kabuki spectacle, theatre of the absurd as vaudevillian buffoonery, and romantic melodrama as campy satire. Thus, at the conception of a theatrical idea today—in the first moments of imagining a specific production—no question can be answered automatically, no style is obligatory, no interpretation is definitive. Jean-Paul Sartre said about the whole of modern life that "man is condemned to be free"; in the theatre the director's freedom in the face of almost limitless possibilities leads to a certain existential anxiety that is both chilling and thrilling in its challenge.

---

*J. L. Styan, *Drama, Stage and Audience* (London: Cambridge University Press, 1975), 3.

## Directors and Producers

The director does not work in a vacuum. Although the director may be said to have final "artistic responsibility" for shaping a production, he or she is usually working within a context established by a producer, whose two chief duties are to provide the production's funding—and to hire the director! So Gordon Craig's perhaps idealistic vision of the director as the sole "true artist of the theatre" occurs in actuality only when the director assumes both roles, as a production's producer-director.

The producer may be a single individual, such as the artistic director of a resident theatre, the dean, chairperson, or artistic director of a university theatre department, a Broadway impresario, or a director who assumes the producing role and becomes a producer-director. Or the producer may be a "producing entity"—a partnership of individuals, particularly on Broadway, where costs range in the multiple millions; a committee (in a university); or a board of directors (of a regional theatre). In all cases, the producer is clearly a major factor in the artistry of the enterprise, for the selection of the director and the allocation of the budget—squarely within the producer's control—create a leverage that is applied to artistic as well as financial issues, for, as the old expression has it, "He who pays the piper calls the tune."

In regional or university theatre, perhaps the most common goal of the producer vis-à-vis the director is to safeguard the long-term interests of the institution that hosts the production—whether it is a regional company, a university department, or a production team. Any of these established groups could face a decline in future attendance if the local audience and press reviewers deemed a single production too shocking or too boring. So, generally, producers maintain a close eye on the productions they oversee, making suggestions during the design development process and giving the director notes after sitting in on rehearsals—particularly technical and dress rehearsals when the production is taking final form. Producers cannot exactly "overrule" a director's decision, but they can certainly fire the director, even at the last moment, and this happens with some regularity in the professional theatre world.

In addition to hiring (or firing) the director, and providing and distributing the financial resources, the producer's functions include creating and managing the budget, choosing and acquiring the theatre facility, and establishing the play's rehearsal and

# PHOTO ESSAY: Director Susan Stroman

No director-choreographer has captured turn-of-this-century Broadway audiences and critics of musical theatre better than Susan Stroman, who won Tony Awards for her choreography of *Crazy for You, Showboat, Contact,* and *The Producers* (plus Tony nominations for *Big, Steel Pier, The Music Man, Oklahoma,* and *Young Frankenstein*), plus a fifth Tony for her *direction* of *The Producers* and yet another nomination for her direction of *Contact*. Quite an achievement for a University of Delaware theatre major from Wilmington who hit the ground running—or at least dancing— following her 1976 graduation.

The author met up with Stroman in Las Vegas, where she was restaging her Broadway production of *The Producers*—which won more Tony Awards (twelve) than any show in history—for the Paris Hotel and Casino. The show had begun its preview performances the evening before, and Stroman was working with a few actors prior to the full rehearsal, which was to begin in the following hour. RC indicates the author; SS, Susan Stroman.

**1.** Directing and choreographing a musical involves close personal interaction, plus great attention to the details of both script and musical score. Here Stroman (*center*) gathers members of her cast around the orchestral score, which she has laid upon the stage in the convenient spotlight so that all can see it (and her) clearly. From left to right behind her are Associate Choreographer Bill Burns and performers Matthew J. Vargo, Shari Jordan, Katrina Loncaric, and Patrick Boyd.

**RC:** When did you start thinking of being a choreographer?

**SS:** Always. I'm not one of the people who dance-dance-dances and then decides to try choreography. Ever since I was a little girl, whether it was classical or rock and roll or an old standard, I visualized music. My father was a wonderful piano player. He would play the piano and I would dance around the living room, but in my head I would be imagining loads of people dancing with lights, sets, and costumes. When I came to New York, I knew I couldn't just "take over"—I would have to come as a song-and-dance gal because I could sing and dance—but I did so always with the idea of going to the other side of the table. So I started to choreograph and direct industrial shows and club acts in small venues—just dabbling in it to see if I could compete. But at a certain point I had to stop being known as a performer, because in New York you have to be either one thing or another. You have to focus on what you want to be. So I stopped performing and decided to go for it. I was in a Broadway show called *Musical Chairs* and with me was another aspiring fellow, Scott Ellis, who wanted to be on the other side of the table. We both knew [the musical Broadway team of composer John] Kander and [lyricist Fred] Ebb, and we decided to go to them and ask if they would allow us to mount an off-Broadway production of their *Flora the Red Menace*. This is a good lesson, because in any business you need to ask yourself "what's the worst that can happen?" They can say "no" or they can say "yes," but you won't get anywhere unless you ask the question. So Scott and I went to Kander and Ebb and they said "yes!" We mounted a production of *Flora,* which developed a cult following and launched our careers. I think we made about three hundred dollars that entire summer. Of course we starved to death, but we had made the leap to the other side. And we have never gone back. It was a wonderful combination of believing in the show, adoring Kander and Ebb, and asking "the question" that led us to get that one really good break. Coincidentally, Kander and Ebb

**2.** Directing often takes the form of one-on-one coaching. Here Stroman works with Burns on the "Ball and Chain" prison number in the final act.

**3.** Studying the script, Stroman and Vargo go over dialogue.

wrote a song in that show called "All I Need Is One Good Break."

That was when things really opened up for me. Hal Prince asked me to choreograph Don Giovanni at the New York City Opera, and then we collaborated on the Broadway show Showboat. Liza [Minnelli] also saw *Flora*. She asked me to choreograph her show *Steppin Out* at Radio City Music Hall. The key is really to be ready for that break when it happens.

**RC:** How did you then make your transition to directing?

**SS:** The transition to directing was very natural. Being a theatre choreographer is very different from being a ballet or modern dance choreographer (although I have done these too—for the New York City Ballet and the Martha Graham company). For choreographing theatre you have to acknowledge the lyric. Everything must center on the plot; your role is to push the plot forward through the choreography. Plus you have to create time period, geographical area, and rich characters. Because of all this, the choreographer is right there with the director from beginning to end. It's not like one job starts where the other one finishes; you're trying to make a total vision together. So it was a very natural transition for me.

The first Broadway show that I directed was *The Music Man,* and that was perfect for me because I love that show. Love it, love it! I grew up in a house filled with music. My father was my real Music Man: he was a salesman and he played the piano. There's a wonderful line in the show where the little boy accuses Harold Hill of lying about being the leader of a band. Harold Hill says, "I always think there's a band, kid." For musical comedy people that line resonates, because we grow up thinking that there's always a band—we're always hoping our band is coming around the corner. So for *The Music Man* to be the first Broadway show I

directed was very meaningful. The movement in *Music Man* is a very important aspect. When you first meet the characters in Iowa they're very stiff, they don't move at all, but by the end, the entire town is dancing the *Shipoopee*. And it's all because Harold Hill has introduced the town to rhythm and music.

**RC:** How did you come up with the terrific ending?

**SS:** Closing the book after one of myreadings of the script during rehearsals I thought, "Well what is this town doing now? What *could* they be doing? Well, perhaps they all took trombone lessons?" So for the curtain call I decided the entire company should play the trombone. What did I have to lose? "I'll hire a trombone teacher, they'll either learn it or they won't, and if they don't they'll just come out and bow." After the second week of rehearsal they sounded like a moose herd, and I thought this is never going to happen. And then *I* became the music man! All of a sudden, they had become my kids, and they were playing seventy-six trombones and it sounded beautiful. I was so pleased and proud! And that's how it ended up as the curtain call.

**RC:** What do you like about directing?

**SS:** It gives me great pleasure to be in the back of the house and see something I've created affect an audience. Whether it makes them laugh from something they saw in *The Producers* or makes them cry from a moment in *Contact* or—in *Crazy for You*—the audience puts their arms around one another (*laughs*). Even last night at the first preview of our Vegas production of The Producers, I saw a lady doubled over with laughter and tumbling into the aisle at the sight of the walker dance with the little old ladies. It gave me such joy to see her laugh.

**RC:** How do you conceive of some of the darker themes you explore, as in *Contact*?

4.

5.

**ss:** Oh, I have a million stories in my head. Being allowed to do something like *Contact* was amazing. Lincoln Center is the only place you can do something like that: take an idea and build it into a show. My production of *Steel Pier* only lasted about six months on Broadway, but [Lincoln Center's artistic director] André Bishop saw it and called me. He loved the choreography and said, "If you have an idea I will help you develop it." And to hear those words from a producer is like hearing a beautiful melody! It's unheard of. Usually, they just want you to do a revival, or something safe. And I said, "Well, as a matter of fact I do have an idea." A few weeks before I had been to a dance club in NYC's meatpacking district, a swing club where everybody wore black. Out of this sea of black stepped a girl in a yellow dress. I got obsessed watching her, and I thought to myself, "She's going to change . some man's life tonight." I thought she was quite bold—a New Yorker wearing yellow—so when André

asked if I had an idea, I said, "I absolutely have an idea," and so I started to develop a story about the girl in the yellow dress. I called my friend John Weidman, who wrote *Assassins* and *Pacific Overtures*. We went into the rehearsal rooms of Lincoln Center with eighteen dancers, and we created a story about someone who, if he doesn't make contact that night, will die. It was remarkable to have the opportunity to develop this work from the visuals and concepts in my mind. Before it opened, I thought, "Well, there'll be a handful of people that will get this," but it took the city by storm. The girl in the yellow dress was on every bus in Manhattan! It clearly has a very universal theme.

**RC:** Do you have any advice for a young person aspiring to be a director?

**ss:** You have to really have a passion and a drive and you can't be afraid to take chances. You can't just wait around for someone to hire you; you've got to create your own work.

And that's the way it should be. There isa collaborative passion in the theatre that I don't think exists in any other business. All of us are in a swimming pool together, and we either drown together or we win an Olympic medal together. It is passion and drive that makes a show work. And the drive toward an opening night: there is nothing like it, nothing like people coming together with a goal to move an audience. It's an amazing feeling. I am very fortunate to be in the theatre. I love the theatre so much!

4. Stroman works individually with the actors as they rehearse, fine-tuning choreographic gestures, expressions, and focus points (where actors are to look).

5. All directors have individual ways of communicating with actors. Stroman's signature style is to write down individual cast notes on three-by-five cards and then pass them out to the actors—Patrick and Katrina in this case—after each rehearsal unit concludes.

performance dates. The producer may also play an important role (and sometimes the dominant role) in selecting the play, negotiating its performance rights, engaging the artistic staff (designers, composers, translators, technicians) and business staff (publicists, accountants, company managers), and casting the actors. In addition, the producer is largely responsible for overseeing publicity, ticketing, the house staff, and the creation of theatre programs. Although some of those functions may seem relatively distant from "theatrical art," each is absolutely crucial to theatrical success and thus plays a critical artistic role. Therefore, when considering the following section on directorial functions, keep in mind that some of them may be handled by a producer and that *all* of them usually take place under a producer's watchful eyes.

# DIRECTORIAL FUNCTIONS

Directing is establishing a point of focus (a "direction") and motivating or persuading all of the production's collaborators to move toward it. The tasks of a play director are not unlike those of a manager of a bank or a corporate division: to set goals, establish priorities and procedures, facilitate communication, maintain the schedule, monitor progress, encourage the timid, rein in the errant, heighten the stakes, build team morale, and inspire excellence from everyone. No two managers fulfill these functions in the same way or to the same degree, but, for theatre directors, a confident, natural, and inspirational way of working with collaborators is at least as important as mastery of staging techniques. Artistic sensitivity, interpersonal skills, and eagerness to accept responsibility and to exercise authority are always expected of professional play directors.

The steps of directing are many. Most are discussed in the following pages. Bear in mind, however, that in practice they are less clearly segmented than they here appear, as each of the separate elements (acting, lights, scenery, costumes, makeup) affects each of the others. And abstract concepts, once they are turned into an actual physical existence (such as a piece of scenery), often generate an unexpected impact on a production's other elements—for either good or bad—and therefore on the production as a whole. So the sequence that you are about to read is rarely as smoothly executed as it is described.

## Preparation

There is first a preparation period, during which the director selects a play, conceptualizes its production in a way that will guide the production team dramaturgically (this is the story we want to tell), intellectually (this is *why* we want to tell it), and aesthetically (this is *how* we want it to look, sound, and feel), and assembles a team of designers technicians, and—of course—actors.

**Play Selection** The selection of a script is unquestionably the most critical decision for any director. The play is the essential theatrical product, so to speak: it is the basic element to which the audience responds—or thinks it responds—and it is universally perceived as the core of the theatrical experience. For this reason, play selection is the one directorial decision over which the producer—the provider of a production's financial support-invariably reserves the right of review.

Three basic considerations go into play selection: the director's interest, the interest of the intended audience, and the capability of the director and producer to acquire, conceptualize, and produce the play. The director's interest is important because no director, save by chance, can create theatrical excitement from a script he or she finds dull and uninteresting. Nonetheless, it is also the director's job to seek the excitement latent in a script and to imagine its various theatrical possibilities. Often a director who can envision the improvements to be gained by script revision, adaptation, or reinterpretation can discover plays that otherwise would be ignored; indeed, one of the marks of a great director is the ability to make us recognize the brilliance or beauty of a script we have unwittingly passed over.

The audience's interest is of even greater importance. It is the audience, after all, that makes the theatre possible, and the ability to assess an audience's needs and wants is absolutely fundamental to directing, both for pragmatic reasons (to ensure that an audience turns out to see the play) and for artistic reasons (to ensure that the play is satisfying and pertinent to those who come to see it). A director directs not only the actors and designers but the audience members as well, by giving direction to their feelings and perceptions through the intellectual focus of the production. A director who discounts or ignores the interests—and the intelligence—of the audience stands little chance of creating any genuine theatrical impact.

Directors are often thought of as commanding presences in a stage production, but Ariane Mnouchkine, the founding director of France's highly distinguished Thèâtre du Soleil (Theatre of the Sun), has always believed in full collaboration, and the members of her company eat and in most ways live together, creating their works in a living artistic ensemble. In Soleil productions, the audience is invited to wander through the actors' makeup rooms before the show, and often—as in *Les Éphémères*-to enjoy beverages and cookies with the actors during intermissions. All Soleil company members are paid identical wages, from the assistant stage managers to Mnouchkine herself, shown here with company members before a *Les Éphémères* rehearsal.

Consideration of audience interest in play selection does not necessarily mean a reliance on the tried and true; quite the contrary, it means providing the audience with theatrical work that is fresh, fascinating, vigorous, and exciting. For some audiences, these ingredients can be provided by musicals, thrillers, and domestic comedies; for others, by works of the European avant-garde, by plays of social protest and reform, or by new plays hot off the laptops of yet unknown authors. There is an audience for every sort of good play, and it is the director's job to find that audience and attract it to the theatre. The audience demands to be challenged as well as confirmed— and, in the long run, directors who lead their audiences are far more likely to gain artistic recognition than are those who either follow the audience blindly or ignore it completely.

The capability of the director to produce the play adequately with available resources is the final requisite for sound play selection. Can the production rights to the play be acquired? Can a suitable cast be brought together? a production staff? a theatre? Is there enough money? Interest alone—the director's and the audience's—will not buy the scripts, rent the theatre, pay for the electricity, or perform the roles. Considerations of quality must also be factored in: Are the available actors experienced enough to master the play's style? Is the costume budget adequate for the size of the cast and the period of the play? And, finally, does the director understand this play well enough to bring out its ideas? A realistic consideration of one's own capabilities, together with an ability to assess the potential of one's expected collaborators, must be a significant factor in the critical decisions of play selection.

**Conceptualizing** More has been written in modern times about the director's role in conceptualizing a play than about any other directorial task; entire books are devoted to the "directorial image," or the creation and employment of a central concept that focuses and informs an entire production. There are two different sorts of directorial concept: the *core concept* and the *high concept*. All plays require the first; not all require the second.

The *core concept* is the director's determination of the most important of the many images, ideas, and emotions that should emerge from the play. Why should there be only one core concept when every play, when read, presents a multiplicity of important images, ideas, and emotions? Chekhov's *The Three Sisters,* for example, can be seen as a play variously about love, ambition, sisterhood, despair, the oppression of women, rivalry between social classes, the social freedom of professional men, the oppression of rural Russian domesticity, the agony of unfulfilled hope, the corruption of provincial czarist bureaucracy, the seeds of a coming revolution. A director who tried to give equal weight to all those themes would create what most audiences and critics would consider a "mess"—a production that is unfocused

In Ariane Mnouchkine's *Les Éphémères* (*Ephemeral Things*), actors often double as scenery shifters. From a squatting or kneeling position, they silently wheel large "chariots" (wheeled platforms, usually circular) on and off the staging area—an alley between two banks of audience seats. Atop the chariots, the company's 27 actors (including children) perform 75 roles in the 29 loosely interrelated scenes of the two-part production that proved the sensation of New York's 2009 Lincoln Center Theatre Festival. Shown here, a Jewish girl, wearing a cross and disguised as a Christian during the Nazi occupation of northern France during World War II, is being questioned by a German officer. Or is she being interrogated? We cannot be certain, but we see every possibility and contingency going through the characters' minds, as they go through our own. In addition to moving the chariots, the scenery shifters provide a nonspeaking chorus of witnesses to the seemingly ordinary but often tragic events that the play depicts. Mnouchkine provided the production's concept and direction, but the play was "dreamed upon, invoked, evoked, improvised and devised" by the Soleil's 50-member company. Everest Canto de Montserrat designed the scenery.

and "all over the place." A production may incorporate most or even all of those themes, and indeed many more, but they must be somewhat prioritized, and one of them should be given the highest priority. That highest-priority image, idea, or emotion becomes the *core organizing principle* that will give the production shape, meaning, importance, and momentum. It will help audience members clarify, at least to themselves, what the play is "about," what it "means." It will ensure that the production *signifies something,* instead of, paraphrasing Shakespeare's Macbeth, being merely "full of sound and fury [but] signifying nothing."

How does a director decide on the core principle? There can be no universally "correct" answer to that question. Although research is important, the decision making is essentially a *creative* task. One way to approach it—to cut through the sound and fury of a complex play and settle on a single focal point before embarking into production—is to ask, "What should a poster for this production look like?" Should it show the image of Masha's final embrace with her lover? the three sisters abandoned by the soldiers at the final curtain? the peasant Natasha hiding in shame from the sisters gossiping about her in the next room? a birthday party of gaily laughing women and military officers, with the image of Vladimir Lenin smirking at them from above? And should the poster's typeface be old-fashioned or modern? Should a few Cyrillic (Russian) letters be used to emphasize the play's Russian setting? Should the colors be primary or pastel, earth-toned or black-and-white, distressed, fragmentary, or faded? Should the design of the poster be clean or grimy, bold or subtle, abstracted or detailed? Should the mood be hopeful or despairing, the style elegant or grim? Answers to these "poster" questions point the director toward a possible core concept of the production.

Taglines—single statements that might serve as an informal subtitle for the play when produced—are

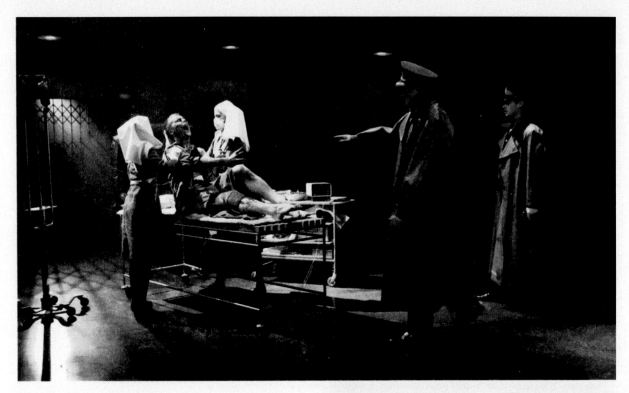

Richard Goold is often considered England's most exciting young director. His highly experimental 2007 *Macbeth,* which after opening at England's Chichester Festival moved on to London and to New York, was set in a Stalin-era war hospital, and the play's famous witches first appear as battlefield nurses. Here they are tending to the Bloody Sergeant whose report opens the play, but they will inject him with fatal poison soon after the observing officers leave. "*The Macbeth* of a Lifetime," as one of London's leading critics called it, starred Patrick Stewart in the title role, seen here opening a bottle of wine as Macbeth tries harder and harder to deaden the terrible anxieties growing within him.

Eastern European theatre—particularly in Romania—produced many brilliantly original high-concept directors during the cold war years because more straightforward plays displaying potentially liberal themes were discouraged by political authorities during the Soviet era. Since the fall of the iron curtain, many of these directors have brought their stylistic innovations to the world stage. Andrei Serban is one of the most distinguished. Here, the trial scene for his Parisian production of Shakespeare's *Merchant of Venice* at the Comédie-Française in 2001 combines words of the text on a blood-red back wall that backs an abstracted courtroom and its symbolically costumed personnel: the Christian defendant Antonio in white; the Jewish plaintiff Shylock in black; and the imposter judge Portia hatless and sporting a white tie beneath her black-and-pinstripe suit.

also useful for creating a production's core concept. A tagline may be a social statement ("this is a play about tyranny") or a philosophical one ("a play about self-knowledge"). It may signal a specific interpretation ("a play about a man who cannot make up his mind") or invoke an invented dramatic genre ("a revenge melodrama"). A director may state the core concept in psychodramatic ("a primitive ritual of puberty"), historical ("a play about fratricide in the Middle Ages"), imagistic ("a play about swords, sables, and skulls"), or metatheatrical ("a play about playing") terms.

Sometimes the tagline mentions a basic tone ("sad," "heroic," "royal") or a basic texture ("rich," "cerebral," "stark"). Diverse as those core-concept examples may seem, they all fall within the range of possibilities for conceptualizing a single play. Indeed, any one of them could be applied to Shakespeare's *Hamlet,* and probably every one of them has been at one time or another, as have hundreds of others besides.

A *high concept* is another matter altogether. Contemporary directors can make a familiar play

Romanian director Gábor Tompa is represented here by this abstract and ritualized 2006 production of *Rhinoceros* by fellow Romanian playwright Eugène Ionesco. A hallmark of the theatre of the absurd that was first written and produced in Paris, *Rhinoceros* is now considered a masterpiece: a savagely comic portrayal of the dehumanization of modern society, which turns humans into the equivalent of clumsy, brawling, thick-skinned animals—portrayed here by masked and trench-coated robotic creatures behind the one remaining human holdout, Ionesco's signature character of Beringer. The performance was produced by the Radu Stanca National Theatre and staged at the Sibiu International Theatre Festival in 2006.

surprising—even astonishing—by introducing highly unexpected insights into character, story, or style. In its most simple form, a high concept may mean nothing more than moving a play out of the period in which it is set and placing it in another: for example, taking *Hamlet* out of medieval Elsinore and setting it in the Victorian era (as Kenneth Branagh did in his popular film version) or producing *Macbeth* with parallels to the Iraq War. But today mere "relocation" hardly makes a play astonishing or even surprising. Twenty-first-century audiences have become quite used to high concepts and even expect them.

Like it or not (and there are many who do not), audiences and critics today are much more likely to admire (and remember) productions, such as those of Peter Brook and Ariane Mnouchkine (see the chapter titled "Theatre Today") and of Romanian directors Andrei Serban and Gábor Tompa (see adjacent images of their respective *Merchant of Venice* and *Rhinoceros* productions), that aim for unique and revelatory rethinkings of major works in the theatrical repertoire. Such productions captivate audiences worldwide by transcending their plays' original conventions and presenting profound, moving, new, and uniquely illuminating theatricalizations that make telling references to current issues. High-concept theatre also avoids the "museum production" onus of traditional staging by taking actors out of, say, Elizabethan

Longtime avant-garde American director Richard Foreman has a directorial "signature"—wires strung across the stage—as seen here in his harshly penetrating production of Bertolt Brecht's *The Threepenny Opera* at New York's Lincoln Center. Brecht's theatre, which is boldly presentational and direct, lends itself to Foreman's technique. Raul Julia (*left*) played Mack the Knife.

doublet and hose (traditional wear of the Shakespearean era) and putting them instead into something more contemporary, or making clearer references to the contemporary: if King Claudius (in *Hamlet*) looks like Saddam Hussein, the audience, without actually thinking about it, will quickly understand that this is a guy who killed to get his throne. A director known for brilliant high concepts will also discourage prospective attendees from declining to see his or her latest production of, for example, *King Lear* on the grounds that "I've already seen it."

It is certainly no exaggeration, therefore, to say that *most* productions of classic plays in the twentyfirst century, not just in experimental theatres but in the theatre's mainstream, seek high concepts. Directors (and directing students) are inevitably drawn to them, and audiences and critics, though sometimes skeptical, are almost always intrigued. Indeed, "So what's your concept for the show?" is likely to be the first question a colleague or a reporter asks a director engaging in a new production.

Arriving at a high concept is no easy task. Once selected, the concept must "work" for the entire play. If *Othello* is set in World War II, what does the actor (or the property designer) do with Othello's "Put up your swords" line? How much can freshness add to a show without diminishing—or even obliterating—it? And how does the high concept actually improve the play—at least for its intended audience? What new ideas, new readings of the text for the actors, new images for the designers, does the high concept arouse? Heavy-duty research, and a comprehensive thinking-through of the entire script, are essential for the director trying to come up with an effective, workable, and genuinely inspiring high-concept production.

When approaching any play, the director should consider both core concepts and high concepts. But because high concepts are prized for their unexpected insights into *familiar* plays, they probably should be avoided in the production of a *new* play. In a new play, it is the playwright who (presumably) is providing the fresh and unexpected insights, and the

# PHOTO ESSAY: The School for Wives

Molière's 1662 comedy, *The School for Wives,* directed by the author of this book, was produced by the Tony Award-winning Utah Shakespearean Festival in the city of Cedar City during the summer of 2008. The production ran from June 27 through August 30 of that year but was put together during a full year preceding its opening performance. These photos show some of the work involved in putting this production together.

**1.** *Conceiving.* The director and principal designers were engaged for this production during the summer and fall of 2007, and each began immediately to conceive the basic look, tone, and feel of the production. Since these artists are based far from Cedar City (New York City, Los Angeles, Tampa, and Ogden, Utah), almost all of the initial collaborations were accomplished by e-mail and attached digital images and sound samples. Here in October, Director Robert Cohen, in his Laguna Beach home, looks over a first "rough model" that Scenic Designer Jo Winiarski digitally photographed and than e-mailed to him from her New York studio.

**2.** *Planning.* In two midwinter meetings, one in Salt Lake City and this one in Cedar City, the director and the principal artistic and technical staffs share and coordinate their ideas for the show. Here, Scene Designer-Winiarski shows her latest model, quite elaborated from her earlier version, to the festival's producers and artistic staff.

**3.** *(Left)* *Detailing.* The show's costume designer, Janet Swenson, shows her rendering of the proposed costume for the character of Enrique, a dandy "recently arrived from New Spain," to the director for his comments and suggestions.

**4.** *(Top right)* *Casting.* The festivals casting director, Kathleen Conlin, discusses with the director the actors whom she is interested in casting in the play's nine roles. `

**5.** *(Bottom right)* *Approvals.* Scott Phillips, the festival's executive director, meets with Cohen to evaluate and approve decisions made at the winter meetings, and also to discuss the proposed "Americanization" of a few words in the new translation, which is by British author Ranjit Bolt. The word changes for the Utah production will be developed by Cohen in consultation with Bolt.

6. *Director's and Designers'* Presentations When cast and artistic staff finally assemble at the Cedar City theatre on May 5, 2008, the director and then the individual designers present their various concepts and plans for the production. Here Costume Designer Swenson shows her costume renderings to the assembled company.

7. *The First Reading.* The directing and design presentations are followed by a reading of the entire play by the actors, seated around a table and working from the scripts mailed to them several weeks previously. Other members of the production team have remained for this reading: they include the casting director, the vocal and dialect coach, the dramaturg, and members of the festival's artistic directorate. This reading is followed by a discussion of the play's details, and everyone around the table is encouraged to speak, comment, and ask questions. The first reading may be followed by a second, third, or even more readings in the ensuing days. In this case, the rehearsals moved directly into the staging of the action.

8. *Staging, or Blocking.* "After th reading phase, the play is given its initial staging. The director, in collaboration with the actors, "blocks" out the play's physical action—each character's entrances and exits, stands and sits, and other major moves. Actors pencil down this blocking in their scripts so as to be able to repeat it the next time through the scene. These rehearsals take place not on the theatre stage but in a nearby rehearsal hall. No scenery or costumes are yet available, so these rehearsals make do with substitutes: a table stands for a railing actors will lean against; a rectangular, stock step unit represents the curvilinear staircase they will descend. The locations of walls and doorways are marked on the rehearsal-room floor with strips of masking tape. If more than one play is rehearsed in the same hall, the different "sets" are indicated by different strip colors: in this case yellow represents the set pieces for *School for Wives,* green those for *Fiddler on the Roof.* Many actors wear "rehearsal costumes" to simulate the bulk of the costumes they will wear in the play. Here Betsy Mugavero wears a billowing rehearsal skirt to mimic the skirt she will wear as Agnès in the production, and Tim Casto has donned a rehearsal cape as her guardian (and would-be husband) Arnolphe. As he stages the play, Director Cohen refers regularly to planned moves he has already penciled into his script, on the music stand; he may change these plans in an instant if the actors make moves he likes better. Visible in the background are a costume rack for the rehearsal garments, a stack of shelves for rehearsal props, and a rehearsal schedule for the entire repertoire of the festival's plays currently ini preparation.

9. (*Right*) *Scenic Construction.* In one of the festival's scene shops, the "deck"—scenic flooring—is being constructed under the oversight of Scenery Supervisor Benjamin Zimmer.

10. (*Below*) *Costume Transfer.* Costume Designer Swenson has transferred her costume designs—the dozen plus individual renderings she has been sharing with the director and cast at various meetings—to the costume shop, where they now hang on the wall to guide the drapers, first hands, seamstresses, and embroiderers who will construct various garments. Here Swenson is giving special instructions to Costume Artisan Jennifer Biehl.

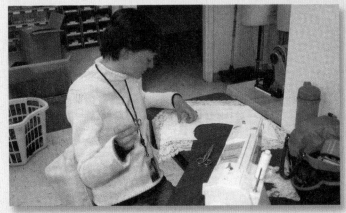

11. *Sewing.* Seamstress Eleanor Kingsley works on the fancy lace collar to be worn by Enrique, a Spanish dandy who arrives in the play's final scenes.

12. *Costume Fitting.* In the costume shop's dressing room, Betzy Mugavero is fitted for her first act Agnès costume by the production's draper, Louella Powell. First Hand Aria Thornton, seen in the mirror, takes notes from Powell on what, if anything, should be changed.

**13.** *Lighting Transfer.* The light plot (instrument chart), designed by Lighting Designer Stephen Boulmetis, lies on the stage floor as Assistant Lighting Designer Michael Pasquini studies it to determine exactly where each instrument should be hung.

**14.** *Hanging.* Lighting Technician Bradley Carson, on a pneumatic lift that hoists him to the lighting battens twenty feet above the stage, hangs and focuses one of the more than three hundred lighting instruments that will be used in this production.

**15.** *Millinery.* In the crafts shop, Assistant Costume Crafts Supervisor Jessica Crowden sews feathers onto the elaborate wide-brimmed hat that Enrique will wear in the last act.

**16.** *Cobbling.* Crafts Artisan Gregory Horton, also in the crafts shop, fashions leather shoes and other accessories that complete the costumes.

**17.** *Sound.* Sound Designer Palmer Jankens, in the sound design studio, records and assembles digital soundtracks of the harpsichord music (by seventeenth-century composer Jacques Duphly) that will be used in the production, along with other offstage sounds, including a horse's hoofbeats and whinnying, crashing dishes, breaking vases, and the footsteps of three persons racing up a flight of stairs.

**18.** *Voice Recording.* The director decided to add to the digital soundtrack Arnolphe's ad-lib grunts and yelps as he runs into a horse offstage, so Sound Designer Jankens has brought Tim Casto into the sound studio to record the actor's voicing of such nonverbal utterances, which Jankens will later combine with the horse whinny and crashing sounds.

**19.** *(Left) Acting Rehearsal.* In the rehearsal room, actors rehearse the second of the four farcical interludes that the director interpolated between the acts of Molière´s play. Here Agnès, at the demand of Arnolphe, is throwing a large "stone down ham her"balcony" at her (Rick Ford and Lillian Castillo) egg her on from each side. These interludes are mimed by the actors, who use exaggerated commedia dell´arte-style movements but do not speak (because Molière wrote no lines for them).

**20.** *(Left)* Fight Rehearsal. This rehearsal of the third interlude, in which Alain and Georgette attempt to beat Horace as he ascends a ladder to rescue Agnès from her guardian's captivity, is overseen by Fight Director Christopher Villa. Trained—and desirably certified—fight directors are employed whenever stage actions involve potentially dangerous movements such as dueling, hitting, or falling, to make such actions theatrically vivid (realistic, convincing, dramatic, and/or hilarious, depending on the production´s style) yet absolutely safe for the actors executing them in performance after performance.

**21.** *Painting.* In the paint shop, Scenic Charge Artist Michelle Fullerton, with Winiarski´s rendering (finished sketch) in hand, paints the "portal" that when erected vertically, will frame the scenic picture.

**22.** *Scenic Assembly.* Now in the Randall Theatre, where the play will be presented, the scenery is being erected and assembled on the actual stage.

**23.** *Scenic Detailing.* Scene Designer Winiarski demonstrates to Scenery Supervisor Zimmer precisely how she intends the window hinges to be fitted.

**24.** *Scenic Revision.* An early version of a stage prop—a portable desk that is to be carried and used by the "Notary"—is tested in rehearsal and found to be too bulky, it must be redesigned immediately. Since Scene Designer Winiarski is completing a project in New York that week, the redesign—as a simpler lap desk—is accomplished through a series of overnight e-mail exchanges. In Cedar City the next morning, Director Cohen approves—and sends to the prop shop—the new version.

**25.** *Props.* In the prop shop, the redesigned lap desk is sanded by Properties Construction Artisan Ryan McAlpine.

**26** *Photo Call.* Neither scenery nor costumes are fully finished, nor have all the lighting instruments been installed, but selected pieces have been completed and temporary lighting has been set up so that key scenes from the play may be photographed for the souvenir program and upcoming; publicity releases. Publications Art Director Phil Hermansen frames a shot that will include Arnolphe and his two servants in front of the house where Agnès is lodged.

**27.** *Tech Rehearsal Setup.* The production is now ready to move into technical rehearsals, in which the acting and the scenery, props, sound, and lighting are brought together on the stage. Here, Scenery Supervisor Zimmer determines with Assistant Stage Manager Nicole Lalonde which upper windows in the scenery the actors will use when making certain appearances.

**28.** *Tech Walk.* Assistant Stage Manager Lalonde invites the actors to "walk the set." Having previously rehearsed only in a bare room with stray tables and strips of masking tape marking out the scenery elements, the actors now have to "feel the scenery" with their hands and feet as they navigate the various doors, windows, and railings that will actually be used.

**29.** *Cue Lights.* Production Stage Manager Angi Weiss-Brandt "calls" the show—that is, she times and calls the lighting, sound, and scene-shift cues to the appropriate operators over an intercom system. She herself blinks the thirty-plus cue lights in different backstage locations, letting individual actors know the precise moments when they should make their entrances or offstage cries and other sounds. Such remote cuing is frequently necessary because actors behind the scenery cannot see the onstage-action. During technical rehearsals the stage manager's console is a table placed across the back rows of the audience, as shown here; by the time the show opens, the stage manager will be at a console in a glassed-in booth in the back of the house.

**30.** *Tech Tables.* Other work tables are set out in the audience so that lighting, sound, and scenic designers can set and adjust cues as the actors "stop and go" through the play during two ten-hour technical rehearsals. In the foreground, Electrics Director Scott Palfreyman, at his table, talks to the stage manager through his intercom system. At the tech table in front of Palfreyman, Sound Designer Jankens readies his cues; other tech tables are to his left and right. Onstage, a crew member tapes the rough edges of a temporary wooden rail that represents a brass railing that has not yet been finished in the scene shop.

**31.** *Setting Light Cue.* At their tech table, Lighting Designer Boulmetis (*foreground*) and Assistant Lighting Designer Pasquini communicate by intercom with the stage manager, light-board operator, and follow-spot operators, while establishing and timing out the more than three hundred light cues that are to be executed in the production.

**32.** *Follow-spot.* Lighting Technician Cristine White operates one of the production's two follow-spots, lighting instruments that are hand-positioned by their operators to follow one or more actors as they move about the stage—or, in this production, up and down the theatre aisles.

**33.** *Gobos.* These oddly named devices are filters placed inside lighting instruments to create patterns that can be projected onto floors and walls to give added texture—to create the impression, for example, of moonlight shining through leafy trees. During technical rehearsal, these gobo-produced patterns will be added to the lighting of a nighttime interlude.

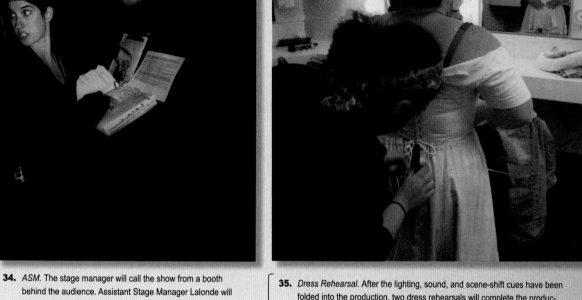

**34.** *ASM.* The stage manager will call the show from a booth behind the audience. Assistant Stage Manager Lalonde will stay backstage, where she can make visual cues to the actors, oversee the placement of the props, and in general trouble-shoot the production and respond to backstage emergencies.

**35.** *Dress Rehearsal.* After the lighting, sound, and scene-shift cues have been folded into the production, two dress rehearsals will complete the production's integration of its many elements. How do the costumes look in front of the set and under the lights? Do the garments overly restrain the actors' movements? Down in a dressing room, Lillian Castillo is being laced into Georgette's undergarment by a costume wardrobe assistant.

**36.** *Makeup.* Stage makeup is added during dress rehearsals. Here Betsy Mugavero, in the dressing room before the rehearsal begins, touches up her makeup after putting on her Agnès costume for the first act.

**37.** *Wig Preparation.* Tim Casto "makes horns" (puts his two forefingers flat againsts his forehead) to make it easier for Wigmaster Karen Craven to slip his Arnolphe wig over his scalp.

**38.** (*Above*) Wig Setting. The wig is securely placed.

**39.** (*Right*) Facial Hair. Asistant Wigmaster Devon Ash secures Castro´s "billygoat" goatee and mustache to his face with spirit gum.

**40.** *Final Adjustments.* Before the first dress rehearsal begins. First Hand Thornton adjust Casto´s costume in his scene with Chrysalde, played by Dennis Elkins.

**41.** *Dress Check.* Rick Ford, in his Alain costume, checks the door handle before practicing, in full costume for the first time, his rapid (and highly comedic) entrances and exits prior to the run.

**42.** *Lights Up!* The audience area is a sea of computers—those of the stage manager and designers and their assistants—as the lights rise on the bare stage for the dress rehearsal's first scene.

**44.** *Publicity Interview.* The play will open tomorrow, and some of the actors—including Betsy Mugavero—have been asked to do interviews on regional television stations.

**43.** *Quick Change.* Backstage, behind the door to Agnès's house, two dressers assist Tim Casto with the costume and wig change he must make in just five seconds.

**45-47.**
*Production Stills.* These three photographs from actual productions show the finished product—scenery, costumes, lighting, wigs, and actors all together. In the first, Rick Ford and Lillian Castillo are seen as the servants Alain and Georgette, and in the second, Tim Casto and Dennis Elkins are seen as Amolphe, the central character, and Chrysalde, his best friend. In the final photo, Kevin Kiler, as Horace, expounds to Arnolphe as the servants watch from separate windows above the arch.

director of a new play probably should concentrate on the *core* concept.

The formation of both core and high concepts takes place at the conscious and unconscious levels. In fact it takes place whether the director wishes it to or not. It simply begins when the director first hears of a certain play, and it grows and develops as she or he reads the play, considers producing it, imagines its effects on an audience, and mentally experiments with possible modes of staging. Either sort of directorial concept is a product not only of the director's intelligence and vision but also of his or her personal experiences that relate to the matters portrayed by the play. Core and high concepts also call into play (and into the play) the director's personal likes and lusts, appreciations and philosophical leanings, and hopes for audience and critical reactions to the final product. A great directorial concept is personal; it is, finally, the director's studied and unique vision. It is also specific, appropriate, evocative, visual, theatrical, concrete, and original, as well as a bit mysterious and a bit amusing. It leads the actors and the designers; and if it is truly inspired, it leads the director as well.

**Director-Designer Collaboration** The concept is the director's own creation, but its refinement and realization finally rest in the hands of collaborators whose personal artistry and inclinations inevitably play an enormous role in the shape and impact of the final product. Hence the selection of these individuals is by no means a mechanical or arbitrary task; it is a central directorial concern of great artistic consequence.

Ordinarily directors make every effort to work with designers with whom they feel not only personal compatibility but also mutual respect and a synchrony of artistic and intellectual vision. Like all true collaborations, the most effective director-designer relationships result in a give-and-take of ideas, plans, feelings, and hypotheses—a sense of sharing and complementary support.

Designing a production marks the first step toward transforming vision into actuality: at this stage, people turn ideas into concrete visual realizations. The director's work in designing a production is generally suggestive and corrective; how well she or he succeeds in this delicate task is highly dependent on the personalities and predilections of the individuals involved. In theory, the director's and designers' goals are identical: actable space, wearable costumes, and an evocative, memorable, and meaningful appearance of the whole. In practice, each of the principals has an independent perspective on what is actable, what is memorable, and what is evocative; moreover, each may have a different sense of the importance of sometimes contradictory values. A costume designer, for example, may place a higher value on the appearance of a garment than does the director, who may be more concerned with the actor's ability to move in it. A lighting designer may be greatly interested in the aesthetics of murkiness, whereas the director may be more concerned that an actor's face be clearly seen at a particular moment. These are the sorts of artistic perspectives that must be reconciled in the design process, which is essentially a collaboration whose decisions are acknowledged to be subjective rather than right or wrong.

Production design normally takes place in a series of personal conferences between director and designers, sometimes on a one-on-one basis and sometimes in group meetings. (Increasingly, in America's regional professional theatres of the 2010s, many of these conferences take place electronically, via e-mail attachments and conference calls, because a given production's freelance director and designers may be working in different parts of the country—or world.) These are give-and-take affairs, for the most part, with the director doing most of the giving at the beginning and the designers taking over shortly thereafter. Often the first step is a collective meeting—the first design conference—at which the director discusses his or her concept in detail and suggests some possibilities for its visual realization: colors, images, spaces, textures, and technological implementations.

In the ensuing conferences, which are often conducted one-on-one and sometimes on an ad hoc basis, designers normally present their own conceptions and eventually provide the director with a progressive series of concrete visualizations: sketches (roughs), drawings, renderings, models, ground plans, working drawings, fabrics, technical details, and devices. During these conferences the design evolves through a collaborative sharing, in which the director's involvement may range from minimal to maximal, depending on how well the initial concept and the developing design seem to be cohering. Periodically— whenever the overall design effort reaches a stage requiring coordinated planning—full design conferences are called to review and compare current plans for scenery, costume, lighting, and properties; these conferences afford opportunities for the designers to collaborate with each other instead of simply with the director.

The director's function at this stage of design is to approve or reject, as well as to suggest. As the person who sits at the top of the artistic hierarchy, the director has the last word on design matters, but that does not mean she or he can simply command the show into being; theatre design, like any creative process, cannot be summoned forth like an obedient servant. Moreover, wholesale rejection of a designer's work after the initial stages inevitably involves serious time loss and budgetary waste—not to mention the risk of provoking some important staff resignations. For these reasons, the directorial effort must be committed from the outset to sound collaborative principles. Once under way, the director-designer collaboration must take the form of shared responsibility in a developing enterprise, not confrontation between warring artists attempting to seize the reins of aesthetic control.

Casting  The cliché "Casting is 90 percent of directing" contains more than a germ of truth. The people in a play—the actors—not only attract more audience attention than any other aspect of the play but also represent what the audience *cares* about and will remember the next day. They garner about 90 percent of all the interest an audience expends on a play, and if they squander that interest they can destroy the effectiveness of any theatrical presentation.

The theatre as a medium has many individual elements that are standardized and predictable: flats are made according to formula, lighting instruments are factory-calibrated to conform to precise specifications, color media are mathematically measured and numbered, and one theatre's black "velours" are nearly identical to those of another. But the one unique ingredient of the theatre—as the audience sees it—is the actor. Actors are people, and as people they are exquisitely individual; moreover, the audience, being human itself, is particularly attuned to the actor's human and idiosyncratic uniqueness. We would never mistake the Hamlet of Mel Gibson for the Hamlets of Kenneth Branagh, Ethan Hawke, Kevin Kline, or Jude Law. The actor's personality, physical and vocal characteristics, technical abilities, and sheer talent and "presence" weigh mightily in the final realization of every individual performance and in every ensemble of performances. A miscast or untalented or untrained actor can mar the effectiveness of any production, even in a minor role; in a major role a poor performance simply ruins the play. Casting may not, in the end, account for 90 percent of the director's

contribution, but there can be no doubt that bad casting renders all other efforts immaterial.

Most casting takes place in auditions, where the actor can be seen and heard by the director and associates either in a "cold reading" of material from the play to be produced or in a prepared presentation of previously developed material not necessarily related to the production at hand: Although "star" performers are often cast apart from auditions, owing to their known ability to attract audiences to any production, most veteran professional actors regularly submit to auditioning. The director's ability to detect an incipiently brilliant performance in the contrived audition format is a critical factor in effective casting.

Depending on the specific demands of the play and the rehearsal situation, the director may pay special attention to any or all of the following characteristics: the actor's training and experience, physical characteristics and vocal technique, suitability for the style of the play, perceived ability to impersonate a specific character in the play, personality traits that seem fitted to the material at hand, ability to understand the play and its milieu, personal liveliness and apparent stage "presence," past record of achievement, general deportment and attitude, and apparent cooperativeness and "directability" in the context of an acting ensemble. And the director might well be looking for a great many other things besides.

What is ultimately astonishing about the casting process is that, in professional auditions, the vast majority of these decisions—which are the dreaded dismissal words "Thank you very much for coming in!"—are made in the first five to thirty seconds of an actor's two- to five-minute audition! That is because experienced directors and casting directors are quick to assess actors as being, in their opinions, wrong for the play, wrong for the part, or lacking in the desired level of proficiency. Others may be winnowed out on the subjective ground of apparent attitude—a dangerous ground, because the director might mistake shyness for hostility or "audition jitters" for an exaggerated reserve.

Actors who survive the first audition then "read" again, sometimes several times, and at this stage the director is involved more and more in the audition process, often coaching the actors to determine how rapidly they can acquire the qualities needed. Such "callbacks" can go on for days and even weeks in the professional theatre, limited only by the union requirement that actors receive pay after a certain point; the frequency with which such payments

# PHOTO ESSAY: Casting Director James Calleri

How can a professional director choose a cast from the more than 150,000 professional actors in the United States with any accuracy—much less seek out newcomers from the even larger number of student actors hoping to enter the professional world? The answer is simple: through the intercession of a casting director.

Casting directors became a vital part of the theatre and film worlds of New York and Los Angeles in the latter half of the twentieth century, and they now exist in theatre companies and, wherever professional theatres and film companies are active, in independent offices. The basic job of the casting director is to study scripts going into production, meet with producers and directors to assess what sorts of actors they're looking for, and, through interviews and preliminary tryouts, assemble a pool of outstanding performers to audition for the directors and producers. James Calleri, founding president of Calleri Casting in New York, has cast dozens of Broadway, off-Broadway, and regional theatre productions as well as hundreds of film and television roles. Your author asked him for his thoughts in 2009, soon after he had cast *33 Variations* on Broadway with Jane Fonda and, off-Broadway, *The Seagull* with Diane Wiest and Alan Cumming (for which he earned his fifth Artios Award for outstanding achievement in casting from the Casting Association of America).

"My interest in casting started when I was in grad school," Calleri began. "I tended to be somewhat opinionated, and a little bossy with my teachers

**1.** James Galleri, founding president of Calleri Casting in New York, in the informal interview room of his lower Manhattan office.

about who should be playing what roles (particularly when I didn't like somebody in something), and I remember speaking up about it. I thought somebody must know how to do this better, and so I packed up my car and moved to New York the day after I graduated. I didn't know anybody when I first got there, but I was lucky to get a job as an assistant at a talent agency, and that put me in the middle of everything. I developed a great relationship with the casting directors I met, and pretty soon I went to work for them, first sweeping floors and filing pictures and soon casting shows myself.

"What do I look for in an actor? Of course, I want to see a person who's terrific in his or her craft, but I'm also hoping to see a fascinating personality, a mystique, a unique point of view about life. Equate this to dating: What is it about a person that keeps '' him or her in your mind? What drives you to ask that person for a second date? Well, an actor having that quality makes me confident that an audience will want to spend two to three hours watching him or her onstage or in multiple episodes of a TV series. For camera media, particularly TV, I'm looking primarily for personality. With theatre casting, it's much more

**2.** With assitant Katya Zarolinski, Calleri looks through headshot photographs of male actors he is considering for a new off-Broadway production.

**3.** Many submissions from actors and agents now come through the Internet. Here Callen examines one of hundreds of headshots of actresses under consideration for the show's initial auditions.

about where you went to school, who you've worked with, what shows you've done, what theatres you've performed in, what type of roles you've played, what your voice is like and your body's like—all those things. And of course on Broadway, name recognition in the cast is pretty crucial. A play doesn't get to Broadway today unless the producers have a name they can hitch it to."

How can a beginning actor break in o New York theatre? "You have to try to find work. Join a company, do a show that our agency would cover, perhaps in the fringe festival [an annual array of low-budget productions mounted around the city in late August], or a showcase, or a downtown theatre company that we frequent. That's where we find most people."

How has modern technology changed the business of casting? "We do a lot more looking at an actor's reels [short compilations of video clips of the actor's performance distributed on DVDs or via the Internet] these days, and we share video clips' of our New York auditions with the producers and directors in other cities. When I started at ABC, we would tape our auditions in New York and ' then ship the reels overnight to our colleagues at the studios in Los Angeles. Now we record them digitally and have them uploaded, edited, and sent out right to the L.A. set, where the producers can go into their trailers, watch the clips on their iPhones, and (we hope) say, 'Yes, that's exactly who I want!' "

How does Callen like his job? "Casting? I love it. It's great, it's always different, it's always challenging, it never gets old."

Trevor Nunn's 2004 production of *Hamlet* at the Old Vic in London employed the revolutionary casting of a very young man, twenty-three-year-old Ben Whishaw, in the title role. Forgoing the standard practice of using a famous older actor, Nunn's production—with a consequently younger-than-usual actress, Imogen Stubbs, as Hamlet's mother—made Hamlet's sulkiness and indecision far more affecting than is customary in this play.

are made amply attests to the care that attends final casting decisions in the professional theatre.

There is good casting and bad casting, of course, and there is also inspired casting. Many of the greatest performances in theatre history have been achieved by actors who at first glance appeared unsuited to their roles. When, for example, director Anthony Page cast the gangly Janet McTeer (the *New York Times* critic called her "a woman of towering height") as Nora (whose husband Torvald calls her his "little lovebird") in his Broadway production of Ibsen's *A Doll's House,* it seemed to many an odd choice; but Page's notion and McTeer's dazzling performance brilliantly underscored Page's notion that Torvald and, by inference, all men of his ilk who shortchange their wives' capabilities are themselves severely diminished. And director Lee Breuer's casting of his Mabou Mines company's production of the same play with actors four

feet tall or less in all the male roles and tall women for the female ones proved an equally brilliant stroke. Breuer's casting was complemented by the show's miniaturized "Alice-in-Wonderland" setting, and it expanded the personal and marital themes of the Page production to a more general social analysis of male-female relations in both Ibsen's and our own times. The ability to see beyond traditional casting options, and to imagine the unique and unexpected relationships actors can create with even "standard repertoire" roles, has always been the mark of the most daring and most successful directors.

## Implementation

With the play selected and conceptualized, with the designers chosen and the designs under way, and with the actors auditioned and cast, the production moves from its preparatory phase to its implementation. The play is read aloud, staged, and rehearsed. The sets, costumes, and props are designed and built. The sound, lighting, and special effect cues are added. The acting is coached, detailed, and drilled into actors' muscle memories. Last, there are the normally intense days when all the production's elements—acting, sets, lights, costumes, props, sound, scene shifts—are integrated into their final form: in tech run-throughs, dress rehearsals, previews on some occasions, and the legendary "opening night" (which may of course be in the morning or afternoon). It is at the start of this phase that the meeting described at the beginning of this chapter occurs; it is then in the silence between the completion of a plan and its execution that conversation and ink on paper turn into blood, sweat, and tears. The pressure is on. The director's ability to maintain both leadership and creative inspiration under pressure—always an important element of professional skill—becomes crucial.

From the time of that first company meeting, the director controls the focus and consciousness of the entire cast and staff. As head of an ambitious and emotionally consuming enterprise, the director will be the repository of the company's collective artistic hopes—the focal point for the company's collective frustration, its anxiety, and, on occasion, its despair. The company's shield against the intrusions of an outside world, the director is also the spokesperson for the enterprise to which the company has collectively dedicated itself. Directorial power or influence cannot be substantially altered by any attempt the director may make to cultivate or repudiate it—it simply comes with the job and with the need for every theatrical company to have a head, a focus, a direction. The manner in which the director uses that power, and the sensitivity with which she or he brings the production into being, determines the nature of each director's individual brand of artistry.

Staging Staging—which essentially involves positioning actors on the set and moving them about in a theatrically effective manner—is the most obvious of directorial functions. It is the one thing directors are always expected to do and to do well, and it is the one they are most often *seen* doing; it is no wonder that traditional textbooks on directing tend to be largely devoted to this function.

The medium of staging is the actor in space and time—with the *space* defined by the acting area and settings and the *time* defined by the duration of the theatrical event and the dynamics of its dramatic structure. The goals of staging are multiple and complementary: to create focus for the play's themes, to lend credibility to the play's characters, to generate interest in the play's actions, to impart an aesthetic wholeness to the play's appearance, to provoke suspenseful involvement in the play's events, and, in general, to stimulate a fulfilling theatricality for the entire production.

The basic architecture of staging is called "blocking," which refers to the timing and placement of a character's entrances, exits, rises, crosses, embraces, and other major movements of all sorts. The "blocking pattern" that results from the interaction of characters in motion provides the framework of an overall staging; it is also the physical foundation of the actors' performance—and many actors have difficulty memorizing their lines until they know the blocking that will be associated with them.

The director may block a play either by preplanning the movements ("preblocking") on paper or by allowing the actors to improvise movement on a rehearsal set and then "fixing" the blocking sometime before the first performance. Often a combination of these methods is employed, with the director favoring one method or the other depending on the specific demands of the play, the rehearsal schedule, rapport with the acting company, or the director's own stage of preparation. Complex or stylized plays and settings and short rehearsal periods usually dictate a great deal of preblocking; simple domestic plays and experienced acting ensembles are often accorded more room for improvisation. Each method can produce highly commendable results in the right hands and at the right time; both can present serious problems if misapplied or ineptly handled. For the most part, the blocking of a play is hidden in the play's action; it tends to be effective insofar as it is not noticed and insofar as it simply brings other values into play and focuses the audience's attention on significant aspects of the drama. By physically enhancing the dramatic action and lending variety to the play's visual presentation, a good blocking pattern can play a large role in creating theatrical life and excitement. But beyond this, there are moments when inspired blocking choices can create astonishing theatrical effects—effects that are not hidden at all but are so surprising and shocking that they compel intense consideration of specific dramatic moments and their implications. Such a coup de théâtre was achieved, for example, by director Peter Brook in his

Staging sometimes begins with a reformulating of the nature of the playing space itself. Particularly in eastern Europe, today's directors may completely redefine the relationship between audience and actor, either by placing the audience on the stage and the actors in the "audience" or by making other variations on the conventional theatrical arrangement. In Mihai Maniutiu's *Job Experiment,* for example, which the director adapted from the Old Testament book of Job, the play's actors—perhaps echoing Satan's Biblical question to God, "Have you not put a fence around him and his house?"—are surrounded by a closed-in polygonal wall (codesigned by Maniutiu and Christian Rusu) that is pierced by forty-four windows through which audience members, one to a window, peer in on the action. Here Job (*kneeling, right*—he "sits among the ashes," says the Bible) is in anguish as an angel of death kills his herd of cattle, represented by gold balloons. Maniutiu explained that his goal was "not to bring old rites to life but to create a ritual fiction." The production was presented at the 2008 Romanian National Theatre Festival in Bucharest.

celebrated 1962 production of *King Lear,* when Paul Scofield, as Lear, suddenly rose and, with one violent sweep of his arm, overturned the huge oak dining table at which he had been seated, sending pewter mugs crashing to the floor as he raged at his daughter Goneril's treachery. This stunning action led to a reevaluation of the character of both Lear and Goneril and of the relationship between this tempestuous and sporadically vulgar father and his socially ambitious daughter. It also instantly established Brook as one of England's greatest living directors and, still talked about to this day, propelled his career to its extraordinary heights.

Some plays require specialized blocking for specialized scenes such as dances or duels. Such scenes require skilled and trained movements (the characters, for example, must ordinarily appear as experienced dancers or duelists), so the director, after determining the basic concept of the dance or fight, may wish to arrange for a dance choreographer or fight director to provide the highly detailed direction that will provide the moment-to-moment moves required. Such specialized dramatic situations are hardly rare. Almost every play written before the nineteenth century includes a dance, a duel, a battle, or some combination of all of them, and the ability to create or at least to oversee a captivating dance number or an exciting battle scene is clearly requisite for any director aspiring to work beyond the strictly modern-realistic mode.

Fight scenes are not always duels or military battles. Here actors Roger Allam and Jodhi May have at each other with ordinary office chairs, as staged by Fight Director Malcolm Ranson in David Harrower's *Blackbird,* an intense drama about pedophilia and its horrific aftermath. The play, directed by the acclaimed German director Peter Stein, was performed at the Edinburgh Festival in 2006.

"Business" is a theatre term that refers to the small-scale movements a character performs within the larger pattern of entrances and crosses and exits. Mixing a cocktail, answering a telephone, adjusting a tie, shaking hands, fiddling with a pencil, winking an eye, and drumming on a tabletop are all "bits of business" that can lend a character credibility, depth, and fascination. Much of the stage business in a performance is originated by the actor—usually spontaneously over the course of rehearsal—although it may be stimulated by a directorial suggestion or request. The director ultimately must select from among the rehearsal inventions and determine what business will become a part of the finished performance; when this determination is made, bits of business become part of the blocking plan.

Staging, then, in the largest sense, includes both hidden and bold blocking effects, specialized movements, and small idiosyncratic behaviors, all combined into a complex pattern that creates meaning, impact, and style. Skillful staging unites the design elements of a production with the acting, creating an omnidynamic spatial interaction between actors, costumes, scenery, and audience, infusing the stage with life. Getting a play "on its feet," as the theatrical jargon puts it, is usually the first step in making it breathe; and the best staging is that which gives the actors the chance to breathe the air of the playwright's world and to awaken to the true vitality of the playwright's characters.

**Actor-Coaching** The director is the actor's coach and both initiates and leads the various activities—discussions, improvisations, games, exercises, lectures, research, blocking, polishing—that will occupy the actors during each rehearsal. Like a football or hockey coach, the director seeks to stimulate proactive

One of the major problems in staging realistic plays is letting the audience see the expressions of important characters—and hence the faces of the actors playing them—while still maintaining the credibility of those characters, who are (supposedly) talking to each other and not to the audience. Director Guy Masterson solves this by having all actors focus on a key prop in this jury-room scene in Reginald Rose's *12 Angry Men,* produced at the Edinburgh Festival in 2003.

teamwork among the "players," as well as developing individual craft excellence and artistry in each one of them. And because the work of the theatre inevitably demands of the actor a good measure of emotional, psychological, even irrational investment, the director has an opportunity (if not an obligation) to provide an atmosphere in which actors can feel free to liberate their powers of sensitivity and creativity. Good directors lead their casts; great directors inspire them.

The ways in which directors go about coaching actors are various and probably more dependent on personality than on planning. Some directors are largely passive; they either "block and run," in the jargon of commercial theatre, or function primarily as a sounding board for actors' decisions about intention, action, or business. Conversely, there are directors closer to the popular stereotype, mercurial

fanatics whose approaches at times verge on the despotic: they cajole, bully, plead, storm, and rage at their actors; involve themselves in every detail of motive and characterization; and turn every rehearsal into a mixture of acting class, group therapy session, and religious experience. Both methods, as experience teaches, can produce theatrical wizardry, and both can fail utterly. Probably the determining factors either way are the strength of the director's ideas and the extent to which the cast is willing to accept his or her directorial authority.

Too little direction, of course, can be as stultifying to an actor as too much. The passive director runs the risk of defeating an actor's performance by failing to confirm it, that is, by withholding constructive response. Similarly, the extremely active director may, in a whirlwind of passion, overwhelm the actor's own creativity and squelch his or her efforts to build a

# Stagecraft

## "This Is How It's Done!"

Publicity photographs taken in rehearsal frequently show a director onstage with !a few actors, demonstrating a bit of business and "showing them how it's done." This kind of publicity has probably fostered a certain misunderstanding of the director's role among the general public, for demonstration is only a- part of directing, and a distinctly small part at that. Indeed, some directors scrupulously avoid it altogether.

Demonstration as a way of teaching an actor a role has a long history in the theatre and was a particularly common ractice in those periods when directing was carried ou chiefly by retired actors. Even today, young actors rehearsing for classical plays at the Comédie-Française (founded in 1680) are expected to learn their parts by mimicking the performance of their elders down to the last detail of inflection, tone, gesture, and timing. And, of course, many contemporary American directors occasionally give "line readings" to an actor or demonstrate the precise manner of gesturing, moving, sitting, or handling a prop if they perceive that a specific desired behavior might not come naturally.

But demonstration as an exclusive method of coaching an actor in a role is very much a thing of the past. Most contemporary directors make far greater use of discussion, suggestion, and improvisation. These methods seek to address the inner actor and to encourage the individual to distill his or her performance out of self-motivated passions and enthusiasms. Because they know that a purely imitative performance is all too likely to be a mechanical performance, today's directors tend to rely on methods more creative than "getting up there and showing how it's done."

sensitive performance, thereby condemning the production to oppressive dullness. For these and other reasons, most directors today strive to find a middle ground, somewhere between task mastery and suggestion, from which they can provide the actor with both a goal and a disciplined path toward it while maintaining an atmosphere of creative freedom.

Directors need not be actors themselves, but they must understand the paradoxes and ambiguities inherent in that art if they are to help the actor fashion a solid and powerful performance. The greatest acting braves the unknown and flirts continuously with danger (the danger of exposure, of failure, of transparency, of artifice). The director must give the actor a careful balance of freedom and guidance in order to foster the confidence that leads to that kind of acting. Directors who are insensitive to this requirement—no matter how colorful their stormings and coaxings or how rational their discussions of the playwright's vision—are almost certain to forfeit the performance rewards that arise from the great actor-director collaborations.

Pacing    Despite all the director's responsibilities, pace is perhaps the only aspect of a theatrical production for which general audiences and theatre critics alike are certain to hold the director accountable. Frequently, newspaper reviews of productions devote whole paragraphs of praise or blame to the actors and designers and evaluate the director's contribution solely in terms of the play's pace: "well paced" and "well directed" are almost interchangeable plaudits in the theatre critic's lexicon; and when a critic pronounces a play "slow" or "dragging," everyone understands he or she is firing a barrage at the director.

To the novice director (or critic), pace appears to be primarily a function of the rate at which lines are said; hence a great many beginning directors attempt to make their productions more lively simply by instructing everyone to speak and move at a lively clip: "Give it more energy!" "Make it happen faster!" But pace is fundamentally determined by a complex and composite time structure that must be developed to accommodate many variables, such as credibility, suspense, mood, style, and the natural rhythms of life: heartbeat, respiration, the duration of a spontaneous sob or an unexpected laugh. How much time is properly consumed, for example, by a moment of panic? a pregnant pause? a flash of remembrance? an agonized glance? a quick retort? These are the ingredients of pace, and they are not subject to the generalized "hurry-up" of the director who has not first discovered the pattern of rhythms inherent in a play.

The pace of a play should be determined largely by the quantity and quality of the information it conveys to the audience, and the director must decide how much time the audience requires to assimilate that information. In a farce, of course, the audience needs almost no time to synthesize information; therefore,

Directing comedy is an art in itself, and Dominique Serrand scored a brilliant success in a Shakespearean play that demands theatrical humor in its very title: *The Comedy of Errors.* Serrand directed this play at the Guthrie Theatre in 2002 with what one reviewer called "fantastical ... madcap panache"—as clearly shown in the mouth-stuffing scene between Laura Esping as an irate Luciana and Judson Pearce Morgan as a bewildered Antipholus.

farce generally is propelled rapidly, with information coming as fast as the actors can get it out. A psychological drama, in contrast, may require a slower pace to foster deeper understanding of its characters and issues; sympathy is engendered when audience members have an opportunity to compare the characters' lives with their own, to put themselves in the characters' situations, and to engage in introspection even as they observe the action onstage. Similarly, political drama commonly demands of us a critical inquiry into our own societies and our own lives as part of our understanding of what is happening onstage; this form, too, demands time to linger over certain perfectly poised questions—and the pace of a production must give us that time.

Just as a symphony is composed of several movements, so a well-paced theatrical production inevitably has its adagio, andante, and allegro tempos. Faster

tempos tend to excite, to bedazzle, and to sharpen audience attention; slower ones give audience members a chance to consider and to augment the play's actions and ideas with their own reflections. Often directors speak about "setting up" an audience with a rapid pace and then delivering a "payoff" with a powerful, more deliberately paced dramatic catharsis. The sheer mechanics of theatrical pacing demand the greatest skill and concentration from both actor and director, and for both, the perfection of dramatic timing (and most notably comic timing) is a mark of great theatrical artistry.

Directors vary in their manner of pacing plays, of course. Some wait until final rehearsals and then, martinet-like, stamp out rhythms on the stage floor with a stick or clap their hands in the back of the house. Some work out intricate timing patterns in the early rehearsals and explore them in great detail with the actors as to motivation, inner monologue, and interpersonal effect. Directorial intervention of some sort is almost always present in the achievement of an excellent dramatic pace; it rarely occurs spontaneously. Actors trained to the realist manner often tend to work through material slowly and to savor certain moments all out of proportion to the information they convey; actors trained in a more technical manner just as often are "off to the races" with the dialogue, leaving the audience somewhat at sea about the meaning or importance of the matters at hand. And when a variety of actors, trained in different schools, come together in production for the first time, they can create such an arrhythmic pace that the play becomes unintelligible until the director steps in to guide and control the tempo.

**Coordinating** In the final rehearsals the director's responsibility becomes more and more one of coordination: of bringing together the concept and the designs, the acting and the staging, the pace and the performance. Now all the production elements that were developed separately must be judged, adjusted, polished, and perfected in their fuller context. Costumes must be seen under lights, staging must be seen against scenery, pacing must include the shifting of sets, acting must coalesce with sound amplification and the size of the performance hall, and the original concept must be reexamined in light of its emerging realization. Is the theme coming across? Are the actions coming across? Can the actors be heard and understood? Do the costumes read? Is the play focused? Is the play interesting? Do we care about the characters? about the themes? about anything? Does the production seem to *work*?

Timing and wholeness are governing concepts in this final coordinating phase of production. In assessing the play's overall timing, the director must be prepared to judge the play's effectiveness against its duration and to modify or eliminate those parts of the production that overextend the play's potential for communicating information, feelings, or ideas. Last-minute cutting is always a painful process—much labor and creative spirit have gone into the parts that will be cut—but many a production has been vastly improved by judicious pruning at this time. And in the interest of providing wholeness—that quality which unifies a play and gives it the stamp of taste and aesthetic assurance—the best and bravest directors are willing in these final moments to eliminate elements that fail to cohere with the play's overall appearance

and significance. Often these elements hold a special meaning for the director; they may even have figured into his or her earliest conception of the production. But now, in the cold light of disciplined analysis, they may rather look painfully like directorial indulgence or extraneous showing off. The best directors are those who can be most rigorous with themselves at this stage, for they are the ones who are capable not only of generating ideas but also of refining and focusing artistic form.

In the final rehearsals—the *technical rehearsals,* when scenery, lighting, and sound are added, and *dress rehearsals,* when the actors don costumes and makeup for the first time—the director arrives at a crossroads: though remaining fundamentally responsible for every final decision about the timing and balance of theatrical elements, she or he must now "give over" the production to the actors and technicians who will execute it. Beyond this junction the director will be consumed by the production and will disappear within it in a matter of days: it will reflect the director's personal conceptions and directorial skills without reflecting the director's own persona. After contributing to everything that appears upon the stage and initiating much of it, the director must accept the fact that he or she will not be recognized in any single moment, any single act, any single costume or lighting cue. In these final rehearsals the director's presence normally becomes more a force for organization than a source of inspiration—clipboard in hand, she or he delivers hundreds of last-minute notes to actors, technicians, and stage managers in an effort to give the production that extra finesse that distinguishes the outstanding from the mediocre.

What an extraordinary exchange of power has taken place between the first meeting of the cast and director and these final days! Whereas earlier the entire production was in the director's head and the cast waited in awe and expectation, now the actors hold the play in their heads and everyone confronts the unknowns of the play's reception. The actors have a new master now: the audience. It is in these days that even the most experienced actors confront their fundamental nakedness in performance: they must face the audience, and they must do it without benefit of directorial protection, with nothing to shield them save their costumes, characters, and lines. To the actor, the director is no longer a leader but a partner, no longer a parent but a friend. Actors may indeed experience a certain feeling of betrayal; the director, after all, has abandoned them to face the audience alone, just as in the medieval play Good Deeds accompanies Everyman only to the brink of the grave. But then acting, like death, is a trial that cannot be shared.

Presenting   It is an axiom of the theatre that nobody is more useless on opening night than the director. If all has progressed without major catastrophe and the production has successfully been "given over" to those who will run it and perform in it, the director's task on opening night consists chiefly in seeing and evaluating the production and gauging the audience response. This night may, of course, prove to be nothing but a calm between storms. Where there are preview performances, as there are in all professional theatres and some academic and community ones, the director has the opportunity (and responsibility) for evaluating the production in terms of its audience response, and instituting changes during the previews where desirable—including cuts and changes in the text if it's a new play and the playwright is on hand and willing—right up to the opening performance. And although in professional theatre a director's contract normally terminates on opening night, most directors try to see performances periodically during the run, and may follow up their visits with notes to the actors—either to encourage them to maintain spontaneity or to discourage them from revising the original directorial plan. One perhaps apocryphal show-business story has it that the American director George Abbott once posted a rehearsal call late in a play's run in order to "take out the improvements."

Just as the actor might feel alone and somewhat betrayed in those empty moments prior to the opening performance, so might the director feel a twinge of isolation at the ovation that follows it. For it is in that curtain-call ovation that the audience takes over the director's critic-mentor function and the director is consigned to anonymity. The actors, heady with the applause, suddenly remember that it is they who provide the essential ingredient of theatre, while the director, cheering the ensemble from the back of the house, suddenly realizes he or she is now just one of the crowd, one witness among many to the realization of his or her own intangible and now remote plans and ideas. In the professional theatre, it is at this moment that the director's contract really expires—a fitting reminder of the "giving over" that occurs in the direction of all plays. Only directors who can derive genuine satisfaction from creating out of the medium of others' performance will thrive

and prosper in directorial pursuits; those who aspire to public acclaim and adulation will most likely face perpetual frustration as practitioners of this, all-encompassing yet all-consuming art.

# THE TRAINING OF A DIRECTOR

Traditionally, directors have come to their craft from a great many areas, usually after achieving distinction in another theatrical discipline: for example, Elia Kazan was first an actor, Susan Stroman a choreographer, Harold Prince a producer, Peter Hunt a lighting designer, Franco Zeffirelli a scene designer, Robert Brustein a drama critic, Harold Pinter a playwright, Mike Nichols an improvisational comedian, and Robert Wilson an architectural student. Still, in addition to a specialty, most of these directors have brought to their art a comprehensive knowledge of the theatre in its various aspects. Having distinction in one field is important chiefly insofar as it gives directors a certain confidence and authority—and it gives others confidence in their exercise of that authority. But it is comprehensive knowledge that enables directors to collaborate successfully with actors, designers, managers, playwrights, and technicians with facility and enthusiasm.

New directors entering the profession today are more likely than not to have been trained in a dramatic graduate program or conservatory—and often they have supplemented this training with an apprenticeship at a repertory theatre. One of the most remarkable recent developments in the American theatre has been the emergence of a cadre of expertly trained directors: men and women with a broad understanding of the theatre and a disciplined approach to directorial creativity.

Well-trained directors will possess—in addition to the craft mastery of staging, actor-coaching, pacing, and production coordinating—a strong literary imagination and an ability to conceptualize intellectually and visually. They will be sensitive to interpersonal relationships, which will play an important role in the onstage and off-stage collaborations under their control. They will have a sound working knowledge of the history of the theatre, the various styles and masterworks of dramatic literature, the potential of various theatre technologies, and the design possibilities inherent in the use of theatrical space. They will have at their command resources in music, art, literature, and history; they will be able to research plays and investigate production possibilities without

While the producer raises funds, the director spends them, to the record tune-in this 2007 London premiere of *Lord of the Rings*—of nearly $50 million. "The parade of images in [director] Matthew Warchus's production ... is ceaseless and astonishing," said the London *Observer,* and this photo of Warchus' production (designed by Rob Howell and lit by Paul Pyant) makes clear that every dollar of the director's budget appears on the stage. An English director who has staged works with the Royal Shakespeare Company and England's Royal National Theatre, among many others, Warchus has also won Tony nominations for his direction of *Art* and *True West* on New York's Broadway.

starting at absolute zero; and they will be able to base ideas and conceptions on sound social, psychological, and aesthetic understandings.

All of these advanced skills can be effectively taught in a first-rate drama program, and for that reason today's top-flight theatre directors, more than any other group of stage artists, are likely to have studied in one or another of the rigorous drama programs now in place across the country. The accomplished director is perhaps the one all-around "expert" of the theatre; this is not to deride the director's function as a creative and imaginative force but to emphasize her or his responsibility over a broad and highly complex enterprise. Nothing is truly irrelevant to the training of a director, for almost every field of knowledge can be brought to bear upon theatre production. The distinctiveness of any production of the contemporary theatre is largely a reflection of the unique but comprehensive training of its director, who is responsible not only for the overall initiative and corrective authority that infuse the production but also for the personal vision that inspires its singular direction.

# Chapter 6

# Designers and Technicians

WHEN AN ACTOR FIRST STEPPED onto the stage as Jocasta in Sophocles' Greek tragedy *Oedipus Tyrannos,* he (and it was a he—all Greek actors of that time being men) wore clothing similar but not identical to what he would wear in the marketplace. It was similar in the sense that it was robelike, but different because the shape and perhaps color of the garments indicated that he was to be seen as a "she." And not only a she, but a *royal* she. This is the basic purpose of design: to transform something so it may be seen, by a willing viewer, as something else, in this case a fifth-century B.C. male commoner as the tenth-century B.C. queen of Thebes.

There would have been other differences too. The robe's sleeves would have been narrower than the sleeves of an everyday gown, so that the actor's movements could be clearly seen from the back of the amphitheatre. And the actor also would have worn a mask, enlarging his face, amplifying his voice, and providing a fixed expression that even from a long distance could be quickly seen as both powerful and tragic.

Thus when the costumed and masked "Jocasta" strode through the giant skene (stagehouse) door onto the sun-drenched stage, the audience saw not an actor walking onto a platform but a tragic queen leaving the royal palace to greet her equally gowned and masked husband, King Oedipus, grieving with his citizens on the palace steps.

Nothing in the text of *Oedipus* refers to the clothing, mask, or door just described. Yet these elements, creating the *look* of the play, are absolutely crucial to the drama in its performance. They constitute its *design:* its costumes (gowns), scenery (door, wall), makeup (mask), lighting (sun), and sound (voice as amplified through the mask). And that design has aesthetic, not only dramatic, characteristics: color, scale, line, balance, harmony, punctuation, surprise. All these design elements came into play with the first drama, and all have even greater importance today.

The playwright creates the play's words, the actors execute its actions and impersonate its characters, but theatre designers determine what both the stage and the characters look like. Design comprises most of what we see when we go to the theatre—and a good deal of what we hear. Designers and the technicians who implement their ideas create what the actors wear, what they sit on, and what they stand before, and they determine how the actors are illuminated and how they—and the play around them—sound. The work of designers and technicians brings to the theatre a play's scenery, costumes, properties, lighting, sound score, sound amplification, and special effects.

## THE DESIGN PROCESS

The initial framework for design is the play itself. The action that Sophocles outlined in *Oedipus* implies a door, and most designers provide one. The action requires a chorus and characters that enter and leave the staging area, so suitable points of entry/exit are created as well. Sometimes—even in ancient times—characters fly in or out of sight, so machines are designed and built to execute these superhuman actions.

Today, of course, scenery, lighting, and costumes can create realistic-looking environments, such as living rooms and Roman piazzas, barrooms and butcher shops—and imagined locales such as Satan's Hell or *Peter Pan's* Never Never Land. They also can create uniquely conceived visualizations that layer interpretations and social, political, or aesthetic references to the scripts they accompany. Sound designs can create scores that enhance (or contrast with) the play's actions by means of musical or other sonic themes, thereby underlining romance, tension, or grief. Or sound designs can punctuate and disrupt the play's actions with the cacophonous noise of traffic, jungle cries, or warfare.

The first stage in creating a play's design is a conceptual one, during which design *ideas* emerge from the designers' reading of the script, researching its historic, intellectual, and stylistic context, and imagining its potential impact on the expected audience. These ideas are shared with the play's director (who may have initiated this process with ideas of his or her own), with the playwright (if a living playwright is part of the conceptual process), and with the production designers in other areas. Although the director normally oversees these conversations, artistic collaboration is absolutely fundamental to this conceptual period of a play production's creation.

For the visual designer, conceptual ideas may be almost instantly translated into mental images, both general and specific. Such images may be expressed first in words—such as "gloomy clouds," "El Greco blues," "delicate archways," "broken bottles," "black, black, black"—but they will soon lead to stabs at representation: quick sketches, photos torn from magazines, color samples and swatches. The sound designer may likewise contemplate resonances of "medieval chanting," "random gunfire," "baroque harpsichords," or "winds in the reeds," and then compose or hunt down sounds that could give others on the design/directing team a sense of where they are heading at this stage.

Gradually, a comprehensive design emerges from the repeated sharing and building upon these contributions, normally guided—with a hand that may be sometimes quite gentle and sometimes quite firm—by the director and, of course, the budget. For the visual designer, a physical presentation of proposed designs normally involves colors (primary, earthy, gloomy, pastel), textures (rough, shiny, delicate, steely), shapes (angular, spiraling, blockish, globular), balance (symmetrical, natural, fractal), scale (towering, compressed, vast), style (realistic, romantic, period, abstract, expressionist), and levels of detail (gross, fine, delicate), as rendered in drawings, digitized representations, three-dimensional models, fabric samples, and other media. For the sound designer, designs may move in the direction of music underscoring (retreating brass bands, lush violins, ominous chords), ambient noises (distant sirens, gunfire, ocean breakers), and enhanced, reverberated, or digitally manipulated live sounds (voices, footsteps, door slams), gathered into digitized recording media.

All these representations are shared among the artistic and technical staff, analyzed for cost and required labor in construction, and evaluated for their individual merit as well as their joint impact. How will the final, synthesized design *look*? How will it propel the *action* of the play? What will it communicate to

The traditional elements—fire and water—can be major scenic pieces, as exemplified in this astonishing 2005 Icelandic production of George Büchner's 1839 *Woyzeck,* staged by Reykyavik's Vesturport Theatre with a water-filled, stage-wide fish tank in which Woyzeck drowns his girlfriend, Marie, and eventually himself. The play is a German pre-expressionist classic about the impoverishment of working-class life in the nineteenth century. Woyzeck, modeled on a real person, is an uneducated army private, tormented by officers and doctors, taunted by his girlfriend, and cuckolded by his company's drum major. His watery murder and subsequent suicide constitute the play's grim climax. Ingvar E. SiQurdsson is Woyzeck; Nina Dogg Filippusdottir, beneath him, is Marie. Gisli Orn Gardarsson directed.

the expected *audience*? How will it tie the actors to the audience, the drama to the theatre in which it is staged, the play's events to the real life that goes on outside the theatre's door?

Those are the questions that the designer considers from the initial moment of conception to the opening performance.

## WHAT DESIGN DOES

Theatrical design is a uniquely *creative* contribution to theatre. Modern plays generally include stage descriptions, but few go into detail and most allow wide designer freedom. At the beginning of *Waiting for Godot,* for example, playwright Samuel Beckett

simply writes, "A country road. A tree. Evening." He then launches directly into the opening dialogue, leaving us to wonder: What sort of road should this be? What sort of tree? Where is it in relation to the road? And how dark an "evening" is it? Later in the play Beckett provides another stage description: "The light suddenly fails. In a moment it is night. The moon rises at back, mounts in the sky, stands still, shedding a pale light on the scene." But how is all this accomplished? How much darker does the stage get? What does the "moon" look like: full? crescent? How quickly does it rise? How suddenly does it stop? And what is it made of: projected light? a wooden cutout on a wire? And if a wire, is it meant to be seen or should it be invisible to the audience? Or is the moon simply a lantern

Most Americans can imagine what a shabby motel room on California's Mojave Desert might look like, but Bunny Christie's scenic and costume design for this 2006 London production, with lighting by Mark Henderson, beautifully sets up the bleak but sensual atmosphere (notice the red dress and the blue and yellow light pouring through the closed blinds) for the action of Sam Shepard's explosive drama of lust and longing, *Fool for Love,* which is set in such a locale. Though deceptively "realistic" in apparent detail, the room looks like no actual motel room in the world. Juliette Lewis is the intensely passionate May, and Martin Henderson is her on-and-off boyfriend Eddie. Lindsay Posner directed at the Apollo Theatre.

carried by an actor—as in the "Pyramus and Thisbe" play embedded in Shakespeare's *A Midsummer Night's Dream*?

And what do *Godot's* actors *wear*? We read in the dialogue of hats, boots, and coats, but what do these garments look like? What colors should they be? How worn? Are they clean or dirty? well-fitted or too large? or too small? What sort of hats?

More questions: How *old* should the characters appear to be? Should any have long hair? facial hair? fat bellies? missing teeth? And what sounds might surround them: birds? wind? passing cars or airplanes? sounds of war? nothing? Should the characters' voices sound natural? be amplified? Should they reverberate?

And what *else* might be there besides the road, tree, and moon?

Those sorts of initial questions are posed and addressed by the production's designers and the technicians who execute their designs. But they also lead to questions of a different order. What are the dominant *feelings* the audience might be expected to experience when they first see the stage? What feelings should be evoked afterward? Should audience members find the environment mundane? shocking? hopeful? depressing? Is the environment human or otherworldly? ancient or futuristic? archetypal or unpredictable? What *world* should the audience enter when the curtain or lights come up and the play begins?

There are certainly as many designs for *Waiting for Godot* as there are designers to tackle this particular script, and the same is true of any play. No matter how detailed the playwright's directions may be, the design team and their collaborators ordinarily shape the production's visual and audio elements as they see fit.

Because of rigorous censorship under Nazi and Communist regimes, innovative playwriting was practically forbidden throughout most of eastern Europe from the mid-1930s until the end of the Soviet era in 1989. So during that period it became the job of directors and designers, when staging the few "approved" classics from past centuries, to introduce the penetrating political analogies and revolutionary aesthetics that would convey deep meaning to an audience while still escaping the censors' wary eyes. Although the iron curtain has since fallen, eastern European directing and design retain their radical slant, as represented by these two twenty-first century productions of Shakespeare's *King Lear* (*Above*) Designer Bertha Jósef, working with Director Lazlo Bocsardi on a 2008 *King Lear* production for the Tamasi Aron Theatre of Romania, augmented Lear's dismay at seeing "poor naked wretches" with "looped and windowed raggedness" by placing near-naked young men in individual glass cages elevated on waist-high stilts and framed within bright brass struts, as if the poor wretches of Lear's kingdom had become mannequins in department store showcases. (*Below*) David Borovsky's design for the same play in Lev Dodin's Russian production at the Maly Drama Theatre of St. Petersburg brutally abstracted the opening court scene by eliminating most of the play's called-for characters and simply presenting the title character—with his back to the audience—facing his three daughters and two sons-in-law, all dressed in white against a skeletal gray setting. Borovsky's design, like Jósef's, does not represent any conceivable real-world environment, but it powerfully conveys the "plainness" with which Cordelia (*standing at center*) hopes to win the approval of her father.

# SCENERY

Scenery is usually what we first see—either when the curtain rises in a traditional proscenium production or as we enter the theatre if there is no curtain—and the scene designer is usually listed first among designers in a theatre poster or program. Scenery, however, is a relatively new design area. Costume, makeup, and masks are far more ancient. Scenery was not needed at all in the Egyptian *Abydos Passion Play* or the Greek dithyramb, and it probably played little part in early Greek or Roman drama, save to afford entry, exit, and sometimes expanded acting space (such as platforms that rolled onto the stage) or to provide a decorative backdrop (by painted panels or rotating prisms) later in the period. In much Asian theatre, scenery remains

Contemporary eastern European design is almost always radically abstracted from realism. In his design for *Waiting for Godot*, Romanian Silviu Purcarete (who also directed) set aside Beckett's stage directions entirely and created a setting of iron scaffolding and plastic sheeting. The plays iconic tree was raised above the actors' heads; only its roots were shown. A prompter sat on the stage, following the script and playing a gong. At the end of each act a three-piece combo appeared at the rear of the stage—at the end of act 1 wearing full-body bunny costumes, at the end of act 2 bare-headed and hacking furiously at their instruments rather than playing them. The staging certainly emphasized the play's "absurdity" but was oddly affecting as well.

rare or even nonexistent; this is the case in most xiqu (Chinese opera) and—apart from the elaborate stage-house itself—in Japanese nō drama as well. Nor was scenery of paramount importance in the outdoor medieval or public Elizabethan theatres, apart from a few painted set pieces made to resemble walls, trees, caves, thrones, tombs, porches, and the occasional "Hellmouth." Prior to the seventeenth century, most of drama's scenic aspects were part of, or dictated by, the architecture of the theatre structure itself.

The development of European indoor stages, artificially illuminated, fostered the first great phase of scene design: initially a period of painted, flat scenery. Working indoors, protected from rain and wind, the scenic designers of Renaissance court masques and public spectacles were for the first time able to erect and position painted canvases and temporary wooden structures without fear of having the colors run and the supports blow away. And with the advent of controllable indoor lighting in the nineteenth century (first by gas, then by electricity), designers could illuminate settings and acting areas as they wished, leaving other parts of the theatre building, such as the audience area, in the dark for the first time. By that time designers could create both realistic illusion and extravagant visual spectacle—and have the audience focus on their work without worrying about the weather outside the theatre doors.

The result was that a new class of theatre artists came to public consciousness. Early designers

such as Sebastiano Serlio (1475-1554), Aristotile da Sangallo (1481-1551), and Giacomo Torelli (1608-1678) in Italy, Inigo Jones (1573-1652) in England, and the Frenchman Jean Bérain (c. 1637-1711) became as prominent as the playwrights whose plays they designed. Indoor stage scenery, painted in exquisite perspective, took on even greater sophistication under the artists of the Royal and romantic eras in the eighteenth and nineteenth centuries. The proscenium format, which was created primarily to show off elegant settings, has largely dominated theatre architecture ever since.

The painted flat scenery that the proscenium gave rise to has been only one of many competing scenic formats in the modern era. Today's scenery is generally realistic or metaphoric or a combination of both. Realistic scenery attempts to depict, often in great detail, a specific time and place in the real world where the play's events are presumed to take place. Metaphoric scenery favors, instead, visual images that seek to evoke (or to suggest, abstract, or make a visual statement about) the production's intended theme, mood, or social/political implications. Metaphoric scenery tends to remind us— at least when we first see it—that we are in a theatre, not in a bedroom or butcher shop; generally its intention is to draw us more deeply into the play's larger issues and concerns. And although stage design today most often combines realism with metaphor—these terms are best described as end points on a continuum rather than

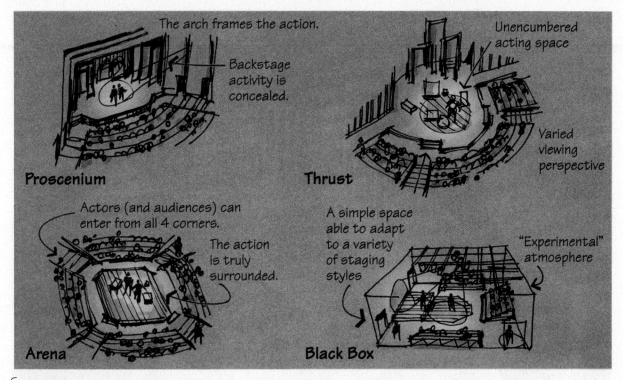

The arch frames the action.

Backstage activity is concealed.

**Proscenium**

Unencumbered acting space

Varied viewing perspective

**Thrust**

Actors (and audiences) can enter from all 4 corners.

The action is truly surrounded.

**Arena**

A simple space able to adapt to a variety of staging styles

"Experimental" atmosphere

**Black Box**

Illustrated here are the four basic staging formats: proscenium, thrust, arena, and black box. Deciding where to locate the stage in relation to the audience is the first consideration in theatre design.

purely exclusive categories—these complementary design goals have each contributed mightily to the important position of scenery in the theatrical experience today.

Realistic settings carry on the tradition of illusionism established in eighteenth-century painted scenery. At that time, an ingeniously arranged assembly of "wings" (vertical, flat scenery pieces standing left and right of the stage), "borders" (horizontal, flat scenery pieces hung above the stage), and "drops" (short for *backdrops:* large, flat scenery pieces at the rear of the stage), painted in perspective, created the lifelike illusion of drawing rooms, conservatories, ballrooms, reception halls, parlors, libraries, servants' quarters, professional offices, and factory yards of many a dramatist's imagination. By the nineteenth century, this "wing-and-drop set," as it was known, yielded to the "box set": a three-dimensional construction of interconnected hard-covered "flats" (representing the walls and occasionally the ceilings of a real room), which was then filled with real furniture and real properties taken from ordinary real-world environments. The box set is very much alive today and is indeed the major scenic format for contemporary domestic drama (particularly comedy) on New York's Broadway, on London's West End, and at many community and college theatres across America. Though no longer particularly voguish (the box set rarely wins design awards), it fulfills the staging requirements of a great many domestic comedies, thrillers, and serious, linearly structured dramas, particularly those requiring interior settings. Advances in scenic construction and technology have made the box set a marvel of lifelike appearance and detail.

Box sets do more than merely designate the locale of a play. By adding three-dimensional features, they allow for acting and playwriting opportunities previously unachievable: staircases to descend, doors to slam, windows to climb through, bookcases to stash revolvers in, and grandfather clocks to hide characters in. Public fascination with realistic scenery reached its high-water mark in the ultrarealistic "theatre of the fourth wall removed" of the late nineteenth century, during which the box set was used to such advantage that it helped foster a uniquely architectural theory of theatre— that it should represent life as it is normally lived, but with one wall removed so that the audience could look in upon it.

Thomas Umfrid's scenery for a production of Noel Coward's *Hay Fever,* set in a well-to-do acting family's English country home in the mid-1920s, is beautifully realized for the 2003 Utah Shakespearean Festival. Umfrid's set forcefully projects the action of the play forward by a skillful arrangement of staircase, doors, and landing. The showy 1920s costumes were designed by Kevin Alberts, and the summery lighting was designed by Lonnie Alcaraz.

Metaphoric scenic design, in contrast, tends to be more conceptual than literal, more kinetic than stable, more theatrical than photographic. The use of scenic metaphor is hardly new. In the 4,500-year-old *Abydos Passion Play*, two maces represent Set's testicles, and a red stone indicates the Eye of Horus. In his prologue to *Henry V,* Shakespeare apologizes for the "unworthy scaffold" of his stage and begs his audience to use their "imaginary forces" to complete his scenic illusion. For example, with the help of two or three scaling ladders placed against the stage balcony the audience could imagine the English army storming a castle wall in France. These are scenic "abstractions" in the most elemental sense: they present reality by a sign rather than *trompe l'oeil* ("eye-deceiving") realism.

The modern sense of metaphoric scenery began with the theoretical (and occasionally practical) works of designers Adolphe Appia (1862-1928) and Edward Gordon Craig (1872-1966), both of whom urged the fluid use of space, form, and light as the fundamental principle of dramatic design. Today, aided by technological advances in motorized, computer-controlled

# Stagecraft

## Quince's "Significant" Moon

Shakespeare understood and at times apologized for the pictorial limitations of the scenery of his time ("Piece out our imperfections with your thoughts," he advised the audience in the prologue to *Henry V*). But he also appreciated its capacity to signify—rather than merely depict realistically—the world of his plays. In Shakespeare's *A Midsummer Night's Dream*, the character Peter Quince is seen directing a production of "Pyramus and Thisbe" with a group of amateur actors and pondering the "hard things" that this play requires, mainly the effect of moonshine in a bedroom chamber. One actor, finding that the moon will be shining on the night of performance, suggests they simply open the window and let the real moon shine in. Quince, however, prefers that an actor hold up a lantern to "disfigure, or to present" the moon. The created "scenic" moon is preferred to the real one because it *signifies* moonshine; it is intentional and consequently meaningful rather than accidental and meaningless. To indicate a "wall" in the same play—the other "hard thing"—Quince refrains from bringing in a real wall and instead has another actor put on "some plaster or some loam" so as "to signify wall."

Life may be a tale, as Shakespeare's Macbeth says, "full of sound and fury, signifying nothing," but the theatre tells tales that signify a great many things. Thus scenery's function is not merely to depict but to signify—to "make a sign, to be "significant."

lighting and scene-shifting, the movement toward a more conceptual, abstract, and kinetic scenography has inspired impressive stylizations around the world. Shafts and walls of light, transparent "scrims," sculptural configurations, wall-size photo projections, mirrored and burlapped surfaces, "floating" walls and rising staircases, and "found" or "surreal" environments have all become major scenic media over the past fifty years. Metaphoric settings (such as Quince's "wall," mentioned in the Stagecraft above) can establish locales, but they are even more effective in establishing moods and styles. Of course, a play's mood can be established by realistic scenery as well. For example, by creating a theatrical space that is tall and airy (or cramped and squat) or by using certain colors or shapes, the designer can create an environment in any mode so that the play's action delivers a strikingly defined tone. But with a determined metaphoric extension, the designer can greatly elaborate upon this tone and translate it into a highly specific sensory impact. For specific examples of such designs, read the captions of photographs of contemporary designs as seen throughout this chapter.

Specifically postmodern design elements made their appearance in the theatre of the 1980s and 1990s. Because the postmodern emphasizes disharmonies and associations, it travels a somewhat different path from the departures of modernist innovators Craig and Appia. Postmodern design is identifiable by its conscious disruption of "unifying" stylistic themes, replacing them with what at first may seem random assemblages of different and unrelated styles, some "quoting" other historical periods or intellectual sources and others disrupting the linear flow of consistent imagery or effect. Postmodern design also tends to reconfigure, or refer to, the theatre facility itself with (for example) painted scenery deliberately made to look scenic, particularly in contrast to seemingly arbitrary found objects strewn about the set, and with designed units meant to comment on—and to mock—their own "theatricality."

Bob Crowley's setting for Tom Stoppard's *The Invention of Love* (see the chapter titled "Theatre Today"), portraying the English poet and classical scholar A. E. Housman, is a postmodern deconstruction of Roman architectural and sculptural forms, reflected in the River Styx in Stoppard's version of the classical Hades (the mythological Greek world of the dead). And Richard Hudson's 1997 *The Lion King* (see "Theatre Today") filled Broadway's New Amsterdam Theatre—stage and house alike—with multiple and ingenious recapitulations of African, Asian, and American avantgarde design in a joyous celebration of the theatre's truly global virtuosity.

The best scenic design today is so much more than mere "backing" for the action of a play. It is instead the visual and spatial architecture of the play's performance, an architecture that when fully realized is *intrinsic to the play's action:* it is the place *where* the play exists; it also determines exactly *how* the play exists and, along with other factors, helps reveal the play's deepest meanings.

The "scenery" designed by Katrin Brack for Chekhov's *Ivanov*, as produced by Berlin's Volksbühne in a 2008 Los Angeles tour, consisted almost entirely of stage fog. Within a towering rectangular surround of white fabric, Brack created a "wall of mist" that billowed up from the floor, dividing the stage in half so that characters could make their entrances and exits by simply walking forward or back through the fog. Because the play, Chekhov's first, is largely about a Russian community beset with depression, despair, and anxiety, Brack's setting—with great support from Henning Streck's lighting—completely captured the confusion of the characters and the malaise of their pre-Revolutionary society. Bulgarian-born Dimiter Gottscheff was the director.

## Scenic Materials

Scene designers begin their work with the words of the text and the images in their minds, but at a certain point they begin to concentrate on the materials with which a design will be physically realized. The traditional materials that they have been using over the past four centuries—wood, canvas, and paint—were in the twentieth century extended to include nearly every form of matter known to (or created by, or found by) humankind: metals, plastics, masonry, and fabrics; earth, stone, fire, and water; fog, smoke, rain, light projections, and live animals.

Platforms, flats, and draperies are traditional building blocks of stage scenery and remain important. The *platform* is perhaps most fundamental: all theatre requires is "two boards and a passion," goes an old adage (variously attributed to Molière, Lope de Vega, and Ben Jonson, among several others), and the boards represent the platform stage that elevates the actor above the standing audience. Platforms create different height levels on the stage, providing actors elevated spaces where they can be seen over the heads of other actors and stage furniture. A stage setting with several well-designed platform levels, normally with the highest at the rear of the (proscenium) stage, permits the audience to see dozens of actors simultaneously. *Flats*—sturdy wooden frames covered in various hard surfaces (such as plywood) and then painted or otherwise treated (pierced with doors and windows, adorned with paintings or moldings)—can realistically represent walls, ceilings, or pretty much any flat surface a designer might wish. *Drapery* is the great neutral stuff of stage scenery: black hanging drapes

Ming Cho Lee's great realistic setting for Patrick Meyer's adventure drama *K-2* portrays a ledge in the Himalaya mountains. It even feels cold.

Bert Neumann's set for the Berlin Volksbühne production of *The Insulted and Injured* (adapted from a Dostoevsky novel of the same title) is a bleak, rotating 1950s German bungalow, topped off with a projection screen that shows events occurring within the bungalow, as well as seemingly irrelevant TV commercials.

are conventional to mask (hide) backstage areas and overhead lighting instruments, and a stage curtain (conventionally but not necessarily dark red) may separate the stage from the audience to indicate, with its rise and fall, the play's (or act's) beginning and end.

In addition to these three primary components of stage settings, unique special objects, or *set pieces,* frequently become focal points for an overall setting

design or even for the action of a play. The tree in *Waiting for Godot,* for example, is the primary scenic feature of that play's setting, symbolizing both life and death. The moment when Vladimir and Estragon "do the tree"—an apparent calisthenic exercise in which each man stands on one leg with the tree between them—is a profound moment of theatre in which set piece and actors coalesce in a single image echoing the triple crucifixion on Calvary, where two thieves died alongside Christ. Similarly, the massive supply wagon hauled by Mother Courage, in Bertolt Brecht's epic play of that name, gives rise to a powerful visual impression of struggle and travail that may last long after the characters' words are forgotten. And what would *Prometheus Bound* be without its striking cliff (however it may be designed), onto which

The horticultural set, dominated by a giant beehive at its center, was designed by Tim Hatley and proved the virtual star of Charlotte Jones's *The Humble Boy,* which played at the New York City Center in 2003.

Prometheus is bound by iron chains? No matter how stylized this element may have been in its original realization, it must have radiated to the Athenian audience a visual poetry every bit as eloquent as the verbal poetry with which the play's author supported it. Such unique set pieces tax the imagination of author, director, designer, and scene technician alike, and the masterpieces of scenic invention can long outlive their makers in the memory of the audience.

A host of modern materials and technological inventions add to the primary components from which scenery is created. *Light* as scenery (as opposed to stage lighting, discussed later) can create walls, images, even (with laser holography) three-dimensional visualizations. Banks of sharply focused light sent through dense atmospheres (enhanced by electronically generated haze that simulates smoke, dust, or fog) can create trenches of light that have the appearance of massive solidity yet can be made to disappear at the

flick of a switch. Image projections can provide visuals either realistic or abstract, fixed or fluid, precise or indefinite. *Scrim,* a loosely woven, gauzy fabric long a staple of theatre "magic," is opaque when lit from the audience's side but almost transparent when lit from behind, and is thus employed to make actors and even whole sets seem to instantly appear or disappear, simply with the flick of a switch on the light board.

*Stage machinery*—power-driven turntables, elevators, hoists, fully tilting stage floors (or "decks"), effortlessly gliding rooms (on "wagons"), and the like—can create a virtual dance of scenic elements to support and accompany the dramatic action. The ancient Greeks understood the importance of such mechanical devices well and used flying machines and rolling carts to deliver gods and corpses to the onstage action. More tricks and sleight-of-hand techniques were invented in the medieval theatre (where they were called "trucs" and "feynts"), imparting a certain sparkle of mystery

Mark Wendland's highly theatrical 2007 setting for *Richard III*, directed on the thrust stage of New York's Classic Stage Company by Brian Kulik and Michael Cumpsty—who also played Richard (seen here being crowned)—was largely made up of hanging chandeliers, which rose and fell to change the varying locales of the play. "Day, yield me not thy light; nor, night, thy rest!" cries Richard, which may have sparked interest in Wendland's design motif.

that was picked up by Shakespeare—whose *Macbeth* includes three mysterious "Apparitions," a reappearing "Ghost," and the stage direction "Witches vanish." Today, the choreography of these appearances and disappearances, and even the gliding of the stage scenery during scene changes, may be as much a part of the performance as the scenery itself.

*Sound* is also considered by the scenic designer, who must plan for the actors' footfalls as well as for the visual elements around them. The floor of a japanese no stage, for example, is meant to be stamped on, and it must be designed and constructed to produce a precisely "tuned" vibration. The European scenographer Joseph Svoboda designed a stage floor for *Faust* that could be either resonant or silent, depending on the

arrangement of mechanisms concealed underneath. When Faust walked upstage, his steps reverberated; when he turned and walked downstage, his steps were suddenly silent—and we knew that the devil Mephistopheles had taken his body.

*Properties (props) and furniture,* which are often handled by separate artists working under the guidance of the scene designer, are crucial not only in establishing realism but also in enhancing mood and style. Although furniture often functions in the theatre as it does in real life—to be sat on, lain on, and so forth—it also has a crucial stylistic importance. Often stage furniture is designed and built in imaginative ways to convey a special visual impact. Properties such as ashtrays, telephones, letters, and tableware are often

(*Above*) Neil LaBute's *The Mercy Seat,* about a couple who were presumed killed in the September 11, 2001, World Trade Center attack but who were actually having a secret affair in an apartment across town, lends itself to both realistic and highly stylized stagings. Robert Jones's entirely realistic setting beautifully sets off Sinead Cusack's effusive exhilaration as Abby (with John Hannah as Ben) in London's Almeida Theatre production of 2003.

(*Left*) Alex Hard's setting for the Zurich Schauspielhaus production of *The Mercy Seat* in the same year (2003) focuses on the situation rather than on the characters, making the play—as directed by Christina Paulhofer—less personal but more intensely political.

functional in realistic plays, but they can have aesthetic importance and are therefore carefully selected or else are specially designed. Frequently, furniture pieces or properties have major symbolic significance, as in the case of the royal thrones in Shakespeare's *Richard III* or the map of England that King Lear divides. Some props are even raised to titular metaphoric importance, such as the glass figurines in Tennessee Williams's *Glass Menagerie* and the adding machines in Elmer Rice's *Adding Machine.* In all these cases, design of properties may be of greatly enhanced importance.

## The Scene Designer at Work

The scene designer's work inevitably begins with a reading and rereading of the play, normally followed by research on the play and its original period (and the periods in which it may be set), a consideration of the type of theatre in which the play is to be produced, and extensive discussions with the director and other members of the design and production team. Scenic design usually is a collaborative process engaging the director, other designers, and the technical staff.

The discussion phase normally proceeds almost simultaneously with the designer's preparation of a series of visualizations, which may begin with collected illustrations (for example, clippings from magazines, notations from historical sources, color ideas, spatial concepts) and move on to sketches of individual settings, *storyboards* that illustrate how the sets will be rearranged or used in each scene, digital or handcrafted color renderings of the set elements, and often three-dimensional models, which will help the director and design team fully understand how the set will work and be put together. Eventually, these lead to a set of *working drawings* and other materials that will guide the eventual scenic construction.

Throughout the process, of course, the designer must gain the approval of the director and producers and reckon with necessary budgetary constraints and the skills of the construction staff that will execute and install the finished design. Part architect, part engineer, part accountant, and part interpretive genius, the scene designer today is one of the theatre's premier artists/craftspeople.

Bob Crowley, one of the leading scenic designers working today, is pleased to share examples of his design process with readers of this book. Pictured here is his model of the basic classroom setting for Alan Bennett's 2004 *The History Boys*. Although the shape of the classroom is unlike any in the real world, it projects the play's action perfectly. The overhead fluorescent tubes dominating the set are not required for actual lighting but convey the institutional rigidity of modern education, against which both teachers and students struggle to engage—and assert—their basic humanity.

(*Above*) Shown here is Crowley's classroom setting as realized for the Royal National Theatre premiere of *The History Boys,* which went on to receive the English Olivier and Broadway Tony best-play awards.

(*Right*) This is Crowley's model showing his design for the Banks family household—emphasizing the kitchen—in the popular 2004 London and 2006 Broadway musical *Mary Poppins,* for which Crowley received the Tony Award for best design of a musical. The meticulous setting, in which individual rooms can be closed off or revealed by the addition of an exterior facade, provides a focus for the individual areas while still maintaining the overall architecture of the play's center: an integrated English family home.

# Scene Designer Tony Walton

**1.**

**2.**

Bitish-born Tony Walton has become, over a forty-plus-year career, one of America's premier theatre designers. In addition to his extraordinary design accomplishments in stage scenery, Walton is noted for his work in stage costumes as well as innumerable designs for films, ballets, operas, posters, books, and record albums.

Born in Surrey in 1934, he found his way to classically oriented Radley College (a prep school near Oxford), London's Slade School of Fine Art, and, at age twenty-one, the hard-knocks post of assistant designer at a provincial theatre in Wimbledon, where he Alas expected to design and paint scenery for a new production every week. British military service took him to Canada the following year, and upon his discharge Walton settled in New York, earning his living by designing caricatures and illustrations for *Harper's* and *Vogue* magazines. He subsequently passed the exam—in all three areas of scenery, costumes,

and lighting—for admission to the United Scenic Artists, America's sole professional union for theatre designers. By 1957 Walton had designed his first New York play, Noel Coward's *Conversation Piece*. By 2009 he had designed, in New York alone, fifty-nine Broadway and thirty off-Broadway productions, receiving sixteen Tony Award nominations and winning the award on three of those occasions (for *Guys and Dolls, Pippin,* and *The House of Blue Leaves*).

Walton, however, is not merely a scenic designer. He has received awards for designing costumes and in recent years he has branched into directing. On a visit to Walton's labyrinthine Upper West Side apartment and studio—a virtual beehive of activity—this author asked Walton what he was working on at the moment. Having prepared himself for this question at a Chinese restaurant the night before, Walton pulled from his pocket a chopsticks wrapper on which he had listed his current projects. "Let's see,"

**1.** Tony Walton is shown here in his New York studio, preparing to unroll a set of plans.

**2.** Walton called his 2008 design of the Broadway *A Tale of Two Cities* "a blend of Shakespeare's Globe Theatre and the infamous French Bastille" Here, Natalie Toro blasts out one of the show's rousing numbers as the cast disports itself on Walton's skeletal but elegant, blood-lit (by Richard Pilbow) setting.

**3.** Walton's set model for *Grand Hotel* shows the orchestra's position above rile play's action.

**4.** Here is the actual set of the play as realized in this 1989 production, directed by Tommy Tune.

he began. "At the moment I'm designing a production of *Noel and Gertie* for the Bay Street Theatre on Long Island, plus an off-Broadway production of a new play by Terrence McNally and Jon Robin Baitz called *House*, plus a production of Harold Pinter's Ashes Ashes for Broadway." While catching his breath, he turned over the wrapper. "Then of course I'm also redesigning this massive *Christmas Carol* for Madison Square Garden again, plus designing the interior of the Roundabout Theatre company's new 42nd Street stagehouse. Also I'm directing a production of my wife, Gen's, new play, *Missing Footage*. I think there's more, but I ran out of room here."

In the studio wing of Walton's apartment, two design assistants — both professional designers themselves-were busily at work. One was touching up the *Ashes* mode!; the other was carefully cutting out some simulated tile squares to use on the model for *House*. Around the room, in addition to stacks of books, drawings, photos, scripts, and material samples, were the models of just-completed projects: the Broadway sets for *Leenane* and *1776*. The workmanship for the latter production was admirable, and one of Walton's assistants said that the ceiling moldings, which had to be precisely carved to account for the forced perspective of the illusion, had been hand-shaped by a team of specialist woodsmiths from Germany. "Getting it right in the model saves countless hours in the shops," Walton explained.

One looks in vain for a "signature style" in Walton's many works, and Walton himself agrees: "For me it is preferable to try and start out as a blank slate—completely available to the special nature of the piece. I hope to let the piece itself—via the director's approach to it—dictate the design," he says in his entry in *Contemporary Designers*. His amazing virtuosity over a wide range of dramatic and aesthetic styles, as well as the sureness of his technique, is illustrated in the photographs of his designs shown here.

5. Walton's set design for Martin McDonagh's 1998 Irish-themed off-Broadway hit *The Cripple* of *Inishman* beautifully captured the dank chill of rural Irish mudplaster.

6. Moldings in Walton's model for the Roundabout Theatre's 1998 revival of the musical *1776* were meticulously carved in perspective, and the furniture was precisely scaled.

7. The actual setting reverses two wall hangings but otherwise retains the balance and scale of the model.

# LIGHTING

The very word *theatre,* meaning "seeing place," implies the crucial function of light. Light is the basic precondition for theatrical appearance. Without light, nothing can be seen. The use of light for dramatic effect, as distinct from pure illumination, can be traced back to the earliest surviving plays. *Agamemnon,* by Aeschylus, was staged so that the watchman's spotting of the signal fire heralding Agamemnon's return to Argos coincided with the actual sunrise over the Athenian skene (stagehouse). It is also probable that the burning of Troy at the conclusion of Euripides' *Trojan Women* was staged to coincide with the sunset that reddened the Attic sky. Modern plays commonly use light in metaphoric and symbolic ways: the blinking neon light that intermittently reddens Blanche's quarters in Williams's *A Streetcar Named Desire* and the searching "follow-spot" (a swivel-mounted lighting instrument that can be pointed in any direction by an operator) demanded by Samuel Beckett to train upon the hapless, trapped characters in his *Play.*

Although it is customary to think of theatre lighting as dating from the invention of electricity, nothing could be more misleading. Lighting has always been a major theatrical consideration. In addition to coordinating the timing of their plays to the sunrise and sunset, the ancient Greeks paid a great deal of attention to the proper orientation of their theatres to take best advantage of the sun's rays. The medieval outdoor theatre, though as dependent on sunlight as the Greek theatre was, made use of several devices to redirect sunlight, including halos made of reflective metal to surround Jesus and his disciples with focused and intensified illumination. In one production a brightly polished metal bowl was held over Jesus' head to concentrate the sun's rays, and surviving instructions indicate that medieval stagehands substituted torches for the bowl in the case of cloudy skies!

It was in indoor stagings, however, that lighting technology attained its first significant sophistication. In a 1439 production of the *Annunciation* in Florence, one thousand oil lamps were used for illumination, and a host of candles were lighted by a "ray of fire" that shot through the cathedral. One can imagine the spectacle. Leonardo da Vinci designed a 1490 production of *Paradise* with twinkling stars and backlit zodiac signs on colored glass. And by the sixteenth century the great festival lighting of indoor theatres, located in manor houses and public halls,

served as a symbol of the intellectual and artistic achievements of the Renaissance itself, a mark of the luxury, technical wizardry, and ostentatious, exuberant humanism of the era. People went to theatres in those times simply to revel in light and escape the outside gloom—in rather the same way that Americans, from early in the twentieth century, populated air-conditioned movie theatres largely to escape the heat of summer days.

By the Renaissance, the sheer opulence of illumination was astonishing —though the entire effect was created simply from tallow, wax, and fireworks. Raphael "painted" the name of his patron, Pope Leo X, with thirteen lighted chandeliers in a 1519 dramatic production; Sebastiano Serlio inserted sparkling panes of colored glass, illuminated from behind, into his flat painted scenery to create glistening and seductive scenic effects. And, as the Renaissance spirit gave way to the lavish Royal theatre of the age of the Sun King, Louis XIV of France, artificial illumination—calculated to match Louis's presumed incendiary brilliance —developed apace: one 1664 presentation at Versailles featured twenty thousand colored lanterns, hundreds of transparent veils and bowls of colored water, and a massive display of fireworks.

The invention of the gaslight in the nineteenth century and the development of electricity shortly thereafter-first in carbon arc and "limelight" electrical lighting, then in incandescence, and now in light-emitting diodes (LEDs)—has brought stage lighting into its modern phase and made it less strictly showy and more pertinent to individual works and dramatic action. Ease and flexibility of control are the cardinal virtues of both gas and electric lighting. By adjusting a valve, a single operator at a "gas table" could raise or dim the intensity of any individual light or preselected "gang" of lights just as easily as we can raise or lower the fire on a gas range with the turn of a knob today. And, of course, with electricity—introduced in American theatres in 1879 and in European theatres the following year—the great fire hazard of a live flame (a danger that had plagued the theatre for centuries and claimed three buildings a year on average, including Shakespeare's Globe) was at last over. The fire crews, which were round-the-clock staff members of every major theatre in the early nineteenth century, were dismissed, and the deterioration of scenery and costumes from the heat, smoke, and carbon pollution similarly came to a halt.

Electrical lighting also had the great advantage of being fully self-starting—it did not need to be relit

Individual pools of light illuminate the parasols and costumes—and the isolation—of ladies waiting for the soldiers' return at the beginning of *Much Ado About Nothing*. This Indiana Repertory Theatre production was directed by LIbby Appel, with lighting design by Robert Peterson.

or kept alive by pilot lights—and it could easily be switched off, dimmed up and down, and reganged or reconnected simply by fastening and unfastening flexible wires. Within a few years of its introduction, electricity became the primary medium of stage lighting in the Western world, and great dynamo generators—for electricity was used in the theatre long before it was commercially available from municipal power supplies—were installed as essential equipment in the basements of theatres from Vienna to San Francisco.

Electricity provides an enormously flexible form of lighting. The incandescent filament is a reasonably small, reasonably cool point of light that can be focused, reflected, aimed, shaped, and colored by a great variety of devices invented and adapted for those purposes, and electric light can be trained in innumerable ways upon actors, scenery, audiences, or a combination of these to create realistic or atmospheric effects through dimensionality, focus, animation, distortion, diffusion, and overwhelming radiance. Today, thanks to the added sophistication of computer technology, LEDs, and microelectronics, it is not uncommon to see theatres with nearly a thousand lighting instruments all under the complete control of a single technician seated in a comfortable booth above the audience.

## Modern Lighting Design

Today, the lighting for most productions is conceived and directly supervised by a professional lighting designer, a species of theatre artist who has appeared as a principal member of the production team only since the mid-twentieth century. By skillfully working with lighting instruments, hanging positions, angles, colors, shadows, and moment-to-moment adjustments of intensity and directionality, the lighting designer can illuminate a dramatic production in a variety of subtle and complex ways. The manner in which the lighting designer uses the medium to blend the more rigid design elements (architecture and scenery) with the evolving patterns of the movements of the actors, the colors and fullness of their costumes, and the meanings of the play is normally a crucial factor in a production's artistic and theatrical success.

*Visibility* and *focus* are the primary considerations of lighting design: visibility ensures that the audience sees what it's meant to see, and focus ensures that it sees this without undue distraction. Visibility, then, is the passive accomplishment of lighting design, and focus is its active accomplishment. The spotlight, a development of the twentieth century, has fostered something akin to a revolution in staging. Contemporary productions now routinely feature a darkened auditorium (a rarity prior to the 1880s) and a deliberate effort to illuminate certain characters (or props or set pieces) more than others—in other words, to direct the audience's attention toward those visual elements that are dramatically the most significant.

*Verisimilitude* and *atmosphere* also are common goals of the lighting designer, and both can be achieved largely through the color and direction of lighting. Verisimilitude (lifelikeness) is crucial in realistic dramas, where the style generally demands that the lighting appear as if emanating from familiar sources: as from the sun, from "practical" (real) lamps on the stage, or from moonlight, firelight, streetlights, neon signs, or perhaps the headlights of moving automobiles. Atmospheric lighting, by contrast, may or may not suggest a familiar source and can be used to evoke a mood appropriate to a scene or to a moment's action: gloomy, for example, or sparkling, oppressive, nightmarish, austere, verdant, smoky, funereal, or regal.

Sharp, bold lighting designs are frequently employed to create highly theatrical effects-from the glittery entertainments of the Broadway musical tradition to harsher experimental stagings like those often associated with the plays and theories of Bertolt Brecht. Brecht's concept of a "didactic" theatre favors lighting that is bright, cold (uncolored), and deliberately "unmagical." Brecht suggested, in fact, that the lighting instruments be made part of the setting, placed in full view of the audience; this "theatricalist" use of the lighting instruments themselves is now widespread even in nondidactic plays. Moodier plays may employ dense or unnatural colors, "gobo" templates that break light beams into shadowy fragments (such as leaf patterns), or atmospheric "fog" effects that make light appear misty, gloomy, or mysterious. The Broadway-type musical, in contrast, often makes splashy use of banks of colored footlights and border

lights, high-intensity follow-spots that track actors around the stage, "chaser" lights that flash on and off in sequence, and a near fuse-busting incandescence that makes a finale seem to burn up the stage. In fact, this traditional exploitation of light has done as much to give Broadway the name "Great White Way" as have the famous billboards and marquees that line the street.

Stylized lighting effects are often used to express radical changes of mood or event; indeed, the use of lighting alone to signal a complete change of scene is an increasingly common theatrical expedient. Merely by switching from full front to full overhead lighting, for example, a designer can throw a character into silhouette and make her or his figure appear suddenly ominous, grotesque, or isolated. The illumination of an actor with odd lighting colors, such as green, or from odd lighting positions, such as from below, can create mysterious, unsettling effects. The use of follow-spots can metaphorically put a character "on the spot" and convey a specific sense of unspeakable terror. Highly expressive lighting and projections, when applied to a production utilizing only a cyclorama (a scenic backdrop at the rear of the stage, often representing the sky), a set piece, sculpture, or stage mechanism and neutrally clad actors, can create an infinite variety of convincing theatrical environments for all but the most resolutely realistic of plays. It is here, in the area of stylization and expressive theatricality, that the modern lighting designer has made the most significant mark.

## The Lighting Designer at Work

The lighting designer ordinarily conceives a lighting design out of a synthesis of many discrete elements: the action and ideas of the play, discussions with the director and other members of the design team about the approach or concept of the production, the characteristics of the theatre building (its lighting positions, control facilities, and wiring system), the scenery and costume designs, the movements and behavior of the actors, and the available lighting instruments. Occasionally the availability of an experienced lighting crew must also be a consideration. Because not all of these variables can be known from the outset (the stage movement, for example, may change from one day to the next right up to the final dress rehearsal), the lighting designer must be skilled at making adjustments and must have the opportunity to exercise a certain amount of control, or at

Lighting Designer Rainer Casper's radically contrasting lighting colors—even in the same scene—create wholly different indoor and outdoor environments in Bert Neumann's set for *The Insulted* and *Injured*.

The lighting by Peter Mumford makes Tim Hatley's setting for Noel Coward's *Private Lives* an enchanting hotel facade, whose Mediterranean-facing balconies offer the promise of an elegant—but perhaps empty—life. Alan Bickman and Lindsay Duncan star in this production on Broadway in 2002.

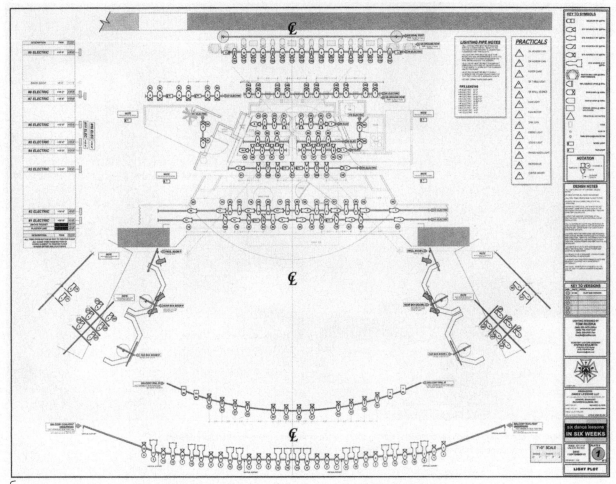

Shown here is Tom Ruzika's light plot for the 2003 Broadway production of *Six Dance Lessons in Six Weeks* (reduced in size to fit this page). You are looking down from the theatre's ceiling; the stage is at the top of the drawing, and the audience area (the "house") is at the bottom. The gray rectangles on each side indicate the vertical sides of the proscenium; the "CL" symbol is the center line of the stage and house, and each bomb-shaped symbol is an individual and specific lighting instrument. "Practicals" are lighting or other working electrical instruments that are part of the scenery but are also connected ("wired") into the lighting control system (the "board"). The light plot tells the electrical staff where instruments are to be hung, where (roughly) they are to be aimed, and how they are wired to the board.

least to voice concerns with regard to areas affecting lighting problems.

Ordinarily, the two major preparations required of the lighting designer are the light plot and the cue sheet. A *light plot* is a plan or series of plans showing the placement of each lighting instrument; its type, wattage, and size; its wiring and connection to an appropriate dimmer; its color; and sometimes its movement—as lighting instruments are increasingly being programmed to pan, tilt, or change color by remote, motorized control. A *cue sheet* is a list of the occasions, referred to by number and keyed to the script of the play (or, in final form, to the fully annotated stage manager's script), when lights change in intensity or in color or move. The light plot and cue sheet are developed in consultation with the director and other members of the design team, who may take major or minor roles in the consultation, depending on their interests and expertise. Inasmuch as some productions use hundreds of lighting instruments and require thousands of individual cues, the complexity of these two documents can be extraordinary; weeks and months may go into their preparation. In today's theatre the cues are almost always programmed into a computer program capable of executing them with the necessary precision.

The lighting designer works with a number of different types of lighting instruments and must know the properties of each well enough to anticipate fully how it will perform when hung and focused on the stage. If you glance up at the grid above the stage or at the pipes above and to the sides of the audience, you will see the huge range of instruments from which the designer makes a selection.

Fixed-focus spotlights are the main instruments for lighting stage action; they come in two main forms. The *ellipsoidal reflector spotlight* (ERS) has a sharply defined conical shape and is the instrument of choice for intense, hard-edged, and closely focused lighting. The circular ERS beam is easy to shape: four shutters can frame it from different sides, an "iris" can tighten its radius, and "gobos"—metal templates—placed into the instrument can project silhouettes of almost any variety. The *fresnel spotlight,* named for its French-designed lens (originally used in lighthouses), has by contrast a generally less defined and less shapeable beam. It is most often used for general (wash) lighting, backlights, and downlights.

Other common lights are even less focused. *Parabolic aluminized reflectors,* or PARs ("cans"), can be used for color washes and general lighting. *Striplights,* banks of PARs or floodlights, are used to light drops, cycloramas, and other broad areas. Specialty instruments include follow-spots—high-intensity spotlights that are operated manually to "follow" an actor (for example, during a solo dance number)—and *automated lights,* which can be computer-programmed to instantly change direction, color, beam size, and "gobo" image at the mere touch of a button. Though more common in the musical theatre, follow-spots and automated lights are beginning to make an impact in straight theatre.

The most exciting new development in lighting technology is the LED (light-emitting diode) light source, which creates an electroluminescence that can now deliver sufficient lighting intensity and color control to rival many incandescent sources (LED light output has doubled every three years since the 1960s). LEDs are also more inexpensive and energy-efficient and, consequently, environmentally friendly, than incandescent bulbs and are widely found in PAR cans, strip lights, moving color washes, and the "LED walls" used in large image and video projections (see the "Projection Design" section later in this chapter). Many believe that in the coming decade LEDs will provide the light source for spotlights and fresnels as well.

Few theatres have the time or space flexibility to permit much on-site experimentation in lighting design; thus the development of the light plot and cue sheet takes place primarily in the imagination and, where possible, in workshop or free experimentation apart from the working facility. This limitation places a premium on the ability of the designer to predict instrument performance from various distances and angles and with various color elements installed. It also demands sharp awareness of how various lights will reflect off different surfaces.

Once the light plot is complete, the lights are mounted (hung) in appropriate positions, attached to the theatre's circuits (wiring system), "patched" to proper control channels (dimmers), focused (aimed) in the desired directions, and colored by the attachment of frames containing plastic color media. Ideally, the stage setting will have been finished and placed in position when all this occurs, but it rarely works this way, particularly on Broadway, where theatres are often rented only a short time before the opening performance. Once the instruments are in place and functioning, the lighting designer begins setting the intensities of each instrument for each cue. This painstaking process involves the programming of thousands of precise numerical directions into the computer software from which an operator will execute the cues during performances.

Finally, the lighting designer presides over the working and timing of the cues, making certain that in actual operation the lights shift as subtly or as boldly, as grandly or as imperceptibly, as desired to support and complement the play's action and achieve the design aesthetic.

Great lighting design springs out of thousands of details, most of them pulled together in a single final week or two. Gradations of light, difficult to measure in isolation, can have vastly differing impacts in the moment-to-moment focus and feel of a play. Because light is a medium rather than an object, audience members are rarely if ever directly aware of it; they are aware only of its illuminated target. Therefore, the lighting designer's work is poorly understood by the theatergoing public at large. But everyone who works professionally in the theatre—from the set and costume designers to the director to the actor—knows what a crucial role lighting plays in the success of the theatre venture. As the Old Actor says as he departs the stage in off-Broadway's longest-running hit, *The Fantasticks:* "Remember me—in light!" The light that illuminates the theatre also glorifies it; it is a symbol of revelation—of knowledge and humanity—upon which the theatrical impulse finally rests.

# PHOTO ESSAY: Lighting Designer Don Holder

With two Tony Awards (for the Broadway production of the 1997 *Lion King* and the 2008 Lincoln Center revival of *South Pacific*) on his shelf, and ten Tony and Drama Desk nominations for his thirty Broadway and seventy-six off-Broadway shows to date—not to mention his innumerable regional theatre productions—Don Holder is clearly at the very top of the American lighting design field. In addition, he has had the opportunity to ride and master the entire new wave of technological sophistication that has propelled a truly revolutionary new era of stage design.

Like many designers, Holder became fascinated by lighting at a very young age. A self-admitted "music and drama addict" from the days his parents drove him from their Long Island home into Manhattan to see symphonies, ballets, and Broadway musicals, Holder began to light shows while still in junior high. "I did band concerts, high school plays, everything I could. I was also the guy at scouting camp who was always lighting the campfires

**1.**

and putting smudge pots on the trails," he remembers. Adoring the outdoors, Holder majored in forestry at the University of Maine's Orono campus, but he also played in jazz bands and the Bangor Symphony during the school year and worked summers as a technician and actor at Maine's Theatre At Monmouth. Inspired by a designer there, he applied for graduate training at Yale Drama School, enrolling first as a stage technician and eventually as a lighting designer under the mentorship of fabled Broadway designer Jennifer Tipton. After Yale, Holder headed directly into a New York career, working first in small off-Broadway and off-off-Broadway companies and then making his Broadway debut with Richard Greenberg's *Eastern Standard* in 1989.

Holder describes his design aesthetic as supportive: "My basic goal is to bring out the play's text, the composer's music, and the director's vision. I strongly feel our job as designers is to adapt our own style and design aesthetic to the specific production; to help tell the story, of course, but also to augment the story's context and style." The path to excellence, however, is in the details. "I suppose I am characterized as meticulous," Holder freely admits. "My work tends to be quite detailed—specific rather

**2.**

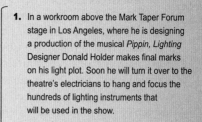

**1.** In a workroom above the Mark Taper Forum stage in Los Angeles, where he is designing a production of the musical *Pippin*, Lighting Designer Donald Holder makes final marks on his light plot. Soon he will turn it over to the theatre's electricians to hang and focus the hundreds of lighting instruments that will be used in the show.

**2.** In the light booth, Holder looks up at stage left (the right side of the stage, as seen from the audience) to see how the lighting will work with the scene as described in his script.

4. As technical rehearsals begin, Holder and his two assistants, in the light booth at the rear of the auditorium, enter the light cues into computers nat will be used to operate the lighting during the show.

3. In the front rows of the audience, Holder discusses the scene with *Pippin* director Jeff Calhoun.

5. What time of day is it? And what mood? These are the issues the lighting designar addresses. Holder created the dawn on a tropical isiand in the South Pacific for the 2007 Broadway revival of the musical by that name, seeking to establish the beauty and tranquillity of the scene before the battles of World War II arrived in this part of the world.

6.

operatic, his storytelling is so rich, his sense of history, religion, and magic have such a depth, and there are so many undercurrents running through the body of his work that there's always much more underneath these plays than what you see on the page. I think my style of lighting is well suited to Wilson's work, since so many of his characters seem like they're stepping out of straight dramatic acting and singing arias. His work has a musicality, an operatic quality, a mythic proportion that I simply love. So there's a certain amount of freedom and liberty I can take by stepping out of reality, heightening things, making things larger than life, and responding to the play emotionally rather than intellectually. And so my work becomes very personal."

Holder's career has taken flight during an extraordinary evolution of lighting technology, which has fit exceptionally well with his careful craftsmanship. "When I broke into the theatre, the theatres I worked at were still employing manual dimming systems, so my work was wholly dependent on the skill of the person running it. Indeed, I was at the mercy of the light board operator. And as my work requires every light to be specifically cued and crafted, I would become despondent when mistakes were made. So I greeted the age of computerized control with open arms. For me it changed everything: my lighting could become more fluid and more creative, and I didn't have to lower my expectations because of technical issues. And then came automated lighting [AL]—motorized moving lights that I first used when I designed *The Lion King*. That show was huge—with scenery constantly flying in and out, an animal parade through the audience to begin the show, and a band that played in the theatre's boxes above the audience. [Director] Julie [Taymor] had conceived the show within a constantly stantly changing skyscape, a " lightscape" actually, that included a whole' spectrum of colors—not just three or four—that were to continuously cross-fade with each other. I needed to have six colors on every single surface of the setting! And since I simply didn't have enough space in the theatre to hang all the lights I wanted, or to provide the level of detail and specificity the

than general, layered rather than spare. I'm certainly obsessive about craft—I start with a strong take on each scene and then detail each moment. This means that my lighting tends to be very densely cued and shaped." Holder cites as an example his 2009 production of the musical *Pippin* at the Mark Taper Forum in Los Angeles on

which he was working at the time of this interview: "It's just two hours long but it has six hundred light cues. But every detail retains the sense of the big picture."

With a strong background in music, Holder finds himself often engaged in shows "that require a romantic, lyrical, and above all musical treatment—but this is not limited to the music in musicals (like *Pippin*) alone. Indeed, he accounts his love of music as a reason why he has often been tapped to design the premieres of August Wilson's "straight" plays. "I think that August's work is so poetic and

7.

6.  It's a later scene in the South Pacific, and the lighting now portrays U.S. Navy soldiers and WAVES (Women Accepted for Voluntary Emergency Service) standing at attention as they await orders against Holder's ominous evening sky.

7.  Holder's lighting for the famous balcony scene in *Romeo and Juliet*, as staged in the New York Public Theatre's outdoor stage in Central Park, isolates the two lovers (played by Oscar Isaac and Lauren Ambrose) against the park's Belvedere Castle and magnificent trees, which are more subtly illuminated. The light also casts subtly romantic reflections in the water-filled seventy-feet round "lake" beneath Romeos feet; a feature of Mark Wendland's scenic design.

8.

**8.** For Arthur Miller's *A View from the Bridge,* staged at Minneapolis's Guthrie Theatre in 2008, Holder has the delicate task of making Miller's realistic characters seem to "pop out of the scenery" without the audience being aware of how the lighting has so focused their attention on the actors. The background (which in an actual living room would be just as bright) all but disappears. John Arnone designed the scenery and Robert Perdziola the costumes for this production.

show required, or even to light the environment—the "dance space on steroids" as we called it—I simply had to use AL. It was incredible—as, for example, in the opening sequence, when several luminous clouds were to rise in sequence while at the same time the sky was changing from twilight to dawn to noon and everything was in a constant state of motion. With AL, one instrument can replace fifty, and so that's how I did it. And when the director wanted to change something, I could do it right from my seat—without ever taking out a ladder or refocusing a light or changing a gel [color agent]. This became a revelation to me!"

Holder thinks of his lighting as both impressionistic and specific. Impressionistic "because the artists I'm most inspired by are the impressionists, they speak to me in a profound way." And specific because "my mantra is craft, sweating the details, really controlling the composition, which must be impeccably crafted." When these two elements are brought together by Holder, the art of stage lighting rises to luminous achievements.

# COSTUMES

Costumes have always been a major element in the theatrical experience. They are vehicles for the "dressing-up" that actors and audiences alike have always considered a requirement for the fullest degree of theatrical satisfaction. Costumes serve both ceremonial and illustrative functions.

## The Functions of Costume

The first theatrical costumes were essentially ceremonial vestments. The himation (a gownlike costume) of the early Aeschylean actor was derived from the garment worn by the priest-chanter of the dithyramb; the comic and satyr costumes, with their use of phalluses and goatskins, were likewise derived from more primitive god-centered rites. The priests who first enacted the *Quem Queritis* trope (liturgical text) in medieval Europe simply wore their sacred albs, hooded to indicate an outdoor scene but otherwise unaltered. And the actors of the classic Japanese no drama even today wear costumes that relate more to spiritual sources than to secular life. Ancient and original uses of costuming have served primarily to separate the actor from the audience, to "elevate" the actor to a quasi-divine status. Thick-soled footwear (kothurnoi) worn by Greek actors in the fourth century B.C. were calculated to enhance this ceremonial effect by greatly increasing the height of the wearers, thereby "dressing them up" both figuratively and literally.

The shift of stress in costuming from a "dressing-up" of the actor to a defining of the character came about gradually. In the Elizabethan theatre, the costumes often had an almost regal, ceremonial quality because the acting companies frequently solicited the cast-off raiment of the nobility. English theatre of this time was known throughout Europe for the splendor of its costuming, but apparently little effort was made to suit costume to characterization. Moreover, it was not unusual in Shakespeare's time for some actors to wear contemporary garb onstage while others wore costumes expressive of the period of the play. In Renaissance Italy, costuming developed a high degree of stylization in the commedia dell'arte; each of the recurring characters wore a distinctive and arresting costume that instantly signified a particular age, intelligence, and disposition. The same characters and the same costumes can be seen today in contemporary commedia productions, and they are still as eloquent and entertaining as they were four hundred years ago.

Plays often indicate design colors for symbolic importance. In *A Streetcar Named Desire,* playwright Tennessee Williams emphasizes the raw sexuality of cardplaying New Orleans workingmen by specifying that they wear "bright primary colors," while the delicate lady who visits them has the name of Blanche—French for "white"—and she dreams of her deceased gay husband, named Grey. In this 2002 London production, designer Bunny Christie underlines Williams's color symbolism by clothing Glenn Close, as Blanche, in a white dress, white hat, and sheer white gloves and accessorizing her with a sheer white handkerchief and white rosebuds in her hair.

Modern costuming acquired much of its present character during the eighteenth and nineteenth centuries, when certain realistic considerations took control of the Western theatre. These centuries witnessed a great deal of radical social change that led to widespread acceptance of science and its methods and great fascination with detail and accuracy. These trends coalesced in the European (and eventually the American) theatre with a series of productions in which historical accuracy served as the guiding principle. For the first time, painstaking effort ensured that the design of every costume in a play (and every prop and every set piece as well) accorded with an authentic "period" source. Thus a production of *Julius Caesar* would be intensively researched to re-create the clothing worn in Rome in the first century B.C., a *Hamlet* would be designed to mirror the records of medieval Denmark, and a *Romeo and Juliet* would seek to recreate, in detail, the world of Renaissance Verona.

The movement toward historical accuracy and the devotion with which it was pursued led to a widespread change in the philosophy of costume design that persists to this day, for although historical accuracy itself is no longer the ultimate goal of costume design, stylistic consistency and overall design control have proven to be lasting principles. Costuming today stresses imaginative aesthetic creativity as well as coordinated dramatic suitability; thus the influence of realism, with its attendant emphasis on historical accuracy, has fostered coherent and principled design in place of the near anarchy that once prevailed.

Modern costume design may be said to serve four separate functions. First, in concert with its ancient origins, it retains at least a hint of the ceremonial magic that ancient priests and shamans once conjured. Costume, even today, bespeaks a primordial theatricality. As Theoni Aldredge said of the costumes she designed for *A Chorus Line,* they "had to look real and yet theatrical enough for an audience to say, `Okay, I'm in the theatre now.'"

Second, in aggregate, the costumes of a play show us what sort of world we are asked to enter, not only its historical place and period but by implication its social and cultural values as well. The word costume has the same root as *custom* and *customary;* as such it indicates the "customary" wearing apparel (or the "habitual habit") of persons living in a particular world. For example, the Mexican American characters in Luis Valdez's *Zoot Suit,* set in the 1940s, are seen as virtual extensions of their overly long pegged trousers and looping watch chains. Tennessee Williams, in *A Streetcar Named Desire,* specifically directed the poker players to wear shirts of "bright primary colors," to contrast their primary sexuality with Blanche DuBois's dead (and gay) husband, whom the dramatist had named "Allan Grey." The ensemble of costumes in a play production generally reveals the production's style, at least as it emanates from the play's characters.

Third, the individual costumes can express the specific individuality of each character's role; they reveal at a glance, for example, the character's profession, wealth, age, class status, tastes, and self-image. More subtly, costume can suggest the character's vices,

Robert Wilson's *Les Fables de La Fontaine* is a hugely imaginative stage re-creation of the stories of France's greatest fabulist. Here Bakary Sangaré plays the Lion and Céline Samie is Circé in "The Lion in Love." The 2005—06 Comédie-Française production, directed and designed by Wilson, was immensely popular with both adults and children at this historic theatre.

virtues, and hidden hopes—or fears. By the judicious use of color, shape, fabric, and even the *movement* and *sound* a fabric makes, costume designers can imbue each character with individual distinctiveness, particularly in contrast to the standard dress in which other characters of his or her class are seen. When Hamlet insists on wearing his "inky cloak" and "suits of solemn black" in his uncle's presence, he silently signifies his refusal to accept his uncle's authority; he refuses to "fit" into the world of the Danish court. The wearing of these garments becomes both a mark of Hamlet's character and a significant action in the play. When Monsieur Jourdain in Molière's *The Bourgeois Gentleman* dons his fancy suit with the upside-down flowers and, later, his Turkish gown and grotesque turban, he is proclaiming (foolishly) to his

(*Right*) "Blood will have blood," says Macbeth after the killing of Duncan. Stage blood is the costume designer's and makeup artist's nightmare, for the costumes (or at least some costumes) have to be worn afresh at the next performance. But blood is fundamental to the theatre, certainly in most tragedies (which stem from rituals involving blood sacrifices), and solutions must always be found. Here Liev Schreiber as Macbeth and Jennifer Ehle as Lady Macbeth try to cover their murderous tracks in Moisés Kaufman's production for Shakespeare in the Park at New York's Delacorte Theatre in 2006.

(*Below*) Blood need not be portrayed realistically. In this *Macbeth* production directed by Mihai Maniutiu at the Romanian National Theatre Festival, the designer Valentin Codoiu created blood that was spewed across the stage floor.

peers that he is a person of elegance and refinement. And Estragon's unlaced shoes in *Waiting for Godot* represent—pathetically, to be sure—his great wish to be unfettered, not "tied to Godot" but simply free, fed, and happy.

Finally, the costume serves as wearable clothing for the actor! For a costume, of course, is indeed clothing; it must be functional as well as meaningful and aesthetic. The actor does not model costumes; he or she walks in them, sits in them, duels in them, dances in them, tumbles downstairs in them. Indeed, unless the character is a prisoner or a pauper, we are supposed to believe that the character actually chose the costume and really *wants* to wear it! Thus the costume designer cannot be content merely to draw pictures on paper but must also design workable, danceable, actable clothing, for which cutting, stitching, fitting, and quick changing are considerations as important as color coordination and historical context. For this reason, costume designers generally collaborate very closely with the actors they dress.

## The Costume Designer at Work

The costume designer begins, as all designers do, with ideas about the play's action, themes, historical setting, theatrical style, and the impact the play might have on the expected audience. Collaboration with the director, who ordinarily takes a leading role from the start, and with the other designers is important even at this early stage, as ideas begin to be translated into thoughts of fabric, color, shape, and period.

Fabrics exist in many textures and weaves and can be cut, shaped, stitched, colored, and draped in innumerable ways. But fabrics are also augmented (and even replaced) by leather, armor, jewelry, feathers, fur, hair (real or simulated), metallic ornamentation—in fact, any material known to exist. The designer selects or at least oversees the acquiring of all materials. Often costumes are acquired whole. For contemporary plays with modern settings, some or all costumes may be selected from the actors' own wardrobes, purchased from thrift shops, or bought at clothing stores. Costumes have even been solicited as gifts. In a celebrated instance, Louis Jouvet appealed to the citizens of Paris after World War II to donate their fancy prewar clothing to provide costumes for the premiere of jean Giraudoux's *The Madwoman of Chaillot*. The spectacular garments that poured into the Athénée theatre for that brilliant 1945 Parisian production signaled to the world that France had survived the scourge of Nazi, occupation with its devotion to the theatre intact.

It is, however, the production that is designed and built entirely from scratch that fully tests the measure of the costume designer's imagination and ability. In such productions, the designer can create a unique design, matching his or her conception of the text with hat-to-shoe originality. The comprehensive design for such a production moves from the conceptual period to a developmental one. The designer usually compiles a portfolio of images from his or her research, creates a series of quick sketches (sometimes called "roughs"), and assembles various "palettes" of possible color samples, all in the service of giving the director and the entire design team a quick idea of the design's direction without, however, including any specific designs. Once this basic direction is approved by the director, and is seen to be consonant with the work of the entire design team (and the show's budget), the designer proceeds to create actual designs. Generally they take the form of "renderings" (drawings, first in black and white and then in color) supplemented with notes about each costume's accessories, hairstyles, and construction details. Enlarged drawings provide information about items too small to show in a single head-to-toe illustration.

The acquisition of fabrics—the basic medium of the costumer's art—is the crucial next stage. Texture, weight, color, suppleness, and response to draping, dyeing, folding, crushing, twirling, and twisting are all considerations. Velvet, silks, and woolens are the costumer's luxury fabrics; cottons, felt, burlap, and painted canvas are less expensive and are often very effective for theatrical use. Dyeing, "aging" (making a new fabric appear old and used), and detailing are often achieved with commercial dyes, appliqués, and embroidery, and sometimes with paint, glues, and other special treatments (for example, the costume designers Motley—three women working under a single professional name—simulated leather by rubbing thick felt with moist yellow soap and spraying it down with brown paints). Before large quantities of fabric are ordered, samples or swatches can be pinned to the renderings to forestall the purchase of material at odds with the desired "look."

Costume accessories greatly affect the impact of the basic design. Occasionally they may stand out in such a way as to "make" the costume—or to obliterate it. Hairstyles (including beards and mustaches) and headdresses, because they frame the actor's face,

# PHOTO ESSAY: Costume Designer Catherine Zuber

With twenty-seven Broadway shows and forty-five off-Broadway ones glimmering on her résumé, along with dozens of regional productions at Baltimore's Centerstage, Chicago's Goodman Theatre, Washington's Shakespeare Theatre and Kennedy Center, Minneapolis's Guthrie Theater, Los Angeles's Mark Taper Forum, San Diego's La Jolla Playhouse, the Hartford Stage Company and Seattle Rep, Catherine Zuber, at the time this interview took place, was probably the most active costume designer in America. These shows have netted her six Tony Awards (*South Pacific, Awake and Sing, The Light in the Piazza,* and all three parts of *The Coast of Utiopia*) plus three additional Tony nominations (*Seascape, Dinner at Eight, Twelfth Night*) and a host of other awards.

1. Catherine Zuber shows some of the research pictures she has collected for her current design of *Impression* to the author in the "costume space" allocated to her in the basement of the Broadway theatre where the play is in technical rehearsals. On the table below the pictures, you can see her black-and-white rendering of the rustumes that are being readied for dress rehearsal.

2. Zuber and First Costume Design Assistant Nikki Moody discuss which of the newly purchased costume items could best be added to the design at this point. "We have been working together for over a year," says Zuber of Moody. 'She's terrific; just out of grad school in Boston and a lot of fun".

3. Going over their collection of fabric swatches for the show, Zuber and Assistant Designer Patrick Bevilacqua are delighted to come up with a swatch they both like. "Patrick and I have a great relationsirip," Zuber explains. "It's a collaboration: I show him a sketch and he interprets it And when really great assistant designers like Patrick take it a step further, it becomes a *great* collaboration!"

1.

2.

3.

**4.** In the basement of the theatre, Zuber and Bevilacqua test whether a new skirt goes with the already-selected jacket.

**5.** One of the roles of the costume designer is to rivet audience attention on the play's key characters and moments. Here, as Kelli O'Hara sings the final bars of "I'm Gonna Wash That Man Right Outa' My Hair" in the Broadway revival of *South Pacific*, the actress's bright turquoise svvimsuit lights up the stage—and the actress—as it pops out from the six mixed red and orange swimsuits behind her.

Your author met with Zuber in the tiny basement costume shop of the Shoenfeld Theatre on 45th Street, where she was making final adjustments to Jeremy Irons's costume for *Impressionism*, for which Irons was

in technical rehearsal on the stage upstairs. This wasn't her only obligation on this day, however. She had just come from a final dress rehearsal of *The Winter's Tale* at the Brooklyn Academy of Music and was about to head to Lincoln Center, where she was designing a gala performance celebrating the Metropolitan Opera's 125th anniversary.

Zuber explained that she had come to her profession from an undergraduate background in art, with a major in photography. But after college graduation and a subsequent move to New Haven, Connecticut, she happened to meet up with several Yale theatre students who, admiring the vintage clothes she liked to wear, encouraged her to design costumes for their extracurricular productions staged at Yale's undergraduate colleges. "I just loved doing this," Zuber exulted, and after a year of designing such shows she assembled a portfolio of her designs and applied to the Yale School of Drama for graduate professional training in the field. Jane Greenwood, a veteran designer who then headed the Yale costume program, was enthusiastic and Zuber was admitted. "I also had a photo portfolio," she adds. "Being a costume designer is not about costumes alone! Learning photography proved extremely helpful, because it taught me how to compose an entire image—a picture of the set with characters wearing my costumes in it. Composing such images taught me how to design a show so that my costumed people would appear to *belong* in that world, to hold their own within it rather than disappearing into the scenery. Costumes then become an ensemble of characters within a rectangular image, not just clothes on a rack."

Zuber now moves easily between classic verse dramas (*Twelfth Night, The Winter's Tale*), musicals (*South Pacific, Dracula, the Musical*), historical dramas (*A Man for All Seasons*, set in sixteenth-century England, *Coast of Utopia*, set in nineteenth-century Russia), and contemporary plays written and set in our own times (*Impressionism, Frozen, Doubt*). "I enjoy going from one style to the other," she says, except that with contemporary plays "it's sometimes harder to convince

**6.**

**7.**

**8.**

**6.** . Sometimes costume uniformity is required as in the case of "uniforms." *In South Pacific, Zuber* has given each sailor a measure of individuality by the way he wears his uniform: with his blue shirt buttoned or unbuttoned and with or without a name or initials printed on it; with his metal dog tags worn or abandoned; with his white hat brim turned up or rolled up or rolled down, or with his hat taken off entirely; and, in the case of one particularly muscular actor (Andrew Samonsky), by sporting a plain white undershirt that stands out in the otherwise "uniform" naval brigade. Lifted by the men and holding a grass skirt is Loretta Ables Sayre as "Bloody Mary," a Polynesian native seller of exotic local products, who wears layered garments and exotic jewelry—all sharply contrasting with the bold masculinity of the sailors

**7. & 8.** Every costume designer faces a challenge in Shakespeare's The Winier's Tale, since the play takes place in two very different locales: the deeply somber and gloom-ridden court of Sicilia, and -the joyous, rustic sheep-shearing festival in far-away Bohemia (*Above*) In Sicilia, young princess Perdita /Morven Cristie) sees what she thinks is a statue of her long-dead mother, Hermione (Rebecca Hall); Zuber has - dressed each in silky white flowing dresses against the black background of the joyless kingdom. (*Below*) In Bohemia, Zuber has costumed the Bohemian country revelry in rough-textured, earth-colored, and multilayered country fabrics that play brilliantly against the scenic background of dark blue sky and red, white, and blue balloons. Ethan Hawke (*center*) plays the shifty but entertaining tradesman Autolycus—a "srapper up of unconsidered trifles," Shakespeare tells us—in an unmatched ensemble of shirt, vest, and trousers, a black hat with a bright yellow flower, tall leather boots, one strapped up to his knee, doubly dark sunglasses, and with hair that straggles down to his shirt pockets. His friends strum their guitars in even more casual garb, and the women, under their loosely tied country aprons, wear rugged red, green, and orange skirts that reach the floor.

**9.**

costumes together on one page, and if I see that one character stands out inappropriately, or doesn't stand out enough, I can change this very quickly. When I was designing the last act of *Cherry Orchard* [at the Brooklyn Academy of Music in 2008], I could show the director all the characters onstage together just as they would be in the play. And on a separate page I can trace each individual character's journey so the director can see the character's trajectory through the play, so the director can say 'this character should be messier here,' or something like that. Photoshop is a fantastic tool to show what the designs will look like onstage in all these formats."

Zuber adores her profession: "I love being a costume designer! You're learning something new with each show, meeting new people, and the greatest thing is that it leaves beautiful, indelible memories. Of course, it's a lot of hard work, and while some people coming to New York may have stars in their eyes, they should know it's not very glamorous. Sometimes we have to laugh at how ridiculous our work conditions can be—just look at this room [referring to the cluttered basement workplace] for instance! But if you really have a love for it, and a passion, there's absolutely nothing like It!"

**10.**

actors to wear certain things, as they all have their own ideas of how they should dress. And that's natural, because in a modern realistic play the actors need to stay connected to who they are. But in a period show, actors are more trusting of the designer: there's enough distance from where they are in their everyday life, and who they are playing as a character." Zuber particularly loves designing fantasy plays, "where I have a project that must come mainly from my imagination, and where I can therefore go more 'over the top.' That's absolutely thrilling!"

But no designer works wholly on her own, and Zuber is quick to point out that costume design is a "real collaboration" with those technicians who actually pattern, cut, drape, and sew the costumes that she draws. "Costume designers are very dependent on the people who make the clothes. We show them the sketch and they interpret and build it—and the really great ones take it a step further."

Technology has come to the aid of costume designers as it has all the design arts, and Zuber now finds her process greatly enhanced by Photoshop in particular. "I sketch freehand, then scan it into the computer, and then add color—and if the director doesn't like the color I can change it right away. After that, I can manipulate it any way I want. I can put all the

9.  Zuber's exquisitely researched historical costumes for this 2008 Broadway revival of Robert Bolt's *A Man for All Seasons* are richly detailed, luxuriously constructed, and subtly indicative of the differing personalities of the play's early-sixteenth-century characters. Frank Langella (*second from left*) plays Sir Thomas More, the "man for all seasons" of the title.

10. Zuber's costume for Sinead Cusack as Madame Ranevskaya in Chekhov's *The Cherry Orchard* fully captures the faded glamour—olf-the-shoulders red dress, red fan, and red scarf, undercut by black elbow-length gloves and red and black jewelry—of the aging actress returning from Paris to her failing estate. Directed by Sam Mendes and presented in the American-English Bridge Project at the Brooklyn Academy of Music in 2009.

# Stagecraft

## Importance of Small Details

The task of subtly distorting formity, without destroying the desired illusion, is a difficult one. Anton Chekhov's play *The Three Sisters* presents a case in point. The characters of the male players are clearly defined in Chekhov's writing, but because the men are all wearing military uniforms they are theoretically similar in appearance. One of the few ways in which the designer can help to differentiate between characters is by the alteration of proportion; alterations such as these, which do not show enough from the "front" to make the uniforms seem strange to the audience, can be extremely effective, as well as helpful to the actor. In a London production of *The Three Sisters*, Sir Michael Redgrave wore a coat with a collar that was too low; Sir John Gielgud one that was too high. No one in the audience was unaware of the characters' individuality, the talents of these actors being what they are, but the small details added to the scope of their performances.

—MOTLEY

convey a visual message every time the actor speaks a line; they are obviously of paramount importance. Jewelry, sashes, purses, muffs, and other adornments, and official badges of various sorts, have considerable storytelling impact: they "read" to the play's audience a character's rank or role in society. The lowly shoe, if unwisely chosen, can destroy the artistry of a production by being unsuitable for the character or style of the play or by being so badly fitted or so unwieldy that the actor exhibits poor posture or stumbles noisily about the stage.

Whether arrived at through design and fabrication or through careful selection from an army surplus store, good costume design creates a sense of character, period, style, and theatricality out of wearable garments. In harmony with scenery, makeup, and lighting, and with the play's interpretation and performance, costuming can have its maximum impact in a subtle way, by underlining the play's meaning and the characters' personalities, or it can scream for attention and sometimes even become the "star of the show." Not a few musicals have succeeded primarily because the audience "came out whistling the costumes," as a Shubert Alley phrase reminds us. Certainly the magnificently attired principals of xiqu, the gloriously patchworked Arlecchino of commedia dell'arte, and the stunningly garbed black-and-white mannequins of Cecil Beaton's *My Fair Lady* have dominated stages past and present. But even in the most naturalistic drama, well-designed and well-chosen costumes can exert a magical theatrical force, lending special magnitude to the actor's and the playwright's art.

## MAKEUP

Makeup, which is essentially the design of the actor's face, occupies a curiously paradoxical position in the theatre. In much modern production, certainly in the realistic theatre, makeup seems sorely neglected. It tends to be the last design field to be considered. In amateur theatre, makeup is likely to be applied for the first time at the final dress rehearsal—and sometimes not until just before the opening performance. Indeed, makeup is the only major design element whose planning and execution are often left entirely to the actor's discretion.

Makeup, however, is one of the archetypal arts of the theatre, quite probably the first of the theatre's design arts, and it was absolutely fundamental to the origins of drama. The earliest chanters of the dithyramb, like the spiritual leaders of primitive tribes today, invariably made themselves up—probably by smearing their faces with blood or the dregs of wine—in preparation for the performance of their holy rites. Their resulting makeup subsequently inspired the Greek tragic and comic masks that are today the universal symbols of theatre itself. The ancient art of face painting remains crucial to xiqu (Chinese opera), as well as to other traditional Asian, African, and Native American theatre forms.

The reason for makeup's paradoxical role resides in the changing emphasis of theatre aims. Makeup, like costuming, serves both ceremonial and illustrative functions. The illustrative function of makeup is unquestionably the more obvious one today—so

Duelist and would-be lover Cyrano de Bergerac has a large nose—indeed, that's the axis on which the entire plot of Edmond Rostand's romantic-era play of the same name turns. But most actors don't have giant noses, so makeup artists need to be experts in prosthesis—the artificial extension or replacement of human body parts. Here normal-nosed Stephen Rea sports a skillfully created prosthetic proboscis, overseen by Costume Designer John Bright, in a 2004 production of the play at England's National Theatre.

Brian d´Arcy James required ninety minutes to put on his makeup to play the title role in *Shrek* when he starred in it for the 2008 family-friendly Broadway musical.

much so that we often forget its ceremonial role entirely. Illustrative makeup is the means by which the actor changes her or his appearance to resemble that of the character—or at least the appearance of the character as the author, director, and actor imagines it. Makeup of this sort is particularly useful in helping to make a young actor look older or an old one look younger and in making an actor of any age resemble a known historical figure or a fictitious character whose appearance is already set in the public imagination. Makeup gives Cyrano his great nose and Bardolph his red one; it reddens *Macbeth's* "bleeding captain" and blackens Laurence Olivier's Othello; it turns the college sophomore into the aged Prospero, the Broadway dancer into one of T. S. Eliot's cats, and Miss Cathy Rigby into Master Peter Pan. Artificial scars, deformities, bruises, beards, wigs, sunburn, frostbite, and scores of other facial embellishments, textures, and shadings can contribute significantly to realistic stagecraft when needed or desired.

A subtler use of makeup, but still within the realistic mode, is aimed at the evocation of psychological traits through physiognomic clues: the modern makeup

Makeup reflects ancient roots. These young African women have applied bold geometric face paint in a centuries-old design for their performance of a traditional dance-drama of the Ivory Coast based on an ancient hunting ritual. The design, originally intended not merely to entertain an audience but to suggest a magical transformation into the spirit realm, continues to carry at least the resonance of that meaning today.

artist may try to suggest character by exaggerating or distorting the actor's natural eye placement, the size and shape of her mouth, the angularity of her nose, or the tilt of her eyebrows. There can be no question that we form impressions of a character's inner state on the basis of observable physical characteristics—as Caesar notices and interprets Cassius's "lean and hungry look," so do we. And the skilled makeup artist can go far in enhancing the psychological texture of a play by the imaginative use of facial shapings and shadings.

Still another use of makeup, also within the realistic and practical spectrum, seeks merely to simplify and embolden the actor's features in order to make them distinct and expressive to every member of the audience. This is known as creating a face that "reads" to the house—a face that conveys its fullest expression over a great distance. To achieve this effect, the

makeup artist exaggerates highlights and shadows and sharply defines specific features such as wrinkles, eyelashes, eyebrows, and jawlines. Such simplified, emboldened, and subtly exaggerated makeup, combined with stage lighting, creates an impression of realism far greater than any that could be achieved by makeup or lighting alone.

An entirely different category of makeup can be described as beyond realism altogether: makeup that is stylized, that is ceremonial, and that represents the actor as a superhuman presence. The face painting of the traditional Chinese xiqu actor, for example, like the mask of the Japanese nōperformer or the African shaman, can endow the person applying it with at least the illusion (and perhaps also the feeling) of spiritual transcendence. Like the war paint applied in tribal rituals, stylized and ceremonial makeup allows

Like many football players, New York Giants tight end Jeremy Shockey applies black grease stripes under his eyes. The technique is often said to protect the player from the glare of the sun, but its real purpose is—as with war paint—to make the player look more menacing, thereby demoralizing the opposition.

the performer, at least in his or her (and hopefully the audience's) imagination, to become larger than life, to assume divine powers, and to ascend to (and lead the audience to) a higher world. This apparent enhancement of the actor may even be thought of as the "up" in "makeup."

Some obvious examples of such traditional makeup and "making up" are still evident, particularly in European and Asian theatre. The makeup of the circus and the classic mime, two formats that developed in Europe out of the masked commedia dell'arte of centuries past, both use bold colors: white, black, and sometimes red for the mimist and an even wider spectrum for the circus clown. Avant-garde and expressionist playwrights also frequently utilize similar sorts of abstracted makeup, as does French dramatist jean Genet in *The Blacks* (which features black

actors in clownish whiteface) and German playwright Peter Handke (whose *Kaspar* features stylized facial painting similar to Genet's conception). And Asian theatre has always relied on the often dazzling facial coloring (and mane-like wigs and beards) of certain characters in Japanese kabuki, Indian kathakali, and Chinese xiqu—not to mention the violently expressive makeup often seen in contemporary avant-garde productions in Tokyo. The American theatre, which sar has witnessed only a small sampling of stylized makeup, is perhaps due for an awakening to this fascinating approach to theatrical design.

The designing of makeup and hairstyle generally begins with the costume designer, whose final renderings usually include all aspects of the character's appearance. But in complex and high-budget productions, the final designs (and sometimes the initial

# Stagecraft

## The Makeup Kit

Basic makeup consists of a foundation, color shadings, and various special applications. The foundation is a basic color that is applied thinly and evenly to the face and neck and sometimes to other parts of the body as well. Creme makeup, formerly (and still commonly) known as grease-paint, is a traditional foundation material; a highly opaque and relatively inexpensive skin paint, it comes in a variety of colors. Cake makeup, or "pancake" as it is also known, is another type of foundation; it is less messy than creme but also less flexible. Cake makeup comes in small plastic cases and is applied with a damp sponge. Most foundation colors are richer and deeper than a Caucasian actor's normal skin color so as to counteract the white and blue tones of stage lights.

Colorshading defines the facial structure and exaggerates its dimensions so as to give the face a sculptured appearance from a distance; ordinarily, the least imposing characteristics of the face are put in shadow and the prominent features are highlighted. Shading colors—universally called "liners"—come in both creme and cake form and are usually chosen to harmonize with the foundation color, as well as with the color of the actor's costume and the color of the lighting. Shadows are made with darker colors and highlights with lighter ones; both are applied with small brushes and blended into the foundation. Rouge, a special color application used to redden lips and cheeks, is usually applied along with the shading colors. When greasepaints are used the makeup must be dusted with makeup powder to "set" it and prevent running. A makeup pencil is regularly used to darken eyebrows and also to accentuate eyes and facial wrinkles.

Special applications may include false eyelashes or heavy mascara, facial hair (beards and mustaches, ordinarily made from crepe wool), nose putty and various other prosthetic materials, and various treatments for aging, wrinkling, scarring, and otherwise disfiguring the skin. A well-equipped actor has a makeup kit that is stocked with glue (spirit gum and liquid latex), solvents, synthetic hair, wax (to mask eyebrows), and hair whiteners—in addition to the standard foundation and shading colors—to create a wide variety of makeup effects.

designs too) are often executed by specialists carrying out the costume designer's general plan. In the Broadway production of *Cats,* for example, costume (and scenic) designer John Napier designed a basic makeup for each "cat" but then collaborated with makeup designer Candace Carell and wig designer Paul Huntley to tweak the individual design for each of the play's feline "characters."

In many cases the makeup design is a major factor in the production. Famous makeup artists include Jon Dodd, who designed the Beast's prosthetics in *Beauty and the Beast* in collaboration with costume designer Ann Hould-Ward, and Jean Begin, who designed the highly stylized makeup of Cirque du Soleil's *Saltimbanco.* More ordinary makeup, however, as for realistic plays, generally relies on the actor's ability to execute the design—and thus a makeup kit is a fundamental part of each actor's professional equipment.

In some realistic productions, particularly in small theatres, actors go onstage with no makeup at all. Directors sometimes say that actors shouldn't do this because their faces will "wash out from the light." But that is nonsense—faces don't wash out. Avoiding makeup altogether, however, bypasses the initial reasons for makeup's creation: to announce the actor as a performer and to establish for acting a milieu that is neither realistic nor practical but rather supernatural, mysterious, and calculatedly theatrical.

In the final analysis, makeup always combines the realistic and symbolic functions of theatre. Even the most stylized makeup is based on the human form, and even the most realistic makeup conveys obvious theatricality. The theatre, after all, is never so immersed in the ordinary that it could—or should—be wholly mistaken for such. So when an American actor sitting at a makeup table opens little bottles and tubes, moistens Chinese brushes, and sharpens eyebrow pencils, more is going on than simple, practical face-making. Atavistic forces are at work, linking the actor not merely to the imagined physiognomy of his or her character or to the demands of facial projection in a large arena but also, and more fundamentally, to the primitive celebrants who in ages past painted their faces to assure the world that they were leaving their temporal bodies and boldly venturing into the exalted domain of the gods.

# SOUND DESIGN

Music and sound effects have been in use in the theatre since ancient times. Aristotle considered music one of the six essential components of tragedy, and offstage thunder, trumpet "flourishes" and "tuckets," and "the noise of a sea-fight" are all called for in Shakespeare's original stage directions. Before the electronic age, theatres were routinely equipped with such devices as rain drums (axis-mounted barrels that, partly filled with pebbles or dried seeds, made rain sounds when revolved), thundersheets (hanging sheets of tin that rumbled ominously when rattled), and thunder runs (sloping wooden troughs down which cannonballs rolled and eventually crashed). Since 1900, most theatres have also used an electric telephone ringer (a battery-powered bell mounted on a piece of wood) and a door slammer (a miniature doorframe and door, complete with latch) to simulate the sounds of domestic life. All of these "sound effects" were ordinarily created by an assistant stage manager, among his or her many other duties. But the rapid development of audio recording and playback technologies starting in the 1970s and 1980s has led to a virtual revolution in the area of sound design and the emergence of an officially designated sound designer in theatres around the world. Like musical underscoring in cinema and sound balancing and enhancement in rock concerts, theatre sound is now almost entirely an electronic art.

Augmented sound is now routinely used in theatrical performances. Musical theatre and larger theatres increasingly employ electronic sound enhancement to reinforce the actors' voices and create a "louder than life" sonic ambiance for almost all musicals and for many "straight" (nonmusical) plays. In such cases the actors usually wear miniature wireless microphones—often concealed, though in the twenty-first century increasingly visible. The use of live or recorded offstage sounds may establish locale (such as foghorns), time of day (midnight chimes), time of year (birdsong), weather (thunder and rain), and onstage or offstage events (a ringing telephone, an arriving taxi, an angel crashing through the ceiling). Stage sounds can be realistic (an ambulance siren), stylized (an amplified, accelerating heartbeat), stereophonically localized (an airplane heard as crossing overhead from left to right), or pervasive and "in-your-head" (a buzzing mosquito, electronic static, a thousand ringing cell phones).

Music, as well as sound, is often used to evoke a mood, support an emotion, intensify an action, or

The Midas XL8 audio mixer is one of the newest and most elaborate sound consoles on the market, providing user-friendly desk operation for the most complex sound-scored productions and concerts, including the 2009 Nobel Prize Ceremony in Dslo and Depeche Mode's "Tour of the Universe," which played worldwide to audiences of up to eight-five thousand in 2009—10.

provide a transition into or between scenes. Music accompanying a play can be composed for the production and played "live" during the performance, or it can be derived from (legally acquired and paid-for) copyrighted recordings, which are then played back through a theatre's sound system (or, sometimes, through onstage "prop" boom boxes). Naturally, many combinations are possible. The sound designer designs and oversees the implementation of all of these elements, and, particularly if she or he is also the play's musical composer, this work may be of immense importance in the overall production.

Sound design has rapidly escalated in importance over the past two decades as playwrights and directors have sought to incorporate the new sound technologies that have swiftly expanded the theatrical potential, first with audiotape recording and now with highly complex digital recording, editing, processing, and playback technologies that grow more sophisticated every year. Contemporary sound design is not without its detractors. The electronic amplification of speaking and singing voices in musicals and nonmusicals alike is often derided by critics who prefer—or believe they prefer—a more natural unamplified sound. The sound-mixing

# PHOTO ESSAY: Sound Designer Scott Lehrer

1.

of synthesizers." Soon he was deep; into electronic music, picking up bits of "found sound" and creating sound collages for classmate directors and choreographers to go with their performances. "I became fascinated by the entire world of sound," he explains. "It was all quite new an wonderful." Not limiting himself to drama or dance productions, he created sound for giant public events like New York's SummerStage in Central Park with 100,000 attendees, along with museum exhibitions, live industrial shows, and corporate media. But theatre beckoned strongly when he took a job as sound engineer for the Colonnades Theatre Lab, an avantgrade off-off-Broadway theatre on New York's Lower East Side. "We all worked together there," he remembers, "blending multichannel 'surround sound' into the rehearsals so that the actors would get used to hearing sounds while rehearsing, and would respond to those sounds like they responded to the other actors. Sound simply became part of their world." Lehrer didn't realize how unusual this was at the time, but in the days when offstage sound was mainly created by stage managers operating wooden, handheld "door-slamming" devices or executing"needle drops" on long-playing records played over a loudspeaker, he and his colleagues were innovating truly revolutionary techniques.

By 1980, Lehrer had moved up the ladder to off-Broadway, where he worked at many of the finest

When Scott Lehrer received the Tony Award for sound design in a musical in 2008, it was an honor not only for him but for theatrical sound design itself, as his award—and a separate one for sound design in a play—were the first Tonys ever awarded in this blossoming field. Yes, Lehrer acknowledges, the Tony was "something of a culmination after working in the mines for many years," but he is also insistent that there have been many other sound design pioneers who should be recognized. "I was just lucky enough to be doing a show the year they initiated these," he modestly declares. But it certainly wasn't just luck: he got his second Tony nomination for designing *Joe Turner's Come and Gone* in 2009, and he received new accolades for his designs for the Broadway productions of *Finian's Rainbow* the following fall and *A View from the Bridge* in 2010.

Lehrer practiced and studied music when he went to college at Sarah Lawrence in the mid-1970s, first expanding his early love of rock, folk, and jazz and then "getting weird sounds out

2.

1. Sound Designer Scott Lehrer in the professional sound studio he has built into his apartment in lower Manhattan, building up possible cues for a new production.

2. Lehrer checks out his extensive CD library for music that might come into play in this new work.

companies: Circle Repertory, Manhattan Theatre Club, the American Place, and, mainly, Playwrights Horizons, where he describes himself as "almost in residence" for many years. "We were still in the Stone Age as far as equipment was concerned," Lehrer recalls. "We had to be really creative, figure out how to do things with very little money, invent new ways of working."

No theatre technology has advanced as rapidly in the past decades as sound, Lehrer says: "Young people coming into this field today have little idea how new it all is. In just the time I've been doing all this, we've gone from records to tape decks to samplers to digital sound and music sequencers. The speed with which we can create sound design, and the level of control we have over it, have increased almost beyond belief." To create the sound of road construction that director Susan Stroman had thought of adding into her production of *Happiness*, at New York's Lincoln Center, for example, Lehrer sent his assistant out to record the jackhammers then hammering away on the street outside. "I handed him my recorder at 10:00, at 10:15 I plugged the recorder into my Pro Tools [digital audio system], by 10:30 I had cleaned it up, and by 10:45 I had it in my QLab [sound software] ready to go into the show. Just a few years ago this would have taken three days!"

By the end of the 1980s, Lehrer was on Broadway, first with Wendy Wasserstein's *The Heidi Chronicles*, which received the Pulitzer Prize and the Tony Award for best play of the year, and soon thereafter designing sound for Tony Kushner's landmark *Angels in America*. The technology he had helped to inaugurate was

**3.**

**4.**

**3.** At his piano, Lehrer composes a new melody that might be inserted into his design.

**4.** In the Mitzi Newhouse Theatre in Lincoln Center, technical rehearsals are about to get started for the world premiere of *Happiness*, with Lehrer as sound designer, and a "sound table" has been placed in the theatre's auditorium where Lehrer and Drew Levy, his assistant, have set up their computers and audio equipment to create the sound cues that will be executed—and adjusted—for this afternoon's rehearsal.

now readily available, and sound design—and Lehrer himself—were poised for a brilliant future.

What, aside from a mastery of technology, does it take to be a sound designer? Lehrer does not pretend to have a single aesthetic style; rather he considers himself something of a chameleon and frames his designs in close concert with the context of the play and the perspective of the director. Working with the playwright/ director Richard Nelson, for example, who asks for the sound "to be a part of the storytelling, to be another character in the play," he investigates the sonic ambience of the text. For Nelson's *Franney's Way*, set in an apartment above a jazz club, Lehrer describes his challenge as creating the unseen people downstairs. "What would they be listening to? Jazz, of course, but what kind of jazz? What tempo? Cool or hot, ballad or uptempo? Saxophone, yes, but Dexter Gordon or John Coltrane? I tried to find the musical style that would convey the ambient emotional feel Nelson

wanted." For Terrence McNally's *A Perfect Ganash*, two older American women are traveling through India. "What sort of music do they hear?" Lehrer asked himself. "There are many regions in India and many local musical forms, and it would be disrespectful to the culture not to represent this. So I have to be an amateur musicologist: I have to listen to everything from t locale, the era, and the culture that the play is seeking to represent."

Lehrer considers sound design a perfect marriage of art and technology. "You have to have something to say. Sound design is not just technical, but you absolutely have to have the skills to do it. While you can't let the technique get in the way, you also have to make it work for you. Sound design takes place in real time. When you're in technical rehearsals, if you don't know the technology you can't keep up with the speed of the rehearsal, and if that happens you simply can't realize your art. You have to control the technology; you can't let the technology control you."

board, now commonplace in the back orchestra rows of most Broadway and larger regional theatres, is a visual reminder of the contemporary technology that some feel mediates the "liveness" of "live theatre." Extended musical underscoring in some plays raises objections that it turns drama into cinema and suffuses the articulation of ideas in the syrup of generalized emotion. Nonetheless, sound design—as well as original music composition that makes use of it—has become absolutely fundamental to the production of today's theatre around the globe and is quite definitely here to stay.

# PROJECTION DESIGN

Perhaps the newest design area in theatre is the creation of visual images projected electronically onto the stage or sometimes throughout the entire theatre. Projections are not exactly new: German designer Erwin Piscator used projected scenery as early as 1924, and Tennessee Williams called for "a screen on which were projected magic-lantern slides bearing images or titles" to be used in the production of his new play, *The Glass Menagerie*, in 1944, so as "to give accent to certain values for each scene." (Director

The projections that Elaine McCarthy designed for *33 Variations* showed various locales where the play takes place, and, as shown here, a handwritten classical piano score by Ludwig von Beethoven that the terminally ill Dr. Brandt, played by Jane Fonda (*right*), is researching in the hopes of discovering the composer's motive for creating it. Susan Kellerman plays Brandt's doctor in this 2009 Broadway production, written and directed by Moises Kaufman.

Tim Bird's projection design forth e 2008 Broadway revival of Stephen Sondheim's *Sunday in the Park with George* was widely considered a major factor in the production's success, spurring a greatly expanded interest in projections as vital contributors to the art of theatrical design.

Eddie Dowling never used the slides in his Chicago and Broadway premieres of *Menagerie,* but many subsequent directors of the play have.) In Europe, Bertolt Brecht used slide projections extensively in his epic theatre productions, and projections have played a major role in European theatre productions ever since. Wendell K. Harrington, credited as Projection Designer (or video designer or multi-image designer) on Broadway since *They're Playing Our Song* in 1979, has designed projections for thirty-four Broadway productions since—winning (along with the set designer) the Drama Desk Award in 1993 for *The Who's Tommy.* Harrington teaches projection design at the Yale Drama School and has played a major role in bringing projected scenery into the American mainstream.

Until recently, projections were limited to small and generally still images that mainly indicated factual details (such as stating the location of a new scene—a technique echoing signboards placed before the audience in Shakespeare's time) or reminiscences of characters mentioned but not seen in the play (such as the absent father in *Glass Menagerie,*

described by Williams as a"mernory play"), or they provided an inexpensive way of changing visual backgrounds without having to move scenic pieces on and off the stage. Today, in part because of new technological developments (digital imaging, video recording, computer-designed animation, LEDs), and in part because of the trend away from straight realism, particularly in directions urged by Brecht, image and video projections are often integral both to theatrical design, replacing what in past eras might have been hard scenery, and to theatrical direction, conveying actions and propelling plots and character relationships. Therefore the projection designer (sometimes called the image designer or video designer) has become a new member of the theatrical design team for productions everywhere.

Signaling this growth, Tim Bird earned the first-ever Drama Desk Award for outstanding projections and video design for his work on the 2008 Broadway revival of *Sunday in the Park with George,* the celebrated musical about French artist Georges Seurat and his influence on modern art. The first act of this work—which received the Pulitzer Prize for Drama—was staged in its 1984 premiere in front of a large painted canvas of Seurat's famous pointillist painting named in the play's title, with the costumed actors taking the positions of the artist's human figures. David Farley's twenty-first-century set design, however, was paired with Bird's animated video of that painting, which was projected on an LED wall at the rear of the stage, allowing the audience to see the painting created from completely blank canvas to finished masterpiece during the act. It was a stunner: *Sunday's* composer-creator Stephen Sondheim was heard to say that "if we had the technology when we first staged the show, this is the way we would have wanted to do it." Yet while Bird's technology was expansive (its 160 separate video cues required three digital media servers and seven projectors, aimed from both front and rear and focused on the side walls, a few small centerstage canvases, and a cutout tree—as as well as on the rear projection screen), his artistry was intense and, by showing Seurat's images constructed from thousands of discrete "points" of color, was instrumental in demonstrating the musical's "pointillist" theme.

All new technologies are controversial, especially when they appear in an art with a five-thousand-year old history. Finn Ross's projection design for the 2008 Broadway revival of Arthur Miller's *All My Sons* (1947), starring John Lithgow, included newsreels of the period, large videos of wartime soldiers, factory workers, and military planes, plus occasional indications of time and scene changes, and was both praised ("surprisingly effective," "insinuating projections") and damned ("[projections do] more to harm the play than bolster it," "don't draw us closer to these people—they push us away"). Similarly, a fellow designer praised the LED screen behind the 2009 Broadway revival of *Guys and Dolls* as "majestic and handsomely humanized," and Destin O'Neill's projections on it as "expertly made," but felt the ultimate impact of the projections was to overwhelm the characters, who were "upstaged by the fancy video.... The wall does all the talking."

But despite the caveats, which are common as new technologies replace older ones, projection design—particularly with video animation—has clearly come into the mainstream. Indeed, more and more playwrights are, as Tennessee Williams did in the early 1940s, writing the new technologies into their scripts. Lisa Loomer's *Distracted*, about a nine-year-old boy with attention deficit disorder, was written to be staged with the media-generated "distractions" the boy faces indicated by projections of multiple media images shown all over the stage—on widescreen TV, a scrolling news marquee, Facebook pages, and iPhones—even before the dialogue begins. It was no wonder that Tal Yarden, the projection designer, was mentioned in the first paragraph of most of the reviews of its 2009 New York premiere. Michael Jacobs's 2009 *Impressionism*, starring Jeremy Irons as an art gallery owner, featured a series of paintings that morphed into personal reminiscences of the play's characters (for instance, an image of impressionist painter Mary Cassatt's *La Toilette* segues to one of a present-day character recalling being bathed by her mother). *Impressionism's* projections were realized by Elaine McCarthy, who also designed the 2009 Broadway premiere of *33 Variations,* starring Jane Fonda as a musicologist researching Beethoven: full-wall projections of Beethoven's handwritten piano scores—along with images of specific locations in Bonn (where the present-day action was set) and imaginary scenes from Beethoven's life—became a fundamental part of that production as well.

As projection design becomes more and more common, will it lick its potential problems, such as upstaging the live actors performing in its midst? Probably, as long as it prioritizes art over technology. "What I know about the technology you can fit in a thimble," says veteran designer Wendell Harrington. "The thinking is much more important."

## SPECIAL EFFECTS

Theatre "magic" implies special effects not easily described as simply lighting or sound—fire, explosions, fog, smoke, wind, rain, snow, lightning, spurts of blood, and mysterious arrivals and disappearances such as what stage directions in Shakespeare's *Tempest* describe as the goddess Juno descending from Mount Olympus and certain nymphs who "heavily vanish" after "a strange hollow and confused noise." And all of these effects must be accomplished without burning down the theatre. (Unless, of course, sometimes they do: the firing of an offstage cannon burned down Shakespeare's Globe in 1613.) Commercial devices can help theatre technicians achieve these effects, but each bit of magic requires its own on-the-spot ingenuity to be both credible and effective. And one-of-a-kind tricks, such as having Hans's armor suddenly fall off his body in jean Giraudoux's *Ondine,* must be individually designed and perfected. Effects designers are not universally employed in the theatre, but since the growth of spectacular musicals and Cirque du Soleil innovations (see the chapter titled "Theatre Today"), they are clearly in a growth industry.

(*Above*) Shown here is Crowley's classroom setting as realized for the Royal National Theatre premiere of *The History Boys*, which went on to receive the English Olivier and Broadway Tony best-play awards.

(*Right*) This is Crowley's model showing his design for the Banks family household—emphasizing the kitchen—in the popular 2004 London and 2006 Broadway musical *Mary Poppins*, for which Crowley received the Tony Award for best design of a musical. The meticulous setting, in which individual rooms can be closed off or revealed by the addition of an exterior facade, provides a focus for the individual areas while still maintaining the overall architecture of the play's center: an integrated English family home.

# DIGITAL TECHNOLOGIES IN THEATRE DESIGN

Designers—like other visual artists—have always used the technologies available to them. For centuries, designers have worked with such basic drawing implements as charcoal, colored paints, rulers, squares, and drafting tables. Complicated "drawing machines" came into play during the Renaissance: Leonardo da Vinci invented a "perspectograph" to help artists transform their perceived earthly realities into two-dimensional sketches and engravings in the early 1500s, and Canaletto's detailed paintings of eighteenth-century Venice were executed with the aid of a room-size "camera obscura." The digital programs of today are only the most recent in a long list of technological tools used by visual artists, but they have become widespread in the theatre.

What does digital design offer that pencil and paper don't? Computers don't think and can't create; they can't (yet) analyze a text, imagine an environment, suggest a costume, conceive a style, or make an audience laugh. But what digital technology *can* do is aid artists who do these things. The capacity for digitally combining and configuring (and then reconfiguring) ideas, angles, shapes, colors, spaces, perspectives, and measurements, which designers uncover through research or create through imagination, makes possible the consolidation of a giant spectrum of experimental and aesthetic possibilities with the speed of light and the assurance of a mathematician. Perhaps no technology of any era has so successfully counterpoised reality's hard facts with the artist's free-floating imagination.

Digital design has become invaluable to contemporary designers on a variety of levels. First, computer-aided-design (CAD) programs can assist with or even replace much of the drudgery of sheer drawing mechanics. With a click of the mouse, straight lines, angles, circles, shapes, colors, and typefaces can be selected from a menu of choices and placed where desired. Moreover, all of these can be shifted in an instant: colors can be changed, lines lengthened, walls thickened, floors raised, furniture moved, sight lines adjusted, dimensions measured, and texts edited and resized. Individual design elements can be instantly replicated: an elaborately drawn banister post can become a dozen posts with two clicks of a mouse. Indeed, whole drawings can be rescaled, zoomed in or out; individual elements can be rotated or relocated freely about the page. And the resulting working drawings can be shared instantly with design team members working anywhere around the world (as designers often do). Global collaboration has become not merely possible in the digital age, it has become routine.

And there's more. Digital storage allows designers to draw upon vast visual databases: "virtual art catalogues" of, for example, eighteenth-century chandeliers, Victorian drapery, Roman togas—all digitized for computer retrieval and available, subject to legal copyright considerations, for incorporation into stage designs. And digitized cutting and pasting allows the designer to *combine* virtual forms. For example, a costume designer can "virtually sew" the sleeves of one digitized garment onto another or even "virtually dress" one digitized actor with a digital costume, giving a view of a fully costumed character without buying a single inch of fabric. Dedicated database programs also permit lighting and sound technicians to save innumerable hours in storing, sorting, and printing the dozens of dimmer schedules, cue sheets, and loudspeaker assignments needed in multiproduction repertory assignments.

Plus, in many theatres digitized scenographic modeling has supplemented traditional drawings by creating, on a computer screen, three-dimensional models of the stage set that can demonstrate perspectives from any vantage: from the left, right, and center of the house or from a bird's-eye position that may clarify lighting and offstage storage positions. Designers, directors, and actors can now "walk through" the set while it exists solely as a virtual reality, and they can "light the scenery" in a variety of ways before anything is built—or even before a theatre is rented. The opportunity to digitally "storyboard" scenery, costumes, and lighting, together with text and music and sound, is an extraordinary advance in the art of production planning wherever time and money are involved, as they almost always are.

Finally, of course, digital technology is not merely a preparatory tool for the designer; it is now the very medium by which sound, lighting, and projections are routinely transmitted to the audience. The music and sound that emanate from house speakers have been fully digitized, the still or moving images projected onto screens or LED walls are now pixelated, and the intensity of the lighting instruments—and increasingly their colors and movements as well—are executed today with the aid of highly specialized computer software. Theatre has definitely entered the digital age, and there seems to be no going back.

Will digital technology reduce the creativity and imagination that go into the designer's art? A few veteran designers voice this concern, apprehensive about the encroachment of binary numbers and microelectronics on what has generally been considered a freehand, soul-expressive art. But young designers are now trained in—and eager to employ—a wide variety of CAD techniques, and most senior designers are switching over to them as well. Imagination is a function not of one's tools—pen and paper or keyboard and screen—but of the mind that guides them. Computers are tools-superpencils, really-not ends in themselves; they provoke experimentation and innovation as well as (or even in lieu of) mere craft precision and mechanics. The computer age already has a substantial history in the theatre; indeed, one of the first commercial uses of computing was in theatrical lighting, which has been computerized since at least the mid-1980s. And the theatre has been one of the testing places for many of the world's emerging technologies, including hydraulic elevators, gas lighting, electricity, and air-conditioning. So it should be no surprise that the computer screen has become a principal conveyor of design creativity and communication in today's theatre.

# THE TECHNICAL PRODUCTION TEAM

Far outnumbering all the others—actors, designers, writers, and directors—put together are the artisans or "technologists" who get the production organized, built, installed, lit, and ready to open, and who then make it run.

Because of their numbers, theatrical technicians are ordinarily marshaled into a hierarchical structure, headed by stage, house, and production managers, technical directors, and shop supervisors, all of whom are charged with guiding and supervising the work of a virtual army of craftspersons. A typical breakdown of these functions—which you might find detailed in the theatre program of any major theatre—could be something like this:

The *production stage manager* (*PSM*)-previously known simply as the *stage manager*—has existed at least since the eighteenth century. The PSM coordinates the scheduling, staffing, and budgeting of every element of the production, from the acting rehearsals to the building, installation ("load-in"), and operation ("running") of all the design and technical elements. Expert in legal codes, safety procedures, and accounting policies, and sensitive to the varying artistic needs of actors, directors, designers, and technicians, the PSM wrestles with the complex problems of integrating the play's disparate elements—determining, for example, whether the lights should be hung and focused before or after the scenery is installed (there can be reasons for going either way on this) and anticipating how long it will take to train the stage crew or to set the light cues.

The production stage manager coordinates the director's work with that of the actors and the technical and design departments. At the beginning of rehearsals, the PSM is involved primarily in organizational matters: scheduling calls and appointments, recording the blocking of actors, anticipating technical problems of quick costume changes, set shifts, and the like, and organizing the basic "calling" of the show—that is, the system by which lighting, sound, actor-entrance, and scene-shift cues are initiated.

During performance, the PSM is in full charge of the show. He or she observes it (either directly from a booth above the audience, or from the side of the stage, or through one or more video monitors) and physically calls each lighting, sound, and scene-moving cue—normally through an electronic intercom system. The production stage manager also signals actor entrances, usually by means of "cuelights," which are tiny backstage lights that the PSM operates to tell an actor when it's time to enter. This task is crucial when an entrance must be timed to an onstage physical action that the actor cannot see from backstage. It is the PSM's job and, more important, his or her art to precisely time these cues to create the theatrical impact intended be the director, while also making adjustments for unexpected interruptions such as sustained audience laughter or applause, electrical outages, or actor or technician accidents onstage.

The production stage manager also maintains the production after its opening performance, conducting understudy and replacement rehearsals when needed, arranging for the cleaning, repair, or replacement of costumes, props, and stage machinery, and in other ways assuming the functions of the director, who, in professional and many amateur productions, is no longer present on a regular basis.

Working for the production stage manager is one or more *assistant stage managers*. In rehearsals, these assistants typically set out props, follow the script, prompt actors who are "off book" (no longer rehearsing with script in hand) when they forget their lines, take line notes when actors memorize lines incorrectly, and substitute for actors who may be temporarily away from the rehearsal hall, as for conflicting publicity or costume-fitting appointments. During the performance, with the production stage manager calling the show from a fixed offstage position, the assistants—on two-way headset connections—implement the PSM's calls to the actors and crew chiefs, often transmitting them as visual "go" signs for scene shifts, actor entrances, and effect cues. Assistant stage managers also serve as the backstage eyes and ears of the PSM, who is always watching the stage.

*Technical director (TD)* is a term that dates from early in the last century, when a person holding that title was responsible for the scenery, lighting, sound, stage machinery, and just about everything "technical" that was designed to operate onstage. Although the title is still used, the TD is usually now only in charge of the building and operation of scenery and stage machinery. The position requires great knowledge and skill in engineering, drafting, construction, budgeting, and team management (of shops and crews). But it is a high art as well, for every construction and operation that the TD oversees is a one-of-a-kind project and must be completed in most cases on an exactly fixed schedule—no small order, given the massive technical complexities of theatre today. (The theatre rarely allows for any variation in the preplanned "opening-night" performance.)

The technical director's first task is to receive the designs—which may simply be drawings augmented by overall dimensions and perhaps supplemented by three-dimensional models—and figure out how each design element will be constructed. Dozens of factors must be considered and, much of the time, traded off. The cost of materials and labor must be carefully reconciled with the available budget; scenery meant to look light and airy must be engineered with critical concerns for stability and safety; scenery meant to look heavy and gargantuan often must be built to roll or fly offstage at lightning speed—or in a choreography of alternate accelerations and decelerations. During this phase the TD drafts the working drawings for the scenery's construction and exact placement and consults, often daily, with the designer and director as to whether the working drawings will lead to the look, and yield scenery that works in the manner that each of them has imagined and is now counting on.

Once the scenery is built, the TD oversees its load-in and establishes the manner in which scenery is to be shifted, either by manual pushing and pulling or by computerized mechanical devices. At the end of the play's run, the TD organizes the "strike"—the removal of scenery into storage or the local dumpster.

During actual production, *technical crews,* working under the production stage manager and trained by the TD, often are a virtual backstage army. They hoist, lower, and push scenery pieces exactly on cue to precisely predetermined locations. They shift props and furniture to the right places at the right times. They relay the PSM's cues to actors awaiting their entrances or offstage cries. In general, they make the carefully preplanned scene changes, prop appearances, and actor entrances appear to flow effortlessly. The skills of the technical crews ensure that the audience concentrates on the play's action rather than on the theatre's mechanics.

One particularly special "tech" assignment is flying actors through the air, which is usually done by only a few professional companies with patented equipment and expertly trained personnel. The most prominent American company, Flying by Foy, was created by Peter Foy in 1950 and has achieved preeminence in aerial choreography of astonishing beauty and complexity.

Working in the scene shop-normally under the technical director, a *shop foreman, or a scenery supervisor*—are production *carpenters* (and master carpenters) and scenic artists (painters). They are joined by welders when steel—commonly used today for weight-bearing constructions—is to be joined.

In the costume shop, a wider array of specialists is required (though many costume designers and technologists assume more than one of these roles):

- *Costume director (or costume shop manager),* who coordinates the entire operation, supervising personnel, work spaces, and schedules.

- *Dyers,* who dye fabrics to the color specified by the design and may also be skilled at fabric painting, aging, distressing, and other fabric modifications.

- *Drapers,* who drape fabrics on an actor or on a dummy, testing and choosing the way the fabric falls—either with the grain or on the bias—to create the desired look of the eventual garment

# PHOTO ESSAY: Broadway Stage Manager Michael McGolf

Michael McGoff has stage-managed five Broadway and eighteen off-Broadway shows since his arrival in New York in 2000, and in 2009 he was stage-managing the world tour of *Rent* with its major Broadway stars. His impressive credits include the American premiere of Caryl Churchill's *Drunk Enough To Say I Love You*, at New York's Public Theatre in 2008, and the Broadway productions of Richard Brinsley Sheridan's The Rivals, Edward Albee's Seascape, David Eldridge's Festen, Shakespeare's *Romeo and Juliet* and *Cymbaline*, and Simon Gray's *Butley*, starring Nathan Lane, at the Booth, where this author interviewed him two hours before curtain time on a weekday evening in early 2007.

**1.**

1. Michael McGoff on the *Butley* set at the Booth Theatre in New York's Broadway Theatre Distict.

2. "The audience is different every night, and so is the play," says McGoff, who must be fully alert to every nuance in the rise and fall of audience laughter and applause, and to the actors' variations in their movements and line deliveries, as he calls cues from his stage manager's console behind the scenes. These cues—for specific (and numbered) shifts in lighting and in sound, for actors' entrances, for the rise and fall of the curtain— all must be timed in precise synchronization with intricate onstage action. The five video monitors on the console capture this action from every possible vantage. Toggle switches above McGoff's hand operate the offstage cue-lights that signal actor entrances. The headset keeps McGoff in continuous contact with the light and sound operators located in distant parts of the theatre and with the stage crew elsewhere behind the scenes. Every two or three days, McGoff turns his console over to an assistant so he can watch the performance from the back of the house and identify moments in the show that may need tweaking to regain their fullest potential.

**2.**

3.

McGoff's work begins ninety minutes before every performance.

"I use this time to check in with my crew and to see if anything needs to taken care of before we turn the house over to the house manager. At that point, while my assistant handles the prop preset, I deal with any of the actors' concerns and give them my notes. Some days there aren't very many; on others I can be continuously running up and down the backstage stairs to keep everyone in the loop. All actors take their notes differently; you learn when to invoke the director, when to appeal to logic, when to cut through with the harsh but important truth, and when to just watch it again and wait until tomorrow."

It's time for the visitor to leave: the actors are arriving, and McGoff is beginning his opening setup.

**3.** "I use my office as a place to focus and communicate with the on-site needs of the show, and also to get in touch with the many off-site service providers, management, producers, public relations and press officers, agents, and so forth," explains McGoff. "The office is placed strategically, allowing me to catch staff going up and coming down the stairs. And when we have guests I can head them off if they are arriving at an inconvenient time. It also puts me where the actors need me, yet it is close to the stage so my crew can call me when they have to.

both at rest and on a moving (and possibly dancing, tumbling, or fencing) actor.

- *Cutters,* who cut the fabric according to the selected grain direction, either from a flat paper pattern or with no pattern at all, often first creating a cheap muslin prototype. (Most often today, draping and cutting are performed by the same person: a draper/cutter.)

- *First hands,* who, working directly for the cutter, correct the pattern after the muslin prototype has been fitted to the actor and then "hand off" the work to stitchers.

- *Stitchers,* who sew the garment.

- *Craft specialists,* who make costumes or costume elements involving more than fabric—armor, belts, masks, and so forth. Specific specialists, such as milliners to make hats and cobblers to make shoes, may be added. Other specialists may be involved in distressing costume elements (making them look older and well used) or adding decorations, such as badges, military ribbons, and gold braid.

- *Hairstylists and wigmakers,* who coif the actors as the designers specify.

- *Wardrobe supervisors,* who ensure that costumes are cleaned and maintained during the run of a show and delivered to the appropriate backstage areas during dress rehearsals and performances. Wardrobe (or storage) supervisors and technicians also oversee the costume storage area and help determine which existing costumes can be taken from storage and rebuilt to serve a new design.

- *Dressers,* who work backstage during dress rehearsals and performances, helping the actors when necessary with quick changes between scenes.

In the area of lighting, *master electricians* and electricians hang, focus, and "gel" (put color media in) lighting instruments prior to and during technical rehearsals, and they maintain the lighting technology during the run of a show. *Lighting-board and follow-spot operators* execute the lighting cues called by the production stage manager. For the sound department, one or more *sound engineers* work with the sound designer in recording the sound cues and placing the speakers, and a *soundboard operator* executes the cues during technical and dress rehearsals and performances. And in the makeup room, *makeup artists* may provide assistance to actors requiring it, or they may indeed apply full makeup to the actors as specified by the designers.

Each of these backstage technicians plays an absolutely crucial role in theatrical presentation. The stage fright of the actor playing Hamlet is not necessarily greater than the nervousness of the stagehand who pulls the curtain, for backstage work, though technical, is never merely mechanical. Every stage production poses a host of problems and situations that are new to the people who deal with them and, sometimes, new to the theatre itself. Technological innovation takes place when sound knowledge of craft combines with creative imagination in the face of unanticipated problems. The technical artists of the theatre have always manifested impressive ingenuity at meeting unprecedented challenges in creative ways. Each of the theatre's shops—scene shop, costume shop, prop shop, and makeup room—is therefore a creative artistic studio and a teaching laboratory for all its members, as well as a theatrical support unit.

Indeed, in contemporary theatre, particularly under the influences of Bertolt Brecht and postmodernism, the theatre's technology—such as lighting instruments and sound-enhancing devices—has increasingly been taken out of hiding and placed right on the stage itself. And when follow-spot operators (and sometimes production stage managers) are placed in direct public view, sound operators are plopped in the midst of the audience, and puppeteers visibly manipulate their animals right on the stage, as often happens nowadays, the theatre's technicians themselves are increasingly drawn into direct public awareness—and in some cases are invited to take onstage curtain calls with the rest of the cast. Popular fascination with technology, together with diminishing interest in mere realism, has led to a scenography that deliberately incorporates technology as a visible aesthetic component of the theatre itself. Given this trend and the theatre's increasing use of the most recent technical innovations—superhydraulics, lasers and holograms, air casters, wall-size video, moving lights, and projections, to name but a few—the theatre technologist is becomingwidely recognized (as cinematographers are in cinema) as not merely implementers but fullfledged stage artists and creators.

Throughout history, the theatrical crafts have been learned through apprenticeship. Even today, although beginning theatre technologists are often trained in universities before their first employment, much of their learning is necessarily on the job, as each job is somewhat unique to the play that prompts it. And although written and unwritten "textbooks" of stage practice can illustrate the traditional means of building a flat, cutting a pattern, organizing a rehearsal, laying out a prop table, and painting a prop, it is artistic sensitivity that ultimately determines the technical quality of a production, and it is artistic imagination that brings about the technical and technological advances that further theatrical creativity.

# Chapter 7

# Theatre Traditions: East and West

THEATRE, WHICH CONSISTS OF LIVE actors who perform in real time before live audiences, is a unique art form because it exists "in the present." Theatre, however, is also deeply rooted in its past; many plays seen today are revivals, adaptations, or parodies of earlier ones. Even when they're wholly original, new plays are inevitably compared to earlier works. Likewise, contemporary actors—like contemporary baseball players—also are compared to their predecessors. Theatre is a living art but also a living tradition.

Some plays travel through time effortlessly, reappearing in new guises at dozens of points throughout history. A fourth-century B.C. Greek comedy named *The Lot Drawers,* by Diphilos, concerning an old man foolishly in love with a young girl, was revised more than one hundred years later by the Roman comic dramatist Plautus under the title *Casina;* and more than one thousand years later it became the basis for a fifteenth-century Italian comedy by Niccolò Machiavelli titled *Clizia.* Thereafter, major elements of the plot appeared in early-sixteenth-century Italian *commedia dell'arte* farces, in the sixteenth-and seventeenth-century plays of Shakespeare and Molière, and more recently in American comedies on stage, film, and television.

Indeed, many of the world's greatest plays—in both East and West—are closely based on preceding ones. Dozens of eighteenth-century Japanese *kabuki* dramas are based on fourteenth-century Japanese *no* scripts (often bearing the same titles), and most traditional Indian and Chinese plays are based on dramas from prior millennia. French neoclassic tragedies of the seventeenth century, as well as French comedies of the twentieth century, were often based on Greek and Roman models more than two thousand years old. At least three of William Shakespeare's best-known plays—*King Lear, Hamlet,* and *The Taming of the Shrew*—were revisions of earlier English plays with nearly the same names by other authors. And Shakespeare's plays, in turn, have been a source for literally hundreds of modern dramas, including Tom *Stoppard's Rosencrantz and Guildenstern Are Dead,* Lee Blessing's *Fortinbras,* Paul Rudnik's *I Hate Hamlet,* Richard Nelson's *Two Shakespearean Actors,* Ann-Marie McDonald's *Goodnight Desdemona (Good Morning Juliet)*, Amy Freed's *The Beard of Avon,* Stephen Sondheim's *West Side Story,* and Neil Simon's *The Goodbye Girl* and *Laughter on the 23rd Floor,* all of which parody or creatively extend portions of Shakespeare's plays. Indeed, the theatre continually resurrects its past traditions, just as it always seeks to extend and surpass them.

Therefore it is helpful, when looking at the theatre of today, to look to the traditions of the theatre in the past, from the West (Europe and the Americas) and the East (Asia and the Indian subcontinent). What follows is a capsule history of eleven important theatre traditions, from both East and West, that together outline the major world developments prior to the start of the modern theatre in the nineteenth century.*

# THE ORIGINS OF THEATRE

How did drama begin?

No one knows for sure, but the theatre, along with human civilization itself, almost certainly began in Africa. The first known dramatic presentations occurred in northern Africa alongside the Nile River in ancient Egypt, at least forty-five hundred years ago and possibly as early as 3300 B.C.

African theatre, however, is far older than that. Indications of ritual performances can be seen in the activities of literally hundreds of African tribal groups

dating as far back as 6000 B.C. Unfortunately, we know very little about such performances, because unlike the arts of painting and sculpture, there are no permanent records. But it is very likely they resembled tribal performances widely seen in rural Africa today. And from such present-day performances, we can see the two foundations of the theatre as it has been known and enjoyed throughout the course of human civilization: *ritual* and *storytelling*. Both have existed since ancient times, and both can be seen—though in different forms—wherever theatre is performed today.

## Ritual

A ritual is a collective ceremony performed by members of a society, normally for religious or cultural reasons. The most ancient rituals were primarily intended to summon gods and influence nature, as with rain dances and healing ceremonies. Tribal rituals also arose to worship important life events, such as the changing of the seasons, and to provide public witness to life passages, such as birth, death, marriage, and the coming of age. Contemporary rituals of Christian baptism and Jewish bar mitzvah (coming of age) and funeral rites in almost all cultures are descendants of these ancient tribal rites-of-passage ceremonies. Other rituals reenact defining moments of a culture's religious history—such as the birth, death, or resurrection of divine beings—allowing adherents to directly experience the passion of their culture's sacred heritage.

The early tribal rituals soon grew to involve elements we now consider theatrical crafts, including staging, costuming, makeup, music, dance, formalized speech, chanting, and singing, as well as specific physical "props" (objects such as staffs, spears, and skulls), often with totemic or spiritual properties that would prove crucial to the staged event. And while initially performed solely for the collective worship of the participants themselves, such theatricalized rituals played a role in impressing, educating, and evangelizing observers, including the children of the tribe and tribal visitors.

Not all rituals are based in religion. Secular rituals exist in Western culture today to give a spiritual or larger-than-life dimension to more worldly events. Such secular rituals may be seen in the black robes of courtroom judges, the precisely choreographed changing of the guard at the Tomb of the Unknown Soldier, the daily recitation of the formal Pledge of Allegiance in certain American classrooms, and even the lowering of the ball in New York's Times Square on

---

*Readers searching for expanded information on the theatre's past should consult the long edition of this book or, for a detailed accounting of the theatre's history, surveys and guides such as those by Martin Banham and Oscar Brockett (see the Brief Bibliography at the back of this book).

DNA studies have shown that the San bushmen, seen here in a ritual trance-dance in their native Botswana, are direct descendants of the first evolved *Homo sapiens* from more than 100,000 years ago. The San remain hunter-gatherers; after a kill, the whole group chants and dances in a prehistoric desert ritual, summoning spiritual powers into each person's stomach so as to heal both physical and psychological illnesses.

New Year's Eve. Perhaps the most common collective ritual in Western culture is the wedding ceremony, with its formal costumes (tuxedo or tie-dyed), elevated language (psalms or sonnets), symbolic gift exchanges (ring or rings), and traditional music (Mendelssohn or McCartney). And the gravely cadenced march down the aisle transmits the ancient symbolism of bride handed from father to groom, even though such symbolism has lost much (if not all) of its original meaning over the years.

Whether sacred or secular, rituals dignify the events they represent, giving them enhanced meaning and authority. Most brides, for example, would feel shortchanged if their intended husband were to respond "uh-huh" instead of "I do," for while the literal meaning of "uh-huh" is perfectly clear, its everyday casualness implies a lack of public—and hence permanent—commitment.

Ritual is at the very origin of theatre. It is the act of performers re-creating, intensifying, and making meaningful the myths, beliefs, legends, and traditions common to their collective lives.

## Storytelling

Coming almost immediately after ritual, and quickly blended into it, is the art of storytelling. Ever since humans developed coherent speech, they have sought to recount their (and others') daily adventures, including stories of the hunt and histories of the tribe. Indeed, such storytelling surely went hand in glove with the development of speech itself, for why invent words like *glorious* and brave and *beautiful* if not to augment a story being told?

Such storytelling is more personal and individual than collective ritual performance, because it generally relies on a single voice—and therefore a single point of view. And while rituals may attract an audience, storytelling *requires* an audience: "hearer-spectators" who either don't know the story being told or are eager to hear it again with new details or fresh expression. Storytelling thus generates elements of character impersonation—the creation of voices, gestures, and facial expressions that reflect the personalities of the individuals portrayed—and seeks means to convey

The mudmen of Papua New Guinea in the South Pacific, isolated from the rest of the world until the twentieth century, still cover their bodies in mud and wear homemade clay masks for their ancient hunting ritual, performed in their villages and also, as shown here, at a biannual September gathering of tribes in the town of Goroka.

Dogon performers of the *dana* ritual, dancing on six-foot stilts, represent larger-than-life forces in the most literal way: by being double human size.

character emotions to the hearer-spectators. It also seeks to entertain, and thus it provides a structured *story*—rather than a random series of observations—which makes the narrative flow so as to compel audience engagement through suspense, varied graphic details, and a calculated momentum of escalating events that, in theatre, is called a *plot*. We can see all of these features in great storytelling today, both in surviving tribal cultures and in modern storytelling performances.

If ritual makes an event larger than life, storytelling makes it personal and affecting. While wedding rituals give wedlock a halo of dignity, marrying couples today generally humanize their own ceremony through their personal decisions about dress, language, music, setting, and staging, so that the resulting event combines collective ritual formality

with the marrying partners' "telling their story" of their own uniqueness—as individuals and as a couple.

## Shamanism, Trance, and Magic

Ancient dramas, or, more commonly, dance-dramas, began in the combination of ritual and storytelling, first on the African continent and afterward in tribal cultures around the world; they continue to be performed in, among other places, Siberia, South America, Southeast Asia, Australia, and Native American enclaves. Storytelling provided these performances with an audience-attracting narrative, a link to events in daily human life, the freshness of detail, and the individuality of each performer's special creativity. But ritual provided the intensity of the celebrants who could commit, body and soul, to the impersonation

Storytelling, an art more ancient than theatre, is still practiced as a public performance form, nowhere more successtuiny than at the annual Jonesborough, Tennessee, storytelling festival.

of divine spirits and the reenactment of what they believed to be real—though otherworldly—events. Belief in the power of such spirits to animate objects has been called *animism*, a catchall term describing the basic religious impulse of tribal culture in the world's prehistory. Humans who assume an animist role, mediating between spirit and earthly realities, are—in a similarly general way—called *shamans* (the word is originally Siberian), or go-betweens to the spirit world.

Shamans have been identified in tribal cultures since at least 13,000 B.C. In the eyes of his community, the shaman (almost always male in the ancient world) can cure the sick, aid the hunter, make the rain come and the crops grow. Shamans may also appear as mediums, taking the forms of otherworldly spirits, often animal or demonic. In most shamanic practices, the shaman performs his mastery—his travel between the human and spirit worlds and his incarnation of spiritual presences—in a state of trance.

Since the shaman's trance leads him to otherworldly presences, his performance takes on a magical

appearance. Ecstatic dancing and rapturous chanting are often primary features of shamanism, usually climaxing in violent shaking at astounding speeds. Astonishing acrobatics are common: in the pegele dance of Nigeria, shamans leap high in the air, spin around horizontally, and then come down far from where they left the ground. Sleight of hand may be involved in this "magic," as when the Formosan shaman "stabs" himself but really only pierces a blood-filled animal bladder hidden beneath his clothes. But genuine transformation, both physical and psychological, apparently takes place as well, permitting normally inhuman feats. The San bushmen of Namibia and Botswana eat live snakes and scorpions during hunting rituals. The Indian fakir (Arabic for "poor man"; the word is not related to fakery) hangs suspended from a hook through his flesh, and the Muslim dervish places glowing coals in his mouth, seemingly anesthetized from pain.

Costumes, body paint, headdresses, and, above all, masks disguise the shaman-performer, sometimes

The antiwitchcraft *kponiugo* mask of the Poro secret society of the Senufo tribe in West Africa's Ivory Coast is believed to protect the community from sorcerers and soul-stealers. Groups of Poro-maskers seem to spit fire between the alligator teeth of their open jaws. Wild boar tusks and antelope horns represent ferocity and gentleness.

completely, transforming him (often to himself as well as to observers) into a spirit presence. The mask, common in nearly all tribal cultures, was initially derived from the ecstatic contortion of the shaman's face during trance and subsequently served to represent the particular spirit that the trance-liberated shaman inhabited. But the mask has outlived the rituals that spawned it and remains today as the primary symbol of drama around the world.

## The Beginnings of Traditional Drama

When spoken dialogue comes into shamanistic rites, true traditional drama begins. For example, the Ceylon *sanniyakuma,* a traditional all-night curing ceremony of drumming and "devil dancing," portrays a suffering patient who seeks exorcism of the devil and includes this exchange:

YAKKA (*demon*): What is going on here? What does this
  noise mean?

DRUMMER: Somebody has fallen ill.

YAKKA: What are you going to do about it?

DRUMMER: We will give him a medicine.

YAKKA: That will not be of any use! Give me twelve presents
  and I will cure him."*

The dialogue creates suspense, conflict, danger, and action.

## Traditional Drama in Sub-Saharan Africa

But it is in sub-Saharan Africa where we can see, even today, the vast variety of traditional drama, where ritual and storytelling continually interweave. More than eight hundred languages are spoken in sub-Saharan Africa, and each represents a culture with roots in the past and social community in the present.

*The source for this dialogue and for other information in this section is largely E. T. Kirby, *Ur-Drama: The Origins of Theatre* (New York: New York University Press, 1975).

Many have long-standing traditions of dance-dramas. The Dogon performers of Mali are celebrated for their stilt walking and brightly colored masks. The Senufo of the Ivory Coast and Burkina Faso have animal masks—with the tusks of wild boars, the teeth of alligators, and the horns of antelopes—to frighten witches, and use brightly colored masks for women characters (played by men). In the Yacouba country of the Ivory Coast, traditional performers may wear elaborate beaded headdresses and full-face makeup instead of masks or, as in the panther dance-drama, cover their entire heads in painted cloth with panther ears. Acrobatics are a feature of Burundi performers, and rain-dance rituals are common in Botswana.

## Egyptian Drama

Theatrical performances almost certainly began in sub-Saharan Africa, but they soon drifted northward, down the Nile River to what we now know as Egypt. From there they spread to Mesopotamia, to Canaan, and eventually throughout the Middle East. The first written records we have of this activity are in Egypt, dating at least as far back as 2500 B.C. and perhaps as much as eight hundred years before that. Known as the *Abydos Passion Play,* this drama was apparently staged each spring in a boat procession along the Nile, with performances taking place at several temples along the way. The play tells the story of the murder of the wheat-god, Osiris, by his enemy Set (death). Scenes of lamentation by the priestesses Isis and Neptys, the tearing asunder of Osiris's body (which is then thrown into the Nile), Osiris's resurrection in the person of the god Horus, and combat between Horus and Set are the ingredients of this drama, portrayed through dialogue, dance, animal sacrifices, mimed violence, a coronation ceremony, and the performance of sacred fertility rites. Bold effects complement the symbolic actions: beads of carnelian (a translucent red stone) represent the great Eye of Horus, which is bloodied when Set plucks it out in the combat between the two demigods. Two maces represent Set's testicles, which Horus tears off and engrafts upon his own body to become stronger. The lowering and raising of ceremonial pillars into the Nile represent the burial and resurrection of Osiris.

Modern anthropology has made clear that this Egyptian springtime resurrection drama derives from even more ancient ritualized reenactments of the coming of spring that celebrated the rebirth of vegetation in the fields. Other similar Middle Eastern texts of that time also employed the same plot elements, such as the Babylonian play *Baal* (in which the god Baal dies, goes to the equivalent of Purgatory, and rises again on the third day) and the Hittite play *Snaring of the Dragon.* The death of Osiris, like the death of the wheat sheaf he represents, is not permanent. When his body is torn apart and thrown into the river, Osiris is resurrected, as is the wheat sheaf when its seeds are scattered by the wind and irrigated by the annual springtime flooding of the Nile. The tragedy of death, therefore, yields life, and the tears of tragic lamentation become nourishment for the seeds of life's renewal. Such tragedy, however painful, brings with it rejuvenation and hope. To emphasize the connection between the drama and nature's annual process of renewal, the *Abydos Passion Play* was performed at temples oriented so that their doorways faced the sun's rising on the vernal equinox, the first day of spring.

# THEATRE IN THE WEST

Drama did not continue to flourish in the Middle East, however. Much of the ancient theatre tradition there had disappeared by the third century B.C.; and the religion of Islam, which originated early in the seventh century A.D., viewed depictions of humans—in both the visual and the performing arts—as irreligious. But dramatic art was not stifled: from its Middle Eastern origins, it spread rapidly both east and west. In both India and Attica (now Greece), cultic rituals took place well before the first millennium B.C. And by the middle of that millennium, there arose in the West a spectacular theatre in the city-state of Athens, which over the course of 150 years produced four of the greatest playwrights and the most important dramatic theorist of the theatre's long history. Greek drama ushered in the Western strain of theatre, establishing its major genres of tragedy and comedy and characters and plotlines that underlie much of Western drama as we know it today.

## Greek Drama

The drama of Athens in the fifth century B.C. Still stands as one of the greatest—some would say *the* greatest—bodies of theatrical creation of all time. A magnificent and vigorous blend of myth, legend, philosophy, social commentary, poetry, dance, music, public participation, and visual splendor, Athenian drama created the forms of both tragedy and comedy, peopling them with characters that have become cultural archetypes in successive eras and laying thereby

Peter Hall's production of Euripides' *The Bacchae* played at England's National Theatre in 2002, and then to an audience of eleven thousand at the ancient theatre of Epidaurus in Greece. Hall and his designers employed bold and uniform colors—blood orange and sea green—to emphasize the masklike uniformity of members of the chorus as they collectively, not individually, wrestle with the play's giant spiritual themes.

the foundation not only of future Western drama but also of continuing debates as to how—and to what purposes—life should be lived.

Aristotle and later scholars tell us that Greek tragedy derived from ancient, orgiastic rites, filled with wine-drinking, phallus-worshipping, and the chanting of ancient poems, called *dithyrambs,* in honor of the Greek demigod Dionysus (the Greek god of fertility and wine and, eventually, the god of theatre as well). Thought to have come to Greece by way of the Middle East, Dionysus was the counterpart of Egypt's Osiris and, like the Egyptian wheat-god, was believed to have been dismembered in the winter and resurrected in the spring, proving a semi-divine analogue to the rebirth of vegetation on the Attic peninsula. And when classic Greek dramas came to be staged on the Athenian acropolis by the latter part of the sixth century B.C., it was at the Great Theatre of Dionysus, during the annual springtime festival known as the City Dionysia (or Great Dionysia), that the demigod's apparent rebirth was celebrated. Dionysus has, ever

since, been considered the founding deity of Western drama.

Although the transition from orgiastic celebrations to tragic drama is decidedly obscure, we do know that by the end of the fifth century B.C. three great tragedians—Aeschylus, Sophocles, and Euripides—had written and produced close to three hundred plays. Thirty-three have come down to us, and most of them are on every theatre scholar's list of the world's greatest dramatic masterpieces. Furthermore, there was a brilliant author of comic dramas—Aristophanes—from whom eleven plays survive, one of which (*The Frogs*) is a biting and vastly informative satire about the three great tragedians who shared his times. Other authors of Greek comedy, including Menander, and literary theorists, including Aristotle (with his Poetics, a treatise on tragedy), plied their trades in the century that followed, making for one of the richest bodies of dramatic work ever created.

Greek tragedies explored the social, psychological, and religious meanings of the ancient gods and heroes

Toe Greek theatre of Priene, in modern-day Turkey, dates from about 300 B.C. Unlike most Greek theatres, Priene was never rebuilt by the Romans and thus remains one of the best examples of a hillside Greek *theatron*. The standing row of columns and connecting lintel once made up the front of the stone *skene*, or stagehouse.

of Greek history and myth, as well as current events; the comedies presented contemporary issues affecting all Athenians. Both types of drama were first staged in a simple wheat-threshing circle on the ground (*the orchestra*), with a dressing hut (*skene*) behind it; the audience was seated on an adjacent hillside (the *theatron*). As Greek culture expanded, however, huge amphitheaters—the largest of which seated upward of fifteen thousand people—were built in Athens and subsequently throughout the growing Greek empire. Many of those later theatres remain today, in various stages of ruin and renovation, in parts of Greece, Italy, and Turkey; and of course the terms *orchestra, scene,* and *theatre* remained to define the theatre of future eras.

Ancient Greek actors were all male. They performed in masks, partly to indicate the age, gender, personality, and social standing of the characters they were playing and partly to amplify their voices. (The word *person* derives from the Latin *per sonum,* or "for

sound," which initially referred to the amplification of the actor's voice and later became the root of the term *dramatis personae,* or "cast of characters"—that is, "persons.") Each tragic actor wore elevated shoes (*kothurnoi*), an elaborate headdress (*onkos*), and a long, usually colorful gown (*himation*) with a tunic over it (*chlamys*) to enhance the larger-than-life struggles between royal heroes, gods, and demigods. Plays were performed with only two (later three) principal actors, who, by changing masks, could play several parts each during the course of a play. The actors were supported by a Greek invention, a chorus of twelve or fifteen singer-dancers (usually representing the local populace) who chanted their lines in unison or through a single chorus leader. When the skene became an elevated stage for the principal actors, the chorus members remained in the orchestra below, separated from the main interactions of the principals.

Greek tragedy was chanted or sung, not spoken; unfortunately, the music has not survived. And the

In the dithyrambs that preceded ancient Greek tragedy, there was a chorus of fifty performers. Romanian director Silviu Purcarete, at the National Theatre of Craiova, employed a chorus of double that number—fifty men and fifty women—in his innovative production of *Les Danaïdes,* adapted from Aeschylus's war tetralogy, *The Suppliants.* Purcarete's highly stylized production, performed (in French) in Manhattan's Damrosch Park as part of the Lincoln Center Theatre Festival in 1997, had clear overtones of current problems in eastern Europe and the Balkans and a strong emphasis on political terrorism, sexual assault, and the ambiguity of gender and cultural identity.

chorus danced, as it did in the dithyrambic ceremonies, sometimes formally, sometimes with wild abandon. Greek tragedy, therefore, is the foundation not merely of Western drama but of Western musical theatre, including opera. Greek comedy, in contrast, is the foundation of burlesque, satire, and television sitcoms. The plays of Aristophanes, referred to as Old Comedy, are filled with broad physical humor, gross sexual gags and innuendos, and brilliant wordplay and repartee, often at the expense of contemporary politicians and celebrities. The later plays of Menander, known as New Comedy, gave rise to "stock characters" (such as the bumbling suitor and the timid warrior) and comic plot devices (such as mistaken identity) that are recurrent elements of thirty-minute network television.

The City Dionysia was a weeklong festival of celebrations and dramatic competitions. On the first day, during introductory ceremonies, each playwright (selected in advance by civic authorities) introduced his cast and announced the theme of his work. The second day featured processions, sacrifices, and the presentation of ten dithyrambs; and on the third day, five comedies were played. On the fourth, fifth, and sixth days, the three competing playwrights presented—each on a separate day—three related tragedies (a *trilogy*), followed by a comic variation or parody (a *satyr play*) on the same theme. The authors served as the directors of their works. On the seventh, and final, day, judging took place, and prizes for the best play and best leading actor were awarded. It appears that the entire population of freeborn males,

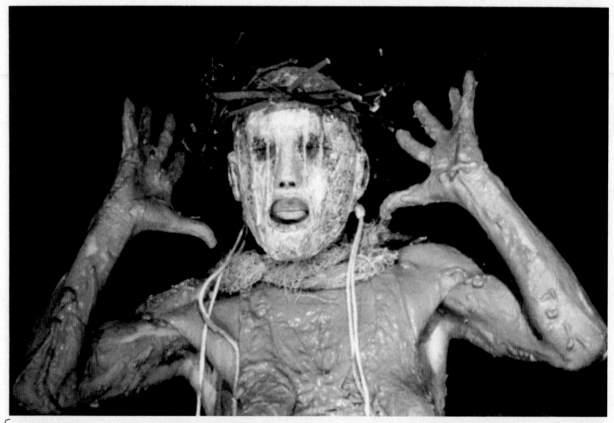

The most ancient theatre is often the most modern. This 1996 English production of Sophocles' Oedipus Tyrannos, with Greg Hicks shown here as Tiresias, premiered at the ancient Greek theatre of Epidaurus before reopening at the National Theatre in London. Packed houses greeted it with rousing acclaim in both locations.

and perhaps of freeborn females (we don't know this for certain), attended these performances and rooted for their favorites; judging by later commentaries, outstanding dramatists and actors were as famous then as are today's best-known film directors and movie stars. Clearly the City Dionysia of fifth-century Athens was a monumental and glorious undertaking that led to some of the most thrilling dramas and theatrical spectacles in history.

## Roman Drama

Greek civilization, battered by internal wars, had lost its leading edge by the end of the fifth century B.C., and the power balance in the Mediterranean shifted, in succeeding centuries, to the growing Roman Empire. Excelling in architecture and engineering more than in dramatic creativity, the Romans created some astonishing stage buildings, of which more than two

hundred (most dating from the first centuries A.D.) survive to the present day. Roman architects dispensed with the Greek hillside theatron and threshing-circle orchestra and designed a theatre that was an entirely integrated structure set on a level plain. They also cut the orchestra in half and created tunnel entrances to it (*vomitoria*) on both sides. The simple Greek skene became an elaborate three-story wall (the *frons scaenae*) decorated by dozens of statues.

Rarely as impressive as Roman architects, Roman dramatists almost always drew upon Greek sources for their work; indeed, most Roman plays are about Greek characters and Greek struggles. The Roman comic playwrights Plautus and Terence were quite popular in their time, however, and many of their works survive and are performed occasionally today, as are (albeit more rarely) the chamber tragedies of Seneca, a protégé (and victim) of Emperor Nero. All three of these Roman dramatists, in fact, were very

As the sympathetic chorus peers out at the audience for help, Prometheus struggles against his imprisonment in New York's Classic Stage Company production of *Prometheus Bound,* a Greek tragedy of unknown authorship but long attributed to Aeschylus.

popular and much admired by writers and audiences during the European Renaissance. Roman theatre, however, degenerated into sheer spectacle and decadence by the end of the empire, as many theatres were converted into arenas for gladiatorial combat, pitched sea battles, and gruesome public massacres. Together, Greek and Roman drama form a "classical theatre" tradition that has been referenced over and over in Western drama from the Renaissance and right up to the present day.

## Medieval Drama

The fall of Rome (around the middle of the first millennium A.D.) brought to an end the classical era of theatre. Both the early Christian and the newly founded Islamic religions banned theatrical representations altogether, partly in reaction to the excesses of late Roman theatre. And when Western drama

reappeared, as it did in Europe shortly before the year 1000, it was an altogether different product, sponsored by the same Christian Church that had once banned it. The earliest known dramatization of that period was not a play in the ordinary sense but rather a brief moment in the church's Easter service, when officiating monks reenact the Biblical story of the Three Marys as they visit the thomb of Jesus. "Whom seek ye?" (*Quem queritis*?) an angel asks. "Jesus of Nazareth," reply the Marys, whereupon they are told, "He is not here, He has risen." They then break into a chorus of hallelujahs. It is fascinating, of course, that medieval European drama, like the drama of ancient Egypt and ancient Greece, began with the springtime celebration of a divine resurrection. This simple liturgical playlet, now known as the *Quem Queritis,* became the first of literally hundreds of church-sponsored dramatizations depicting and celebrating the Judeo-Christian story of humankind—from the Creation of

Adam and Eve (Alessandro Mastrobuono and Erin Jellison) take their instructions from God (Tom Fitzpatrick) in Brian Kulick's 2003 *The Mysteries* in Los Angeles. The actors would probably have worn flesh-colored body stockings in medieval times, but contemporary theatre is able, on this occasion, to express their innocence before the Fall more literally.

the Universe and Adam and Eve to Doomsday and the Harrowing of Hell.

Medieval drama remained in church liturgy for nearly two centuries, but by about 1250, Bible-based drama had moved outdoors into the churchyards and then into the public streets of every country in Europe. By this time the medieval "mystery plays," as they were then called, were performed in the emerging modern languages of French, English, Spanish, German, and Italian rather than Latin, and included scenes that were more secular than purely religious, often with contemporary political overtones. The actors were no longer monks but ordinary citizens, some of them—those who had mastered the leading parts—well paid for their efforts. Though anonymous to us, the authors were highly prized by their communities, as they converted the formal prose of the Bible to comic interplay, jesting repartee, swashbuckling bluster, and intricate versification.

Entire festivals of such plays, numbering in the dozens, were presented in hundreds of European towns every spring, dominating city life where and when they were played, and attracting rural audiences from all around. On the European continent, such drama festivals lasted for many days or even weeks, with huge casts performing on a series of stages (known as *mansions*) set up next to each other in the town plaza or marketplace. Audiences could stroll from one play to the next, as the plays were performed in sequence. In England, however, the plays were performed on wagon-mounted stages, one for each playlet, that were wheeled from one audience site to another during a daylong springtime festival known as Corpus Christi.

At first glance, these mystery plays may appear stylistically primitive, at least in contrast to the splendor of the classic Greek tragedies, but twenty-first-century productions have demonstrated their tremendous

Passion plays, centering on Jesus's trial and crucifixion, were among the most powerful dramas of medieval times. Such plays are still seen in countries around the wo rld, notably in cities and villages throughout Mexico during *semana santa* (Easter Holy Week). Here, in the crucifixion scene of the 2009 passion play of Tlalixtac, a suburb of Oaxaca, Mexico, Jesus has been nailed to the cross by Roman soldiers, one of whom raises "vinegar" (sour wine mixed with myrrh) to his lips. The play's spectators surround the action on all sides.

and published, their influence—on all arts and culture, not merely the theatre—proved overwhelming. This period in which ancient culture was "reborn" and fused—sometimes uneasily—with the medieval and Gothic forms that had been dominant for centuries is called the Renaissance.

By most reckonings, the Renaissance began in Italy, where the plays of Plautus and Seneca were first translated in the 1470s. Amateur productions of these Italian translations soon became popular, giving rise to freer adaptations, which are now known as *commedia erudita,* or "learned comedies." By the 1520s, the Florentine diplomat and essayist Niccolò Machiavelli was famous throughout Italy for his learned comedies based on—and taking off from—Roman forebears, and by the middle of the sixteenth century a semi-improvised variation of that comedy, known as *commedia dell'arte,* was performed by itinerant professional actors throughout the Italian peninsula and even beyond. Soon both commedia dell'arte and scripted plays in modern European languages—based on classic or current themes, not Biblical ones—were common throughout Europe.

It was in England that the Renaissance brought forth the greatest dramatic masterpieces of that (or perhaps any) era, in the works of William Shakespeare. Coming of age during the reign of Queen Elizabeth I(1558-1603), Shakespeare began his career in a vibrant world of palatial court theatres, freestanding outdoor "public theatres" that dominated the London skyline, and companies of professional actors who entertained court and public at home and on tour. This "Elizabethan" theatre featured dozens of playwrights whose works remain popular today; Christopher Marlowe, Ben Jonson, and John Webster are three of Shakespeare's most prominent contemporaries, but none, however, was fully comparable to Shakespeare himself. Alone among the world's great authors, Shakespeare was equally adept at producing exemplary postclassical masterpieces of both comedy and tragedy. Four centuries after they were written (from approximately 1580 to 1610), his plays are the most-produced dramas in literally thousands of theatres around the world; they are, indeed, the primary repertoire of over a hundred theatre companies named after him.

Shakespeare was not only an author; he was also an actor and part owner of his own theatre company, the King's Men, and of The Globe theatre in London, which his company built and operated; a new Globe, in fact, has been built near the original site and, since

dramatic impact, even to a religiously diverse contemporary audience. And the scale of medieval theatre production—with its mansions, rolling stages, and casts of hundreds-was simply astonishing. Like the great Gothic cathedrals—also created anonymously and at roughly the same time—the Bible-based medieval theatre was a monumental enterprise that affected the lives of the entire culture that created and experienced it.

## Renaissance Drama

Medieval drama was created in ignorance of its classical predecessors, but when, in the High Middle Ages, Roman and then Greek texts began to be translated

An eighteenth-century illustration of Italian *commedia dell'arte*.

its 1997 opening, has been used for the presentation of Shakespearean-era (and occasionally other) plays. With its "thrust stage" and standing-room "pit" open to the sky and surrounded by thatched-roof seating galleries on three levels, the modern Globe may not—because of fire regulations—seat the three thousand people accommodated by the original building, but its restoration helps us better understand the vigor of Shakespearean-era staging and the potential of the drama to electrify a large and diverse audience with profound intelligence and passion, as well as comically expressive hijinks. Shakespeare's plays are well known to literary scholars for their poetic brilliance, relentless investigation of the human condition, and deeply penetrating character portrayals, but they are also filled with music, dancing, ribaldry, puns, satire, pageantry, and humor, which only performance brings to life. They are both great dramatic art and magnificent theatrical entertainment.

## The Royal Theatre

If the Renaissance was the rebirth of classical civilization, the age that followed was a vast consolidation and refinement of what had come before; it was an era organized intellectually by the then-emerging empirical sciences and rational philosophies and politically by the increasing importance of European royalty. The seventeenth-century theatre of this so-called Royal era featured the dramas of Pedro Calderón de la Barca at the court of King Philip IV in Spain, the tragedies of jean Racine and Pierre Corneille and the comedies of Moliere under King Louis XIV in France, and the Restoration comedies of William Wycherley and William Congreve under English king Charles II, who was crowned when the royal family was restored to the throne after eighteen years of English civil war and Puritan rule.

Royal era plays were generally aimed more at the aristocracy than at the general populace and reflected the gentility of the seemingly refined taste of courtly patrons. Rational sensibility dominated the times: theories of drama, adapted from Aristotle and hence called "neoclassic," sought to regularize plays within "reasonable" frameworks of time and place, establish strictly measured structures for dramatic verse, unify styles around set genres, and eliminate onstage depictions of physical violence. Indoor theatres,

Like its predecessor, the modern Globe Theatre replica in London schedules performances by daylight, come rain or shine. As in Shakespeare's day, a sizable portion of the audience (the "groundlings," as they were called in Elizabethan times) observes from a standing-room pit in front of the stage; everyone else sits on hard wooden benches in the surrounding galleries. Shown here, the concluding dance of the Globe's 1998 *As You Like it* enchants the audience on all sides of the stage, which is "thrust" into their midst.

The Comedy of *Errors* may be Shakespeare's first play. In this work, based on a comedy/farce by the Roman playwright Plautus—but even funnier—Shakespeare clearly proved that he could entertain an audience in the 1590s, and he can certainly do so today. This scene in the 2009 Chicago Shakespeare Theatre adaptation shows the stock characters, exaggerated physical characterizations, hilarious costumes and makeup, and super-rambunctious action that have always been factors of farcical performance. Pictured are Kymberly Mellen (*center*) as the (presumed) wronged wife, Kevin Gudahl as the quavering servant who faces her wrath, and Angela Ingersoll as the terrified servant peeking through the kitchen cupboard. David Bell adapted and directed.

The balcony scene from the 2006 Royal Shakespeare Company production of Romeo and *Juliet* took an athletic turn within and without Katrina Lindsay's unconventional design, up and down which the actors—Rupert Evans and Morven Christie—clambered with alacrity and grace. Nancy Meckler directed. Katrina Lindsay designed the spare scaffold that represented the balcony and much more.

Matthew Rhys (*left*) as Romeo and Tam Mutu as Tybalt duel in this 2004 Royal Shakespeare Company production of *Romeo and Juliet,* directed by Peter Gill.

Calderón's *Life Is a Dream* is one of the great classics of the seventeenth-century Spanish stage. Noted Cuban American playwright Nilo Cruz (*Anna and the Tropics*) adapted the play, and Kate Whoriskey directed it for its world premiere at South Coast Repertory in Costa Mesa, California. "I've always adored the poetic language of *Life Is a Dream* and its mythical landscape," said Cruz. "The play is full of questions, and I think Calderón's greatness as a playwright lies in the rich humanity of his characters, and the questions they pose." Daniel Breaker is the hero, the banished prince, Segismundo; designers were Walt Spangler (sets), Ilona Somogyi (costumes), and Scott Zielinski (lighting).

lit by candles instead of sunlight, replaced the outdoor public theatres of earlier times, providing more intimate and comfortable surroundings for an increasingly well-dressed audience. Furthermore, protection from wind and weather permitted elaborately painted scenery and stage machinery. Several of these theatres are architectural gems that have remained in continuous use to the present day. Style, wit, grace, and class distinction became not merely the framework of drama but its chief subject, and the fan and the snuffbox became signature props. This was also the Western world's first era of extensive theatrical commentary and thus the first from which we have detailed reports and evidence—both textual and visual—of the era's dramatic repertoires, acting styles, artists' lives, and manifestos and controversies that continue to define, in sum, the art of drama.

## The Romantic Theatre

Every era in theatre is, to some extent, a rebellion against the previous one, and the romantic theatre of the eighteenth and nineteenth centuries was, in the main, a bold rejection of the rational decorum of the preceding Royal era and its spirit of ordered, elegant, and enlightened debate. Romanticism, in contrast, was florid, exotic, grotesque, sprawling, and imbued with the free-flowing spirit of the individual rather than the social organization of class, court, or scientific or aesthetic academy. Compassion, rather than style and wit, was central to the romantic creed, and authors, such as Johann Wolfgang von Goethe and Friedrich von Schiller in Germany and Victor Hugo in France, intrigued audiences with their deep humanitarian concerns in plays that dealt with devils

# Spotlight

## Did Shakespeare Write Shakespeare?

Students occasionally wonder about the so-called authorship question, which challenges the commonly held belief that Shakespeare's plays were written by Shakespeare. Several books have argued against Shakespeare's authorship, and some distinguished thinkers (among them Mark Twain and Sigmund Freud) have shared their doubts as well, but there is simply no question to be posed: the evidence that Shakespeare wrote Shakespeare's plays is absolutely overwhelming. Nor has a shred of evidence appeared thus far to indicate that anyone else wrote them. Not a single prominent Elizabethan scholar has accepted the "anti-Stratfordian" (as proponents of other authors are called) argument, which America's most noted Shakespearean scholar, Harold Bloom, simply dismisses as "lunacy."

How can there be a question? Shakespeare is named as author on the title page of seventeen separate publications during his lifetime and is cited as the author of eleven known plays in a book published when he was thirty-four. He is credited as the author of the First Folio in its title, *Mr. William Shakespeare's Comedies, Histories, and Tragedies,* published just seven years after his death; the Folio's editors were his acting colleagues, who describe Shakespeare as fellow actor, author, and friend, and their preface also includes four poems—one by dramatist Ben Jonson—each unequivocally referring to Shakespeare as the author of plays. Surviving records show him performing in his plays at the courts of both Queen Elizabeth and King James, and he was buried, along with his wife, daughter, and son-in-law (and no one else), in the place of greatest honor in his hometown church. An inscribed funeral monument, mentioned in the Folio and showing him with pen in hand, looks down on Shakespeare's grave and was regularly visited in the coming years by persons wishing to see, as one wrote, the last resting place of "the wittiest poet in the world." Birth, marriage, death, heraldic, and other legal records, plus dozens of citations during and shortly after his life tell us more about dramatist William Shakespeare than we have collected for all but a few common-born citizens of his era.

So, what is left to argue? Anti-Stratfordians maintain that the evidence doesn't paint the picture we should expect of such a magnificent playwright: he apparently didn't go to college; his name was spelled in several different ways and sometimes hyphenated; his signatures indicate poor handwriting; his wife and daughters were probably illiterate; he didn't leave any books in his will; no ceremony marked his death; he never traveled to Italy, where many of his plays were set; and an early engraving of the Stratford monument looks different—lacking its pen—than the monument does now.

Little of this is provable, however, and none of it is remotely convincing even if true. Aeschylus, Euripides, and George Bernard Shaw didn't go to college, either. Shakespeare's knowledge of Italy is nothing an intelligent person couldn't have picked up in an afternoon's conversation—and it wasn't that accurate (Shakespeare writes of one who could "lose the tide" facilitating a trip from Verona to Milan—where no water route exists). Many people have unreadable signatures, and in Shakespeare's day neither spelling nor hyphenation was standardized, nor was literacy a norm among country women. That we don't know of a memorial ceremony doesn't mean there wasn't one, and evidence clearly indicates the engraving of a penless monument was simply one of many errors in a too-hastily-prepared book. And if Shakespeare maintained a library, he could simply have given it to his son-in-law (a doctor) before his death or left it to be passed on to his wife along with his house and furnishings, or perhaps he kept books in a private office at The Globe theatre in London, which burned to the ground three years before his death. And who actually knows that he didn't travel to Italy or even study at a university for that matter? We know next to nothing about Shakespeare between the ages of twenty-one and twenty-eight; he could have been anywhere and done anything.

But we do know he was a man of the theatre. And obviously a genius. What else need we know? Why must we insist that he have good handwriting? or literate relatives? Because we do? But we're not Shakespeare, and Shakespeare doesn't have to be like us.

And absolutely no evidence exists that anyone elsewrote any of the plays—which explains why there are nearly a half dozen claimants to this phantom position of the "real" Shakespeare.

It is impossible to represent the entirety of either argument in a few paragraphs (one of the books, proposing the Earl of Oxford, runs over 900 pages), but the entire anti-Stratfordian case, diverting as it may be, is painstakingly and effectively refuted in Irvin Leigh Matus's relentlessly straightforward Shakespeare, *in Fact* (1994).

It is, of course, possible that all the evidence we now have—all of it—has somehow been fabricated. This would mean Shakespeare managed to fool—or buy off—almost everyone in his town, everyone in his church, everyone in his theatre company, everyone at two royal courts, everyone in the London theatre world, most of the printers and booksellers in England, and everyone they talked to. We would be asked to believe that this gigantic lie (for which we have not a trace of evidence) never got out, not through the revival of his plays after his death and then later during the Restoration era. It would have been the most stupendous hoax in human history, incomparable to the insignificant hoax proffered to us by anti-Stratfordians today.

Michel Vuillermoz is the famously hook-nosed poet-warrior Cyrano de Bergerac, kneeling above his young friend Christian (Éric Ruf), who is dying in the arms of Roxanne (Françoise Gillard), who is tragicall, fated to love them both. This Comédie-Française production of Edmond Rostand's magnificent late romantic classic of 1897, titled with its hero's name, was directed by Denis Podalydès in 2006; Ruf served also the scenic designer.

and monsters, robbers and priests, hunchbacks and heroes. Romanticism gave rise to melodrama and grand opera and to much of the anarchic passion and sprawling sentiment of modern realism as well. Moreover, the romantic quest for the foreign and exotic represented Western drama's first serious reengagement with the theatre of the East. This, then, is a good point at which to return to drama's earlier years—to the Eastern strain of theatre that sprang from Egyptian and Canaanite beginnings and soon resurfaced on the Indian subcontinent and thereafter throughout Asia.

## THEATRE IN THE EAST

It is misleading to refer to an "Asian theatre," for drama in Asia is as rich and diverse as theatre in the West, if not more so. Asia, after all—with three-fifths of the world's population—comprises dozens of countries, hundreds of languages, and thousands of identified theatre forms. Nevertheless, although Asian dramatic forms differ markedly from each other, they generally adhere to many fundamental principles, mostly in strong contrast to Western traditions:

- Asian drama is almost never just "spoken"; rather, it is danced, chanted, mimed, and very often sung. Mere spoken drama, when it does occur in the East, is generally recognized as Western in origin or influence.

- Asian dramatic language is invariably rhythmic and melodic; it is appreciated for its sound as much as (or more than) for its meaning. Alliteration, imagery, rhyme, and verbal juxtaposition are often as important in Asian dramatic dialogue as logic, persuasive rhetoric, and realism are in Western drama; and the sonic value of words is as valued by an Asian audience as their semantic value is by a Western audience.

- Asian theatre is ordinarily more visual and sensual than literary or intellectual. Although some Asian dramatists are known for their literary gifts (and several are mentioned in the following discussion), few Asian plays have been widely circulated for general reading or academic study. Most Asians would consider the act of reading a play—separate from seeing it in performance—a rather odd pastime. Rather, Asian drama is inextricable from the arts of performance that bring it to life: dance, song, mime, gesture, acrobatics, puppetry, music, sound, costume, and makeup.

- Asian theatre has a strong emphasis on storytelling and myth, yet it is not tightly plotted, as Western drama is, and rarely leads to escalating incidents, stunning reversals, crescendoing climaxes, or elaborate plot closures. Asian theatre, whose metaphysical roots lie in those timeless meditations on human existence that are at the very heart of Hindu and Buddhist cultures, instead may seem, to Western tastes, leisurely and almost wandering. Certainly, Asian theatre's dramatic appeal is more continuous and rapturous than cathartic or arresting.

- Asian theatre is broadly stylized. As one might expect of a dramatic form imbued with music and dance, slice-of-life realism is practically unknown. Brilliantly colored costumes and makeup, long and obviously artificial beards, elegantly danced battle scenes, and live instrumental accompaniment are almost standard in traditional Asian theatre.

- Actors train in traditional Asian dramatic forms through an intense apprentice system beginning in early childhood and lasting into early middle age. Most Asian actors, indeed, are born or adopted into their trade.

- The Asian theatre is deeply traditional. Although there are modern and avant-garde theatre movements in most Asian countries—and some Western influence is evident in many of them— what is most remarkable about Eastern theatre is its near-universal consonance with folk history, ancient religions, and cultural myths.

## Indian Sanskrit Drama

Asian drama began in India, where it sprang from the same Middle Eastern roots as its Western counterpart; some scholars even believe that the Greek Dionysus had an Indian heritage. Indeed, tantalizing connections between ancient India and Greece, one scholar argues, suggest an "Indo-Greek theatre" of the first millennium B.C.* These include fragments of Indian archeological remains that seem to be based on Greek dramatic texts and intriguing anecdotes of Greek theatre productions mounted by officers of Alexander the Great during his Indian invasion in 326 B.C.

Despite its connections to Greek theatre, Indian theatre is very much an independent Asiatic creation, which was first known to us in the form of a native Sanskrit dance-theatre that achieved a solid foothold on the subcontinent somewhere around 200 B.C. and remained popular for more than a thousand years thereafter.† Sanskrit plays survive from about A.D. 100, and a comprehensive book of dramatic theory, the

Natyasastra, or "treatise on theatre," ascribed to Bharata Muni, dates from somewhere between 200 B.C. and A.D. 200. The most comprehensive study of theatre surviving from the ancient world, the Natyasastra contains detailed analyses of Sanskrit dramatic texts, theatre buildings, acting, staging, music, gesture, dance, and even theatre-company organization. The treatise describes ten major genres of Sanskrit drama, including two primary ones: the *nataka*, which was based on well-known heroic stories of kings or sages, and the *prakarana*, based on the theme of love. The greatest Sanskrit poet, Kalidasa, wrote his masterpiece, *Sakuntala and the Ring of Recollection*, in the nataka style somewhere around the fifth century A.D. *The Little Clay Cart*, attributed to Sudraka, is the best known of two surviving examples of prakarana.

Sanskrit theatre, as far as we can tell (no ruins or drawings survive), was performed indoors, within roofed buildings. Rectangular in structure and fitted with a stage of about forty-eight by twenty-four feet, these buildings could seat somewhere between two hundred and five hundred spectators. Two doors, with an onstage orchestra between them, provided access to the dressing area behind the stage, and four columns held up the roof or an upper pavilion. Carved wooden elephants, tigers, and snakes adorned the pillars and perhaps the ceiling. Sanskrit drama was danced and acted with an onstage instrumental and percussion accompaniment. Performers, all from priestly castes and trained from early childhood, were virtuosos of their demanding art. Sanskrit drama died out around the tenth century, as the broad-based Hindu court culture fragmented in the wake of repeated Mongol invasions and the peoples of India fell back into preexisting regional cultures and languages. In succeeding centuries, an abundance of provincial theatre forms became popular throughout the subcontinent, a vast number of which remain to the present day. Despite their many differences, all Indian drama forms share many of the fundamental theatre aesthetics of their Sanskrit predecessors and the doctrines of the ancient *Natyasastra*.

## Indian Kathakali

Today the most widely known regional dance-drama form is the *kathakali* ("story play"). It originated in rural villages in the province of Kerala in the seventeenth century, and currently plays in many urban centers in province and that abroad. Kathakali is a

---

*M. L. Varadpande, *Ancient Indian and Indo-Greek Theatre* (New Delhi: Abhinav, 1981).

†All dates in early Indian drama are extremely approximate, within a plus-or-minus margin of sometimes up to four or five *centuries*.

In the Indian *kathakali* dance-drama, royal characters wear an elaborate *kiritam*, or crown, which frames the actor's eye movements—one of the most intensively studied skills of kathakali performers. Kalamandalam Gopi, a senior kathakali maestro, is shown here in the role of King Rugmangada in *Rugmangadacharitam*, performed in Trichur, Kerala (India), in 1993.

contortions, they reveal subtleties of meaning and characterization that are barely suggested by the text. Consequently, actors train rigorously for kathakali performance from early childhood, achieving mastery—if at all—only by about age forty. Highly stylized makeup and costuming also convey characterization and attitude: red- or black-bearded characters represent evil, white-bearded ones the divine. No scenery is used in kathakali, as plays are presented in arbitrary sites, with four simple poles defining the acting area.

## Chinese Xiqu

China, Asia's largest nation, is Asia's oldest continuous culture, as well as the home of Asia's oldest continuous theatre tradition. Like all Asian drama, Chinese theatre is more sung than spoken, but since Chinese speech itself is semimusical—it is based on tonal changes as well as syllabic pronunciation—all traditional Chinese theatre is known by the Chinese term *xiqu* ("tuneful theatre"), which we translate as "Chinese opera."

Although forms of xiqu existed in China before the first century A.D., the first well-defined Chinese opera form, known as *zaju* ("various plays"), appeared in China during the Song dynasty in the tenth century, reaching its golden age in the thirteenth century under the Mongol emperor Kublai Khan. Zaju was a comedic music-dance-drama, with acrobatics and clowning; it was so popular that a single amusement park in thirteenth-century Keifeng (then China's northern capital) featured at least fifty indoor zaju theatres, the largest holding several thousand people.

By the end of the Ming dynasty, in 1644, zaju had been succeeded by a more stately, aristocratic, and poetic opera known as *kunqu*, originating from the town of Kunshan; soon thereafter kunqu became the favored theatre entertainment of the Chinese court. Kunqu is still performed today. More popular theatre developed around the same time in the form of a more boisterous "clapper opera," characterized by the furious rhythmic beating of drumsticks on a hardwood block. And in subsequent years, many regional theatre styles, influenced by the zaju, kunqu, and clapper-opera forms, arose throughout the country. Today there are as many as 360 variations of Chinese opera in the People's Republic, most of them—such as Cantonese opera, Sichuan opera, Hui opera—known by their regional origins.

The most famous Chinese opera in modern times is Beijing (Peking) opera, which is known in Chinese as *jingju*, or "theatre of the capital." Jingju was founded in

drama based on any of thousands of stories from the two great Indian epics, the *Ramayana* and the *Mahabharata*. Kathakali performance itself is somewhat of an epic as well, with its outdoor performances lasting from about ten at night until well past dawn the next day. Traditionally, audience members are free to leave, take naps, and eat during the performance; today, however, kathakali is more often performed in the three-hour evening time blocks common to Western theatre.

In kathakali, the text is sung—to a percussion accompaniment of gongs, drums, and cymbals—by two singers seated at the side. Actors dance and pantomime the dramatic action; by employing precise and elaborate hand gestures, footwork patterns, distinctive eye and eyebrow movements, and postural

Professional-level acrobatics are a fundamental part of all *kunqu*, and indeed of all Chinese opera. Here, in Hell, a devil leaps high over Du Liniang to terrorize her in the Suzhou Kun Opera production of *Peony Pavillion* at the University of California—Irvine in 2006.

performers' individual skills (*gong*); in particular, actors must master the classic fourfold combination of singing (*chang*), speech (*nian*), acting and movement (zuo), and martial arts and acrobatics (*da*). Nearly all Chinese opera performers are proficient in all four of these arts; the greatest performing artists—who are famous throughout China—have mastered each of them to virtuoso standards. Indeed, it might be said that the equivalent of a great Chinese actor in the West would be someone who could perform for the American Ballet Theatre, La Scala Opera, the Royal Shakespeare Company, the Ringling Brothers Circus, and the French Foreign Legion—all on the same evening.

Chinese opera offers a spectacular visual feast, with dazzling costumes, huge glittery headdresses, and brilliantly colorful face painting. Actors of both sexes wear multilayered gowns in bold primary colors; many of them have "water-sleeves," which fall all the way to the floor. Chinese opera singing, much of it in an extreme falsetto (originally employed so that actors could be heard over the din of people talking during the performance), is accompanied by the near-constant clanging of gongs and cymbals, clapper claps, drumbeats, and the furious strumming of various two-stringed fiddles. Movement skills include a rapid heel-to-toe walk, contortionist bendings and swayings, sudden jerks and freezes, and thrilling displays of full-stage acrobatics: continuously back-springing performers bound across the stage in a literal blur, and in battle scenes combatants repel spear thrusts—sixteen at a time, all from different directions—with both hands and both feet. Chinese opera has never been dependent on scenery—an actor who enters holding a paddle behind him is assumed to be on a boat; an actor entering with a riding crop is assumed to be on horseback—but its storytelling conventions and its spectacular musical, visual, and acrobatic displays offer audiences one of the world's most thrilling and magnificent theatrical experiences.

## Japanese Nō

The island nation of Japan has created two great theatre forms, *nō* and *kabuki*. Each is virtually a living museum of centuries-old theatre practice. No and kabuki are performed today in very much the same fashion as in earlier times, yet each is also an immensely satisfying theatre experience for modern audiences attuned to the Japanese culture.

Nō is Japan's most revered and cerebral theatre. It is also the oldest continuously performed drama in

1790, when, in celebration of the emperor's eightieth birthday, a group of actors from the mountains of Anhui—led by one Cheng Chang-geng—came to Beijing and amazed the court with their brilliant and innovative style of singing, music, and (in particular) acrobatics and martial arts. As local actors assimilated the Anhui style with their own, a new "capital" style was developed, reaching its current form by about 1850, by which time it had become the dominant popular theatre of all China. Beijing opera remains not just one of the great glories of the world's traditional performing arts but-after a nearly thirteen-year hiatus occasioned by the Cultural Revolution in China in the 1960s and 1970s—a highly popular national entertainment in China and around the world.

Because the stories and plots of Chinese opera are normally ancient and well known, the actual staging of such works becomes, above all, a celebration of the

The Monkey King-a ferocious scamp—is the most enduring character in *xiqu;* he is always dressed in yellow, as shown here in this Shanghai Jingju Theatre production of *Pansi Cave.*

the world. Perfected in the fourteenth and fifteenth centuries almost solely by a single father-son team (Kan'ami and Zeami), who between them wrote and produced approximately 240 of the surviving plays, no is a highly ceremonial drama, mysterious and tragic, that almost always portrays supernatural events and characters. All nō plays center on a single character, the *shite* (the "doer"), who is interrogated, prompted, and challenged by a secondary character, called the *waki*. Whereas waki characters are always living male humans—usually ministers, commoners, or priests—shite characters may be gods, ghosts, women, animals, or warriors. The shite role, unlike the waki, is played in a mask. Nō actors—all of them male—train for only one of these role types, which they normally perform throughout their careers. Long training provides actors with the precise choreography and the musical notations required of their danced and chanted performance.

The actual no stage is a precisely measured square of highly polished Japanese cypress flooring, about eighteen feet across, supported from below by large earthenware jars that resonate with the actors' footstompings. A bridgelike runway (*hashigakari*) provides stage access from stage right; it is used for the solemn entrances and exits particularly characteristic of nō. An ornate, curved roof covers the stage and is reminiscent of the time when the stage was housed in a separate building, which the audience observed from a distance. The nō roof is supported by four wooden pillars, each with its own name and historic dramatic function. A wooden "mirror wall" at the rear of the stage bounces back the sounds of music and singing to the audience; on the wall, a painted pine tree, delicately gnarled and highly stylized, provides the only scenery. A four-man orchestra—whose instruments include a flute, small and large hand drums, and a stick drum—provides continuous musical

Nō actors usually come from long-standing nō families that operate nō schools. Here one of Japan's "living national treasures," the venerable Otoshige Sakai of the Kanze Nō-gakudo school, which was founded in the fourteenth century, helps mask his son, Otaharu, before a 2004 performance in Tokyo.

accompaniment at the rear of the stage, and a chorus of six to ten singer-chanters is positioned on a platform addition at stage left. The absolute precision of the theatre design and the stately performance choreography and musicality give nō a ceremonial quality that is unique in world drama.

Nō has never been a theatre of mass entertainment, and first-time patrons today—including many Japanese—often find it bewildering. Plotting, even in comparison to other Asian forms, is weak or almost nonexistent. The language is medieval, elliptical, and often forbiddingly obscure. The cast is small, the action relatively static, and the pace, by modern standards, nearly glacial: the basic nō walk, said to be derived from tramping through rice paddies, is an agonizingly deliberate slip-slide shuffle, with the feet barely leaving the ground. The actors are trained to keep their faces immobile and expressionless at all times, even when unmasked. Certainly nō is produced today more for enthusiasts than for the general public, but the number of such enthusiasts—at least in Japan—is currently growing, not falling. Like the study of martial arts, flower arranging, and the tea ceremony, nō remains a Japanese national passion. Its sublime mystery and serenity—reflective of deep Buddhist and Shinto values—resonate profoundly in contemporary Japanese life and have proven increasingly influential to Japanese as well as Western dramatists of the current era.

## Japanese Kabuki

Created two hundred years after nō, kabuki has always been a more spectacular and accessible form of theatrical entertainment. Whereas nō is refined, dignified, and designed for small, studious audiences, kabuki is gaudy and exhilarating; from its earliest days, it was created to delight large crowds of merchants, traders, courtesans, and ordinary city dwellers. Whereas nō is sober and ascetic and staged on a relatively small, bare

In kabuki's famous dance-drama *Kagami Jishi* (*The Lion Dance*), the lion (played by Nakamura Kankuro V) is teased by butter-flies (played by his sons Nakamura Kantaro II and Nakamura Schichinosuki II).

platform, kabuki is a theatrical extravaganza of dazzling colors, flamboyant dance and recitation, passionate emotion, and elaborate stage machinery and effects. Japanese audiences often respond by shouting their favorite actors' names or other words of encouragement at key moments in the play.

Kabuki was created in Kyoto around 1600 by the legendary shrine maiden Izumo Okuni, whose flamboyant and dramatic style of dancing became hugely popular in Kyoto's brothels and teahouses. The outlandish extravagance of Okuni's costumes and the fact that women performed both male and female parts invited the term *kabuku,* meaning "askew" (today we might translate it as "punk"). This fast-developing and exotic entertainment was transformed by midcentury through a series of government edicts from an all-female to an all-male performing art. More complex dramatic storytelling—with themes based on traditional myths, historical incidents, local sex scandals and suicides, and already-ancient nō drama—was adapted into the evolving format, which

was by then renamed *kabuki,* a term made up of three ideographs: *ka* ("song"), *bu* ("dance"), and *ki* ("skill"), the three major ingredients of kabuki.

By the century's end, kabuki staging had incorporated curtains and scenery, playwrights' names were being printed in kabuki programs, and star actors had emerged, creating the two principal kabuki acting styles: *wagoto* (the elegant and naturalistic "soft style" of actor Sakata Tōjūrō I, from Kyoto) and *aragoto* (the thundering "rough style" of Ichikawa Danjūrō I, from Edo, now Tokyo). The traditions of both these actors remain central to kabuki to the present day, as all kabuki actors are members of but eleven famous families and all can trace their lineage—familial and professional—back to their kabuki-performing ancestors. The current star Ichikawa Danjūrō XII, for example, is the great-great-great-great-great-great-great-great-great-grandson of Ichikawa Danjūrō I, born in 1660; the celebrated Danjūrō style has been directly passed, father to son, down through the centuries.

This *bunraku* version of *Yoshitsune and the Thousand Cherry Trees* was performed at the National Bunraku Theatre in Osaka, Japan. As many as three puppeteers, dressed in black, operate each puppet in bunraku. The principal operator of each major-role puppet is usually unmasked, though he remains expressionless throughout the performance. Most other operators, such as the one barely seen here on the far right, are covered in black from the head down, making them all but invisible. In bunraku, the puppet is the star.

There are many types of kabuki dramas, but the major works fall generally into two categories: history plays (*jidaimono,* or "period things") and domestic plays (*sewamono,* or "common things"). The history plays dramatize—usually in spectacular fashion—major political events of the remote past; often, however, the historical distance was little more than a protective cover for past playwrights and actors, who were in fact reflecting—under the guise of an apparently historical depiction—various controversial issues of nobles and political officials of their own time. Domestic plays, in contrast, deal with the affairs of the townspeople, merchants, lovers, and courtesans of the playwright's own era, often focusing on the conflicts—intense throughout Japanese culture—between affairs of the heart and the call of duty. A great many domestic plays end in suicide (many, in fact, end in double suicides), with the lovers vowing to meet again in the world to come; such plays have been the subject of attempted bannings, as they have led to real suicides in consequence.

Kabuki is mainly an actor's theatre; many of its plays are of unknown authorship and have been augmented over the centuries by actors' additions. One notable exception, however, is the kabuki author Chikamatsu Monzaemon (1653–1725). Considered the greatest Japanese dramatist of all time, Chikamatsu was also a famous playwright of the Japanese puppet-theatre *bunraku.*

## THE THEATRICAL TRADITION TODAY: EAST AND WEST

These eleven great theatre traditions of the past—Greek, Roman, medieval, Renaissance, Royal, and romantic in the Western world; Sanskrit, kathakali, xiqu, nō, and kabuki in the East—are all alive today, either in the form of regular and careful revivals or, happier yet in the case of the last four (and, to some extent, the plays of the Royal and romantic eras as well), by a continuous tradition of performance. All of these traditions have influenced the modern theatre, as we will see in the next chapter. Increasingly, that influence crosses and recrosses the East-West divide that has existed in theatre history since the decline of the Egyptian resurrection dramas two thousand years ago.

# Chapter 8

# The Modern Theatre

THE THEATRE HAS EXPERIENCED MANY great periods, and one of its greatest is still going on. This is the period we call "modern," to which can be added the onrush of avant-garde movements we call (for the time being) "postmodern." Together, these make up the theatre of our times, a theatre that will likely be heralded for *all times.*

Modern drama can be said to date back to about 1875, and its roots lie deep in the social and political upheavals that developed in the eighteenth and nineteenth centuries, a time characterized by revolution. Political revolution in the United States (1776) and France (1789) irrevocably changed the political structure of the Western world, and industrial-technological revolution cataclysmically overhauled the economic and social systems of most of the world. In the wake of these developments came an explosion of public communication and transportation, a tremendous expansion of literacy, democracy, and public and private wealth, and a universal demographic shift from country to town. These forces combined to create in Europe, the United States, and elsewhere mass urban populations hungering for social communion and stimulation: a fertile ground for the citified and civilized theatre of our times.

Simultaneously, an intellectual revolution—in philosophy, in science, in social understanding, and in religion—was altering human consciousness in ways far transcending the effects of revolutionary muskets and industrial consolidation. The intellectual certainty of Louis XIV, whose divine right to rule was unquestioned in the seventeenth and early eighteenth centuries, appeared ludicrous in an age governed by secular scientific investigation. The clear-sightedness of a playwright such as Molière seemed simplistic in an age of existentialism signaled by the soul-searching, self-doubting analyses of Søren Kierkegaard. The intellectual revolution was an exceedingly complex phenomenon that occurred in many spheres of thought and was to gain momentum with each passing decade. It continues to this day.

The Copernican theory had already made clear that human beings do not stand at the geographic center of the universe but rather that our world, indeed our universe, is swept up in a multiplicity of interstellar movements. Later scientists would press further than that, until eventually the revelations of Albert Einstein, Werner Heisenberg, and others would remove all of our "hitching posts in space" and establish the human animal as little more than a transformation of kinetic energy, wobbling shiftily in a multigravitational atomic field marked by galaxies and black holes, neutrinos and quarks, matter and antimatter, all in a vast dance of inexplicable origin and doubtful destiny.

Nor was that "human animal" so vastly privileged over other species, it would seem. Darwin would argue that we Homo sapiens are directly linked to other mammals—descended not from Adam and Eve or pre-Hellenic demigods but from primal apes and prehistoric orangutans. Our morals and religions, anthropologist Ruth Benedict would argue, were not handed down to all humanity from a single source but are instead a ranging complex of laws and traditions wholly relative to the climes and cultures we inhabit. The work of Freud would posit the existence of the unconscious, a dark and lurking inner self aswarm with infantile urges, primordial fantasies, and suppressed fears and rages. The writings of Karl Marx would contend that all social behavior has its basis in economic greed, class struggle, and primal amorality. "Everlasting uncertainty and agitation" is the nature of human intercourse, according to Marx, and society comprises "two great hostile camps" continually engaged in civil war.

These and scores of other serious challenges to traditional thinking were accompanied everywhere by public debate and dispute. By the turn of the twentieth century, an investigative ferment had seized Western civilization: data were being collected on every conceivable topic, and scientific questioning and testing replaced intuition and dogma as the accepted avenues to truth. Experimentation, exploration, documentation, and challenge became the marching orders of the artist and intellectual alike.

The modern theatre has its roots in these political, social, and intellectual revolutions. Ever since its outset it has been a theatre of challenge, a theatre of experimentation. It has never been a theatre of rules or simple messages, nor has it been a theatre of demigods or of absolute heroes and villains. It has reflected, to a certain degree, the confusions of its times, but it has also struggled to clarify and to illuminate, to document and explore human destiny in a complex and uneasy universe.

# REALISM

Thus far, the movement that has had the most pervasive and long-lived effect on modern theatre is, beyond question, realism. Realism has sought to create a drama without conventions or abstractions. *Likeness to life* is realism's goal, and in pursuit of that goal it has renounced, among other things, idealized or prettified settings, versifications, contrived endings, and stylized costumes and performances.

Realism is a beguiling aesthetic philosophy. Indeed, the theatre has *always* taken "real life" as its fundamental subject, so realism seems at first glance to be an appropriate style with which to approach the reality of existence. Instead of having actors represent characters, the realists would say, let us have the actors *be* those characters. Instead of having dialogue stand for conversation, let us have dialogue that *is* conversation. Instead of having scenery and costumes that convey a sense of time and place and atmosphere, let us have scenery that is genuinely inhabitable and costumes that are real clothes.

But, of course, realism has its limits: any dramatic piece must inevitably involve a certain shaping and stylization, no matter how lifelike its effect, and advocates of theatrical realism are well aware of this inevitability. Nevertheless, the ideology of realism was tested, during the last years of the nineteenth century and the first years of the twentieth, in every aspect of theatre—acting, directing, design, and playwriting—and the results of those tests form a body of theatre that is both valid and meaningful and a style that remains enormously significant.

## A Laboratory

In essence, the realistic theatre is conceived to be a laboratory in which the nature of relationships, the ills of society, the symptoms of a dysfunctional family are "objectively" set down for the final judgment of an audience of impartial observers. Every aspect of realistic theatre is to strictly adhere to the "scientific method" of the laboratory; nothing must ring false. The setting is to resemble the prescribed locale of the play as closely as possible; indeed, it is not unusual for much of the scenery to be acquired from a real-life environment and transported to the theatre. Costumes worn by characters in the realistic theatre follow the dress of "real" people of similar societal status; dialogue recreates the cadences and expressions of daily life.

Early on in the realist movement, the proscenium stage was modified to accommodate scenery constructed in box sets, with the walls given full dimension and with real bookcases, windows, fireplaces, swinging doors, and so forth, built into the walls just as they are in a house interior. In the same vein, realistic acting was judged effective insofar as it was

Tennessee Williams's *A Streetcar Named Desire* maybe the most popular American play ever; since its 1947 opening there have been seven Broadway revivals. Here, at London's Donmar Warehouse Theatre in 2009, Rachel Weisz (*center*) plays Blanche DuBois in what critics have called a "radiant" and "mesmerizing performance." Williams's writing, says Weisz, "is out of this world. I have never come across a female character that is written with Blanche's level of complexity: she's vulnerable, she's pathetic, she's a monster, she's nasty, she's tender, she's kind—she's so many things that you never know quite what she's going to do next." Ruth Wilson plays Blanche's sister Stella, and Elliot Cowan plays Stella"s glowering husband Stanley, the role made famous in the play's Broadway premiere by Marlon Brando.

drawn from the behavior of life and insofar as the actors seemed to be genuinely speaking to each other instead of playing to the audience. A new aesthetic principle was spawned: the "theatre of the fourth wall removed," in which the life onstage was conceived to be the same as life in a real-world setting, except that, in the case of the stage, one wall—the proscenium opening—had been removed. Thus the theatre was like a microscope and the stage like a biologist's slide: a living environment set up for judicious inspection by neutral observers.

Realism presents its audience with an abundance of seemingly real-life "evidence" and permits each spectator to arrive at his or her own conclusions. There is some shaping of this evidence by author and performer alike, to be sure, but much of the excitement of the realistic theatre is occasioned by the genuine interpretive freedom it allows the audience and by the accessibility of its characters, whose behaviors are familiar enough to the average spectator that they may be easily assimilated and identified.

Moreover, in presenting its evidence from the surface of life, realism encourages us to delve into the mystery that lies beneath—for the exploration of life's mystery is the true, though perhaps unspoken, purpose of every realistic play. Realism's characters, like people in life, are defined by detail rather than by symbol or abstract idealization: like people we know, they are ultimately unpredictable and humanly complex rather than ideologically absolute.

The success of realism is well established; indeed, realism remains one of the dominant modes of drama to this day. At its most profound, when crafted and performed by consummately skilled artists, realistic theatre can generate extremely powerful audience empathy by virtue of the insight and clarity it brings to real-world moments. In giving us characters, the realist playwright gives us *friends:* fellow travelers on the voyage of human discovery with whom we can compare thoughts and feelings. In the uncertainties and trepidations, the wistfulness, the halting eloquence and conversational syntax of these characters we recognize ourselves, and in that recognition we gain an understanding of our own struggles and a compassion for all human endeavors.

## Pioneers of Realism

The realistic theatre had its beginnings in the four-year period that saw the premieres of three shocking plays by Norwegian playwright Henrik Ibsen: *A Doll's House* (1867), Ghosts (1881), and *An Enemy of the People* (1882). Already famous for historical and poetic dramas, including the magnificent *Peer Gynt* (1867), Ibsen (1828-1906), soon to be known as the "father of dramatic realism," in these works turned his attention to more contemporary and day-to-day themes: woman's role in society, hereditary disease and mercy killing, and political hypocrisy. Ordinary people populate Ibsen's realistic world, and the issues addressed in these dramas affect ordinary husband-wife, motherson, and brother-brother relationships and are played out in the interiors of ordinary homes. Controversial beyond measure in their own time, these plays retain their edge of pertinence even today and still have the power to inform, move, and even shock. The reason for their lasting impact lies in Ibsen's choice of issues and his skill at showing both sides through brilliantly captured psychological detail.

The realistic theatre spread rapidly throughout Europe as the controversy surrounding Ibsen's plays and themes stimulated other writers to follow suit. The result was a proliferation of "problem plays," as they were sometimes called, which focused genuine social concern through realistic dramatic portrayal. In Germany, Gerhart Hauptmann (1862-1946) explored the plight of the middle and proletarian classes in several works, most notably in his masterpiece *The Weavers* (1892). In England, Irish-born George Bernard Shaw (1856-1950) created a comedic realism through which he addressed issues such as slum landlordism (in *Widowers' Houses,* 1892), prostitution (in *Mrs. Warren's Profession,* 1902), and urban poverty (in *Major Barbara,* 1905). In France, André Antoine (1858-1943) created his Théâtre Libre in 1887 to encourage stagings of realistic dramas, including Ibsen's *Ghosts* and *Wild Duck,* Hauptmann's *Weavers,* and the French plays of Eugène Brieux (1858-1932), including *Damaged Goods* (1902), about syphilis, and *Maternity* (1903), about birth control. By the turn of the century, realism was virtually the standard dramatic form in Europe.

If the realistic theatre came to prominence with the plays of Henrik Ibsen, it attained its stylistic apogee in the major works of Anton Chekhov (1860-1904). Chekhov was a physician by training and a writer of fiction by vocation. Toward the end of his career, in association with realist director Konstantin Stanislavsky (1863-1938) and the Moscow Art Theatre, he also achieved success as a playwright through a set of plays that portray the end of the tsarist era in Russia with astonishing force and subtlety: *The Seagull* (1896),

Lee Breuer's celebrated production of *Dollhouse* with the Mabou Mines company, which he coheads in New York, was remarkable for casting all the male roles in this adaptation of Ibsen's play (usually translated as *A Doll's House*) with actors four feet tall or less, and with the play's women towering two feet above them. The setting (by Narelle Sisson) was also a "doll house," with miniature walls and furniture. Maude Mitchell plays Nora in this performance, seen at the 2007 Edinburgh Festival, with Mark Povinelli as her husband, Tonrald.

*Uncle Vanya* (1899), *The Three Sisters* (1901), and *The Cherry Orchard* (1904). The intricate craftsmanship of these plays has never been surpassed; even the minor characters seem to breathe the same air we do.

Chekhov's technique was to create deeply complex relationships among his characters and to develop his plots and themes more or less between the lines. Every Chekhovian character is filled with secrets that are never fully revealed by the dialogue.

As an example of Chekhov's realist style, examine particularly the dialogue in the following scene from *The Three Sisters*. In this scene, Vershinin, an army colonel, meets Masha and her sisters, Irina and Olga, whom Vershinin dimly remembers from past years in Moscow:

VERSHININ: I have the honor to introduce myself, my name is Vershinin. I am very, very glad to be in your house at last. How you have grown up! Aie-aie!

IRINA: Please sit down. We are delighted to see you.

VERSHININ: (*with animation*) How glad I am, how glad I am! But there are three of you sisters. I remember— three little girls. I don't remember your faces, but that your father, Colonel Prozorov, had three little girls I remember perfectly. How time passes! Hey-ho, how it passes! . . .

IRINA: From Moscow? You have come from Moscow?

VERSHININ: Yes. Your father was in command of a battery there, and I was an officer in the same brigade. (*To* MASHA) Your face, now, I seem to remember.

MASHA: I don't remember you.

VERSHININ: So you are Olga, the eldest—and you are Masha—and you are Irina, the youngest—

OLGA: You come from Moscow?

VERSHININ: Yes. I studied in Moscow. ... used to visit you in Moscow.

Masha and Vershinin are destined to become lovers; their deepening, largely unspoken communion will provide one of the most haunting strains in the play. And how lifelike is the awkwardness of their first encounter! Vershinin's enthusiastic clichés ("How time passes! ") and interjections ("Aie-aie!") are the stuff of everyday discourse; the news that he comes from Moscow is repeated so that it becomes amusing rather than informative, a revelation of character rather than of plot.

Masha's first exchange with Vershinin gives no direct indication of the future of their relationship; it is a crossed communication in which one character refuses to share in the other's memory. Is this a personal repudiation, or is it a teasing provocation? The acting, not simply the text, must establish their developing rapport. The love between Vershinin and Masha will tax to the maximum the capabilities of the actors who play their parts to express deep feeling through subtle nuance, through the gestures, glances, tones of voice, and shared understandings and sympathetic rhythms that distinguish lovers everywhere. It is a theme that strongly affects the mood of the play but is rarely explicit in the dialogue.

## Naturalism

Naturalism represents an extreme attempt to dramatize human reality without the appearance of dramaturgical shaping. The naturalists flourished primarily in France during the late nineteenth century. Émile Zola (1840-1902) was their chief theoretician. The naturalists based their aesthetics on nature, particularly humanity's place in the natural (Darwinian) environment. To the naturalist, human beings were merely biological phenomena whose behavior was determined entirely by genetic and social circumstances. To portray a character as a hero, or even as a credible force for change in society, was anathema to the naturalists,

Realistic plays do not necessarily require realistic scenery. In Alfred Uhry's Driving Miss Daisy, the elderly southern Jewish woman of the title is driven around town by her African American chauffeur; over the years, they develop a profound—though mostly unstated—emotional relationship. It would be impossible to stage the moving car realistically, so this vital element must simply be mimed. But the costumes, dialogue, and acting are acutely realistic. Patricia Fraser and Ernest Perry Jr. are the actors in this 2000 Utah Shakespearean Festival production.

Perhaps the seminal play of mid-century American realism is Clifford Odets' *Awake and Sing!* Initially produced by the Group Theatre in 1935, it led the development of a down-to-earth, gritty style of both playwriting and acting that dominated the American theatre for the next fifty years. The play, which details the hopes and dreams and emotional crises of a Jewish immigrant family living in a cramped Bronx apartment, established an American pattern of domestic dramas of working-class, urban life, while the actors who starred in the original production—Group members Luther and Stella Adler, Sanford Meisner, and Morris Carnovsky—became legendary acting teachers of "the method" that was to inspire future generations of American performers. The production pictured was staged in 2010 by A Noise Within in Los Angeles: from left to right are Alan Blumenfeld as Uncle Morty, Len Lesser as Jacob, and Deborah Strang as Bessie Berger; Andrew Traister directed.

who similarly eschewed dramatic conclusions or climaxes. Whereas realist plays at that time tended to deal with well-defined social issues—women's rights, inheritance laws, worker's pensions, and the like—naturalist plays offered nothing more than a"slice of life." The characters of the play were the play's entire subject; any topical issues that arose served merely to facilitate the interplay of personalities and highlight the characters' situations, frustrations, and hopes.

The naturalists sought to eliminate every vestige of dramatic convention: "All the great successes of the stage are triumphs over convention," declared Zola. Their efforts in this direction are exemplified by August Strindberg's (1849-1912) elimination of the time-passing intermission in *Miss Julie* (instead, a group of peasants, otherwise irrelevant to the plot, enter the kitchen setting between acts and dance to fill the time Miss Julie is spending in Jean's offstage bedroom) and by Arthur Schnitzler's (1862-1931) elimination of conventional scene beginnings, endings, and climaxes in the interlocking series of cyclical love affairs that constitute the action of *La Ronde*.

Inasmuch as sheer verisimilitude, presented as "art-lessly" as humanly possible, is the primary goal of the naturalist, the term *naturalism* is often applied to those realistic plays that seem most effectively life-like. This is not a particularly felicitous use of the term, however, because it ignores the fundamental precept of naturalism—that the human being is a mere figure in the natural environment. Naturalism is not merely a matter of style; it is a philosophical concept concerning the nature of the human animal. And naturalist theatre represents a purposeful attempt to explore that concept, using extreme realism as its basic dramaturgy.

Eugene O'Neill (1888-1953), America's first great playwright, pioneered an earthy naturalistic style in his early plays, returning to that style in his autobiographical masterpiece, *Long Day's Journey into Night*—a play so true to life that O'Neill forbade its production or publication until many years after his death. In our times, the dramas of Arthur Miller, Tennessee Williams, August Wilson, Wendy Wasserstein, David Mamet, and Neil LaBute are all strongly influenced by both realism and naturalism, which continue to have a commanding presence on the American stage.

# ANTIREALISM

Realism and naturalism were not the only new movements of the late nineteenth century to make themselves strongly felt in the modern theatre. A counterforce, equally powerful, was to emerge. First manifest in the movement known as symbolism, this counterforce evolved and expanded into what we will call antirealistic theatre, which moved across Europe and quickly began contesting the advances of realism step-by-step.

## The Symbolist Rebellion

The symbolist movement began in Paris during the 1880s as a joint venture of artists, playwrights, essayists, critics, sculptors, and poets. If realism was the art of depicting reality as ordinary men and women might see it, symbolism would explore—by means of images and metaphors—the *inner* realities that cannot be directly or literally perceived. "Symbolic" characters, therefore, would not represent real human beings but instead would symbolize philosophical ideals or warring internal forces in the human (or the artist's) soul.

Symbolism had another goal as well: to crush what its adherents deemed to be a spiritually bankrupt realism and to replace it with traditional aesthetic values—poetry, imagery, novelty, fantasy, extravagance, profundity, audacity, charm, and superhuman magnitude. United in their hatred for literal detail and for all that they considered mundane or ordinary, the symbolists demanded abstraction, enlargement, and innovation; the symbolist spirit soared in poetic encapsulations, outsized dramatic presences, fantastical visual effects, shocking structural departures, and grandiloquent speech. Purity of vision, rather than accuracy of observation, was the symbolists' aim, and self-conscious creative innovation was to be their primary accomplishment.

The first symbolist theatre, founded in 1890 by Parisian poet Paul Fort (1872-1960), was intended as a direct attack on the naturalistic Théâtre Libre of André Antoine, founded three years earlier. Fort's theatre, the Théâtre d'Art, was proposed as "a theatre for Symbolist poets only, where every production would cause a battle." In some ways, the theatres of Antoine and Fort had much in common: both were amateur, both gained considerable notoriety, and each served as a center for a "school" of artistic ideology that attracted as much attention and controversy as any of its theatrical offerings.

But the two theatres were openly, deliberately, at war. While Antoine was presenting premieres of naturalistic and realistic dramas by August Strindberg, Émile Zola, and Henrik Ibsen, Fort presented the staged poems and poetic plays of both contemporary and earlier writers such as the French Arthur Rimbaud and Paul Verlaine, the Belgian Maurice Maeterlinck, and the American Edgar Allan Poe. Whereas Antoine would go to great lengths to create realistic scenery for his plays (for example, he displayed real sides of beef hung from meat hooks for his presentation of *The Butchers*), Fort would prevail upon leading impressionist easel painters—including Pierre Bonnard, Maurice Denis, and Odilon Redon—to dress his stylized stage. Silver angels, translucent veils, and sheets of crumpled wrapping paper were among the decors that backed the symbolist works at the Théâtre d'Art.

Fort's theatre created an immediate sensation in Paris. With the stunning success in 1890 of *The Intruder*, a mysterious and poetic fantasy by Maeterlinck, the antirealist movement was fully engaged and, as Fort recalled in his memoirs, "the cries and applause of the students, poets, and artists overwhelmed the huge disapproval of the bourgeoisie."

The movement spread quickly as authors and designers alike awakened to the possibilities of a theatre wholly freed from the constraints of verisimilitude. Realism, more and more critics concluded, would never raise the commonplace to the level of art; it would only drag art down into the muck of the mundane. It ran counter to all that the theatre had stood for in the past; it throttled the potential of artistic creativity. In fact, such naturalistic and realistic authors as Henrik Ibsen, August Strindberg, Gerhart Hauptmann, and George Bernard Shaw soon came under the symbolist influence and abandoned their social preoccupations and environmental exactitude to seek new languages and more universal themes. As an added element, at about this time Sigmund Freud's research was being published and discussed, and his theories concerning dream images and the worlds of the unconscious provided new source material for the stage.

By the turn of the century, the counterforce of theatrical stylization set in motion by the symbolists was established on all fronts; indeed, the half decade on either side of 1900 represents one of the richest periods of experimentation in the history of dramatic writing. Out of that decade came Hauptmann's archetypal fairy tale *The Sunken Bell* (Germany, 1896), Alfred Jarry's outrageously cartoonish and scatological *Ubu Roi* (France, 1898), Ibsen's haunting ode to individualism *When We Dead Awaken* (Norway, 1899), Strindberg's metaphoric and imagistic *The Dream Play* (Sweden, 1902), William Butler Yeats's evocative poetic fable *Cathleen ni Houlihan* (Ireland, 1903), Shaw's philosophical allegory Man and Superman (England, 1903), and James Barrie's whimsical, buoyant fantasy *Peter Pan* (England, 1904). Almost every dramatic innovation that has followed since that time has been at least in part prefigured by one or more of these seminal works for the nonrealist theatre.

The realist-versus-symbolist confrontation affected every aspect of theatre production. Symbolist-inspired directors and designers, side by side with the playwrights, were drastically altering the arts of staging and decor to accommodate the new dramaturgies that surged into the theatre. Realist directors such as Antoine and Stanislavsky suddenly found themselves challenged by scores of adversaries and renegades: a school of symbolist and poetic directors rose in France, and a former disciple of Stanislavsky, the "constructivist" Vsevolod Meyerhold (1874-1940), broke with the Russian master to create a nonrealist "biomechanical" style of acting and directing in sharp contrast to that established at the Moscow Art Theatre; by 1904 Stanislavsky himself was producing the symbolist plays of Maeterlinck at the Moscow Art Theatre. With the advent of electrical stage lighting, opportunities for stylizing were vastly expanded: the new technology enabled the modern director to create vivid stage effects, starkly unrealistic in appearance, through the judicious use of spotlighting, shadowing, and shading. Technology, plus trends in postimpressionist art that were well established in Europe by 1900, led to scenery and costume designs that departed radically from realism. Exoticism, fantasy, sheer sensual delight, symbolic meaning, and aesthetic purity became the prime objectives of designers who joined the antirealist rebellion.

In some respects, the symbolist aim succeeded perhaps beyond the dreams of its originators. Fort's Théâtre d'Art, although it lasted but a year, now has spiritual descendants in every city in the Western world where theatre is performed.

## The Era of Isms

The symbolist movement itself was short-lived, at least under that name. *Symbolism,* after all, was coined primarily as a direct contradiction of *realism,* and movements named for their oppositional qualities—called for what they are *not*—are quickly seen as artistically limited, as critiques of art rather than as art itself.

Within months of the symbolist advances, therefore, symbolism *as a movement* was deserted by founders and followers alike. Where did they go? Off to found newer movements: futurism, Dadaism, idealism, impressionism, expressionism, constructivism, surrealism, and perhaps a hundred other ism-labeled movements now lost to time.

The first third of the twentieth century, indeed, was an era of theatrical isms, an era rich with continued experimentation by movements self-consciously seeking to redefine theatrical art. Ism theatres sprang up like mushrooms, each with its own fully articulated credo and manifesto, each promising a better art—if not, indeed, a better world. It was a vibrant era for the theatre, for out of this welter of isms the aesthetics of dramatic art took on a new social and political significance in the cultural capitals of Europe and America. A successful play was not merely a play but rather the forum for a *cause,* and behind that cause was a body of zealous supporters and adherents who shared a deep aesthetic commitment.

Robert Wilson (the director) and John Conklin (the costume designer) codesigned the scenery for this dreamlike American Repertory Theatre production of Ibsen's *When We Dead Awaken* in 1991.

Nothing quite like that ism spirit exists today, for we have lost the social involvement that can turn an aesthetic movement into a profound collective belief. But the experiments and discoveries of those early days of the twentieth century and the nonrealistic spirit of symbolism itself survive and flourish under a variety of formats: ritual theatre, poetic theatre, holy theatre, theatre of cruelty, existentialist theatre, art theatre, avant-garde theatre, theatre of the absurd, and theatre of alienation. These present-day groupings, unlike the isms, are critic-defined rather than artist-defined; indeed, most theatre artists today reject any "grouping" nomenclature whatever. However, the formats these groupings pursue can be shown to reflect the general approach to structure, style, and

experimentation that began with the symbolists in the late nineteenth century.

## Stylized Teatre

We have chosen the rather loose term *antirealistic theatre* or, occasionally, *stylized theatre* to embrace the entire spectrum of nonrealistic modern theatre, which, although disparate in its individual manifestations, exhibits a universal insistence on *consciously stylizing reality* into larger-than-life theatrical experience. Any theatre mode in any era, of course, has its distinctive style, but in past eras that style was always largely *imposed* by current convention and technological limitations. Modern dramatists, in contrast, have consciously selected *and created* styles to satisfy their aesthetic theories, their social principles, or simply their desire for novelty and innovation.

Antirealistic theatre attempts to create new theatrical formats, not merely to enhance the portrayal of human existence but also to disclose fundamental patterns underlying that existence: patterns of perception, patterns of association, patterns of personal and environmental interaction. The styles employed by this modern theatre come from anywhere and everywhere: from the past, from exotic cultures, and from present and futuristic technologies. The modern theatre artist has an unprecedented reservoir of sources to draw upon and is generally unconstrained in their application by political edict, religious prohibition, or mandated artistic tradition. The modern stylized theatre is undoubtedly the freest in history: the dramatist, director, actor, or designer is limited only by physical resources and individual imagination. Almost anything can be put upon a stage, and in the twentieth century it seems that almost everything was.

Antirealistic theatre does not altogether dispense with reality but wields it in often unexpected ways and freely enhances it with symbol and metaphor, striving to elucidate by parable and allegory, to deconstruct and reconstruct by language, scenery, and lighting. Further, it makes explicit use of the theatre's very theatricality, frequently reminding its audience members, directly or indirectly, that they are watching a performance, not an episode in somebody's daily life. Stylization inevitably reaches for universality. It tends to treat problems of psychology as problems of philosophy, and problems in human relations as problems of the human condition. Stylization reaches for patterns, not particulars; it explores abstractions and aims for sharp thematic focus and bold intellectual impact.

In the stylized theatre, characters usually represent more than individual persons or personality types. Like the medieval allegories, modern stylized plays often involve characters who represent forces of nature, moral positions, human instincts, and the like—entities such as death, fate, idealism, the life force, the earth mother, the tyrant father, and the prodigal son. And the conflicts associated with these forces, unlike the conflicts of realism, are not responsive to any human agency; they are, more often than not, represented as permanent discords inherent in the human condition. The stylized theatre resonates with tension and human frustration in the face of irreconcilable demands.

But that is not to say the antirealistic theatre is necessarily grim; on the contrary, it often uses whimsy and mordant wit as its dominant mode. Although the themes of the antirealistic theatre are anxious ones—for example, the alienation of humanity, the futility of communication, the loss of innocence, the intransigence of despair—it is not on the whole a theatre of pessimism or of nihilistic outrage. Indeed, the glory of the stylized theatre is that, at its best, it refuses to be swamped by its themes; it transcends frustration; it is the victory of poetry over alienation, comedy over noncommunication, and artistry over despair. The antirealistic theatre aims at lifting its audience, not saddling them; and even if it proffers no solutions to life's inevitable discords, it can provide considerable lucidity concerning the totality of the human adventure.

The diversity of stylized theatrical works precludes further generalization about their shared characteristics. To help us understand this diversity, however, we will examine brief examples from plays written over the past hundred-plus years that serve to establish the main lines of the antirealistic theatre.

**The French Avant-Garde: *Ubu Roi*** The opening of Alfred Jarry's *Ubu Roi (King Ubu)* at the Théâtre de l'Oeuvre in Paris on December 10, 1896, was perhaps the most violent dramatic premiere in theatre history: the audience shouted, whistled, hooted, cheered, threw things, and shook their fists at the stage. Duels were even fought after subsequent performances. The avant-garde was born.

The term *avant-garde* comes from the military, where it refers to the advance battalion, or the "shock troops" that initiate a major assault. In France the term initially described the wave of French playwrights and directors who openly and boldly assaulted realism in the first four decades of the twentieth century. Today the term is used worldwide to describe any adventurous, experimental, and nontraditional artistic effort.

Jarry (1873-1907), a diminutive iconoclast ("eccentric to the point of mania and lucid to the point of hallucination," says critic Roger Shattuck), unleashed his radical shock troops from the moment the curtain rose. Jarry had called for an outrageously antirealistic stage—painted scenery depicting a bed, a bare tree at its foot; palm trees, a coiled boa constrictor around one of them; a gallows with a skeleton hanging from it; and falling snow. Characters entered through a painted fireplace. Costumes, in Jarry's words, were

Mother Ubu pokes her strikingly made-up face through an abstractly colored backdrop in Babette Masson's 1993 French production of Jarry's *Ubu Roi.*

of romanticism; far from trying to sneak them back in, Jarry simply threw them up, schoolboylike, in the face of the astonished audience. The added "r" in *merdre,* far from "cleansing" the offending obscenity, only called more attention to it and to its deliberate intrusion onto the Parisian stage.

*Ubu Roi* was, in fact, a schoolboy play; Jarry wrote the first version at the age of fifteen as a satire of his high school physics teacher. Jarry was only twentythree years old when the play astounded its Parisian audiences, and the juvenile aspects of the play's origins were evident throughout the finished product, which proved to be Jarry's sole masterwork.

*Ubu Roi* is a savage and often ludicrous satire on the theme of power, in which Father (later King) Ubu—a fat, foul-mouthed, venal, amoral, and pompous Polish assassin—proves one of the stage's greatest creations. The play sprawls; its thirty-three scenes are often just crude skits barely linked by plot, but the interplay of farce and violence is inspired, as in the famous dinner scene:

FATHER UBU, MOTHER UBU, CAPTAIN BORDURE *and his followers.*

CAPTAIN BORDURE: Well, Mother Ubu! What have you got that's good today?

MOTHER UBU: Here's the menu. Polish soup, roast ram, veal, chicken, chopped dog's liver, turkey's ass, charlotte russe...
FATHER UBU: Hey, that's plenty.

MOTHER UBU: (*continuing*) Frozen pudding, salad, fruits, dessert, boiled beef, Jerusalem artichokes, cauliflower  à la shrit.

FATHER UBU: Hey! Do you think I'm the Emperor of China, to give all that away?

MOTHER UBU: Don't listen to him, he's feeble-minded.

FATHER UBU: I'll sharpen my teeth on your shanks.

MOTHER UBU: Try this Father Ubu. Polish soup.

FATHER UBU: Crap, is that lousy!

CAPTAIN BORDURE: Hmm—it isn't very good, at that.

MOTHER UBU: What do you want, you bunch of crooks!

FATHER UBU: (*striking his forehead*) Wait, I've got an idea. I'll be right back. (*He leaves.*)

MOTHER UBU: Let's try the veal now, gentlemen.

CAPTAIN BORDURE: It's very good—I'm through.

MOTHER UBU: To the turkey's ass, next.

CAPTAIN BORDURE: Delicious, delicious! Long live Mother Ubu!

ALL: Long live Mother Ubu!

FATHER UBU: (*returning*) And you will soon be shouting, "Long live Father Ubu." (*He has a toilet brush in his hand, and he throws it on the festive board.*)

"divorced as far as possible from [realistic] color or chronology." And the title character stepped forward to begin the play with a word that quickly became immortal: "*Merdre!*" or "Shrit!"

This mot *d'Ubu* ("Ubu's word") more than anything else occasioned scandal, for although Ibsen had broken barriers of propriety in subject matter, no one had tested the language barriers of the Victorian age. Vulgar epithets, common enough in the works of Aristophanes and Shakespeare, had been pruned from the theatre in the Royal era and abolished entirely in the lofty spirit

MOTHER UBU: Miserable creature, what are you up to now?

FATHER UBU: Try a little. (Several try it, and fall, poisoned.) Mother Ubu, pass me the roast ram chops, so that I can serve them.

MOTHER UBU: Here they are.

FATHER UBU: Everyone out! Captain Bordure, I want to talk to you.

THE OTHERS: But we haven't eaten yet.

FATHER UBU: What's that, you haven't eaten yet? Out, out, everyone out! Stay here, Bordure. (Nobody moves.) You haven't gone yet? By my green candle, I'll give you your ram chops. (He begins to throw them.)

ALL: Oh! Ouch! Help! Woe! Help! Misery! I'm dead!

FATHER UBU: Shrit, shrit, shrit! Outside! I want my way!

ALL: Everyone for himself! Miserable Father Ubu! Traitor! Meanie!

FATHER UBU: Ah! They've gone. I can breathe again—but I've had a rotten dinner. Come on, Bordure.

They go out with MOTHER UBU.

The elements of deliberate scatology, toilet humor, juvenile satire, and a full-stage food fight make clear that *Ubu Roi* is a precursor of American teen films such as *American Pie 2*. It is a little more difficult, however, to see the play as a precursor of a serious art and literary movement like surrealism, but such is the case. *Surrealism,* a word that means "beyond realism" or "superrealism," was officially inaugurated by André Breton in 1924 but can be said to date from this play—which, its advocates claim, reaches a superior level of reality by tracing the unconscious processes of the mind rather than the literal depictions of observable life.

**Expressionism: *The Hairy Ape*** Of all the isms, expressionism is the one that has given rise to the most significant body of modern theatre, probably because of its broad definition and its seeming alliance with expressionism in the visual arts. The theatrical expressionism that was much in vogue in Germany during the first decades of the twentieth century (particularly in the 1920s) featured shocking and gutsy dialogue, boldly exaggerated scenery, piercing sounds, bright lights, an abundance of primary colors, a not very subtle use of symbols, and a structure of short, stark, jabbing scenes that built to a powerful (and usually deafening) climax.

In America, expressionist writers addressed the growing concern that the country's rapid industrial and financial successes were crushing human freedom—and human nature itself. During the 1920s, in the boldly expressionist dramas *Subway, The Adding Machine,* and *Street Scene,* Elmer Rice (1892-1967) angrily attacked what he considered the dehumanization of modern American life. And Eugene O'Neill, who had begun as a realistic playwright in the previous decades, wrote a play that became a landmark of expressionist theatre in 1921. O'Neill's *The Hairy Ape* is a one-act play featuring eight scenes. Its workingman-hero Yank meets and is rebuffed by the genteel daughter of a captain of industry. Enraged, Yank becomes violent and eventually crazed; he dies at play's end in the monkey cage of a zoo. Scene 3 illustrates the tenor of the writing:

> The stokehold. In the rear, the dimly outlined bulks of the furnaces and boilers. High overhead one hanging electric bulb sheds just enough light through the murky air laden with coal dust to pile up masses of shadows everywhere. A line of men, stripped to the waist, is before the furnace doors. They bend over, looking neither to right nor left, handling their shovels as if they were part of their bodies, with a strange, awkward, swinging rhythm. They use the shovels to throw open the furnace doors. Then from these fiery round holes in the back a flood of terrific light and heat pours full upon the men who are outlined in silhouette in the crouching, inhuman attitudes of chained gorillas. The men shovel with a rhythmic motion, swinging as on a pivot from the coal which lies in heaps on the floor behind to hurl it into the flaming mouths before them. There is a tumult of noise—the brazen clang of the furnace doors as they are flung open or slammed shut, the grating, teeth-gritting grind of steel against steel, of crunching coal. This clash of sounds stuns one's ears with its rending dissonance. But there is order in it, rhythm, a mechanical regulated recurrence, a tempo. And rising above all, making the air hum with the quiver of liberated energy, the roar of leaping flames in the furnaces, the monotonous throbbing beat of the engines.
>
> As the curtain rises, the furnace doors are shut. The men are taking a breathing spell. One or two are arranging the coal behind them, pulling it into more accessible heaps. The others can be dimly made out leaning on their shovels in relaxed attitudes of exhaustion.

PADDY: (from somewhere in the line—plaintively) Yerra, will this divil's own watch nivir end? Me back is broke. I'm destroyed entirely.

YANK: (from the center of the line—with exuberant scorn) Aw, yuh make me sick! Lie down and croak, why don't yuh? Always beefin', dat's you! Say, dis is a cinch! Dis was made for me! It's my meat, get me! (A whistle is blown—a thin, shrill note from somewhere overhead in the darkness. YANK curses without resentment.) Dere's de damn engineer crackin' de whip. He tinks we're loafin'.

Elmer Rice's *The Adding Machine* (1923) is one of America's most important expressionistic plays, showing the dehumanization of employees trapped in a corporate accounting department. Anne Bogart directed this rambunctious version for the 1995 Classics in Context festival of the Actors Theatre of Louisville.

PADDY: (*vindictively*) God stiffen him!

YANK: (*in an exultant tone of command*) Come on, youse guys! Git into de game! She's gettin' hungry! Pile some grub in her. Trow it into her belly! Come on now, all of youse! Open her up! (*At this last all the men, who have followed his movements of getting into position, throw open their furnace doors with a deafening clang. The fiery light floods over their shoulders as they bend round for the coal. Rivulets of sooty sweat have traced maps on their backs. The enlarged muscles form bunches of highlight and shadow.*)

YANK: (*chanting a count as he shovels without seeming effort*) One—two—tree—(*His voice rising exultantly in the joy of battle*) Dat's de stuff! Let her have it! All togedder now! Sling it into her! Let her ride! Shoot de piece now! Call de toin on her! Drive her into it! Feel her move. Watch her smoke! Speed, dat's her middle name! Give her coal, youse guys! Coal, dat's her booze! Drink it up, baby! Let's see yuh sprint! Dig in and gain a lap! Dere she go-o-es. (*This last in the chanting formula of the galley gods at the six-day bike race. He slams his furnace door shut. The others do likewise with as much unison as their wearied bodies will permit. The effect is of one fiery eye after another being blotted out with a series of accompanying bangs.*)

PADDY: (*groaning*) Me back is broke. I'm bate out—bate— (*There is a pause. Then the inexorable whistle sounds*

again from the dim regions above the electric light. There is a growl of cursing rage from all sides.*)

YANK: (*shaking his fist upward—contemptuously*) Take it easy dere, you! Who d'yuh tink's runnin' dis game, me or you? When I git ready, we move. Not before! When I git ready, get me!

VOICES: (*approvingly*)  That's the stuff!
Yank tal him, py golly!
Yank ain't affeerd.
Goot poy, Yank!
Give him hell!
Tell 'im 'e's a bloody swine!
Bloody slave-driver!

YANK: (*contemptuously*) He ain't got no noive. He's yellow, get me? All de engineers is yellow. Dey got streaks a mile wide. Aw, to hell wit him! Let's move, youse guys. We had a rest. Come on, she needs it! Give her pep! It ain't for him. Him and his whistle, dey don't belong. But we belong, see! We gotter feed de baby! Come on! (*He turns and flings his furnace door open. They all follow his lead. At this instant the SECOND and FOURTH ENGINEERS enter from the darkness on the left with MIL-DRED between them. She starts, turns paler, her pose is crumbling, she shivers with fright in spite of the blazing heat, but forces herself to leave the ENGINEERS and take a few steps nearer the men. She is right behind YANK. All this happens quickly while the men have their backs turned.*)

YANK: Come on, youse guys! (*He is turning to get coal when the whistle sounds again in a peremptory, irritating note. This drives YANK into a sudden fury While the other men have turned full around and stopped dumbfounded by the spectacle of MILDRED standing there in her white dress, YANK does not turn far enough to see her. Besides, his head is thrown back, he blinks upward through the murk trying to find the owner of the whistle, he brandishes his shovel murderously over his head in one hand, pounding on his chest, gorilla-like, with the other, shouting.*) Toin off dat whistle! Come down outa dere, yuh yellow, brass-buttoned, Belfast bum, yuh! Come down and I'll knock yer brains out! Yuh lousy, stinkin', yellow mut of a Catholic-moiderin' bastard! Come down and I'll moider yuh! Pullin' oat whistle on me, huh? I'll show yuh! I'll crash yer skull in! I'll drive yer teet' down yer troat! I'll slam yer nose trou de back to yer head! I'll cut yer guts out for a nickel, yuh lousy boob, yuh dirty, crummy, muck-eatin' son of a—(*Suddenly he becomes conscious of all the other men staring at something directly behind his back. He whirls defensively with a snarling, murderous growl, crouching to spring, his lips drawn back over his teeth, his small eyes gleaming ferociously. He sees MILDRED, like a white apparition in the full light from the open furnace doors. He glares into her eyes, turned to stone. As for her, during his speech she has listened, paralyzed with horror, terror, her whole personality crushed, beaten in, collapsed, by the terrific impact of this unknown, abysmal brutality, naked and shameless. As she looks at his gorilla face, as his eyes bore into hers, she utters a low, choking cry and shrinks away from him, putting both hands up before her eyes to shut out the sight of his face, to protect her own. This startles YANK to a reaction. His mouth falls open, his eyes grow bewildered.*)

MILDRED: (*about to faint—to the ENGINEERS, who now have her one by each arm—whimperingly*) Take me away! Oh, the filthy beast! (*She faints. They carry her quickly back, disappearing in the darkness at the left, rear. An iron door clangs shut. Rage and bewildered fury rush back on YANK. He feels himself insulted in some unknown fashion in the very heart of his pride. He roars.*) God damn yuh! (*And hurls his shovel after them at the door which has just closed. It hits the steel bulkhead with a clang and falls clattering on the steel floor From overhead the whistle sounds again in a long, angry, insistent command.*)

O'Neill's forceful combination of visual and auditory effects lends this expressionistic play a crude, almost superhuman power. The use of silhouette in the staging and lighting, the "masses of shadows everywhere," the "tumult of noise," the "monotonous throbbing beat of the engines," the "fiery light," the "rivulets of sooty sweat," the massed chanting and the movements in unison, the "peremptory, irritating note" of the "inexorable whistle," the shouting of curses and bold ejaculations, the animal imagery, and the "horror, terror ... of ... unknown, abysmal brutality, naked and shameless" are all typical of the extreme stylization of early-twentieth-century expressionism. The scene also demonstrates how O'Neill and his followers in the American theatre turned away from realism and romanticism in their effort to arrive at a direct presentation of social ideology and cultural criticism.

Metatheatre: *Six Characters search of an Author* First produced in 1921, *Six Characters in Search of an Author* expresses from its famous title onward a "meta-theatrical" motif by which the theatre itself becomes part of the content of play production, not merely the vehicle. "All the world's a stage," said Shakespeare, but in this play Luigi Pirandello (1867-1936) explores how the stage is also a world—and how the stage and the world, illusion and reality, relate to each other. In this still-stunning play, a family of dramatic "characters"—a father, his stepdaughter, a mother, and her children—appear as if by magic on the "stage" of a provincial theatre where a "new play" by Pirandello is being rehearsed. The "characters," claiming they have an unfinished play in them, beg the director to stage their lives in order that they may bring a satisfactory climax to their "drama." This fantasy treats the audience to continually shifting perceptions, for clearly a play-within-the-play is involved, but which is the real play and which real life? There are actors playing actors, actors playing "characters," and actors playing "actors-playing-characters"; there are also scenes when the actors playing "characters" are making fun of the actors playing actors-playing-"characters." It is no wonder that most audiences give up trying to untangle the planes of reality Pirandello creates in this play; they are simply too difficult to comprehend except as a dazzle of suggestive theatricality.

Pirandello contrasts the passionate story of the "characters"—whose "drama" concerns a broken family, adultery, and a suggestion of incest—with the artifice of the stage and its simulations. In the course of this exposition Pirandello's performers discuss the theatricality of life, the life of theatricality, and the eternal confusions between appearance and reality:

THE FATHER: What I'm inviting you to do is to quit this foolish playing at art-this acting and pretending—and seriously answer my question: WHO ARE YOU?

THE DIRECTOR: (*amazed but irritated, to his actors*) What extraordinary impudence! This so-called character wants to know who I am?

**THE FATHER:** (*with calm dignity*) Signore, a character may always ask a "man" who he is. For a character has a true life, defined by his characteristics-he is always, at the least, a "somebody." But a man-now, don't take this personally—A man is generalized beyond identity—he's a nobody!

**THE DIRECTOR:** Ah, but me, me-I am the Director! The Producer! You understand?

**THE FATHER:** Signore—Think of how you used to feel about yourself, long ago, all the illusions you used to have about the world, and about your place in it: those illusions were real for you then, they were quite real—But now, with hindsight, they prove to be nothing, they are nothing to you now but an embarrassment. Well, signore, that is what your present reality is today—just a set of illusions that you will discard tomorrow. Can't you feel it? I'm not speaking of the planks of this stage we stand on, I'm speaking of the very earth under our feet. It's sinking under you—by tomorrow, today's entire reality will have become just one more illusion. You see?

**THE DIRECTOR:** (*confused but amazed*) Well? So what? What does all that prove?

**THE FATHER:** Ah, nothing, signore. Only to show that if, beyond our illusions (*indicating the other characters*), we have no ultimate reality, so your reality as well—your reality that touches and feels and breathes today—will be unmasked tomorrow as nothing but yesterday's illusion!

These lines illustrate Pirandello's use of paradox, irony, and the theatre as metaphor to create a whimsical drama about human identity and human destiny. By contrasting the passion of his "characters" and the frequent frivolity of his "actors," Pirandello establishes a provocative juxtaposition of human behavior and its theatricalization—and the whole fantastical style is nothing but an exploitation of the theatrical format itself.

**Theatre of Cruelty:** *Jet of Blood*   Antonin Artaud (1896-1948) was one of drama's greatest revolutionaries, although his importance lies more in his ideas and influence than in his actual theatrical achievements. A stage and film actor in Paris during the 1920s, he founded the Théâtre Alfred Jarry in 1926, producing, among other works, Strindberg's surrealist *A Dream Play* and, in 1935, an adaptation of Shelley's dramatic poem *The Cenci*. His essays, profoundly influential in the theatre today, were collected and published in 1938 in a book titled *The Theatre and Its Double*.

The theatre envisaged by Artaud was a self-declared theatre of cruelty, for, in his words, "Without an element of cruelty at the root of every performance, the theatre is not possible." The "cruel" theatre would flourish, Artaud predicted, by "providing the spectator with the true sources of his dreams, in which his taste for crime, his erotic obsessions, his savagery, his illusions, his utopian ideals, even his cannibalism, would surge forth."

In Artaud's vision, ordinary plays were to be abolished; there should be, in his words, "no more masterpieces." In place of written plays there should be

cries, groans, apparitions, surprises, theatricalities of all kinds, magic beauty of costumes taken from certain ritual models; ... light in waves, in sheets, in fusillades of fiery arrows. ... Paroxysms will suddenly burst forth, will fire up like fires in different spots.

In a famous metaphor, Artaud compared the theatre to the great medieval plague, noting that both plague and theatre had the capacity to liberate human possibilities and illuminate the human potential:

The theatre is like the plague ... because like the plague it is the revelation, the bringing forth, the exteriorization of a depth of latent cruelty by means of which all the perverse possibilities of the mind, whether of an individual or a people, are localized....

One cannot imagine, save in an atmosphere of carnage, torture, and bloodshed, all the magnificent Fables which recount to the multitudes the first sexual division and the first carnage of essences that appeared in creation. The theatre, like the plague, is in the image of this carnage and this essential separation. It releases conflicts, disengages powers, liberates possibilities, and if these possibilities and these powers are dark, it is the fault not of the plague nor of the theatre, but of life.

Artaud's ideas were radical, and his essays were incendiary; his power to shock and inspire is undiminished today, and many contemporary theatre artists claim an Artaudian heritage. It is not at all clear, however, what final form the theatre of cruelty should actually take in performance, and it is readily apparent even to the casual reader that the theatre Artaud speaks of is much easier to realize on paper than on an actual stage. Artaud's own productions were in fact failures; he was formally "expelled" from the surrealist movement, and he spent most of his later life abroad in mental institutions. His one published play, *Jet of Blood* (1925), illustrates both the radically antirealistic nature of his dramaturgy and the difficulties that would be encountered in its production. This is the opening of the play:

**THE YOUNG MAN:** I love you, and everything is beautiful.

**THE YOUNG GIRL:** (*with a strong tremolo in her voice*) You love me, and everything is beautiful.

THE YOUNG MAN: (*in a very deep voice*) I love you, and everything is beautiful.

THE YOUNG GIRL: (*in an even deeper voice than his*) You love me, and everything is beautiful.

THE YOUNG MAN: (*leaving her abruptly*) I love you. (Pause) Turn around and face me.

THE YOUNG GIRL: (*she turns to face him*) There!

THE YOUNG MAN: (*in a shrill and exalted voice*) I love you, I am big, I am shining, I am full, I am solid.

THE YOUNG GIRL: (*in the same shrill tone*) We love each other.

THE YOUNG MAN: We are intense. Ah, how well ordered this world is!

> *A pause. Something that sounds like an immense wheel turning and blowing out air is heard. A hurricane separates the two. At this moment two stars crash into each other, and we see a number of live pieces of human bodies falling down: hands, feet, scalps, masks, colonnades, porches, temples, and alembics, which, however, fall more and more slowly, as if they were falling in a vacuum. Three scorpions fall down, one after the other, and finally a frog and a beetle, which sets itself down with a maddening, vomit-inducing slowness ...*
>
> *Enter a knight of the Middle Ages in an enormous suit of armor, followed by a nurse holding her breasts in both hands and puffing and wheezing because they are both very swollen.*

Artaud's apocalyptic vision has stimulated many subsequent theatre directors, including Jean-Louis Barrault and Roger Blin in France, Peter Brook in England, Jerzy Grotowski in Poland, and André Gregory in America; his influence can also be seen in the plays of jean Genet and the productions of Robert Wilson. His notion of a theatre of cruelty, though not fully realized onstage in his lifetime, has been more closely approached by each of these artists and may still be achieved.

### Philosophical Melodrama: *No Exit*

*No Exit* is one of the most compelling short plays ever written. In this one-act fantasy written in 1944, jean-Paul Sartre (1905-1980), the well-known French existentialist philosopher, establishes a unique "Hell," which is a room without windows or mirrors. Into it come three people, lately deceased, all condemned to this netherworld because of their earthly sins. The three are brilliantly ill matched: Garcin, the sole man, tends toward homosexuality, as does Inez, one of the two women; Estelle, the final occupant of this bizarre inferno, tends toward heterosexual nymphomania. Estelle pursues Garcin, Garcin pursues his fellow spirit, Inez, and Inez pursues the beautiful Estelle in a triangle of misdirected affection that, one presumes, will continue maddeningly through all eternity. The infinite bleakness of this play's fantastical situation and the numbing futility of each character's aspirations provoke Garcin to beg for some good old-fashioned torture—but nothing quite so simple is forthcoming. Instead, he is forced to conclude: "Hell is other people." And the play ends with a curtain line that is characteristic of the modern stylized theatre:

GARCIN: Well, well, let's get on with it.

This line suggests that although the play concludes, the situation continues, eternally, behind the drawn curtain.

*No Exit* is a classic dramatic statement of existentialism, of which Sartre was the twentieth century's leading exponent. Remove the fantastical elements—that this is Hell and the characters are ghosts—and we have Sartre's vision of human interaction: every individual forever seeks affirmation and self-realization in the eyes of the Other. Each character in the play carries with him or her some baggage of guilt and expectation, each seeks from another some certification of final personal worth, and each is endlessly thwarted in this quest. We are all condemned to revolve around each other in frustratingly incomplete accord, suggests Sartre; we are all forced to reckon with the impossibility of finding meaning in the unrelated events that constitute life.

One can accept or reject Sartre's view—which is perhaps more than usually pessimistic for having been written during the Nazi occupation of Sartre's Paris—but no one can dispute the brilliance of his dramatic stylization: the fantastical Hell, an amusing "valet" who brings each character onto the stage, and the highly contrived assemblage of mismatched characters all serve to focus the intellectual argument precisely. Sartre's characters are philosophically representative rather than psychologically whole; there is no intention on Sartre's part to portray individual people with interesting idiosyncrasies, and there is no feeling on our part that the characters have a personal life beyond what we see in the play. Biographical character analysis would be useless for an actor assigned to play one of these roles, and the interlock of psychological motivation, even in this sexually charged atmosphere, is deliberately ignored by the author. What Sartre presents instead is a general understanding of human affairs: a philosophy of interpersonal relations.

**Theatre of the Absurd: *Waiting Godot*** The name *theatre of the absurd,* coined by English critic Martin Esslin in his 1962 book of that name, applies to a grouping of plays that share certain common structures and styles and are tied together by a common philosophical thread: the theory of the absurd as formulated by French essayist and playwright Albert Camus (1913-1960). Camus likened the human condition to that of the mythological Corinthian king Sisyphus, who because of his cruelty was condemned forever to roll a stone up a hill in Hades, only to have it roll back down upon reaching the top. Camus saw the modern individual as similarly engaged in an eternally futile task: the absurdity of searching for some meaning or purpose or order in human life. To Camus, the immutable irrationality of the universe is what makes this task absurd. On the one hand, human beings yearn for a "lost" unity and lasting truth; on the other hand, the world can only be seen as irrecoverably fragmented—chaotic, unsummable, permanently unorganized, and permanently unorganizable.

The plays that constitute the theatre of the absurd are obsessed with the futility of all action and the pointlessness of all direction. These themes are developed theatrically through a deliberate and selfconscious flaunting of the "absurd"—in the sense of the ridiculous. Going beyond the use of symbols and the fantasy and poetry of other nonrealists, the absurdists have distinguished themselves by employing in their dramas, for example, clocks that clang incessantly, characters that eat pap in ashcans, corpses that grow by the minute, and personal interactions that are belligerently noncredible.

The theatre of the absurd can be said to include mid-twentieth-century works by Jean Genet (French), Eugéne Ionesco (Romanian), Friedrich Dürrenmatt (Swiss), Arthur Adamov (Russian), Slawomir Mrozek (Polish), Harold Pinter (English), Edward Albee (American), Fernando Arrabal (Spanish), and the Irish poet, playwright, and novelist Samuel Beckett. And although Paris is the center of this theatre—so much so that the works of Ionesco, Adamov, Arrabal, and Beckett are all written in French rather than in their native tongues—its influence is felt worldwide.

Samuel Beckett (1906-1989), the unquestioned leader of the absurdist writers, eschewed all realism, romanticism, and rationalism to create works that are relentlessly unenlightening, that are indeed committed to a final obscurity. "Art has nothing to do with clarity, does not dabble in the clear, and does not make clear," argued Beckett in one of his earliest works, and his theatre was based on the thesis that man is and will remain ignorant regarding all matters of importance.

Born in Dublin, Beckett emigrated in 1928 to Paris, where he joined a literary circle centered on another Irish émigré, James Joyce. Beckett's life before World War II was an artistic vagabondage, during which he wrote several poems, short stories, and a novel. After the war and his seclusion in the south of France during the Nazi occupation, he produced the masterworks for which he is justly famous: the novels *Molloy, Malone Dies, and The Unnamable,* and the plays *Waiting for Godot* and *Endgame.* By the time of his death in 1989, Beckett had received the Nobel Prize in Literature, and his works had become the subject of hundreds of critical books and essays. It was *Godot* that first brought Beckett to worldwide attention: the play's premiere in Paris in 1953 occasioned a great stir among French authors and critics, and its subsequent openings in London and New York had the same effect there.

*Waiting for Godot* is a parable without a message. On a small mound at the base of a tree, beside a country road, two elderly men in bowler hats wait for a "Mr. Godot," with whom they have presumably made an appointment. They believe that when Godot comes they will be "saved"; however, they are not at all certain that Godot has agreed to meet with them or if this is the right place or the right day or whether they will even recognize him if he comes. During each of the two acts, which seem to be set in late afternoon on two successive days (although nobody can be sure of that), the men are visited by passersby—first by two men calling themselves Pozzo and Lucky and subsequently by a young boy who tells them that Mr. Godot "cannot come today but surely tomorrow." The two old men continue to wait as the curtain falls. Although there are substantial references in the play to Christian symbols and beliefs, it is not clear whether these imply positive or negative associations. The only development in the play is that the characters seem to undergo a certain loss of adeptness while the setting blossoms in rebirth (the tree sprouts leaves between the acts).

What Beckett has drawn here is clearly a paradigm of the human condition: an ongoing life cycle of vegetation serving as the background to human decay, hope, and ignorance. Beckett's tone is whimsical: the characters play enchanting word games with each

In a poll of eight hundred playwrights, actors, directors, and theatre journalists taken by the Royal Shakespeare Company in 1998, Samuel Beckett's *Waiting for Godot* was voted "the most important play of the twentieth century." Yet its American premiere, at the Coconut Grove Playhouse in Miami, Florida, in 1956, was a complete disaster. On opening night, half the audience left at intermission, and the next morning when the box office opened, dozens of people were standing in line to return tickets they had bought for future performances! Times have certainly changed for this play about two elderly tramps who wait for a mysterious figure who never shows up. In 2009, major theatres in both New York and London presented *Godot productions* with superb casts, and each was completely sold out for its entire run. (*Above*) The American production with Nathan Lane (*left*) and Bill Irwin as the hapless tramps, Estragon and Vladimir, and between them John Goodman as the bullying pseudo-aristocrat, Pozzo. (*Below*) The London production with Patrick Stewart as Vladimir and Ian McKellan as Estragon.

other, they amuse each other with songs, accounts of dreams, exercises, and vaudevillian antics, and in general they make the best of a basically hopeless situation. Beckett's paradigm affords a field day for critical investigators: *Waiting for Godot* has already generated a veritable library of brilliantly evocative discussions, and few plays from any era have been so variously analyzed, interpreted, and explored for symbolic meaning and content. Owing largely to the international critical acceptance of this play and its eventual public success, absurdist drama, as well as the whole of modern stylized theatre, was able to move out of the esoteric "art theatre" of the world capitals and onto the stages of popular theatres everywhere.

### Theatre of Alienation: *The Good Person of Szechuan*

Contrasting vividly with the theatre of the absurd is the theatre of alienation (or of distancing). Whereas the hermetic, self-contained absurdist plays highlight the essential futility of human endeavors, the sprawling, socially engaged "epic" theatre of alienation concentrates on humanity's potential for growth and society's capacity to effect change.

The guiding genius of the theatre of alienation was Bertolt Brecht (1898-1956): theorist, dramatist, and director. No single individual has had a greater impact on post-World War II theatre than Brecht. This impact has been felt in two ways. First, Brecht introduced theatre practices that are, at least on the surface, utterly at variance with those in use since the time of Aristotle. Second, his accomplishments invigorated the theatre with an abrasive humanism that reawakened its sense of social responsibility and its awareness of the capacity of theatre to mold public issues and events.

Brecht, who was born in Germany, emerged from World War I a dedicated Marxist and pacifist. Using poems, songs, and eventually the theatre to promote his ideals following the German defeat, Brecht vividly portrayed his country during the Weimar Republic as caught in the grips of four giant vises: the military, capitalism, industrialization, and imperialism. His *Rise and Fall of the City of Mahagonny,* for example, an "epic opera" of 1930, proved an immensely popular blending of satire and propaganda, music and expressionist theatricality, social idealism and lyric poetry. It was produced all over Germany and throughout most of Europe in the early 1930s as a depiction of a rapacious international capitalism evolving toward fascism.

Brecht was forced to flee his country upon Hitler's accession to the chancellorship. Thereafter he moved about Europe for a time and then, for much of the 1940s, settled in America. After World War II he returned in triumph to East Berlin, where the East German government established for him the Berliner Ensemble Theatre. There Brecht was allowed to consolidate his theories in a body of productions developed out of his earlier plays and the pieces he had written while in exile.

Brecht's theatre draws upon a potpourri of theatrical conventions, some derived from the ancients, some from Eastern drama, and some from the German expressionist movement in which Brecht himself played a part in his early years. Masks, songs, verse, exotic settings, satire, and direct rhetorical address are fundamental conventions that Brecht adopted from other theatre forms. In addition, he developed many conventions of his own: lantern-slide projections with printed "captions," asides and invocations directed to the audience to encourage them to develop an objective point of view, and also a variety of procedures aimed at demystifying theatrical techniques (for example, lowering the lights so that the pipes and wires would be displayed) became the characteristics of Brecht's theatre.

Brecht deplored the use of sentimentality and the notion of audience empathy for characters and attempted instead to create a performance style that was openly "didactic": the actors were asked to alienate themselves, or distance themselves, from the character they played—to "demonstrate" a character rather than to embody that character in a realistic manner. In Brecht's view, the ideal actor was one who could establish toward his or her character a *critical objectivity* that would make clear the character's social function and political commitment. In attempting to repudiate the "magic" of the theatre, he demanded that it be made to seem nothing more than a place for workers to present a meaningful "parable" of life, and he in no way wished to disguise the fact that the stage personnel—actors and stagehands—were merely workers doing their jobs. In every way possible, Brecht attempted to prevent the audience from becoming swept up in an emotional, sentimental bath of feelings: his goal was to keep members of the audience "alienated" or "distanced" from the literal events depicted by the play so that they would be free to concentrate on the larger social and political issues that the play generated and reflected. Brecht considered this theatre to be an "epic" one because it attempted, around the framework of a parable or an archetypal event, to create a whole new perspective on human history and to indicate the direction that political dialogue should take to foster social betterment.

Brecht's theories were to have a staggering impact on the modern theatre. In his wholesale renunciation

Jane Horrocks plays Shen Te pretending to be her male cousin Shui Ta as she bars her door to the family of freeloaders whom, as Shen Te, she had earlier welcomed into her shop. This production of *The Good Soul of Szechuan*, as Brecht's play was retitled and staged by Richard Jones at London's Young Vic Theatre in 2008, is set outside a cement factory that becomes a heroin distribution center. Scenery and costume designs by Miriam Buether.

of Aristotelian catharsis, which depends on audience empathy with a noble character, and his denial of Stanislavsky's basic principles concerning the aims of acting, Brecht provided a new dramaturgy that encouraged playwrights, directors, and designers to tackle social issues directly rather than through the implications of contrived dramatic situations. Combining the technologies and aesthetics of other media—the lecture hall, the slide show, the public meeting, the cinema, the cabaret, the rehearsal—Brecht fashioned a vastly expanded arena for his *dialectics:* his social arguments that sought to engender truth through the confrontation of conflicting interests. These ideas were played out, in Brecht's own works and in countless other works inspired by him, with bold theatricality, an open-handed dealing with the audience, proletarian vigor, and a stridently entertaining, intelligently satirical, and charmingly bawdy theatre. This theatre has proven even more popular today than it was in Brecht's time, because since then the world seems to have grown even more fragmented, more individualistic, and more suspicious of collective emotions and sentimentality.

No play better illustrates Brecht's dramatic theory and method than *The Good Person of Szechuan* (1943). This play, set in western China (of which Brecht knew practically nothing, thus adding to the "distancing"

of the story), concerns a kindhearted prostitute, Shen Te, who is astounded to receive a gift of money from three itinerant gods. Elated by her good fortune, Shen Te uses the money to start a tobacco business. She is, however, quickly beset by petty officials seeking to impose local regulations, by self-proclaimed creditors demanding payment, and by a host of hangers-on who simply prey upon her good nature. At the point of financial ruin, Shen Te leaves her tobacco shop to enlist the aid of her male cousin Shui Ta, who strides imperiously into the tobacco shop and rousts the predators, making it safe for Shen Te to return. But the predators come back, and Shen Te again has to call on the tyrannical Shui Ta to save her. A simple story—but Brecht's stroke of genius is to make Shui Ta and Shen Te the same character: Shui Ta is simply Shen Te in disguise! The aim of the play is not to show that there are kindhearted people and successful people but that a person must choose to be one or the other. What kind of society is it, Brecht asks, that forces us to make this sort of choice?

Brecht was no mere propagandist, and his epic theatre is not one of simple messages or easy conclusions. At the end of *The Good Person of Szechuan*, Shen Te asks the gods for help, but they simply float off into the air reciting inane platitudes as the curtain falls. The gods do not have the answer—so the audience must provide it. In the play's epilogue, a character comes forward and addresses us:

Hey, honorable folks, don't be dismayed
That we can't seem to end this play! You've stayed
see our shining, all-concluding moral,
And what we've given you has been this bitter quar-
rel.
We know, we know—we're angry too,
To see the curtain down and everything askew.
We'd love to see you stand and cheer—and say
How wonderful you find our charming play!
But we won't put our heads into the sand.
We know your wish is ever our command,
We know you ask for more: a firm conclusion
To this alarming more-than-mass confusion.
But what is it? Who knows? Not all your cash
Could buy your way—or ours—from this mishmash.
Do we need heroes? Dreams? New Gods? Or
None?
Well, tell us—else we're hopelessly undone.
The only thing that we can think to say
Is simply that it's you must end this play.
Tell us how our own good woman of Szechuan
Can come to a good ending—if she can!
Honorable folks: you search, and we will trust
That you will find the way. You must, must, must!

Brecht's parables epitomize the conflicts between social classes they do not presume to solve these conflicts. Indeed, the social problems Brecht addresses are to be solved not on the stage but in the world itself: the audience must find the appropriate balance between morality and greed, between individualism and social responsibility. Brecht's plays reenact the basic intellectual dichotomy posed by Marx's dialectical materialism; thus they are, in a sense, Marxist plays, but they certainly are not Leninist, much less Stalinist. They radiate faith in the human potential. Yet although they are both socially engaged and theatrically eclectic—qualities not particularly noticeable in the theatre of the absurd—they still resound with the fundamental human uncertainty that pervades all of modern stylized theatre.

## Comedy of Contemporary Manners: Bedroom Farce

Comedy has always been one of the greatest staples of the theatre; since the days of Aristophanes in ancient Greece and Plautus in Rome, comedians have entertained the public with puns, antics, lighthearted social commentaries, and a host of other amusing reflections on the human struggle. It is an axiom of the theatre that "comedy is serious business," and the true comedian is understood to be as inspired an artist as any who labors under the lights. Yet comedy is rarely accorded its fair share of academic consideration, partly because comedy tends to be topical and therefore less than universal and partly because the very thing that makes comedy popular—its accessibility—also makes it relatively simple, and academicians adore complexity. But simple does not mean simple-minded, and the relative scarcity of fine comic plays originating in any generation attests to the enormous talent it takes to write, direct, and act comedically.

In America, Neil Simon (born 1927) has for four decades exhibited enormous talent and success as a writer of light comedy for the stage (and film), and in England, Alan Ayckbourn (born 1939) has demonstrated comparable skill at the form. Ayckbourn's *Bedroom Farce* was first produced in 1975 by the Library Theatre in Scarborough, England, with which Ayckbourn is associated; the play was subsequently produced by the National Theatre in London in 1977 and came to Broadway and various other American cities shortly thereafter.

Like all of Ayckbourn's works, *Bedroom Farce* is an ingenious comedy of current manners, novel in its dramatic structure and reasonably true to life in its concerns. The setting for *Bedroom Farce* is three bedrooms, all in view simultaneously. The characters consist of four couples who, for reasons cleverly worked out in the plot, find themselves in one bedroom after another by turns. Although the innuendos of this play are highly sexual, the action consists primarily of animated verbal exchanges and comic business and pratfalls; thus the play lives up to the farcical structure promised by its title.

The opening scene of *Bedroom Farce*-an exchange of dialogue between Ernest and Delia, the oldest couple in the play—typifies the witty and very British repartee mastered by Ayckbourn. The scene takes place in a bedroom described as a "large Victorian" room "in need of redecoration":

... DELIA sits in her bedroom at her dressing table mirror She is going out. She is in her slip and finishing her make-up. An elaborate operation. ERNEST wanders in. Birdlike, bumbling, nearly sixty He is in evening dress. He stares at DELIA. They are obviously going to be late but ERNEST has learnt that impatience gets him nowhere.

DELIA: It would appear that things between Susannah and Trevor are coming to a head.
ERNEST: Ah.
DELIA: He was always a difficult boy. I sometimes think if you hadn't ignored him quite as much -
ERNEST: I did?

Shown here is Alan Ayckbourn's delightful three-bedroom comedy, Bedroom Farce, as directed by Loveday Ingram for London's Aldwych Theatre in 2002.

DELIA: Of course you did. You hardly said a word to him all the time he was growing up.

ERNEST: I seem to remember chatting away to him for hours.

DELIA: Well. Chatting. I meant conversation. Conversation about important things. A father should converse with his son. About things that matter deeply.

ERNEST: Doesn't really leave them much to talk about then, does it?

DELIA: And that if I may say so is typical. No. Let's admit it. We weren't good parents. You did nothing and I tried to make up for it, and that's why he's like he is today. I mean if he'd had a stable childhood, he'd never have completely lost his sense of proportion and married Susannah. I mean, I sometimes feel on the rare occasions one does see them together that she's not really—awful thing to say but-not really resilient enough for Trevor. He wants somebody more phlegmatic. That Jan girl for instance would have been ideal. Do you remember her?

ERNEST: Jan? Jan? Jan?

DELIA: Nice little thing. Beautifully normal. She came to tea, do you remember? You got on very well with her.

ERNEST: Oh yes. She was jolly, wasn't she? She was very interested in my stamps. What happened to her?

DELIA: Oh, she married—someone else, I think. She still writes occasionally.

ERNEST: I must say I preferred her to Susannah. Never really hit it off with her, I'm afraid.

DELIA: Well, she's a very complex sort of girl, isn't she? Hasn't really made up her mind. About herself. I mean, I think a woman sooner or later has simply got to make up her mind about herself. I mean, even if she's someone like Carolyn—you know, Mrs. Brightman's Carolyn—who looks at herself and says, right, I'm a lump. I'm going to be a lump but then at least everyone can accept her as a lump. So much simpler.

ERNEST: I think he should have married this other one.

DELIA: Jan? I don't think she was that keen.

ERNEST: She was altogether much jollier.

DELIA: Well, we're saddled with Susannah as a daughter-in-law—at least temporarily. We'd better make the best of it—I think I've put these eyes on crooked—we'd better make the best of it.

ERNEST: It's their bed. They can lie on it.

DELIA: Yes. I think that's one of the problems.

ERNEST: Eh?

DELIA: B—E—D.

ERNEST: B—E—D? Bed?

DELIA: Enough said.

ERNEST: Good lord. How do you know?

DELIA: One reads between the lines, darling. I've had a little look around their house. You can tell a great deal from people's bedrooms.

ERNEST: Can you? Good heavens. (*He looks about.*)

DELIA: If you know what to look for.

There is nothing obscure or difficult in *Bedroom Farce,* which stands out in the contemporary theatre mainly for its capacity to entertain, to titillate, and to dazzle with cleverness. Indeed, Ayckbourn makes clear his purely comedic intentions in the selection of his title, which suggests an even more frivolous diversion than Ayckbourn actually provides. What the author has created in *Bedroom Farce* is, ultimately, something more than just another series of hijinks, physical incongruities, and dramatic clichés: it is a wry combination of social satire, middle-class insights, and boisterous good fun. The modern stylization can be seen in the intricacy of the plot design, which is echoed if not exceeded in Ayckbourn's other plays (*Absurd Person Singular* takes place, successively, in the kitchens of three married couples; *The Norman Conquests* consists of three interlocking plays, occurring simultaneously, involving the same cast of characters in three parts of the same house) and reflects a skill at construction that borders on pure genius. This kind of craftsmanship alone would suffice to elevate any comedy far beyond the usual level of television skit or sitcom; in Ayckbourn's case, it enables his stage works to reach the heights of inspired farce.

**Political Satire: Serious Money** Since at least the time of Aristophanes, playwrights have used the theatre as a broad public platform to criticize the social world of their times—most often in a way that is both caustic and entertaining. Causticity gives such criticism its necessary bite, but a playful or whimsical tone renders even the harshest criticism palatable—and, in exceptionally dangerous times, may also protect a playwright from political retribution. We use the term *satire* to distinguish such works, which have been popular in the theatre of most cultures.

British playwright Caryl Churchill (born 1938) has been a unique exemplar of socially conscious dramatic satire since the 1970s, with trenchant and brilliantly innovative works on a wide variety of issues: sexual orientations and their attendant prejudices and hypocrisies (*Cloud 9*), gender discrimination throughout history (*Top Girls*), British-American attractions and antipathies (*Ice Cream*), and the postcold war chaos in eastern Europe (*Mad Forest*). In each of these works, Churchill has reinvestigated—and in some cases reinvented-the dramaturgical format itself. In *Cloud 9,* for example, she double-casts actors in both male and female—and youthful and elderly—roles, putting a wholly new slant on the complex perspectives that gender and age cast on our notions of personal identity. And in all of her plays, Churchill reexamines the syntaxes of stage dialogue, often creating new conversational punctuation systems to identify just how characters— like people in real life—frequently overlap, interrupt, and self-abort their own and each other's speeches.

In *Serious Money* (1987), Churchill employs a racy rhyming verse—in an exceptional glib patter that lies somewhere between e. e. cummings and gangsta rap— to explore the vagaries of arbitrage stock trading on the London market and of international finance:

ZACKERMAN [an international banker in London]:
There's some enterprising guys around and here's an
    example.
You know how if you want to get a job in the
    states you have to give a urine sample?
    (This is to show you're not on drugs.)
There's a company now for a fifty dollar fee
They'll provide you with a guaranteed pure,
    donated by a churchgoer, bottle of pee.
    (They also plan to market it dehydrated
    in a packet and you just add water.)
And AIDS is making advertisers perplexed
Because it's no longer too good to have your
    product associated with sex.
But it's a great marketing opportunity.
Like the guys opening up blood banks where
    you pay to store your own blood in case of an
    accident and so be guaranteed immunity.
    (It's also a great time to buy into rubber.)
Anyone who can buy oranges for ten and sell at
    eleven in a souk or bazaar
Has the same human nature and can go equally
    far.
The so-called third world doesn't want our charity
    or aid.
All they need is the chance to sit down in front
    of some green screens and trade.

The witty rhymes, punctuated by parenthetical "ad libs," and the complicated frenzy of *Serious Money's* plot and staging (much of the play takes place on a stock brokerage's trading floor, bursting with stock

Telephone calls come fast and furious in Caryl Churchill's *Serious Money,* a savage and satirical comedy about stock trading. This 2004 production at the Yale Repertory Theatre was directed by Jean Randich, with costumes by Daniel Urlie and lighting by Paul Whitaker.

monitors, telephone banks, and continuous, shouted deal-making) create a mesmerizing enchantment. Yet Churchill's views of economic exploitation on an international level beam through loud and clear. Satire is a topical dramatic form that often does not outlive its topics, but when the content is compelling and the form brilliant—as it was with Aristophanes and is with Churchill—the play usually survives its merely political utility and makes its way into the lasting theatrical repertoire.

# The Musical Theatre

# Chapter 9

Musical theatre—a theatre that includes music and songs, and usually dance—is certainly "antirealistic" in the most obvious sense. However, its particularity derives not from a rebellion against verisimilitude (thus it does not fit into the category "antirealistic theatre," as described in the preceding chapter) but rather from its basis in an aesthetics unique to its performance. Hence we treat musical theatre (or music theatre as it is increasingly called) in a chapter of its own.

## THE ROLE OF MUSIC IN THEATRE HISTORY

It could be argued that drama has always been at least partly musical. Aristotle, as we saw in the "What Is a Play?" chapter, considered music the fifth component of tragedy (by which he meant all serious drama). Classic Greek tragedy was sung and danced; it was accompanied by the *aulos* (flute) and other instruments, and Aeschylus, who directed his own plays, was particularly noted for his choreography in the choral entrance of *The Eumenides*. Most Renaissance and commedia dell'arte plays included songs and instrumental music, and twenty-five of Shakespeare's thirty-eight plays contain at least some singing (*The Tempest* alone has nine scripted songs). Moreover, Shakespeare's comedies, as well as those of his

247

contemporaries, seem to have ended with full-stage company dances. In the seventeenth century, English dramatist Ben Jonson wrote musical masques (dance-dramas) for the court of King James I, and in France, Molière wrote *comédie ballets* for King Louis XIV. Each of the five acts of *The Bourgeois Gentleman*, for example, ends with a fully orchestrated and choreographed mini-opera. And, of course, all major Asian dramatic forms involve singing, dancing, and instrumental music—sometimes continuously throughout the performance.

Although spoken text predominates in modern Western drama, singing and dancing make frequent appearances there too, certainly in the antirealistic theatre. Most of Bertolt Brecht's theatre of alienation plays involve songs (his *The Threepenny Opera, Happy End*, and *The Rise and Fall of the City of Mahagonny* are fully orchestrated musical works), and brief songs are included in the texts of Samuel Beckett's theatre of the absurd plays *Waiting for Godot* and *Happy Days*.

Still, musical theatre has become a distinct genre over the past 150 years of Western drama, not so much as a reaction to (or against) prevailing theatre traditions but as a medium calculated, at first anyway, to provoke audience merriment. Absorbing elements of light opera and ballet and, even more significantly, of popular nineteenth-century entertainments such as the English music hall and American minstrel and variety shows, the modern musical theatre brings to the contemporary dramatic repertory a proven and widely enjoyed form of entertainment with global commercial appeal.

Nowhere is that commercial and entertainment success better known than in New York, which remains the international capital of the world's musical theatre—although London, Toronto, and even Sydney are currently hot competitors. In New York, during the past two decades, as much as 80 percent of Broadway's box-office income has derived from musicals alone. Several of them (*Phantom of the Opera, The Lion King, Wicked*) seem all but permanently installed in the theatres where they play eight times a week. At the time of this writing, twenty-five full-scale musicals were performing on Broadway, and more were waiting in the wings. And the income from "road" (touring) versions of these shows attests to an even greater dominance of musicals in larger performing halls around the country. Furthermore, New York's less-capitalized off-Broadway theatres are also home to musicals, many of them smaller musical theatre pieces with simpler stagings, reduced casts, and less-than-complete orchestras. *The Fantasticks*, with an eight-member cast and an "orchestra" of piano and harp, opened in 1960 and ran for forty-two years, closing in 2002 after 17,162 performances—and then reopening in 2006!

Not-for-profit regional theatres are increasingly drawn to musicals too, as are university, community, and dinner theatres and even Shakespeare festivals. Musical theatre is also now a staple of major theatres abroad, including government-subsidized houses such as the National Theatre of England, which in the past three decades has become a major producer of American musicals (*Guys and Dolls, Carousel, Oklahoma!, My Fair Lady, South Pacific, Anything Goes,* and *Caroline, or Change*). Indeed, up to a third of the main theatres in Berlin, Budapest, London, Tokyo, Sydney, and Stockholm (many of them government subsidized) are at any given time hosting engagements of such world-popular musicals as *Phantom of the Opera, Rent, Chicago, Jekyll and Hyde, The Lion King, Les Misérables,* and *The Sound of Music*. Such musical theatre engagements, often (but not always) spectacularly produced, can form the commercial backbone of an entire theatre community's offerings.

But commercial appeal is hardly the sum of musical theatre's international importance. Musical theatre is a dramatic form of great variety, vitality, and—on many occasions—artistic significance. The Pulitzer Prize has been awarded to numerous musical dramas (*Of Thee I Sing, South Pacific, Fiorello!, How to Succeed in Business without Really Trying, A Chorus Line, Sunday in the Park with George, Rent*). Using techniques as old as Greek tragedy and as inspired as those of Mozart and Wagner, musical theatre authors and artists have created both aesthetic innovations and social impact through brilliantly integrated disciplines of melody, cadence, choreography, and rhyme.

# THE DEVELOPMENT OF THE BROADWAY MUSICAL: AMERICAS CONTRIBUTION

What we now know as the Broadway musical has roots deep in the nineteenth century, beginning with singing and dancing shows known as *extravaganzas*— such as *The Seven Sisters,* marketed as a "Grand Operatic, Spectacular, Musical, Terpsichorean, Diabolical, Farcical Burletta" when it premiered in 1860 at the fabled Niblo's Garden in downtown New York City (Broadway and Prince Street). Such lavish extravaganzas were soon joined by increasingly popular *vaudeville* entertainments (collections of musical and variety acts, originally performed in brothels and drinking parlors but becoming more respectable by that time) and by *burlesques* (broadly comedic parodies of serious musical works, often involving cross-dressing). All of these led to a rapidly growing profession of musical performers adept at singing, dancing, acting, and comedy.

Burlesque and vaudeville lasted well into the twentieth century. Florenz Ziegfeld became one of America's great showmen with his annual Ziegfeld Follies—a musical review dedicated to "Glorifying the American Girl" that made stars of vaudevillian comics W. C. Fields, Eddie Cantor, Will Rogers, and Fanny Brice. But it was at Niblo's Garden that what is regarded as America's first true musical, *The Black Crook,* opened in 1866. This play was a rather ordinary melodrama, but when a French dance company, stranded in the city, was added to the show to give it some extra spice, *Crook* became a rather sexy spectacle, with dances, songs, and a bevy of scantily clad young women.

The popularity of staged musical entertainments featuring a wide diversity of performers grew by leaps during the nineteenth and early twentieth centuries. Challenging the old custom of white actors' "blacking up" (with burnt-cork makeup) for minstrel shows, a new black musical comedy arose, employing the emerging ragtime musical syncopations of earlier black vaudeville reviews. Bob Cole's 1898 *A Trip to Coontown* (*coon* was, at the time, a common and generally offensive term for blacks) was one of the most successful: a full-length black musical comedy written and performed by African Americans (some in whiteface!), it played to large mixed-race audiences in New York. Though an unapologetic farce—with ethnic humor, girlie numbers, and neooperatic inserts—Cole's play included at least one song of direct social protest: "No Coons Allowed!" tells of a young man unable to bring his date to the "swellest place in town" on account of the club's racist policy.

New York also proved a hospitable site for sophisticated musical theatre works from abroad at the end of the nineteenth century. The super-witty and still-popular satirical light operas of the English duo W. S. Gilbert and Arthur Sullivan (*HMS Pina fore, The Pirates of Penzance, and The Mikado*), the *opéra bouffe* (satirical comic opera) of French composer Jacques Offenbach (*La Périchole, La Belle Hélène, Orpheus in the Underworld*—which introduced the cancan), and the Viennese operetta of Franz Lehar (*The Merry Widow*) all demonstrated that musical theatre could tell a story in a delightfully appealing way. Audiences flocked to these musicals, and American writers and composers emerged to create homegrown products that could compete with these imports. Irish-born Victor Herbert, an émigré to the United States at twenty-seven, became America's first great composer for the stage. Herbert's major hits, *Babes in Toyland* (1903) and *Naughty Marietta* (1910), proved immensely successful, introducing songs such as "Ah, Sweet Mystery of Life" to America's popular music repertoire. More prominent still was Rhode Island-born vaudevillian George M. Cohan, whose *Little Johnny Jones* (1904), in which Cohan also starred, provided what became his—and some of his country's—signature songs: "I'm a Yankee Doodle Dandy" and "Give My Regards to Broadway." By the first decade of the new century, American musical theatre was becoming the world leader in a newly defined theatrical form: musical comedy.

## Musical Comedy: Gershwin, Kern, *Darktown Follies,* and Rodgers and, Hart

The first third of the twentieth century was the great age of *musical comedy*—a genre that, of course, emphasized comedy as well as singing but also youthful romance. It featured sexy (and lightly clad) girl choruses, liberal doses of patriotic jingoism, and, in response to the "dance craze" of the early 1900s, spectacular dancing—including the show-offy "tap"—to a jazzy or ragtime beat.

By the 1920s and 1930s, American musical comedy had dozens of starring composers, lyricists, and performers. Tourists from all over the country flocked to midtown Manhattan to see such musical works as the brothers George (music) and Ira (lyrics) Gershwin's cool and still-memorable *Lady Be Good, Oh, Kay!, Funny Face,* and *Girl Crazy;* Vincent Youmans's sweetly romantic *Hit the Deck* and *No, No, Nanette* (with "Tea for Two"); Jerome Kern's bouncy *Very Good Eddie* and *Sunny;* Cole Porter's wittily engaging *Anything Goes* and *DuBarry Was a Lady;* and a series of especially droll and delightful musical comedies by Richard Rodgers (music) and Lorenz Hart (lyrics), including *A Connecticut Yankee, On Your Toes,* and *Babes in Arms.* What all these works had in common were a laughably simple plot, a cast composed strictly of romantic and comedic characters, a wholly unchallenging theme, lots of pretty girls in revealing costumes, and abundantly cheerful singing and dancing that had little or no connection to the plot. And although these works were often silly as dramas, there can be no mistaking the musical glories of the best of them, with music that remains enchanting to the present day. The Gershwin songs ("Embraceable You," "'S Wonderful," and "The Man I Love") and those of Rodgers and Hart ("The Lady Is a Tramp," "Small Hotel," and "Bewitched, Bothered and Bewildered") and the shows they came from have been regularly revived; the songs themselves have become a staple of the repertories of literally hundreds of modern jazz singers.

Up in Harlem, meanwhile, Bert Williams and J. Leubrie Hill drew large mixed-race audiences for their *Darktown Follies of 1914* (introducing the hit number "After the Ball"). And in 1921 a black musical dominated a full Broadway season for the first time: composer Eubie Blake and lyricist Noble Sissle's wildly successful *Shuffle Along* ran more than five hundred performances and introduced such songs as "In Honeysuckle Time" and "I'm Just Wild about Harry." Popular high-stepping, side-slapping "black-bottom" dancing was a feature of many black musicals of the 1920s, as was the epoch-defining dance known as "the Charleston," which, introduced in the 1923 black musical *How Come?* (composed by Maceo Pinkard), started a national craze in the hit show *Runnin' Wild* (by James P. Johnson and Cecil Mack) later that year.

## A Golden Age

By 1925 the American musical was beginning to dominate New York's cultural life—and the country's. That September, four great musicals opened on Broadway in four days: Vincent Youmans and Irving Caesar's *No, No, Nanette*, Rudolf Friml's *The Vagabond King*, Jerome Kern and Oscar Hammerstein II's *Sunny*, and Rodgers and Hart's *Dearest Enemy*. Each of these shows was wildly popular and went on to run well into the following year—from almost three hundred performances (Dearest Enemy) to more than five hundred (The Vagabond King and Sunny). What is widely considered a "golden age of musicals" had begun.

The golden age ushered in a new genre—musical drama—characterized by increasingly serious plots and sophisticated musical treatments. *Show Boat*, written by Jerome Kern (music) and Oscar Hammerstein II (book and lyrics) in 1927, was an early masterpiece of musical drama (though its authors insisted on calling it a musical comedy). It represents one of the great pieces of fully acted—and not just sung—vocal literature in the American theatre. Adapted from a gritty novel by Edna Ferber, *Show Boat* has a complex plot that is carried by the music and dancing as well as by the work's spoken dialogue; the musical touches significantly on race relations in America. Indeed, the famous "OF Man River" aria (though viewed by some as patronizing at the time of its successful 1993 revival) referred pointedly to the then-current racial divisions as sung by a black actor in front of the show's (largely white) 1927 audience:

Colored folks work on de Mississippi,
Colored folks work while de white folks play,
Pullin' dem boats from de dawn to sunset,
Gittin' no rest till de Judgment Day—
Don' look up
An' don' look down—
You don' dast make
De white boss frown.
Bend your knees
An' bow your head,
An' pull dat rope Until yo' dead.

Meanwhile, the Gershwin brothers' *Strike Up the Band* and *Of Thee I Sing* moved this fraternal team into the arena of political satire and proved so successful that the latter production received the 1932 Pulitzer Prize for Drama—the first musical to do so. The Gershwins followed with the full-out folk opera *Porgy and Bess* (1935), which remains a staple of international opera companies today.

The second serious phase of the musical's golden age came into full flower with Rodgers and Hart's startling *Pal Joey* (1940), adapted from grimly ironic and sophisticated *New Yorker* stories by John O'Hara and featuring an amoral gigolo and his often unsavory companions in a musical pastiche of the contemporary urban nightclub scene. Tame by today's standards, *Joey* shocked prewar audiences with its blithely suggestive lyrics about sexual infidelity and shady business ethics and with a show-stopping song ("Zip!") belted out by an intellectual stripteaser—who sang out her thoughts while doing her act.

Many serious musicals followed, straining the word *comedy* wholly out of the musical's nomenclature. Marc Blitzstein's *The Cradle Will Rock* (1938), concerning the struggle to organize a union of steelworkers in "Steeltown" against the opposition of one Mr. Mister, the town's leading capitalist, was canceled an hour before its New York opening by U.S. government officials who objected to the play's "left-wing propaganda" (the government provided funding for the sponsoring theatre). The play was performed later that night at another theatre, oratorio-style and without scenery or costumes, to tremendous enthusiasm—as memorialized in Tim Robbins's film *Cradle Will Rock* in 1999. Lady in the Dark (1941)—with a book by dramatist Moss Hart, lyrics by Ira Gershwin, and music by Kurt Weill (Brecht's colleague, who, like Brecht, had fled to America from Nazi rule in Germany)—concerned itself with psychoanalysis and dream analysis and the perilous situation of a career woman (Liza Elliott) in a world dominated by old-fashioned ideas of marriage and women's roles; the musical numbers were all contained in Liza's three long dream sequences. Oklahoma! (1943), with music by Richard Rodgers and lyrics by Oscar Hammerstein II, dealt with social and sexual tensions in the opening of the western states. Dispensing with the accepted convention of decorative dancing girls, *Oklahoma!* featured content-laden balletic choreography by Agnes de Mille to advance the plot and treated its historical subject—which included an onstage killing and the quick dispensing of frontier justice—with romantic passion and a new level of social intensity.

By the end of the Second World War, seriously themed Broadway musicals dominated the commercial American theatre. Rodgers and Hammerstein followed *Oklahoma!* with one success after another: *Carousel* (dealing with spousal abuse), *South Pacific* (racial prejudice), *The King and I* (gender prejudice and ethnocentricity), *Flower Drum Song* (East-West assimilation), and *The Sound of Music* (Nazism), all marked with social and intercultural conflict, richly romantic settings and songs, beautiful solo numbers and love duets, and thrilling choral, choreographic, and orchestral ensembles. Leonard Bernstein, one of America's leading orchestral conductors and composers, left a considerable mark on the musical's golden age with his *On the Town*, about World War II sailors on leave in Manhattan, and *West Side Story* (with lyrics by Stephen Sondheim), a powerfully emotional retelling of the *Romeo and Juliet* story, with a contemporary Polish American (Tony) as his Romeo and a Puerto Rican American (Maria) as Juliet. And Jerry Bock and Sheldon Harnick conveyed a profoundly moving version of Jewish shtetl life in tsarist Russia with *Fiddler on the Roof.*

Not all musicals were deeply sober and serious, of course. More-lighthearted and satirical musicals of the 1940s and 1950s—first-rate works that still featured well-integrated plots, characters, themes, and musical styles—included Frank Loesser's *Guys and Dolls,* based on the idiosyncratic urban stories of Damon Runyon; Cole Porter's *Kiss Me Kate,* based on a backstage romance during a tour of Shakespeare's *The Taming of the Shrew;* and Irving Berlin's Annie Get Your Gun, based on the life of American folk heroine Annie Oakley. Richard Adler and Jerry Ross's *Pajama Game* (about union organizing in a pajama factory) and *Damn Yankees* (a Faustian tale about baseball) featured superlative jazz dancing choreographed by Bob Fosse. Alan Jay Lerner (book and lyrics) and Frederick Loewe (music) first successfully collaborated on the fantasy *Brigadoon,* about a mythical Scottish village, and then followed up with their brilliant musical revision of George Bernard Shaw's *Pygmalion,* renamed *My Fair Lady,* which wittily explores and exploits heroine Eliza Doolittle's proper and improper pronunciation of spoken English.

The best of these musicals during Broadway's golden age were commercially successful beyond anything in the theatre's previous history. Hit plays ran not for weeks or months, as before, but for years. They were, indeed, more than just "plays"; they were world-renowned cultural phenomena. For the first time, theatre tickets were sold as far as six months in advance, and business travelers returning from Manhattan were expected to provide a full report on "the new musicals in town." Touring companies brought the best of these shows to the rest of the country: first-class national tours, with the Broadway stars intact, and, subsequently, "bus and truck" tours, with less-familiar performers—nonetheless advertising "straight from Broadway!"—traveled around the nation. It is likely that most Americans during these years first experienced live theatre in the form of a road version of a Broadway musical, as did the author of this book. Songs from the best musicals—and even from some mediocre ones-routinely made the radio "hit parade" (forerunner of the "top ten" or "top forty" listings of today) and gained an instant national audience. Film versions of many musicals—*Oklahoma!, Carousel, My Fair Lady, Guys and Dolls, The Sound of Music*—were also widely popular. For a couple of decades, at least, it seemed as if everyone in America was whistling the latest creation from the tunesmiths of Broadway. And the stars of Broadway musicals past and present—Jimmy Durante, Eddie Cantor, Mary Martin, Ethel Merman, Julie Andrews, Carol Charming, Pearl Bailey, Bob Hope, and John Raitt—achieved national celebrity status; many became the pioneer performers on America's new entertainment medium, television. It is certain that the theatre had never played such a central role in American popular culture before; it is questionable if it ever will again.

# THE CONTEMPORARY MUSICAL

No golden age lasts forever, and in retrospect no such age is unquestionably remembered as golden; the glittery epithet may in fact become little more than a quaint historical milepost. It is unquestionable, however, that the bulk of musicals produced in America today, not just by amateur groups but on Broadway as well, are revivals of the great musicals of mid-twentieth-century America. Today, however, a new and more contemporary musical theatre—at once less sentimental and more ironic, less rhapsodic and more choreographic—has come onto the scene.

## The Emergence of Choreographer-Directors

The past half century has seen a tremendous escalation in the importance of choreography in American musicals. Agnes de Mille was instrumental in initiating this movement with her plot-advancing dance numbers in Rodgers and Hammerstein's *Oklahoma!* But later years saw the emergence of several choreographers who became more widely known than the directors they worked with—indeed, who became their productions' directors.

Jerome Robbins (1918-1998), trained in both ballet and acting, was the first of these. His "Small House of Uncle Thomas" ballet—a deliberately quaint, Siamese-themed version of *Uncle Tom's Cabin*-in *The King and I* and his vigorous teenage "street rumble" dances in *West Side Story* earned him national critical fame, leading to his combining directorial and choreographic chores in the seriocomic Broadway musicals *Gypsy,* about the lives of striptease artist Gypsy Rose Lee and her mother, and *Fiddler on the Roof,* about Jewish life in prerevolutionary Russia. In 1989 Robbins put together a retrospective collection of his dances in *Jerome Robbins' Broadway,* winning the Tony Award for best musical.

Gower Champion (1921-1980) and Bob Fosse (1927-1987) were of Robbins's generation but utterly unalike. Champion, a veteran dancer (with his wife, Marge)

in many Broadway shows and Hollywood films, returned to the stage in 1960 to both stage and choreograph the energetic, crowd-pleasing *Bye Bye Birdie.* He followed this up with the romantic *Carnival* (1961) and the brashly presentational *Hello, Dolly! (1964),* in each case placing dance at the center of his dramatic entertainment. Champion's final show—he died tragically on its opening night—was *42nd Street* (1980), a virtual valentine to the Broadway theatre and particularly to tap dancing; the show enjoyed a long run and was brought back in a Tony Award-winning revival in 2000-01. Fosse, also a golden-age choreographer (*Pajama Game* and *Damn Yankees,* 1954 and 1955), went on to develop a highly idiosyncratic style—quick, jerky moves that suddenly segue to slow, sinuous come-ons; bumps and grinds from the striptease; white gloves and black bowler hats from minstrel and vaudeville; dance-as-sex and sex-as-dance—in, particularly, *Chicago* (1975) and *Dancin'* (1978), as well as in the film of *Cabaret* and his own filmed autobiography, *All That Jazz.* A posthumous retrospective of Fosse's dances, simply titled *Fosse,* opened on Broadway in 1999, running two years and winning the Tony Award for best musical.

Tommy Tune (born 1939) and Michael Bennett (1943-1987) are of a later generation. The lanky Tune, a brilliant tap dancer, even performs in some of the productions he also choreographs or directs; indeed, he is the only person to have won Tony Awards in four categories—director, choreographer, leading actor, and featured actor. Tune's *My One and Only* (1988), in which he also starred, *Grand Hotel* (1989), and *Will Rogers Follies* (1991) were celebrations of dance entertainment. Bennett's artistic goals were somewhat more conceptual: his masterwork (after choreographing and codirecting Stephen Sondheim's *Company* and *Follies*) was *A Chorus Line* (1975), a musical that, conceived, staged, and choreographed by Bennett, takes place in a dance audition and consists largely of dances interspersed with "interviews" of the auditioning dancers. It was initially developed off-Broadway using improvisations with performers, many of whom landed in the show itself. *A Chorus Line* was for many years Broadway's longest-running show.

At the top of the twenty-first century, Susan Stroman practically seized at least temporary control of the Broadway musical stage, winning every award in sight for her extraordinary direction and choreography of the hit Broadway production of Mel Brooks's

The iconic "musical about musicals" is Michael Bennett´s *A Chorus Line* (1975), which portrays New York musical performers auditioning for a show—in part created from true-life stories told to Bennett by just such performers. This 2006 Broadway revival was directed by Bob Avian (the original production's choreographer); the costumes were designed by Theoni V. Aldredge, who also designed the original.

*The Producers,* which won a record-shattering twelve Tony Awards; plus awards for her choreography and direction of the wordless, all-dance *Contact,* which she also conceived, and for a notable revival of *The Music Man;* plus awards for her choreography for a revisionist revival of Rodgers and Hammerstein's *Oklahoma!*—all within a three-year period! What is remarkable about Stroman's choreography is its combination of humor, exuberance, inventiveness, and down-to-earth accessibility across an enormously wide-ranging stylistic palette. The clever deployment of "dancing props" is as close as Stroman comes to having a trademark: rustic farm implements in *Crazy for You,* hurtling trays of dishes in the restaurant scene of *Contact,* eye-popping rope tricks in *Oklahoma!,* tap dancing by old ladies hanging on to metal walkers in *The Producers,* and a "Putting on the Ritz" chorus dressed in top hats, tails, and rugged combat boots in the 2008 *Young Frankenstein.*

## Stephen Sondheim

No one has had greater influence on the modern musical than the composer and lyricist Stephen Sondheim (born 1930), whose first important work, mentioned earlier, was the composition of lyrics for Leonard Bernstein's 1957 *West Side Story.* After one more assignment as a golden-age lyricist (for Jule Styne's *Gypsy*), Sondheim turned composer as well, winning high praise and success for both the lyrics and music to the songs in the highly novel *A Funny Thing Happened on the Way to the Forum,* drawn from the Roman comedies of Plautus.

But in his work from 1970 onward, Sondheim departed from the standard formats of those early shows to develop a new style, marked by a disturbing plot, an ironic and sometimes even cynical tone, brutal skepticism about conventional morality, and highly sophisticated, adult, intricately rhymed lyrics

# Spotlight

## Musical Lyrics through the Eras

This sampling of lyrics from different eras clearly indicates the changing styles of musical theatre popular in America.

W. S. Gilbert's lyrics tend toward lighthearted satire and revel in their own cleverness and literary showmanship. With multisyllable rhymes and a mocking attitude toward all pomposity, Gilbert amusingly skewers official British pretension, as in the Major General's self-explanatory "patter song" (so called because its singing requires rapid enunciation) from The Pirates of Penzance (1879):

STANLEY: I am the very model of a modern major general,
  I've information animal and vegetable and mineral,
  I know the kings of England and I quote the fights
    historical,
  From Marathon to Waterloo in order categorical.
  I'm very well acquainted too with matters mathematical,
  I understand equations both the simple and quadratical,
  About binomial theorems I am teaming with a lot of
    news,
  With many cheerful facts about the square of the
    hypotenuse!...

Ira Gershwin's lyrics are openly romantic and tender; rather than call attention to the lyricist's own wit, the clever wordplay is more hidden within the feelings of the characters. The following excerpt from "'S Wonderful" was coau-thored by Ira and his brother George (music) for the musical Funny Face (1927). Like most songs, it is divided into a verse, which sets up the situation, and a refrain, which is the musical (and emotional) heart of the song:

PETER: Life has just begun:
  Jack has found his Jill.
  Don't know what you've done,
  But I'm all a-thrill.
  How can words express
  Your divine appeal?
  You could never guess
  All the love I feel.
  From now on, lady, I insist,
  For me no other girls exist.

(Refrain)
  'S wonderful! 'S marvelous
  You should care for me!
  'S awful nice! 'S Paradise—
  'S what I love to see!
  You've made my life so glamorous
  You can't blame me for feeling amorous.
  Oh, 'S wonderful! 'S marvelous—
  That you should care for me! ...

Perhaps no lyricist in the field has conveyed thwarted love and ironic longing as well as Lorenz Hart, the first partner of Richard Rodgers. In "Bewitched, Bothered and Bewildered" (Pal Joey, 1940), Vera, a society lady, drunkenly sings of her going-nowhere affair with a sexy but good-for-nothing night-club owner:

VERA: After one whole quart of brandy,
  Like a daisy I awake.
  With no Bromo Seltzer handy.
  I don't even shake.
  Men are not a new sensation;
  I've done pretty well, I think.
  But this half-pint imitation's
  Put me on the blink.

(Refrain)
  I'm wild again,
  Beguiled again,
  A simpering, whimpering child again—
  Bewitched, bothered and bewildered am I.
  Couldn't sleep
  And wouldn't sleep
  Until I could sleep where I shouldn't sleep—
  Bewitched, bothered and bewildered am I.
  Lost my heart, but what of it?
  My mistake, I agree.
  He's a laugh, but I love it
  Because the laugh's on me ...

By the time of Hart's death in 1943, Rodgers had begun a new partnership, with Oscar Hammerstein II, already the lyricist for Jerome Kern's Show Boat and many other musicals. Hammerstein wrote that he barely dared "place a timid encroaching foot on the territory" of the "masters" Gilbert and Hart and sought to write instead what he himself termed "a more primitive type of lyric ... expressing my own true

that are integrated with a score that brings surprising new rhythms to popular music. Sondheim's first works in this style include *Company* (1970; Broadway revival 2006), a devilishly clever and incisive look at sexual pairings and partings in the Manhattan of the time; *Follies* (1971; Broadway revival 2001), set at an onstage reunion of able but aging musical theatre

performers, also set in Manhattan ("I'm Still Here!" is the famous number from this show); and *A Little Night Music* (1973), adapted from an Ingmar Bergman film about summer sexual dalliances on a country estate in Sweden. These works were widely heralded for their brilliantly acerbic but always entertaining portrayal of the inevitable and eternal conflicts between convictions and feelings." His lyrics for the opening song in *Oklahoma!* (1943) clearly convey this:

CURLEY: There's a bright, golden haze on the meadow,
   There's a bright, golden haze on the meadow.
   The corn is as high as an elephant's eye,
   An' it looks like it's climbin' clear up to the sky.

(*Refrain*)

   Oh, what a beautiful mornin'!
   Oh, what a beautiful day!
   I got a beautiful feelin'
   Ev'rythin's goin' my way ...

Hammerstein derived the verse of this song from a written stage description in Lynn Riggs's *Green Grow the Lilacs,* the source play for *Oklahoma!* Riggs had described the scene as "a radiant summer morning ... cattle in the meadow, blades of the young corn ... their images giving off a visible golden emanation that is partly true and partly a trick of imagination." Deciding it was a shame to waste Riggs's images on the reading audience only, Hammerstein made them the source of his famous opening lyric.

   Stephen Sondheim, who enlarged the musical's palette more profoundly, perhaps, than any artist in the field, is most noted for a deeply ironic and antiromantic tone that, nonetheless, remains amusing and surprisingly good-spirited. Somehow he has managed to leaven his gloomy message with buoyant music, penetrating observation, and fiendishly clever rhymes and rhythm breaks. In "The Little Things You Do Together" (*Company,* 1970), Sondheim mocks the too-easy sentimentality of marital "relationships":

JOANNE: It's the little things you share together,
   Swear together,
   Wear together,
   That make perfect relationships.
   The concerts you enjoy together,
   Neighbors you annoy together,
   Children you destroy together,
   That keep marriage intact.

(*Refrain*)
   It's not so hard to be married
   When two maneuver as one
   It's not so hard to be married,
   And, Jesus Christ, is it fun.

Jonathan Larson in Rent (1996) brought a new style to lyric writing altogether and, with it, a new audience for the Broadway musical. With a rock and rap beat (Larson wrote his own music) and with a script and staging that derived in part from cast improvisations, the musical scored an enormous success. "Contact" is one of the show's closing songs. Because it does not easily divide into verse and refrain stanzas, none are noted here:

ROGER, MARK, JOANNE, & BENNY: Hot-hot-hot-sweat-sweet
   Wet-wet-wet-red-heat
   Hot-hot-hot-sweat-sweet
   Wet-wet-wet-red-heat
   Please don't stop please
   Please don't stop stop
   Stop stop stop don't
   Please please please please
   Hot-hot-hot-sweat-sweet
   Wet-wet-wet-red-heat
   Sticky-licky-trickle-tickle
   Steamy-creamy-stroking-soaking
COLLINS: Touch!
MAUREEN: Taste!
MIMI: Deep!
COLLINS: Dark!
MAUREEN: Kiss!
COLLINS: Beg!
MIMI: Slap!
MIMI, MAUREEN, & COLLINS: Fear!
COLLINS: Thick!
COLLINS, MIMI, & MAUREEN: Red, red
   Red, red
   Red, red—please
MAUREEN: Harder!
ANGEL: Faster!
MAUREEN: Wetter!
MIMI: Bastard!
COLLINS: You whore
MAUREEN: You animal
MIMI & ANGEL: More
MAUREEN, COLLINS, & MIMI: Fluid no fluid no contact yes no
   contact
ALL: Fire fire burn—burn yes!
   No latex rubber rubber
   Fire latex rubber latex bummer lover bummer

social mores and romantic idealism (or, more bluntly, between laws and lust). Furthermore, they established Sondheim's supremacy in the American musical form for the entire generation that followed.

   Sondheim continued to break new boundaries in three amazing creations. *His Pacific Overtures* (1976) employs kabuki-inspired music and stage techniques to trace the history of relations between Japan and the United States since Commodore Perry's "opening" of Japan in 1853. His *Sweeney Todd* (1979) integrates Brechtian alienation techniques and blends elements from Italian grand opera, the English music hall, and Victorian melodrama in a wildly morbid story of a barber's revenge. *Sweeney's* score is so powerful and its actions and images so compelling that the work has been staged by several European opera companies. Conversely, his *Sunday in the Park with George* (1984) is an elegant musical play about the pointillist painter Georges Seurat; for this production, Sondheim invented a "pointillist" style of music to echo Seurat's painting style.

Sondheim's most controversial works are *Assassins* (1991) and *Passion* (1994). *Assassins* is a musical review of presidential assassinations (and assassination attempts), which cascades through two centuries, portraying the quirks and oddities of John Wilkes Booth, Lee Harvey Oswald, Squeaky Fromm, and John Hinckley Jr., among other unlikely musical theatre protagonists (if not heroes). *Passion,* a nineteenth-century gothic tragedy ("one long love song," Sondheim calls it) tells the strange story of Giorgio, a handsome Italian army officer who, though deeply in love with his beautiful mistress Clara, is relentlessly pursued by his superior's cousin Fosca, a homely, ailing, and pathetically obsessive woman. The play begins with Giorgio and Clara naked in bed, singing to each other: "I'm so happy, / I'm afraid I'll die / Here in your arms." But Giorgio soon yields to the intensity of Fosca's passionate fixation, much to Clara's (and the audience's) despair. There being little for the Broadway audience to "root for" in this romantic tangle, Passion closed soon after its Broadway premiere. Its innovations, however, are exhilarating, and the nationally televised 2005 Lincoln Center concert version won great praise. *New York Times* critic Charles Isherwood declared that in this slimmed-down version Passion "may have found its purest, most persuasive and most powerful form."

## Black Musicals

More than a dozen major "black musicals" (musicals largely by, about, and performed by African Americans) have excited Broadway audiences since the 1970s, attracting large "crossover" (i.e., black and white) audiences and indeed helping to pave the way for cultural integration at every level of the country's social structure. These include Charlie Smalls's *The Wiz* (an African American version of *The Wizard of Oz*), *Bubbling Brown Sugar* and *Eubie* (both based on the music of ragtime composer/ pianist Eubie Blake, who in 1921 wrote Broadway's first black musical, *Shuffle Along*); *Ain't Misbehavin'* and *Sophisticated Ladies* (featuring, respectively, the

music of Fats Waller and Duke Ellington); *Dreamgirls* (celebrating a Supremes-like singing group and their struggles to succeed in an environment of racism and civil strife); *Jelly's Last Jam* (about jazz pioneer Jelly Roll Morton, written and directed by George C. Wolfe); and *Bring in 'Da Noise, Bring in 'Da Funk* (a capsule history of racial injustice in America, conceived and directed by George C. Wolfe and choreographed by Savion Glover, who also performed). These musicals have increasingly explored—in addition to African American music—black American history, culture, and cultural issues, often passionately and always engagingly. Tours and local revivals of all these productions, plus the 2006 hit film and 2010 Harlem (NY) stage revival and national tour of *Dreamgirls,* have extended the earlier stage productions' themes to broad multicultural audiences.

## Foreign Invasions: British, French, Swedish, and Disney

American-born musicals dominated Broadway's musical theatre scene for the first six decades of the twentieth century. Then, beginning in 1970, European composers, lyricists, and directors came to the musical theatre forefront. Leading the "foreign invasion" of America's music theatre capital was English composer Andrew Lloyd Webber, first with his Bible-themed *Joseph and the Technicolor Dreamcoat* in 1982, followed by *Cats* (also 1982, based on poet T. S. Eliot's *Old Possum's Book of Practical Cats*) and the now nearly legendary *Phantom of the Opera* (1988), the latter two becoming the longest-running musicals in Broadway history. Lloyd Webber's works—also including the successful *Jesus Christ Superstar, Evita, Starlight Express,* and *Sunset Boulevard*-are known for their lush musical scores more than for their books or lyrics. Most are "sung-through" (with no spoken dialogue), so they are easily accessible to global audiences who need little in the way of translation. The staging of these musicals has also tended to extravagance: *Starlight Express* featured a cast speeding on roller skates around an elevated track encircling the audience. In *Phantom,* a chandelier seems to fall right in the midst of the audience, and the masked Phantom and his beloved cruise in a gondola on a fiery subterranean "lake" in the basement of the Paris Opera House.

Following closely in Lloyd Webber's trans-Atlantic steps were French composer Claude-Michel Schödnberg

*Mary Poppins* is only one of the spate of Disney musicals that have transformed Broadway in recent years (others are *The Lion King, Beauty and the Beast, Tarzan,* and *Aida*). The show's designs by Bob Crowley (see the chapter titled "Designers and Technicians" for some of Crowley's working process on this show) and its choreography by the innovative Matthew Bourne made the stage production, which is darker than the Disney movie on which it is based, a success in its 2005 London premiere (pictured herewith Laura Michelle Kelly as Mary) and even more popular on Broadway in 2006.

and lyricist Alain Boublil. Their *Les Miserables* (1987, revived 2006) and *Miss Saigon* (1991) both became megahits, rivaling Lloyd Webber's productions with both their luxuriant scores and their spectacular staging, capped by the helicopter descending onto the roof of the American Embassy to rescue fleeing diplomats in *Miss Saigon.* Not only were composers and lyricists of these shows European, but the productions were in the main staged by top-tier British directors: Nicholas Hytner (for *Miss Saigon*) and Trevor Nunn (for *Cats, Les Misérables, Sunset Boulevard,* and *Starlight Express*).

Other European composers have joined the invasion of New York's famed theatre district. *Mamma Mia!,* which opened on Broadway in 2001, was based on the music of the popular Swedish singing group ABBA (Benny Andersson, Björn Ulvaeus, Agnetha Faltskog, and Anni-Frid Lyngstad); it was still running strong at the time of writing. Englishmen Eric Idle's and John Du Prez's *Monty Python's Spamalot,* a burlesque of the King Arthur legend adapted from their film, *Monty Python and the Holy Grail,* won the 2005 Tony Award for best musical. And, though not yet on Broadway, the Viennese (and German-language) *Elisabeth* has been performed for more than eight million attendees in eight countries in Europe and Asia. A musical about the Austrian empress Elizabeth of Bavaria, it was written by

Germans Michael Kunze (lyrics) and Sylvester Levay (music), whose two 2006 musicals, Rebecca and *Marie Antoinette,* excited critics and audiences in Vienna and Tokyo, respectively.

No one has more mastered the global theatrical musical, however, than the very American corporation known as Disney, which since the 1990s has all but saturated theatres worldwide with its productions of *The Lion King, Beauty and the Beast, Tarzan, Aida, Mary Poppins, The Little Mermaid,* and, in Berlin only, *The Hunchback of Notre Dame.* Disney musicals, mostly adaptations of very successful Disney films, profit commercially from Disney's bottomless financial resources and worldwide name recognition. The celebrated "Mouse" also has been credited with great theatrical art, however, particularly in the designs of Bob Crowley for *Mary Poppins* and the amazingly innovative designs and staging of *The Lion King* by longtime avant-garde director-designer Julie Taymor. This show (with music by Elton John), opening on Broadway in 1997 and currently playing in London, Hamburg, Shanghai, Tokyo, and Holland, employs live actors and hugely overscaled puppets that perform in a stunning mix of African, Asian, and American performance styles, creating a unique blend of African jungle and universal myth that has won Taymor top artistic awards and netted Disney giant box-office income from around the world.

The musical *Spring Awakening,* based on Frank Wedekind's 1891 play, astonished audiences and critics in its 2006 Broadway opening, won eight Tony Awards, and had reviewers arguing over whether it was the best musical of the year or the best in a generation. The genius of the show—directed by Michael Meyer and previously seen at the off-Broadway Atlantic Theatre—was to retain the basic story, characters, and oppressive social-sexual morality of the nineteenth-century German original while coupling them with modern (and postmodern) elements: a brazenly contemporary rock score by Steven Slater and Duncan Sheik, electrifying modern choreography by Bill T. Jones, Christine Jones's "theatre-within-a-theatre" setting with its onstage band and onstage audience, and furious lighting by Ken Adams that pulses with the music and cavorts with the performers. The performers, whose average age at the time of opening was between eighteen and nineteen, are onstage all the time and create an impressive ensemble. "I can't think of a better bonding experience than to be able to sit on stage and to watch your fellow performers perform on stage every night," says Jonathan Groff, who plays Melchior.

Clearly the musical theatre, in the twenty-first century, has become a global phenomenon.

## Musicals of the Twenty-first Century

This century's musicals have had their share of great commercial success, as noted above, and offered comedy as broadly entertaining as in any previous age—Mel Brooks's *The Producers,* Marc Shaiman's *Hairspray!,* and David Yazbek's *Dirty Rotten Scoundrels* being prime examples. But the musicals of this century are increasingly tackling serious subjects. Gang violence (*The Beautiful Game,* 2000), unemployment and its sexual consequences (The Full Monty, 2000), infidelity and betrayal (*The Wild Party,* 2000),

environmental degradation (*Urinetown,* 2001), immigration and assimilation (*Flower Drum Song,* revised version by David Henry Hwang, 2002), the exploitation of scandal and sexual anomalies in American popular culture (*Jerry Springer, the Opera,* 2003), oppression in race relations (*Caroline, or Change,* 2004), sexual ignorance and its ramifications (*Spring Awakening,* 2006), and violence, oppression, and government corruption in contemporary Nigeria (*Fela,* 2009) have been explored in today's musical dramas with sharp, even brutal, insight and penetration.

Some of these plays have been not only serious but downright grim. John Lachiusa and George C. Wolfe's *The Wild Party* (the second of two Broadway musicals in the 2000-01 season with that title, each derived from the same 1928 poem) cynically depicts the raucous goings-on at a late-night drinking party, providing a menu of sexual infidelities and emotional betrayals. "People like us, we take lovers like pills / Just hoping to cure what we know we can't fix," says one character at the party. "You're out in the clubs / Paradin' your meat / Spending all your advance / On snatch off the street / You seen more ass / Than a toilet seat," says another. And the party ends with the conclusion:

> You can make a fortune doing next to nothing:
> You can sit there on your ass and screw your
> friends:
> But you better know how to kick—kick—kick your
> way
> Outta the burning room
> When it ends.

The Hell of *The Wild Party*, conveying the message of the medieval *Everyman* with a contemporary American bite, is echoed by Ben Elton's lyrics for the ironically named *The Beautiful Game* (with music by Andrew Lloyd Webber) as it addresses English-Irish terrorism with this prisoner's lament:

> You're in the death zone. Satan sits on his throne.
> Even the strongest are frightened.
> This is the dark zone. We see in monochrome.
> Nothing is good or enlightened.
> Happiness is ended. All hope is suspended.
> We are the damned, we are all despised.

Other recent musicals extend cultural malaise to social protest and personal anguish. The 2005 *Billy Elliott*, written by Lee Hall and with music by Elton John, tells the story of an English coal miner's son who wants to become a ballet dancer during the raucous turmoil of labor unrest and violent class antagonism in the north of England during 1984. Termed a "protest musical," it became an enormous success on London's West End and won thirteen Tony Awards when it opened on Broadway in 2008. Richard Thomas's *Jerry Springer* presented—only to London and Chicago audiences thus far—the chamber of horrors existing on America's outermost sexual fringes, with rambunctious (and scatological) song titles and lyrics such as "Chicks with Dicks," "Sex with My Sister," and "I got shit pouring outta my ass" in the first act alone. And the second act takes place in Hell. It was "the most explosive theatrical event in years" said the *London Observer*. Tony Kushner's *Caroline, or Change* is awash in bleak depression from beginning to end. Its characters' hopes are continually dashed,

Billy Elliott an immensely popular British musical with music by Elton John (2005), retells the story of the film of the same name: an eleven-year-old boy from a northern British mining community secretly aspires to become a ballet dancer in the midst of a bitter labor strike polarizing the town. Liam Mower, pictured, is one of the three boys with natural Scots-accented dialects who alternated as Billy in the original cast. The show opened on Broadway in 2008, winning ten Tony Awards, including Best Musical.

and the title character—a black maid working for a white Jewish family in the American South—never smiles during the entire play (nor, in the performance this writer attended, even during the curtain call ovation). Caroline's defining solo, at her ironing board, is practically a funeral dirge:

> I'm gonna slam that iron
> down on my heart
> gonna slam that iron
> down on my throat
> gonna slam that iron
> down on my sex
> gonna slam it slam it slam it down
> 'til I drown the fire out
> 'til there ain't no air left anywhere!

Dare we applaud? Of course, we do—but we sure don't feel like it.

(*Left*) *Avenue Q,* an ironic and risqué musical of current life—animated by both humans and puppets—walked away with five Tony Awards in 2004.

(*Below*) The "jukebox musical," a hugely popular musical theatre entertainment in the twenty-first century, gathers its songs from composer-performers (as *The Buddy Holly Story, Ring of Fire*), from popular singing groups (*Mamma Mia!, The Jersey Boys*), or even from musical eras. The 2009 Tony-nominated *Rock of Ages* is in that last category, building its deliberately sketchy story line (the characters make fun of the plot as they perform it) around a compilation of MTV-Sunset Strip pop numbers of the 1980s. Here James Carpinello plays bad-boy superstar Stacee Jaxx, and Amy Spanger is Sherrie—a would-be actress who relocates from Kansas to Hollywood in hopes of scoring her big break. The spot-on period costumes are by Gregory Gale.

Alice Ripley won the Tony for Best Actress in a Musical for her leading role as a mother with bipolar disorder in the 2009 *Next to Normal*. Here Ripley is seated next to Robert Spencer, who plays her stage husband, while Aaron Tveit, as the living image of their grown son—a son who had actually died in infancy—hovers over them both, as a nightmare that simply will not go away. Directed by Michael Greif; the scenic design is by Mark Wendland.

*Spring Awakening*, based on Frank Wedekind's 1891 German drama about teenagers kept sexually ignorant by their parents and teachers with disastrous results, received outstanding reviews for its pop-rock score by Duncan Sheik (music) and scalding lyrics by Stephen Slater, as from the song "Totally Fucked":

> There's a moment you know you're fucked
> Not an inch more room to self destruct
> No more moves, oh yeah, the dead end zone
> Man you just can't call your soul your own
> But the thing that makes you really jump
> Is that the weirdest shit is still to come
> You can ask yourself, "Hey what have I done?"
> You're just a fly the little guys, they kill for fun.

And *Next to Normal* (music by Tom Kitt, book and lyrics by Brian Yorkey) is a powerfully realistic musical about a housewife with bipolar disorder bordering on schizophrenia, and the dreadful impact her illness has on her husband and teenage daughter, Natalie, who sings:

> So it's times like these I wonder how I take it
> And if other families live the way we do?
> If they love each other or if they just fake it
> And if other daughters feel like I feel too?
> 'Cause some days I think I'm dying
> But I'm really only trying
> To get through
> For just another day . . .

This musical, ten years in development on its road to winning four Tony Awards shortly after its 2009 Broadway premiere (out of twelve nominations), was greatly prized for its alternately delicate and soaring portrayal of a deeply troubled but ultimately admirable family battling with tragic psychic ailments and the hope and anguish that come with them.

Seriousness, of course, need not be conveyed through profanity or mental breakdowns, but the intensity of passion that radiates through most of these works leads to an unpitying vigor that makes the current musical theatre angrier and more genuinely shocking than the musicals of previous eras. And the rock-inspired music that is increasingly employed by the composers of these shows—which were preceded in this regard by the epoch-making *Hair* (1968)—has created a contemporary musical context (even for *Spring Awakening's* nineteenth-century setting), and it has brought to Broadway a younger audience as well as the technology of the contemporary rock concert era, with its heart-pumping sound amplification and lighting dazzle. The music theatre of the twenty-first century in all likelihood will continue to intrigue and entertain and perhaps will spread its influence deeper into the general populace of an increasingly interracial and intercultural American community.

# Chapter 10

# Theatre Today

THE THEATRE OF TODAY EXISTS ONSTAGE, not in the pages of this or any other book. The theatre of today is being performed right now, in the multi-million-dollar theatres of the world's great cities as well as on simpler stages at schools, community theatres, night-clubs, roadhouses, and experimental theatre clubs everywhere.

The theatre of today is all around us, waiting to be discovered, seen, heard, felt, and experienced. The best way to tap into its fundamental impulse is to go out and see it.

## WHAT'S HAPPENING?

It's not easy to say what's happening in the theatre today. We cannot evaluate the current theatre with the same objectivity that we bring to the theatre of the past—even the recent past. Theatre is a business as well as an art, and the promotion, publicity, and puffery that surround each current theatrical success make a cool perspective difficult. Whereas poets and painters are often ignored until years following their deaths, the opposite is more often true of theatre artists: they may be lionized in their own time and forgotten a few years later. A permanent place in the repertory of world theatre is the achievement of very few; among the playwrights once deemed equal to Shakespeare are such dimly remembered figures

The 2009 Broadway revival of *Hair*— by James Rado and Gerome Ragni (book and lyrics) and Galt McDermot (music)—brought back to New York the iconic musical that boldly introduced nudity, profanity, rock music, and interracial casting to mainstream American theatre in the mid-1960s. Originally a product of the hippie era's sexual revolution and virulent antiwar protest, this 2009 Broadway revival—pictured above with Will Swensen (*center*) as Berger and Alison Case (*kneeling at his right*) as his sometime girlfriend Crissy—went on to receive the Tony Award for Best Revival and then to have a London triumph as well, with critics and audiences alike acknowledging that while *Hair* may have been a creation of its rambunctious era, neither its social impact nor entertainment value had lessened over the ensuing decades.

as John Fletcher, Joseph Addison, and Maxwell Anderson. Which of our present-day writers and actors and other theatre artists will achieve more than ephemeral glory? Which, if any, will leave a mark on future generations? No one can answer either question with any certainty.

From a practical point of view—looking at stage practice rather than theory—theatre is a fairly conservative institution. Theatre companies around the world present plays from the past as well as from their own time and also conserve many of the theatre's traditional ways of working. Nearly all the plays mentioned in the previous chapters will be performed somewhere in the world this season, and the vigorous debates among today's actors and directors often repeat dialogues from the days of Aristophanes,

Shakespeare, and Stanislavsky. Nevertheless, in the twenty-first century, a new era seems to be emerging. The previous century was a violent one: two world wars and one cold war, assassinations of political and cultural leaders (Mohandas Gandhi, Martin Luther King Jr., John and Robert Kennedy, Anwar Sadat, Yitzhak Rabin, John Lennon), Nazi and nuclear holocausts, the proliferation of alluring but dangerous drugs and sex-linked diseases, and the threatened destruction of Earth's vital resources. The arts responded to these social changes with an artistic freedom often frightening in its extremity—nowhere more so than in the theatre, where by the 1970s Dionysian ecstasy had returned to the stage with a force almost equal to that of the ancient dithyramb. As play-licensing laws fell in England and legal censorship became locally unenforceable in America, profanity, nudity, at least simulated copulation, violence, and libelous accusation—all unknown on the legitimate stage since ancient times—became almost commonplace. Plays popular in America in the last third of the twentieth century included one accusing the sitting president of murder (*MacBird*), another accusing a recent pope of genocide (*The Deputy*), another featuring a farm boy copulating with his pig (*Futz*), another featuring teenage boys stoning a baby to death in its crib (*Saved*), and another that concluded with the actors and some of the audience undressing and marching naked out into the street (*Paradise Now*). Some of this Dionysian frenzy reached right into the theatre's mainstream when the rock Broadway musical *Hair* (1968) ended its first act with its actors—who had already sung rapturously about sodomy, fellatio, and cunnilingus—brazenly stripping off their clothes and facing the audience in a posture of mocking defiance.

Nor were theatre audiences themselves immune from such changes in theatrical convention. In the experimental theatre of the 1970s and 1980s, spectators almost routinely found themselves sat upon, fondled, assaulted, hurled about, handed lit joints (of marijuana), and, in at least one case (in Finland), urinated upon. These and other extreme behaviors had become part of the license claimed by a theatre purportedly trying to make itself heard above the societal din of war, riots, and corruption. Or, as many asked, were its adherents merely "acting out" to get attention? In any event, it was an era of dramaturgical violence and abandon that brought the age of "modernism" to a crisis, if not to a conclusion.

Well before the century's end, however, this mood of violent protest was largely spent. Profanity and nudity no longer seemed novel and, having lost their power to shock, became new tools for addressing serious social issues not only in the theatre's experimental avant-garde but on its mainstream stages, both academic and professional.

And just what were those social issues? Foremost among them were assaults on longtime (and largely knee-jerk) prejudices and privileges associated with gender, race, class, and sexual orientation that came under fire in various movements—civil rights, women's and gay liberation, ethnic pride—that began in earnest in the 1960s and gained breadth and depth in succeeding decades. By the turn of the twenty-first century, at least half the new plays appearing on American stages touched on, or were even devoted to,

issues that those movements had brought to public consciousness.

On the international scene, the end of the twentieth century saw an explosion of new social and political alignments and an often overwhelming spectrum of new technologies. With the cold war ended and its empires and alliances dissolved or reconfigured, the newly globalized economy challenged local cultures with enhanced but often troubling prospects, and astonishing advances in telecommunications—e-mail, weblogs, satellite telecasting, text-messaging, and iPhones—revolutionized the way the world's populations were interconnecting. A mere year into the new millennium, whatever political stability seemed to have been achieved at the century's end was staggered by a terrorist attack on New York and Washington that was said to have "changed everything" and that soon led, if indirectly, to military invasions, suicide bombings, regime changes, civil wars, insurrections, threats of nuclear proliferation, a "global war on terror," and a staggering recession.

The theatre—a tool of live communication—has responded quickly to a vast store of new subjects and fresh opportunities. Once again, as in the days of the ancient Greeks and Shakespearean England, the stage has surfaced as an arena in which new thoughts, fashions, feelings, morals, theologies, and aesthetics can be enacted, and new technologies explored, in order to bring lucidity and structure to the confusions that beset us all.

Although generalizations about an era still upon us must be tentative, some major themes have clearly emerged in today's theatre, and we look at several of them in the ensuing pages.

## A Theatre of Postmodern Experiment

The label "postmodern" is often applied to the non-traditional theatre forms that have gained prominence in the past two or three decades. The label, however, refers not to a specific style as much as to a way of thinking, or of nonthinking. It defies comprehensive analysis because it essentially defies the act of analyzing itself. Not all—perhaps not even most—of today's theatre can be considered postmodern, but the creative forces that go into writing, directing, and designing plays are increasingly affected by postmodern impulses.

These impulses motivate the artist (in the theatre and elsewhere) to rely less on logic or cause-and-effect determinism, and more on creating sequences of related—or unrelated—reflections. Such reflections are of two sorts: *self-reflections,* whereby the work of art pays homage to itself, and *reflections of the past,* whereby a work of art absorbs and refashions earlier models. The first form of postmodernism is evident in surrealist René Magritte's seemingly realistic painting of a pipe, which sports directly below the image the legend "Ceci n'est pas une pipe" ("This is not a pipe"). The legend is thus a reflection *of* the painting *in* the painting—in this case, a reflection that rejects precisely what it reflects. The second form of postmodernism may be seen in Andy Warhol's repeated images of Campbell's soup cans, electric chairs, and head shots of Marilyn Monroe, which embrace, quote, and recycle the past, instead of repudiating it as modernism seeks to do.

A postmodernist work of art is not about "something" as much as it is about itself—about "art." And about ourselves—about "us." Such a work is sometimes said to "deconstruct" itself as we view it, so that we are asked to think as much about the idea of art, and of ourselves, as we are about what we're seeing. How do we view art? the artist asks. How do we view ourselves? Do our assumptions about what art "is," or what we "are," help us or prevent us from enjoying art—or from living comfortably with ourselves? These are the essential questions of the postmodern theatre.

Postmodern drama springs directly from the antirealistic theatre, but unlike most of that theatre, it rejects the modernist's aesthetic sense and social optimism. Whereas symbolists and surrealists tried to reveal higher orders of reality, and Brecht's theatre struggled to change the world and raise social expectations, the postmodernist artist does neither. The postmodernist rather eliminates all symbols (the postmodern, one critic suggests, is the art of the "missing metaphor") and, having no expectation of social progress, contemplates the future warily if at all. Postmodern playwrights and directors therefore are more likely to explore the *discontinuity* of reality as we know it than to try to create an integrated synthesis or "meaning" through their works. Thus Aristotle's "theme" often takes a beating in twenty-first-century-theatre, where plays are unlikely to be held together by an overarching central idea or message but rather are collated as a mélange of ideas, images, and sensory discoveries.

Indeed, postmodern art celebrates the seeming randomness of arbitrary juxtapositions. It prides itself not on logic and conviction but on delightful surprises and tantalizing (often bewildering) irrelevancies. Students of the postmodern find its main features in, for example, the largely improvised, haphazard, and disjunctive movements of break dancing, hip-hop, rapping, and DJ-ing. Postmodern impulses can be experienced in one's own home: in the concatenation of video clips, dramatic fragments, promos, ads, newsbreaks, and home movies we find—often on split screen—while speed-surfing over any of a hundred-odd TV channels.

Postmodernism is not new to the theatre. Its first appearance may be considered the short-lived performance phenomenon called *dada,* a stew of random folk music, "chance poetry" (words recited as they were drawn out of a hat), spasmodic dance numbers, and snippets of classical recitations—as performed with great enthusiasm by rebel poets and political exiles in a café in Zurich, Switzerland, during the dark days of World War I. Today's postmodernism follows more in the wake of theatre of the absurd. The late plays of Samuel Beckett exemplify a nihilistic postmodern retreat from meaning. In his short *Rockaby* (1981), Beckett's sole visible character is an old lady with "huge eyes in white expressionless face" who sits alone on a dark stage and, rocking in a rocking chair, says but a single word ("More"), in what is apparently a beyond-the-grave dialogue with her prerecorded voice. The play ends with the recorded voice saying:

> rock her off
> stop her eyes
> fuck life
> stop her eyes
> rock her off
> rock her off

And the rocking stops and the lights fade out.

But contemporary postmodernism also owes a debt—and certainly a larger one—to Brecht's theatre of alienation. If Beckett's theatre stimulates pessimism, Brecht's stimulates a delight in breaking out of the dramatic situation: deconstructing drama into social discourse and disconnecting actors from the characters they play. Postmodern directors and dramatists influenced by Brecht's views openly, even gaily, employ the theatre itself as an ironic metaphor, jumping back and forth between simulations of reality and comments on that very simulation. Deliberate cross-gender casting, for example—as when actors switch both roles and genders between the acts of Caryl Churchill's *Cloud Nine* (1983), or when a young actress with an obviously fake beard plays the ancient Jewish rabbi in the first scene of Tony Kushner's *Angels in America* (1993)—forces us to confront a profound separation between the actor and his or her role, and the "role" that one's gender plays in society.

And increasingly, as Brecht foresaw, the raw mechanics of theatrical practice are openly shown on the stage today. Undisguised microphones are now commonly visible taped onto an actor's forehead, and the "sound mixer" who adjusts volume levels is plunked in the midst of the audience in musicals seen on larger stages—both on Broadway and in the university theatre. In the postmodern theatre, the "showing" of show business is part of the "show."

Plays also now comment on their own dramaturgy. In *The Producers*, one character asks another, "Why did you just walk downstage right?" In *Urinetown*, one character asks another, "Is this where you tell the audience about the water shortage?" Other plays adopt the theatre or its repertory as their primary subjects. The opening scene of Tom Stoppard's *The Real Thing* is revealed to have been a staged play when, at the second scene, we see the "characters" of the first appear as the actors who played them earlier. Other plays are about older—and real—plays. Amy Freed's *The Beard of Avon* shows the "character" of Shakespeare writing plays attributed to him. Lee Blessing's *Fortinbras* and Tom Stoppard's *Rosencrantz and Guildenstern Are Dead* tell the stories Shakespeare didn't get around to telling in his version of *Hamlet*, while Jeff Whitty's *Further Adventures of Hedda Gabler* takes off from where Henrik Ibsen's play about that complicated lady leaves off. Even commercial playwright Neil Simon takes off on classical theatre productions; his *Laughter on the 23rd Floor* and stage version of *The Goodbye Girl* each include scenes parodying Shakespearean performances—of *Julius Caesar* and *Richard III*, respectively.

And it seems that postmodern-era musicals are increasingly about other musicals, as, for example, *The Drowsy Chaperone*, *The Producers*, *George Gershwin Alone*, *A Class Act*, *The Boy from Oz*, *Urinetown*, *Curtains*, *[title of show]*, and *The Musical of Musicals—The Musical!* It is certainly clear that twenty-first-century postmodernist drama is delightedly cannibalizing—ingesting, chewing, and eventually regurgitating, in various ironic transformations—the theatre's past glories.

Aristotle said that plays should have a beginning, middle, and end, and they generally still do—but

Perhaps no play reaches the minimafism, and the nihilism, of Beckett's *Rockaby*, in which "W," the sole character (played here by Siân Phillips), is alone onstage for the play's duration, rocking and saying but one word while listening to a recording of "V"—her own voice. Directed by Loveday Ingram at London's Barbican Theatre, 2006.

no longer always in that order. The conventional development of plot—from an inciting incident through intensifying action, climax, and denouement—is no longer uniformly presented in linear fashion. Temporary flashbacks, of course, have been used in drama, as well as in film, for several decades. They appear prominently in Arthur Miller's *Death of a Salesman*, for example, and the action of Tennessee Williams's *The Glass Menagerie* is, in effect, almost entirely a flashback. But in such linear works flashbacks are generally framed as such, as by a narrative or musical transition or, in film, by a blurry cross-dissolve, which makes clear that the story is shifting to an earlier time period. In postmodern nonlinear drama, however, movement from one time zone to another is usually instantaneous and rarely narrated: the audience is simply

Tom Stoppard's *The Invention of Love* portrays various events in the life of the English classical scholar and poet A. E. Housman from age eighteen to seventy-seven, not only by jumping backward and forward in time but also through intriguing same-time conversations between the young Housman (played by Robert Sean Leonard, *right)* and Housman as a just-deceased old man (played by Richard Easton), here shown—along with their reflections—sitting on a fallen antique monument (another postmodern touch) on the River Styx in Hades (the land of the dead). Both Leonard and Easton won Tony Awards for their Housman portrayals in the 2001 Broadway season. Sets and costumes are by Bob Crowley; lighting is by Brian MacDevitt.

expected to figure it out. Moreover, the audience is not necessarily "returned" to the present when a postmodern flashback concludes.

A postmodern play proceeds in almost any order the playwright wishes to construct, and such time-warping no longer seems surprising. When Harold Pinter, in *Betrayal* (1978), organized his play's nine scenes in mostly reverse chronological order, the decision was considered revolutionary and reviewers talked of little else. Two decades later, when David Auburn, in his 2001 Pulitzer Prize-winning *Proof,* began act 2 with a scene chronologically four years earlier than act 1 (requiring that a ghost appearing in act 1 be instantly seen—with no change of costume or makeup or explanation—as a living man in act 2), very few reviewers thought this reordering of events even worth mentioning. Indeed, the *New York Times* theatre critic called the play "as accessible and compelling as a detective story." Postmodern plays are freed from the necessity to align themselves with a forward-moving arrow of time, and even from the need to explain when the arrow reverses direction.

Jefferson Mays, as German transvestite Charlotte von Mahlsdorf, holds a treasured antique record player in Doug Wright's multiple-award-winning *I Am My Own Wife*. Charlotte is one of thirty-three roles Mays plays in the show, which crosses gender, linguistic, and time barriers.

Here are a few other examples of postmodern nonlinear theatre:

- In Tony Kushner's Pulitzer Prize-winning 1993 *Angels in America,* the action makes quantum moves in time—between previous centuries, the present, and the afterlife—with never so much as a program note, while actors jump back and forth between different roles and occasionally between different genders as well (also see the chapter titled "The Playwright").

- In Tom Stoppard's 1998 *The Invention of Love,* the principal character, poet and scholar A. E. Housman, is divided into younger and older selves, each self played by a different actor; the play's scenes alternate back and forth between

Housman's student days, professorial years, and boat-borne journey to Purgatory after death. The younger and elder Housmans even cross paths for conversation as the eras of their lives intertwine.

- In Doug Wright's *I Am My Own Wife* (2003), we continually swing forward and back through the life of the play's main character, German transvestite Charlotte von Mahlsdorf. The play's sole actor performs Charlotte not only in two genders but in two languages and at multiple ages—as well as playing playwright Wright (and thirty-two other characters) besides.

None of these nonlinear—or gender or language or character—shifts represents dramaturgical novelty. Rather, each indicates a theatre—and an audience—prepared for instant cross-association and able to keep several ideas and chronologies in mind at the same time, melding them into a satisfying dramatic experience.

## An Open Theatre

It is safe to say that, in the United States, theatre audiences and practitioners alike have opted for an "open" theatre—open, that is, for an infinitely wider range of interests, cultures, and individuals than existed during any other period in theatre history. This openness—the word comes from Joseph Chaikin's short-lived but extremely influential Open Theatre company of the American 1960s and 1970s—made us painfully conscious of the theatre's challenge, after two world wars, to fully reflect the humanity inside us and the society around us. For although Shakespeare (for instance) was certainly able to create magnificent female and ethnic characters (Beatrice and Cleopatra, Othello and Shylock) and his acting company was apparently skilled at bringing them vividly to life, the notion of an all-white (and all-male) theatre company claiming, in a speech of Hamlet's, to hold "a mirror up to nature" has proven in the current age generally unsustainable. How can an exclusively male or an exclusively white—or even an exclusively single-ethnicity company—wholly "mirror" the hopes and concerns of all human nature: women as well as men, gays and straights, Asians and blacks and Native Americans as well as whites?

Postwar authors and directors, therefore, have increasingly sought to open the theatre to all comers. The postmodern disconnect between actor and

(*Left*) The Propeller is an all-male acting company directed by Edward Hall; in this 2006 production of Shakespeare's *The Taming of the Shrew*, Dugald Bruce Lockhart plays Petruchio (the tamer) and Simon Scardifield plays Katherine (the "shrew"). This is no mere novelty: as critic Ron Dungate aptly notes, "*The Taming of the Shrew* is OK as a play as long as you don't take the violence against Kate seriously. But then you have to take it seriously—the play does. The play is seen to be what it is—a cruel play about making women do what you want by beating them up. The remarkable thing about this production is that the maleness of Propeller and its physical style enables the actors to fully confront this violence; we are more able to take the violence since we see Petruchio and Kate are both men and, crucially, the male Kate can give equal violence back. It doesn't make it acceptable, it makes it possible to bear. The play becomes an intricate, multi-layered event and the message is truly disturbing." The production, stirringly designed by Michael Pavelka, toured to London, New York, Perth (Australia), and Hong Kong after its Stratford-upon-Avon opening.

(*Bottom*) In Shakespeare's time, men played all the roles. In 2002, at the Globe Theatre in London, which was designed to appear as Shakespeare's theatre did in 1600, Globe artistic director Mark Aylance continued the all-male acting tradition by playing Lady Olivia in *Twelfth Night,* for which he received England's Olivier Award, the equivalent of the American Tony.

Cultural diversity is the thematic territory of playwright David Adjmi's *Stunning,* which explores relations between New York's Syrian-Jewish community (where Adjmi was raised) and its relationship with other ethnic groups in multicultural America. The play's 2009 premiere at off-Broadway's Duke Theatre featured Cristin Milioti as the unhappily married Syrian-Jewish teenager Lily and Charlayne Woodard as her black lesbian maid Blanche.

character is helpful in creating this openness, as playwrights or directors tend now to create "roles" more than characters, inviting the audience to see an actor not as a character but rather as an actor *playing* a character. So today a woman may play King Lear, a white actor may play a black Othello, and a black actor can play the English King Henry V, without at all compromising the integrity of the theatrical experience. Casting considerations have broadened to radically bend gender distinctions, cross racial lines, and span age ranges.

Chaikin's Open Theatre pioneered in this development for little more than a decade, combining social improvisation with Brechtian techniques, developing plays in which performers glided into and out of the characters they played (they also played scenery and props, and often played themselves), and using story and character merely as vehicles for direct interactions with audiences. These plays, which included Megan Terry's *Viet Rock,* Susan Yankowitz's *Terminal,* and the company-authored *Mutation Show,* were continually evolving workshop performances that addressed immediate audience concerns. The Open Theatre toured Europe, as well as American campuses and prisons, making alliances with the New Lafayette Theatre in Harlem, El Teatro Campesino in California, and the Women's Collective Theatre. Although it ended its existence in 1973, the Open's influence lasts to this day, and its name may well stand to represent the larger "opening" of our contemporary stage to the great diversity of our contemporary cultures, and to our diverse personal and sexual identifications and orientations.

## A Diverse Theatre

From top to bottom, in gender, race, and ethnicity, in playwrights, performers, producers, and directors, American theatre is now broadly diverse.

Women were practically unrepresented in the theatre until the seventeenth century (except in the commedia dell'arte and some medieval English pageant productions), and even afterward women were relegated mainly to acting, copying scripts, and building costumes. Now they are a major force at every level of the American theatrical arts. Since the 1980s, seven women playwrights (Paula Vogel, Beth Henley, Marsha Norman, Wendy Wasserstein, Margaret Edson, Suzan-Lori Parks, Lynn Nottage) have received Pulitzer Prizes and four (Anna Deveare Smith, Naomi Wallace, Mary Zimmerman, Sarah Ruhl) have been honored with MacArthur "genius" awards. Women directors, once a rarity, now represent at least one-third of the nation's total field and a comparable percentage are now artistic directors as well. Meanwhile, feminist theatre ensembles—groups of women presenting plays by, about, and for women—have been founded throughout the United States, with the stated goal of writing and presenting plays about gender-role stereotyping, abortion, pregnancy, motherhood, rape,

*Joe Turner's Come and Gone* is often thought (by your author, certainly) to be August Wilson's masterpiece. Set in a Pittsburgh boarding house in 1911, the play is a deeply resonant study of the unsettled aftereffects of slavery on American culture, both black and white. In this Tony-nominated 2009 Broadway revival, Roger Robinson plays the spellbinding healer Bynum Walker, a freed slave with mysterious insights, and Marsha Stephanie Blake is Mattie, a lost young woman seeking love but not knowing where to find it. Costumes are by Catherine Zuber.

El Paso-born Octavio Solis moved into the top tier of American playwrights with his brilliant, Pulitzer-nominated *Lydia* in 2009. This production, directed by Juliette Carrillo and performed in a mixture of English and Spanish at the Mark Taper Forum in Los Angeles, starred Onahuoa Roderiguez (*left*) as Ceci, a young girl whose brain was shattered in a car accident days before her *quinceañera* (traditional fifteenth birthday celebration). We mainly see Ceci in her dreams, where she acts like a vivacious young woman. Stephanie Beatriz plays the mysterious Lydia, a young Mexican "illegal" (unlawful immigrant) who uses magical powers to comfort Ceci and translate her unexpressed thoughts to her bewildered parents and brothers.

the mother-daughter relationship, lesbianism, domestic violence, historically important women, battered women, and women in prison.

Racial diversification of American theatre shows a similar development. Until the mid-1950s, the American dramatic repertoire was almost entirely written by, for, and about whites. Talented black writers were hardly ever able to secure productions, and even the best black actors were often reduced to playing the roles of servants and "exotics." But in the decades following World War II, black-themed, black-authored, and black-acted drama began to surge forward in American culture. Lorraine Hansberry's

1959 *A Raisin in the Sun,* a realistic study of black family life, became the first black-authored play to appear on Broadway, and its director, Lloyd Richards, became the first black director in the American theatrical mainstream. Soon, a vigorous black theatre had become a truly revolutionary force with the startling plays of African American Amiri Baraka, whose *Dutchman* and *The Toilet* appeared off-Broadway in 1964 and confronted American racism with astonishing ferocity. Bakara (then known as LeRoi Jones) refused to shrink from his subject's violent ramifications, and his gut-wrenching urban plays—set, respectively, in a subway car and a high school

This Broadway revival of Lorraine Hansberry's classic A Raisin in the Sun—directed by Kenny Leon and starring Sean Combs (*left*) as Walter Lee Younger, Audra McDonald as his wife, and Sanaa Lathan as his sister, Beneatha—attracted large crossover audiences on Broadway in 2004.

latrine—provided a startling wake-up call not only to American society but to the American stage. In 1967, actors Robert Hooks and Douglas Turner Ward created the Negro Ensemble Company, bringing forth dramatist Lonne Elder III's eloquent *Ceremonies in Dark Old Men* in 1969 and continuing to flourish to the present day, and in 1982 Charles Fuller's *A Soldier's Play,* about the murder of a black soldier in the American South, received the Pulitzer Prize.

The early 1980s brought to the fore the extraordinary August Wilson, whose ten-play dramatic cycle (see the chapter titled "The Modern Theatre: Realism") is an unparalleled achievement—treating, as it does, aspects of American black life in each of the ten decades of the twentieth century. Wilson's plays received dozens of awards—including two Pulitzer Prizes—and have been regularly revived on

Broadway and in regional theatres since his untimely death in 2005. And in the current century, two African American women dramatists have received Pulitzer awards: Suzan-Lori Parks for *Topdog/Underdog* in 2002 and Lynn Nottage for *Ruined* in 2009. As black playwrights, directors, and actors increasingly populate mainstream Broadway and regional American theatre, the movement to create dedicated black ensembles has faded though certainly not disappeared.

Latino theatre, often distinguished by its language as well as its ethnic roots, has also blossomed in today's open environment. Spanish-speaking theatre is hardly a newcomer to North America—indeed, the first play staged on this continent was *Los Moros y Los Cristianos* (*The Moors and the Christians*) at the San Juan Pueblo near Santa Fe in the sixteenth century.

Gloria Garayua is Gracie in Octavio Solis's Christmas play, *La Posada Mágica* (*The Magic Journey*), which echoes the traditional Latin American procession honoring Joseph and Mary's search for lodging to bear the Christ child. This 2008 production, directed by playwright Solis himself, was presented for the fifteenth consecutive year at South Coast Repertory in Costa Mesa, California.

But the 1965 founding of El Teatro Campesino by Mexican American Luis Valdez became the impetus to a truly national movement to create homegrown Latino theatre in the United States. Created in conjunction with the United Farm Workers union in rural California, Valdez's Teatro and its powerful creative and political thrusts electrified California audiences and won national acclaim, particularly for its ground-breaking *Zoot Suit* (1978), written by Valdez about riots in the Los Angeles barrio that pitted Mexican American migrants against the Los Angeles police and politicians in the early 1940s. In this work, Valdez employed theatre of alienation techniques to make social, political, and economic points, while retaining the music, whimsy, and verve of full-blooded theatrical entertainment. The play went on to Broadway (making a star out of Edward James Olmos) and was eventually adapted into a feature film. "In a Mexican way," wrote Valdez in 1966, "we have discovered what Brecht is all about. If you want unbourgeois theatre, find unbourgeois people to do it."* The Teatro Campesino continues to perform, at least intermittently, at its permanent home in San Juan Bautista, California.

Today, the works of dozens of Latina and Latino dramatists are seen around the country. Cubanborn Nilo Cruz received the 2003 Pulitzer Prize

for his enchanting *Anna in the Tropics,* portraying Cuban émigré workers in a Florida cigar factory. His rapturous adaptation of Calderón's classic *Life Is a Dream* was successfully premiered in California in 2007. Octavio Solis, born of Mexican immigrant parents in El Paso, Texas, was nominated for a 2009 Pulitzer for his intense *Lydia.* This realistic yet often mystical drama of a family not unlike Solis's own had earned extravagant praise in its initial productions in Denver and Los Angeles. Puerto Rican-born José Rivera is another nationally heralded Latino playwright. His *Marisol* (1992), a fantasy about a woman and her guardian angel in the tradition of magic realism, has been produced throughout the country, as has his *References to Salvador Dali Make Me Hot* (2003). And Chicana author Josefina López is known for, among other works, her *Real Women Have Curves* (1990), which after its stage success became an award-winning entry at the Sundance Film Festival.

Since Latino theatre is closely linked to its Spanish-speaking roots (*Lydia* and Luis Valdez's *Zoot Suit* and *I Don't Have to Show You No Stinkin' Badges* are all a spoken mixture of Spanish and English), permanent and semipermanent bilingual Latino theatre companies flourish throughout the country, particularly in areas where there are significant Spanish-speaking populations. Based in California, Culture Clash, cofounded in San Francisco in 1984 by

---

*Abel Franco, "Teatro Campesino," *New World, 2* (Fall 1974), 22.

# PHOTO ESSAY: Theatre in the Borderlands

1. In a public assembly room in the city center, the audience gathers, sitting on folding chairs that surround the acting area. A handful of lights illuminate the hand-painted setting.

2. In the performance, "Little Brother" (Bryant Ranier Enriquez, *standing*) thinks he sees a ghost in his bedroom, as "Big Brother" (Rafael E. Martinez) rolls over in mock dismay.

1.

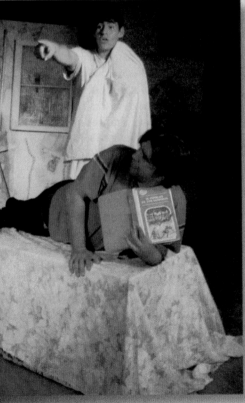

2.

Not all—or even most—Latino theatre activity in the United States is found in America's largest cities. The Borderlands Theatre was founded in Tucson, Arizona, in 1986, with the express purpose of producing and stimulating productions in Spanish and English, to provide theatrical entertainment for the local Mexican American population and to create interchange among members of the Latino and Anglo communities in the Arizona-Sonora "borderlands" that at times link and at other times divide Mexico and the United States.

Borderlands has no permanent theatre and owns minimal equipment, but it recruits plays, performers, and directors from both countries with the aid of National Endowment of the Arts funding along with a body of loyal community supporters. The pictured production, presented in English and Spanish versions on alternate nights, is Mexican playwright Javier Malpica's *Papá está en la Atlántida* (*Our Dad Is in Atlantis*), directed by Eva Tessler. It was a great success for the company in 2009, telling the heartbreaking story of two preteen Mexican brothers— played by adult actors Rafael E. Martinez and Bryant Ranier Enriquez—who, after their mother's death, try to walk through the Sonoran desert to find their father, who has illegally crossed the border to Atlanta (which the younger brother thinks is the magical kingdom of Atlantis).

Similar bilingual theatre companies can be found in most cities along America's southern frontier—Teatro Promoteo in Miami, Latino Teatro in Los Angeles, the Latino Theatre Alliance in Austin, Texas—as well as in northern cities including Teatro Pregones in New York's Bronx, the Gala Hispanic Theatre in Washington, and the all-female Teatro Luna in Chicago.

Richard Montoya, Ric Salinas, and Herbert Siguenza, has become the most noted Chicano/Latino performance company in the United States, producing a wide-ranging repertoire in major theatres around the country (Lincoln Center, Kennedy Center, Seattle Repertory, Mark Taper Forum) comprising plays that range from *Water and Power,* an exposé of the hidden influence of business on local Los Angeles politics, and a riotous adaptation of Aristophanes' comedy *The Birds.* The Culture Clash founders—who are also the company's leading actors and directors—describe their methods as making a "performance collage" of "history, geography, 'urban excavation,' 'forensic poetry,' and storytelling—together in a contemporary, movable theater narrative through a Chicano point of view." And in New York, Repertorio Español, founded in 1968 by René Buch, regularly produces classical Spanish drama (including plays by Garcia Lorca, Calderón de la Barca, and Lope de Vega), along with contemporary Latino works (as by Nilo Cruz and Carmen Rivera) in both English and Spanish, seeking to fulfill artistic director Buch's dream to create a theatre that "instills cultural pride among Hispanics from all Latin American countries, challenges misconceptions and ignorance about Spanish language, culture and traditions, and hopefully, creates and inspires the next generation of theatergoers and theatre artists."

Asian American theatre has claimed its share of the American theatrical scene as well, its quantum leap forward being David Henry Hwang's *M. Butterfly,* which received both a Tony Award and a Pulitzer Prize during its 1988 Broadway premiere. Hwang's play boldly reinterprets the Madame Butterfly story, as well as its political and sexual prejudices, by incorporating both Western and Beijing opera (xiqu) techniques into a contemporary, highly postmodern play that explodes "Orientalist" stereotypes about Asians as viewed by Westerners. Hwang's career continues to flourish (see the chapter titled "The Playwright") with his new book for the 2002 Broadway revival of the Rodgers and Hammerstein musical *The World of Suzie Wong,* on Chinese immigration to the United States, and his *Golden Child,* on the same subject, which was nominated for a best-play Tony Award. Hwang's semiautobiographical 2008 *Yellow Face,* however, may be his most provocative work since M. Butterfly. It traces his own career as an Asian American playwright, including his winning the Tony and then losing his battle to keep a white actor from playing the lead role of an Asian character in the Broadway *Miss Saigon.*

Hwang is only the most prominent of the many Asian Americans now solidly ensconced in the American repertoire, however. Philip Kan Gotanda, Lonnie Carter, and Elizabeth Wong are among the others writing about relations between American and, respectively, Japanese, Filipino, and Chinese cultures.

## A Global Theatre

Theatre today is increasingly global. Of course during much of its history theatre has crossed regional and national borders. In ancient Greece, nearly all of the diverse and often warring city-states on the Hellenic peninsula participated in the Great Dionysia in Athens, which, held in the spring, also attracted traders and visitors from throughout the Mediterranean world. Shakespeare's London audiences also included a broad mix of foreigners (some of whom, indeed, provided us with much of the information we now possess about English theatres and staging of that era). And Shakespeare's plays were set in many foreign lands—Italy, France, Egypt, Bohemia, Greece, Austria, Denmark, Scotland, and (apparently) Bermuda—so his audiences must have had an interest in faraway places.

In the nineteenth century, with the advent of steamships, actors and even entire theatre companies began touring the world. American audiences became accustomed to seeing celebrated foreign actors (Italy's Tomasso Salvini and Eleanora Duse, France's Jean-Mounet Sully and Sarah Bernhardt, England's Henry Irving and Ellen Terry, and Poland's Helena Modjeska) performing in the great classic roles, some even in their own native languages. The 1923-24 American tours of Konstantin Stanislavsky's Moscow Art Theatre, which eventually played—in Russian—380 performances in Manhattan, Brooklyn, Newark, New Haven, Hartford, Chicago, Boston, Cleveland, Detroit, Pittsburgh, and Washington, provided an opportunity for American audiences to discover modern Russian theatre and revolutionized this country's acting style for decades to come. And the vastly increased speed and lowered cost of global travel in recent decades have allowed many of the world's greatest theatre companies to perform not only in the major centers of New York (at the Brooklyn Academy of Music and the summer Lincoln Center Theatre Festival) and Los Angeles (at UCLA-Live) but also in smaller cities such as Ann Arbor (Michigan) and Davidson (North Carolina).

And for Americans able and willing to travel abroad, literally dozens of major international theatre festivals provide vast samplings of some of the greatest theatrical achievements of our time in a host of cities: Amsterdam, Edinburgh, Singapore, Berlin, Paris, Avignon (France), Spoleto (Italy), Tampere (Finland), Gdansk (Poland), Ibiza (Spain), Toga (Japan), Adelaide (Australia), Pècs (Hungary), and Curitiba (Brazil), and, in the most globally ambitious country of them all, Romania, the cities of Sibiu, Cluj, Craiova, and Bucharest. In some cases these festival productions are provided with English translations (by earphones or supertitles), but most often the productions brought to international festivals are well-known classic plays that audiences can appreciate without proficiency in the production's language.

Nothing could prove more valuable for the world today than such cultural exchanges, for drama's capacity to serve as a vehicle for international communication goes beyond mere rhetoric and allows theatre artists and audiences from around the world to share alike in the universals of human experience—hopes, fears, feelings, and compassion for the living.

## A Macaronic Theatre

Nor is a single language sacrosanct in the theatre of today, as plays, now, are increasingly written in multiple tongues. Critic Marvin Carlson uses the term *macaronic*—originally referring to the *maccarone* (macaroni) of Latin and Old Italian as they were interwoven in the speech of medieval Italy—to describe plays that employ such a mingling mix of languages.*

The European theatre has long been macaronic: even Shakespeare's plays include many lines (and a large part of two entire scenes) in French, Italian, Latin, or Welsh. Postmodern plays take this multilingualism much further. Canadian playwright David Fennario's *Balconville,* about the relationship of French-speaking and English-speaking Canadians, is presented in both languages of officially bilingual Canada. The French comedy *Les Aviateurs* is performed entirely in English—the language of aviation—although it is a thoroughly French play that (so far) has been performed only in France. *Endstation Amerika,* Frank

Castorf's adaptation of Tennessee Williams's *A Streetcar Named Desire* for Berlin's Volksbühne ("People's Theatre"), was performed in a roughly equal mixture of German, French, and English. British dramatist David Edgar's *Pentecost* (the word refers to the Biblical "tongues of fire" of multiple languages) portrays a mix of frightened Kurdish, Romani, Azeri, Mozambican, Hindi, Afghan, and Bosnian refugees, all speaking their own languages along with their individual versions of ESL. The American macaronic theatre has recently generated Octavio Solis's Spanish-English *Lydia,* Lonnie Carter's English-Tagalog (Filipino) *The Romance of Magno Rubio,* and Tony Kushner's French-Arabic-Pashto-Dari-English-Esperanto *Homebody/Kabul.*

It is both realistic and poignant for the characters in all those plays to speak in different languages, for in each case linguistic variety conveys differing aspects of cultural identity—as well as the difficulties inherent in intercultural communication—while still propelling the dramaturgical basics of plot, character, and the creation of audience empathy. Many of us face these linguistic challenges in our increasingly multicultural lives, and a macaronic theatre mirrors our evolving nature. It is hard to overestimate the importance of this movement, which can powerfully depict conflicts between cultural survival and assimilation, and give voice to the multiple perspectives of societies rent with factionalism and longing for harmony.

## A Theatre of Difference

Gender, race, ethnicity, geography, and language are not the only sources of the new voices entering the theatre's mainstream in the current era. Sexual preference has emerged as a defining issue for many theatre groups, theatre festivals, and theatre publications, each seeking to examine the political, cultural, and aesthetic implications of gay- and lesbian-themed drama. Sexual preference remained buried deeply in the closet during most of the theatre's history. As recently as 1958 the representation of homosexuality was illegal in England and widely (though not legally) suppressed in America. The love that "dared not speak its name" came to the stage only through authors' implications and audiences' inferences. Gay playwrights, such as Oscar Wilde, Tennessee Williams, Gertrude Stein, Edward Albee, William Inge, and Gore Vidal, were forced to speak—at certain critical moments in their work—only by innuendo and through oblique code words.

---

*Marvin Carlson, "The Macaronic Stage," in *East of West: Cross-Cultural Performance and the Staging of Differences,* ed. Claire Sponsler and Xiaomei Chen (New York: Palgrave, 2000), 15-31.

Macaronic (multilingual) theatre reaches a high point in Ariane Mnouchkine's production with her Théâtre du Soled company production of *Le Dernier Caravansérail* (*The Last Caravan*), presented at the Lincoln Center Theatre Festival in New York in 2005. Mnouchkine and her company have been the greatest French theatre innovators over the past three decades, with Asian- or East Asian—inspired productions of plays by Shakespeare (*Richard II, Twelfth Night*), Aeschylus (the Oresteia), and Molière (*Tartuffe*), among others. Here she tackles an original subject—the global crisis of immigration—with a text developed from interviews she and her colleagues conducted all over the world. The six-hour production—portraying current immigrants from Afghanistan, Iraq, Kurdistan, and Iran crossing to Europe on the ancient Silk and Spice Roads—includes forty-two scenes, actors traveling by carts, boats, and other conveyances so that they never set foot on the ground, and a wide variety of languages totally unfamiliar to theatre audiences, even when they are heard above the screams and sounds coming from the stage. In this opening scene, "La Fleuve Cruel" ("The Cruel River"), immigrants in a wicker basket are smuggled across violent and roaring "waves" created by a gigantic span of billowing fabric. The cacophony of multiple languages, together with the roar of the river and the screams of those thrown overboard, greatly intensifies the realism of this global catastrophe.

Dramatic changes occurred in the late 1960s, when gay and lesbian life and gay and lesbian issues began to be treated as serious dramatic subjects, most notably by Mart Crowley in his groundbreaking American comedy *The Boys in the Band* (1968). Since then, sexual-preference issues have become principal or secondary topics in hundreds of plays, including mainstream Broadway musicals (*La Cage aux Folles, Falsettos, Kiss of the Spider Woman, The Wild Party, Avenue Q*), popular comedies (*Love! Valour! Compassion!, Jeffrey, The Little Dog Laughed*), and serious dramas (*Bent, M. Butterfly, Gross Indecency, Breaking the Code,*

*The Laramie Project, Take Me Out, I Am My Own Wife*). Gay actors have come out of the closet (most of them theatrically) to advocate gay rights worldwide, as did the British classical star Ian McKellen in his one-man performance "A Knight Out" at the Gay Games in New York in 1994.

In the wake of a new and terrible illness, a growing genre of AIDS plays (*The Normal Heart, As Is*) addressed the tragic human consequences of this disease, whose initial victims in the United States and Europe were predominantly gay. In 1992, Tony Kushner's extraordinary *Angels in America*, subtitled

## Nontraditional Casting

Across the country, color-blind or deliberately cross-color casting—once thought of as daring—has become almost routine, particularly in the classics. As audiences more easily accept the notion that they are watching "performances of characters" rather than "characters" themselves, the theatre has increasingly cast African Americans in roles once thought to be reserved for whites, and, conversely, the white actor Patrick Stewart has played the black Othello (without makeup or changing any lines) opposite a black actress playing the white Desdemona.

The New York Shakespeare Festival has been a leader in nontraditional casting, choosing Angela Bassett for Lady Macbeth, Morgan Freeman for Petruchio, and Denzel Washington for Richard III. In Los Angeles, meanwhile, the black actress Fran Bennett played King Lear, and in a state with less than 4 percent African Americans and Asian Americans *combined,* the Oregon Shakespeare Festival recruits and engages an acting company in which a full one-third of the members are non-Caucasian. Black, Asian, and Hispanic actors are often cast in American and European productions today in roles that represent, say, Elizabethan royalty, French aristocrats, Greek gods, or Judeo-Christian Bible figures, thus dispensing fully with stereotypes of received images.

Cross-gender casting is also commonplace in the postmodern age, as in the case of Bennett's King Lear or, at London's Globe Theatre, Mark Rylance's Cleopatra and Olivia. The New York Shakespeare Festival has also proved a pioneer in this area, featuring New York's first female Hamlet in modern times. By now, female Hamlets, Prosperos, Richard IIs, and Richard Ills are everywhere apparent—as are male Rosalinds and Lady Bracknells. And in *Bridge and Tunnel* on Broadway in 2006, the black, Baltimore-born actress Sarah Jones played fourteen different roles—male and female, black and white, Pakistani, Lithuanian, Mexican, Russian, Jamaican, Jordanian, Chinese, and African American—all with uncanny accuracy, charm, and respectful admiration of the shared problems and challenges of immigration and assimilation, the "bridges and tunnels," that affect a great majority of our current national corpus.

## A Spectacular Theatre

Aristotle considered spectacle one of the six components of theatre, but the past decades have seen theatre

Martin Sherman's 1979 *Bent* received a Tony nomination for its harrowing tale of the treatment of German homosexuals during the rise of Adolf Hitler, and it paved the way for the serious—even tragic—theatrical treatment of homophobia. In this 2006 English revival at the Trafalgar Studios in London, Max (Alan Cumming, *right*) and Rudy (Kevin Trainor) are gay men imprisoned by the Nazis. Max pretends to be Jewish under the misapprehension that he will be treated less harshly. Costumes are by Mark Bouman.

"a gay fantasia on national themes," proved the most celebrated American stage production of the 1990s.

Differently-abled persons are also represented by new plays as well as by theatre companies that were created specifically for these voices and for expanding differently-abled audiences. In New York, Theatre by the Blind employs sightless actors for all of its productions. The National Theatre of the Deaf is one of several groups that create theatre by and for the hearing-impaired, employing American Sign Language (ASL) as their primary verbal dramatic medium. With Mark Medoff's prize-winning *Children of a Lesser God,* the hearing-impaired reached a broad popular audience, and a number of hearing-impaired actors and actresses found national recognition.

Deaf West is a Los Angeles theatre for the hearing-impaired, and its production of the musical *Big River*, in which characters alternately speak, sing, and sign their roles, began on the company's tiny home stage. From there it moved to the much larger Mark Taper Forum and then to Broadway, winning critical acclaim not merely for overcoming its "handicapped" label but for creating an altogether new theatre aesthetic of hearing and "seeing" musical drama at the same time. Tyrone Giordano (*left*) plays Huckleberry Finn, with Michael McElroy as Jim, at the American Airlines Theater in 2003.

move from mere spectacle (that which is seen) to the totally spectacular (that which astounds). In part, this shift reflects the development of new technologies, affecting both visual and sound design; and in part, it reflects the emergence of a new arts aesthetic.

Some of the new theatre technology (see the chapter titled "Designers and Technicians") comes from cinema, with its dazzling computer graphics, animations, and digitized motion-capture, and from the contemporary circus. The effects to be seen in films like *Star Wars and Lord of the Rings,* and in Cirque du Soleil productions like *O* and *Kà,* have encouraged stage directors and designers to discover computerized technologies that in a matter of nanoseconds can create and remove lakes and replace them with tall buildings or vast cauldrons of hellfire, can move lights and change their colors second by second, and can produce seemingly magical illusions and even upend whole stages, plunging the actors into the unknown

below. And the pop/rock concert stage has created sound systems capable of reaching ear-blasting volume while still maintaining clarity of tone and mellowness of timbre, reaching every seat in the house simultaneously and in the process overthrowing, as it were, the very speed of physical sound.

Such spectacular effects reach their apex in the high-budget (and high-ticket) Broadway musicals, with their falling chandeliers and descending helicopters, or in Cirque du Soleil extravaganzas with their gyrating stages and loudspeakers fitted behind every seat in the audience. But audiences have come to expect these effects in such shows—pricey as they are—to the extent that audiences for Broadway musicals willingly accept that the "characters" whose lives and fortunes they're presumably following have visible microphones pasted on their foreheads (or, on the naked actors in Stephen Sondheim's *Passion,* wires running down their backs), in return for

English playwright David Hare's *The Power of Yes* is a verbatim work, examining—through the words of real-life economists, politicians, and financiers—the economic conditions that lay behind the near-total collapse of the world banking system in the fall of 2008. "This isn't a play, it's a story," says a character representing the author in the play's opening moments. Here Jonathan Coy plays Sir Howard Davies, real-world director of the London School of Economics, as he explains to his colleagues—and to the theatre audience—what he believes are fundamental economic principles. The play was commissioned shortly after the crash by England's Royal National Theatre and premiered at the Lyttelton Theatre in the fall of 2009. Angus Jackson directed.

the amplified and digitally processed sound they enjoy in return.

There is also an aesthetic behind the theatre's current turn from spectacle to spectacular. The French theorist Antonin Artaud argued fiercely in the 1930s that theatre should have "no more masterpieces," that words in dramas should be valued more for their vibrations than for their meanings and have only the importance they have in dreams. Artaud's proposed theatre was one of overwhelming sounds and visual images that would dominate the stage. His arguments, not fully tested in his own time, have proven greatly influential in ours, starting with the unscripted *happenings* of the 1960s and the more lasting *performance art* that followed in the 1980s and continues to this day.

Performance art is not normally spectacular in the technological sense. It is, however, intensely visual and generally unconcerned with dramatic matters of plot structure, logical argument, or character development—preferring instead explosive, arresting, shocking, provocative, or hilarious imagery. Such art tends by its nature to be transitory; its individual performances are often brief (fifteen minutes, say), attended by small audiences, and not usually meant to be repeatable other than for occasional short runs. Most performance artists prefer it this way. But several have moved into the more rigorous demands of full theatrical presentation, often in national or international tours. Laurie Anderson, one of the most noted such artists today, pushes the envelope with advanced visual and sound technologies and with elements of

the conventionally dramatic: she has performed her *Moby Dick*, after Melville's novel, around the world. Karen Finley's best-known solo performances have a strong political thrust. One piece, in which Finley smeared her naked body with chocolate to represent the exploitation and sexual abasement of women, led the National Endowment for the Arts to revoke the artist's funding, and so, for her subsequent Shut *Up and Love Me,* Finley again smeared herself with chocolate, this time inviting audience members to lick it—at twenty dollars a lick, to compensate for the loss of her NEA grant. By confronting viewers with their own lust—and disgust—Finley creates a vividly memorable unease.

## Verbatim Theatre

Theatre has always dealt with current politics. Indeed, the potentially short lead time between initial conception and finished product is one of the advantages live theatre has over film. But the twenty-first century has seen a virtual explosion of up-to-the-minute dramas performed on major stages, particularly in England and America. Many of these may be called "verbatim theatre," as they have been developed from transcripts of real-life speeches and interviews. Here are a few examples:

- *My Name Is Rachel Corrie* was compiled from the diaries and e-mail messages of American peace activist Corrie, who died in Gaza in 2003 while trying to stop an Israeli bulldozer from demolishing a Palestinian home. Despite its success at London's Royal Court Theatre in 2005, its scheduled New York opening was "postponed" (in effect canceled) the following year in deference to reactions from persons opposed to the play's theme. A resulting furor in the English and American theatre communities, however, led to the play's subsequent mounting later that season at a different off-Broadway theatre.

- Robin Soams's *Talking to Terrorists,* a transcription of interviews with persons involved in terrorism and torture around the world, also premiered at London's Royal Court in 2005. The play's graphic accounts of torture are recounted in the words of torturers and their victims alike. The play has since been produced in Boston and Tehran. Soams's equally verbatim *Arab-Israeli Cookbook* has run successfully in London, Los Angeles, and Toronto.

- *Stuff Happens,* by celebrated British playwright David Hare, deals with the creation of the British-American coalition during the buildup to the Iraq War; the play's title comes from U.S. Defense Secretary Donald Rumsfeld's response, during a press conference, to the looting of Baghdad. It has played widely in England and America since its 2004 London premiere.

- *Sin, a Cardinal Deposed* was created by playwright Michael Murphy from a thousand pages of court deposition by Boston's Cardinal Bernard Law, plus letters and public documents from priests, doctors, and sexual-abuse victims. The verbatim script was performed by six actors of the Bailiwick Theatre in Chicago in 2004 to great—and often tearful—acclaim.

In addition to those new plays of immediate political pertinence, the current theatre is home to new stagings of classic dramas, particularly Greek tragedies, that are openly reflective of current world crises. Such productions include Kate Whoriskey's *Antigone* at South Coast Repertory in California, Katie Mitchell's *Iphigenia at Aulis* at the National Theatre of England, and Tony Harrison's *Hecuba* for the Royal Shakespeare Company. All of these productions have drawn direct parallels between the wars of the ancient Greeks and those of our own era. *Hecuba,* for example (which starred Vanessa Redgrave and played engagements in London, New York, and Washington in 2005), was set in a modern, Middle Eastern refugee camp run by an all-powerful "coalition force" that had been organized against Trojan "terrorists."

## Dangerous Theatre

A theatre that is drawn directly from today's news, that is open and diverse, experimental and macaronic, is likely to be shocking as well. And so the late modern and postmodern theatre has increasingly been seen as a dangerous one.

The nudity and sensory assault of contemporary theatre stagings no longer cause much consternation. Audiences in the twenty-first century generally take these in stride; indeed, the 2009 revival of *Hair* proved a mainstream Broadway hit, with most of the audience considering its famous full-cast frontal nudity tableau ending the first act more quaint than electrifying. Today the theatre's shock rather comes from current events—and particularly current violence—as in Christopher Durang's *Why Torture Is Wrong, and the People Who Love Them.* In this 2009 play, Durang frames the brutality of his subject into a genre that might be termed lunatic farce, and virtually turns members of the audience into pretzels as they find themselves laughing hysterically—despite themselves—at the cruelest scenes imaginable. Other recent plays on torture, such as Martin McDonagh's *Lieutenant of Inishmore* and *The Pillowman* (both nominated for Tony Awards), also are dark, ironic comedies in which the agonies of the victims are emotionally distanced from the audience, in Brechtian fashion, so that the plays' political message is evoked indirectly rather than through empathy alone. Other, more direct plays about actual human savagery—during the Holocaust, at Abu Ghraib prison, on the battlefield—have also proliferated. Violent and unwanted sex in Africa is the central subject of Lynn Nottage's *Ruined,* the 2009 Pulitzer Prize-winner (the title refers to the mutilation of a young woman's genitalia when she is raped with a bayonet); and rapes, killings, dismemberments, and cannibalism are the subjects of the late Sarah Kane's *Blasted,* which, though premiering in 1995, became a worldwide success with its 2001 London revival following Kane's suicide.

Stage nudity may be old hat; but the simulated homosexual intercourse in Angels in America, and the incessantly vulgar language of many recent plays (starting perhaps with David Mamet's 1983 *Glengarry Glen Ross*—with lines like "*Fuck* marshalling the leads. What the fuck talk is that?"), and even the title of

(*Above*) No playwright in recent years has caused more controversy than England's Sarah Kane, whose postmodern, largely expressionistic works are filled with gruesome violence and carnality. Her first play, *Blasted,* presents shocking images of rape, racism, and cannibalism that caused a theatre scandal unknown in England since the 1960s, which led to hundreds of productions of this and her four other plays throughout the theatre world. Kane was certainly England's most talked-about new playwright when, tragically, she took her own life in 1999, just weeks after her twenty-eighth birthday. In this production, directed by Thomas Ostermeier at Berlin's Schaubünne am Lehniner Platz in Berlin in 2005 and photographed at its Avignon Theatre Festival tour later that season, Katharina Schüttler plays Cate, kneeling over her rapist Ian (played by Ulrich Mühe), who by this time has himself been raped, blinded, and battered to near-death by a soldier in the play's wartime environment. Scenery is by Jan Pappelbaum; costumes are by Almut Eppinger.

(*Bottom*) Nudity had firmly entered serious mainstream theatre by 1973, when Peter Shaffer's *Equus* proved a solid success at London's National Theatre and then received a Tony best-play award for its Broadway version. Based on a true story, Shaffer's play treats an engaging but disturbed teenage boy, Alan Strang, whose passion for horses has displaced his more conventional sexual development. *Equus* (Latin for "horse") achieves its astonishing climax when, totally naked in a horse barn, Alan fails to consummate an impromptu sexual encounter with an equally naked girl and, in a fit of maniacal despair, blinds the onlooking "horses" with a hoof pick. The play's immensely successful 2007 London revival, with Daniel Radcliffe as Alan, made clear that staged nudity, though perhaps no longer shocking, retains its tremendous power to create an intense theatrical impact. Radcliffe reprised his performance in the Broadway production in 2008-09.

(*Left*) One of the most gripping contemporary plays about urban British violence is Mark Ravenhill's shockingly titled *Shopping and Fucking*. Andrew Clover is the besieged actor in the original London production, at the Royal Court Theatre, in 1996.

(*Below*) The director of Howard Brenton's *Romans in Britain* was hauled into Old Bailey—the venerable British court—when the play first opened at England's National Theatre in 1980. He was accused of creating an act of "gross indecency" when actors simulated the rape of a naked Celt male by a naked Roman soldier during the Roman occupation two thousand years previously. The director (Michael Bogdanov) won his case, but Brenton's powerful play, which draws parallels with modern-day English rule in Northern Ireland, still sparks furious controversy. This Sheffield, England, revival in 2006, with its luxuriously verdant setting by Ralph Koltai, may suggest an even deeper parallel that the author did not consider: the rape of the natural planet by civilization. Samuel West directed.

(*Facing page*) A theatre of community can also comprise communal *living*, and the Living Theatre—created in the 1950s in New York by Julian Beck and his wife Judith Molina—pioneered in both creating experimental theatre and building a theatrical collective where the artists lived as well as worked together. The company's politically radical 1963 production of Kenneth H. Brown's *The Brig,* about brutality in a U.S. Marine base prison, became a landmark of American experimental theatre. But the Becks' difficulties in New York with public officials—who closed their theatre and briefly imprisoned them—caused the entire company to leave the United States and live and perform abroad for decades to follow. In 2006, the "Living," as it is popularly known, returned to New York under Molina's direction and presented this revival of *The Brig,* which earned the company excellent reviews—and no prison sentences.

Mark Ravenhill's *Shopping and Fucking,* have shocked viewers into writing angry letters to the theatres that produced them and the newspaper critics who reviewed them. Religious defamation was the accusation that led to bomb threats that caused the cancellation of a planned 1998 New York opening of Terrence McNally's *Corpus Christi,* in which a Jesus-like character was to have sexual relations with his disciples. (The play finally opened in New York ten years later, causing no disturbance at all.) And Neil LaBute's violent, baby-murdering *The Distance from Here* was met with outrage by some subscribers and loud screams from at least one audience (as well as plaudits from many critics) at its Manhattan Theatre Club premiere. Theatre today continually treads on toes—and sometimes the toes kick back.

## A Theatre of Community

Although most of the theatre discussed and pictured in this book was created by trained professional artists, we must never forget that theatre's origins are located in performances created not by theatre professionals but by social communities—religious and ethnic—whose works were intended not for the entertainment of spectators but for the benefit, and often the rapture, of their own participants. The African dance-drama, the Egyptian resurrection plays, the Greek dithyrambs, and the medieval *Quem Queritis* trope were basically celebrations of their societies' cultures, and their performers were the primary celebrants. Such theatres—whose works are created not only *for* a community but *by* it—continue today. They eventually may attract audiences, attain box-office income, and pay professional salaries, but they are primarily expressions, celebrations, and sometimes critiques of the cultures of their creators.

In America, such groups have existed in tribal Native American cultures since, before the landing of Columbus. In twentieth-century America, several "workers' theatres" in the 1930s created theatre pieces by and for the American worker. The most famous, Clifford Odets's *Waiting for Lefty,* was produced in 1935 by the Group Theatre, which became one of the country's first prominent theatre ensembles dedicated to social causes. Other focused theatre ensembles followed, many devoted not merely to creating theatre works by and for members of their community but also to touring their productions to localities previously unserved by the theatre at all, including Luis Valdez's El Teatro Campesino (the "farmworkers' theatre," mentioned earlier) and the Free Southern Theatre founded in New Orleans by African American playwright John O'Neal in 1965.

Unique in this movement, however, is the Cornerstone Theater, founded in 1986 by Harvard graduates

Bill Rauch and Alison Carey and now headed by Michael John Garcés. The Cornerstone's goal has been to engage with local cultural groups in creating new theatrical works (often based on classic dramas) adapted to each group's interests, fears, and aspirations. These works are then performed—by the merged Cornerstone and community groups—within the community, usually on a free or pay-what-you-can basis. The response is usually electric: not only are these works heralded as absorbing and entertaining, but they initiate new cultural discourse and even social change in almost every community where they have been engaged. Examples of Cornerstone's work are as varied as American culture itself, as, for example,

- *Tartoof Molière's Tartuffe,* adapted to portray a disintegrating farm family with a cast and crew of fifty-five Kansans; performed in Norcatur, Kansas (population 215).

- *Romeo & Juliet:* performed by a racially integrated cast in Port Gibson, Mississippi (population 2,371).

- *The House on Walker River:* an adaptation of Aeschylus's trilogy *The Oresteia,* staged on an Indian reservation in Schurz, Nevada (population 325).

- *Steelbound:* adapted from the tragedy *Prometheus Bound,* featuring steelworkers at a defunct Bethlehem Steel plant in Pennsylvania and staged in a vacant factory.

- *The Toy Truck:* adapted from a Sanskrit epic and performed in English, Spanish, Mandarin, and Korean with residents of the nation's largest low-income housing complex for seniors.

- *Touch the Water:* written by Julie Hébert, directed by Juliette Carrillo, and created in collaboration with, according to the Cornerstone, "local river residents, engineers, biologists, environmentalists, activists, advocates and patrons who walk, fish, bike and ride horses on the Los Angeles River." Staged in 2009 next to the river—which is mostly a vast ribbon of concrete through the city's downtown, with barely a trickle of water—the play seeks to explore the ways laws "shape and disrupt communities.".

Theatre, Cornerstone's founder Rauch believed, is "a rehearsal for changing the world." In asserting this goal, Rauch reached back to the most ancient role of theatre as the broadest possible community forum—not merely an entertainment for an elite "theatergoing" class but a participatory ceremony involving truth, fiction, struggle, and art, welded together into performance and witnessing. His successors are clearly continuing in this tradition.

## Movement Art and Dance-Theatre

With emphases in postmodern performance shifting from verbal semantics to the sheer sensory impact of images and sound, contemporary "theatre" listings now often include stage events consisting almost entirely of expressive movement, dance, music, and lighting—events in which rhythm, color, sound, and athleticism reign over plot, character, and language. Many of these groups enjoy enormous popularity and have been fully embraced by the commercial as well as the experimental theatre communities.

At least in the popular mind, *movement art* might be said to date from the early 1990s when Luke Cresswell, a percussionist and composer, and Steve McNichols, an actor and writer, created *Stomp,* a storyless and purely percussive performance piece in 1991; it proved a great success in both London and New York and has run ever since in those cities and many others around the world. Stomp employs an assortment of garbage-can lids, pipes, brooms, and other everyday objects for its drumming; its rhythms are furious, its choreography is explosive, and its intensity is relentless—and often comic.

Blue Man Group, which followed, is a similar plotless percussive enterprise that also employs riotous clowning, interaction with the audience, and amazing food fights; it is performed by three headshaved actors covered from the neck up in superglossy blue goop. The avant-garde group was created in New York City by former school pals Chris Wink, Matt Goldman, and Phil Stanton, who opened their first show, *Tubes,* at the tiny off-Broadway Astor Place Theatre in 1991. They (and their professional heirs) are now a near-permanent fixture in the New York, Boston, Chicago, Berlin, Oberhausen, London, and Amsterdam theatre centers and are ensconced in their own huge, permanent theatres in Las Vegas and, since 2007, in Florida's Universal Orlando Resort.

*Dance-theatre* was popularized by Pina Bausch with her German Tanztheater Wuppertal during the 1970s. Adding words to her choreography (and thus popularizing the term *dance-theatre*), she created dramatic dance work that is both playful and experimental yet underlain with strains of contemporary human

The Argentine movement art company De La Guarda was founded in 1993 by a group of theatre students who, unable to find acting jobs upon graduation, created their own, highly original form of expression in interactive aerial ballet. Company performers mostly fly over and into their standing, swaying audience—which is simultaneously assaulted by rain, smoke, and wind and blasted by pummeling music and sound. The company's most recent production, *Fuertzabruta* (*Brute Force*)—seen here in its run at the Edinburgh International Festival in Scotland—has elements of circus, rave, rock concert, striptease, and fraternity party and has been performed around the world.

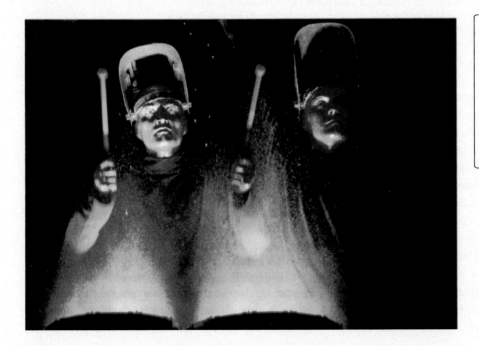

Blue Man Group, now running lavish and apparently permanent productions in nine cities in the United States and Europe, began as an unknown three-man percussion ensemble performing in the streets and eventually in a tiny off-Broadway theatre. Extraordinary drumming, lighting, physical dexterity, and the now-famous iridescent blue makeup have characterized Group performers since the beginning.

The Studio is truly a dance-drama, which is to say a play about dance and the role of the relationships, personal and professional, between choreographer and dancer. Written, directed, and choreographed by Christopher d'Amboise, a former principal dancer with the New York City Ballet and choreographer of fifty ballets in Europe and America (and the son of legendary ballet star Jacques d'Amboise), the play treats the creation of a new work by the fictional choreographer Emil (played by Terrence Mann, *left*) working with an eager ballet aspirant Lisa (Nancy Lemenager) and her more seasoned dance partner, Jackie (John Todd). This South Coast Repertory premiere in 2006 concludes with the ballet that the fictional actors, after many struggles, have created: a genuine case of reality and art inextricably intermixed.

anguish. Revivals of her historic *Sacre du Printemps* (1975; about youthful sexual desire and its complications), *Café Müller* (1978; taken from her own childhood when she hid under the tables at her parents' restaurant), *Nelken* (1982; "Carnations," performed on a stage covered with the red flowers), and her more recent and intercultural productions of *Nefes* (2003; based on Turkish themes and music) and *Bamboo Blues* (2008; with Indian themes and Indian music), were touring the world at or just before her sudden death in 2009.

Martha Clarke, a veteran of the Pilobolus dance troupe, became Bausch's American match with her dance-theatre pieces in the late 1980s, particularly *The Garden of Earthly Delights,* based on the famous

painting by Hieronymus Bosch; Clarke refashioned and revived this production to wide acclaim in 2008-09. Her major works in the current century include *Vienna: Lusthaus,* which evoked the artistic and sexual ferment of Vienna at the time of painter-designer Gustav Klimt, and *Kaos,* a dance-theatre piece based on stories by Italian playwright Luigi Pirandello, which includes a spoken Italian text (with projected English translations) conveying tales of tragic madness, sexual passion, and despair among the inhabitants of a dusty Sicilian village.

The dance-theatre of the present has also been enhanced by two innovative choreographers also active in music theatre. Susan Stroman, distinguished on Broadway for her choreography and direction of

Susan Stroman directed and choreographed *Contact,* one of the first musical hits of the twenty-first century. Debra Yates is the dazzling dancer in the yellow dress who attracts the life-changing attention of Boyd Gaines (*spotlighted behind her*), who plays a burnt-out advertising exec.

Martha Clarke's *The Garden of Earthly Delights,* based on a painting (about 1503) by Hieronymus Bosch, was a seminal creation in American dance-theatre in 1984. Shown here is Clarke's re-creation of the work in 2008 in the same theatre (the off-Broadway Minneta Lane), where it (and she) sparked even greater public enthusiasm.

*The Producers* and a revival of *The Music Man,* scored an immense success with her all-but-wordless *Contact* in 2000, which surprisingly won the Tony Award for best play while Stroman took the Tony for best director. Billed as a "dance play," *Contact* consists of three separate pieces connected only by the theme of romantic linkups: "Swinging," in which Fragonard's famous eighteenth-century French painting of a girl on a swing comes to life as a three-way sex romp; "Did You Move?", a housewife's seriocomic fantasy in a chaotic, outer-borough, 1950s New York restaurant; and the title piece, "Contact," in which an alcoholic and burnt-out advertising executive tries to commit suicide after failing to make contact, in a high-voltage dance club, with a supersexy lady dazzlingly dressed in brilliant yellow. (For more on Susan Stroman, see the photo essay in the chapter titled "The Director.")

English-born Matthew Bourne, who had been choreographing for the stage since the late 1980s, moved from conventional assignments at the start of his career to startlingly radical adaptations of classical nineteenth-century ballets in the 1990s, including the *Nutcracker* and *Swan Lake* (for which Bourne replaces the airy and delicate swan-ballerinas with bare-chested, buzz-cut men), and then (in the following decade) even more surprising stagings, including *Car Man: An Auto-Erotic Thriller. Car Man* adapted Bizet's Carmen from its Spanish setting to a rural American diner/auto-repair shop of the 1960s; it is

Matthew Bourne's *Car Man,* a sexy, powerful dance-drama using music from Bizet's opera *Carmen,* is set in a diner that doubles as an auto-repair shop in a mythic Harmony, USA, of the 1960s. Ewan Wardrop plays the "car man" Luca, in the 2000 London premiere, and Michaela Meazza plays his girlfriend, Lana.

flagrantly sexual, violent, and raw, with characters copulating on kitchen tables and bloody fights reddening the stage. Bizet's opera has been reorchestrated into a percussion-heavy score, which blares forth (presumably) from an onstage jukebox in this version, and the story has been changed entirely, with the character of Carmen replaced by two lovers, Luca, an auto mechanic, and Lana, his tempestuous girlfriend. Bourne's more recent *Play without Words* is a dance-drama portraying social and sexual relationships during Britain's "swinging sixties," combining jazzy eroticism with a penetrating cultural critique.

## Solo Performance

Although Anton Chekhov wrote a short play for a single actor (*On the Harmfulness of Tobacco*, in which the character is a lecturer addressing his audience), only in recent times have authors seriously entertained the possibilities of full-length plays employing a single actor. Sometimes these are little more than star vehicles or extended monologues, often based on historical characters, as, for example, Hal Holbrook's long-running portrayal of America's great writer in *Mark Twain Tonight*, James Whitmore's rendition of America's feisty thirty-third president in *Give 'Em Hell, Harry!*, and Julie Harris's recurrent tours as Emily Dickinson in *The Belle of Amherst*. More fully dramatized works followed in the 1990s, however, when Jay Presson Allen wrote two intriguing and generally successful Broadway plays for solo actors, the most noted being *Tru*, about novelist and society darling Truman Capote in his last, despairing days. Also noteworthy in the 1990s were Willy Russell's *Shirley Valentine*, in which a frustrated middle-aged housewife tells us of leaving her English husband for a boatman on a Greek island; Lily Tomlin's portrayal of all seventeen characters in Jane Wagner's wonderfully amusing and affecting *Search for Signs of Intelligent Life*; and Patrick Stewart's one-man presentation of Charles Dickens's *A Christmas Carol*, in which the celebrated Shakespearean actor (and *Star Trek* star) played all the roles.

More socially engaged solo performances, however, have redefined the genre. Jeff Weiss's epic narratives of (presumably) his life on the Lower East Side, *... And That's How the Rent Gets Paid*, probably began the trend at the Wooster Theatre in New York's SoHo during the 1970s and 1980s. In the next decade, Eric Bogosian's series of intense and penetrating performances, savage and comic by turns, with their indelible cast of American low-life characters—pimps and whores, addicts and agents, executives and rock stars, panhandlers and jocks (*Drinking in America; Sex, Drugs, and Rock & Roll; Pounding Nails in the Floor with My Forehead; and Wake Up and Smell the Coffee*)—created a giant social panorama of life on the social fringes. Anna Deveare Smith's *Fires in the Mirror* and *Twilight: Los Angeles 1992* were solo narratives, in multiple voices, that respectively portrayed the days of rage in Crown Heights, Brooklyn, following the violent deaths of an African American and a Hassidic Jew, and the Los Angeles riots following the acquittal of white police officers charged with the beating of the black motorist, Rodney King.

Smith's work creates a more complex dramaturgy than do most solo performances, as does Sherry Glaser's seemingly plain but dramatically astonishing *Family Secrets*, which recounts the author's family story through the lively and racy monologues of five characters: Glaser, her mother, her sister, her father, and her grandmother—all played by Glaser, who transforms herself on stage, often in mid-sentence, with simple costume and makeup changes. Glaser's family secrets—some hilarious, some painful, and all provocative—revolve around sexual identity and ambiguity, religious absorption and assimilation, mental illness, menstruation, and childbirth. Many of these subjects also are addressed by Colombianborn and New York University-educated John Leguizamo, who has become another of America's leading solo writer-performers. His performances of *Freak* and *Sexaholix,* both set in Leguizamo's childhood borough of Queens (New York), are hugely comic and often deeply poignant autobiographical journeys.

Perhaps the most exciting solo performer at the time of writing, though, is Danny Hoch, whose *Taking Over,* a series of eight monologues on the theme of urban gentrification (elite classes "taking over" ethnic urban neighborhoods), thrilled audiences in its 2008 Berkeley Repertory Theatre (California) premiere and subsequent engagements at New York's Public Theatre and Los Angeles' Mark Taper Forum. Hoch, who came to public attention with his *Jails, Hospitals & Hip Hop* in the late 1990s, specializes in luminous portrayals of loudmouthed social outcasts—of all sexes, races, and persuasions—who mainly habituate New York's working-class boroughs. Fluent in both English and Spanish, and in many of the dialects spoken in Latin America, Hoch conveys almost everything discussed in this chapter: the postmodern, nonlinear, multicultural, macaronic, foul-mouthed, and politically engaged level of shock performance that characterizes

Danny Hoch is one of today's most exciting solo performers. He is seen here in a collage of three of the nine characters—black and white, male and female, English— and Spanish-speaking-that he plays, without change of makeup, in his *Taking Over.* The play premiered at Berkeley Repertory Theatre in 2008, then was performed in the Bronx, in Queens, and at the Public Theatre in Manhattan. The play concerns the gentrification—too rapid in Hoch's opinion—of his Williamsburg neighborhood in Brooklyn.

our times. "What a diverse group of people," he—as a half-Polish, half-Puerto Rican American—greets us with at the start of the play. "Get the fuck out! You suck! Nobody wants you here!" he continues. We're hooked; Hoch has taken over.

## THREE THEATRE-MAKERS IN THE THEATRE TODAY

Three theatre artists—generally described as directors although their artistic contributions include the creation of entirely new styles and even theories of performance—have profoundly shaped the theatre of our times and are likely to shape the theatre of the future as well. The names of these contemporary "theatre-makers" are Peter Brook, Robert Wilson, and Julie Taymor.

## Peter Brook

No one has more influenced the theatre in the past half century, and no one is more provocative in it today, than the English-born director and theorist Peter Brook, born in 1925. Beginning his directorial career with freshly conceived experimental productions of Shakespeare, Marlowe, Jean-Paul Sartre, and Jean Cocteau, Brook received sufficient attention to be appointed, at age twenty, to direct at the Shakespeare Memorial Theatre at Stratford-upon-Avon, where his 1955 *Hamlet* was a sensation and became the first English play to tour the Soviet Union. Within a few years, Brook was staging plays, musicals, and operas at major performing venues on both sides of the Atlantic (New York's Broadway and the Metropolitan Opera; London's Covent Garden).

Peter Brook continues to pioneer in bringing global theatre to audiences around the world. His production of the groundbreaking *Sizwe Banzi Is Dead,* a play that exposed apartheid to an international community in its 1972 South African premiere, was staged at the Avignon Theatre Festival in 2006 and subsequently toured to festivals in Toronto, Jerusalem, Adelaide (Australia) and, shown here, the Barbican Theatre in London in 2007. Written by South Africans Athol Fugard, John Kani, and Winston Ntshona, the play was performed in this production by Malian actor Habib Dembélé (*left,* as Styles) and Congolese actor Pitcho Womba Konga in the title role.

Brook's heart remained in experimental stagings of new and classical drama, however, and in three landmark productions with the newly founded Royal Shakespeare Company in the 1960s he received immense international acclaim. These productions—Shakespeare's *King Lear* (1962), strongly influenced by Beckett and the theatre of the absurd; Peter Weiss's *Marat/Sade* (1964), a production blending Artaud's notion of a theatre of cruelty with Brecht's theatre of alienation; and US (1966), a company-improvised documentary commenting on American ("U.S." as "us") involvement in Vietnam—toured widely. Both *Lear* and *Marat/Sade* were later filmed, receiving even wider exposure.

Moreover, Brook's essays on drama in Encore magazine in the 1960s, and his publication of *The Empty Space* in 1968 (now translated into fifteen languages), presented a brilliant recategorization of theatre that remains pertinent today. Brook divided the current theatre into three distinct branches: "deadly, holy, and rough"—which basically correspond to conventional, Artaudian, and Brechtian. Rejecting all three, Brook concluded his study with a manifesto on behalf of an "immediate" theatre, one not preplanned by the director but developed through a creative and improvisational process, "a harrowing collective experience" rather than a dispassionate assemblage of the separate contributions of cast and designers. Brook then proved his point with an amazingly comic, penetrating, original, and "immediate" version of *Shakespeare's A Midsummer Night's Dream* in 1971, a production that—staged on a bare white set and without the play's usual sentimentality—combined circus techniques with uninhibited sexual farce and created fresh interactions between the play's very familiar (though often shallowly realized) characters. Brook's

Peter Brook's 2009 production of *Fragments*, a compilation of short plays by Samuel Beckett, included Beckett's *Act Without Words II*, a pantomime of two men who live in big white "sleeping bags" and are seen to wake when prodded, go about their business, and then go back into their bags. Here Marcello Magni plays the first, and more slovenly of the two men, in a performance seen in Wroclaw, Poland, in 2009.

*Dream* was truly revolutionary, captivating critics and audiences alike throughout Europe and America during the early 1970s and further establishing its director as one of the most creative and talented theorist/ theatrical practitioners of all time.

In 1971, however, Brook walked away from all of this, moving to Paris and creating the International Center of Theatre Research. Engaging a company of actors from every continent to perform mostly in French, in a long-abandoned, dirt-floored theatre (the Bouffes du Nord, located in the North African quarter of Paris), Brook has produced a series of intercultural works of extraordinary interest, including *The Iks* (about a northern Ugandan tribe), *The Conference of the Birds* (based on a twelfth-century Persian poem), an abridged version of Georges Bizet's Carmen, a production of Shakespeare's *The Tempest,* and, most remarkable, *The Mahabharata,* which opened in Paris in 1986 and was filmed in 1991.

*The Mahabharata* is the national novel of India, ancient, archetypal, and immense (it is the longest single work of world literature). Brook had it adapted into a nine-hour play, which he initially staged with an international cast in a rock quarry in the south of France, then at his Bouffes du Nord. Brook blends the text with a myriad of natural (but not naturalistic) elements: actors wade in pools and rivers of real water and are trapped by circles of real fire; chariot wheels are mired in real mud; armies clash by torchlight; candles float in the pond. The multifaceted reality of this Indian epic—directed by an Englishman, in French, with an intercontinental cast—lends to the production a universality that leaves the audience fulfilled in ways previously unrealized in the theatre's history.

Brook's stage work in the 1990s studied the individual human mind and included notable and highly original productions such as *The Man Who,* an adaptation of Dr. Oliver Sacks's study of neurological illness, and *Le Costume,* a South African play by Can Themba about a ménage á trois that consists of a man, his wife, and her lover's suit of clothes! At the start of the twenty-first century, Brook's severely abridged and intermissionless *Hamlet,* his first production in English in decades, toured Europe and America with an intercultural cast: Jamaican-born Adrian Lester played the title role, the Indian Shantala Shivalingappa played Ophelia, and the English Natasha Parry (Brook's wife) played Gertrude, all accompanied by a string and percussion score composed and performed by Japanese musical artist Toshi Tsuchitori. Brook's more recent productions include those certifying his intercultural commitment: *Tierno Bokar* (2004), based on the writing of the late African writer Amadou Hampaté Bâ, which takes place in an Islamic African village torn asunder in World War II, *Sizwe Banzi Est Mort* (2006) as adapted from the South African play of Athol Fugard, John Kani, and Winston Ntshona. But

Brook remains keen on the classical literature with which his career began, and in 2009 he premiered his own adaptation of Shakespeare's sonnets under the title *Love Is My Sin* at the International Center of Theatre Research, bringing it to America (at the Ringling International Arts Festival in Sarasota, Florida) later that year. Brook did announce, in 2008, that he was retiring from the Center—but only in 2011! Clearly, Brook, eighty-three at the time, is on track to remain as active as ever, both as director and as author/theorist.

And to remain as unique. In an interview with *The Guardian,* Brook warned against anybody trying to perpetuate his particular vision: "The first thing I wanted to establish [in picking a successor]—having spent all my life fighting against tradition and saying everything in the theatre must always be in a state of evolution, must always refuse to have a method, a way of working—was to avoid a successor who would have to try and prove my line, which is against the whole life force of the theatre."

## Robert Wilson

No director has more successfully explored—and essentially renovated—the visual elements of current avant-garde theatre than Texas native Robert Wilson. Born in Waco in 1941 and initially trained as an architect, Wilson emerged in the European avant-garde in the early 1970s as a brilliantly innovative creator (a playwright-designer-director-producer) of what at the time were considered performance-art pieces, or *tableaux vivants* ("living pictures"), rather than dramas. The extraordinary duration of these pieces earned Wilson considerable notoriety: *The Life and Times of Joseph Stalin* (1973) lasted twelve hours; *Ka Mountain* (1972) lasted twenty-three, performed (on the top of a mountain in Iran) over a period of seven days. Wilson became widely known in his home country only when he was invited to create the central performance work of the 1984 Los Angeles Olympic Arts Festival, for which he composed a twelve-hour piece to be entitled *the CIVIL warS,* which was to be rehearsed in several countries around the world. Unfortunately, sufficient funding could not be raised, but he became widely admired for the extent of his vision and artistic ambition.

Since the mid-1970s, Wilson's work has been more focused within practical time-and-space limits, and he has begun to direct—however unconventionally—more conventional works, including classic dramas, operas, and original pieces of mixed genres. His first dramatic production, Euripides' *Alcestis* at the American Repertory Theatre in Cambridge, Massachusetts, in 1986 proved a visually stunning, almost magical production of the Greek tragedian's eerie work. Wilson's staging featured a mountain collapsing in slow motion, a river in which women slowly washed their hair in choreographic unison, and a goat sacrificed so that its spurting blood colored the actors' arms red. Original music by performance artist Laurie Anderson, the addition of a Japanese kyōgen epilogue, innovative laser lighting effects, and what has become Wilson's trademark—glacially slow actor stage crossings—created intense mystery and engagement, at least for audiences willing to set aside their interests in fast-paced plots and empathetic characters. In *Alcestis,* Wilson created a "spectacular" theatre of the avant-garde, not conventional or commercial but visually thrilling and often wonder-inspiring.

Wilson continues to work in every aspect of the theatre: he is the director, author, or adapter of the text and the principal designer of all his productions, several of which are depicted in photographs elsewhere in this book. In his 1995 adaptation of *Hamlet,* Wilson also performed the title and other roles. The play was set in a minimalist construction of black slabs against a horizon shifting from white to blue to red according to the prince's mood, presenting Shakespeare's text as a deathbed meditation on the play's confounding events and discoveries.

For his immensely popular 2004 production of *Les Fables de La Fontaine* at the Paris Comédie-Française, Wilson turned to the world of animals, adapting nineteen children's stories by the seventeenth-century French fabulist jean de La Fontaine, and clothing his cast in brilliantly imaginative animal masks and costumes. Backed with vivid lighting and stunning geometric designs, and staged with bold and sprightly movements, the fifteen members of France's oldest and most celebrated theatre company leaped and whirled their way through ancient fables such as "The Crow and the Fox," "The Grasshopper and the Ant," and "The Frog Who Wanted to Be as Big as the Ox." The avant-garde, Wilson had apparently discovered, does not have to be grim.

Wilson continues to innovate, particularly in the area of boldly color-saturated lighting and contemporary music, which he explores in new stagings of modern theatre classics including *Woyzeck, Peer Gynt, Happy Days,* and the German fable *The Black Rider,* in

which he incorporates music by Tom Waits, played by a stage band featuring a toy piano, a pocket trumpet, a glass harmonica, and a musical saw. Wilson's most recent work (like Brook's) is an elaborate staging of Shakespeare's sonnets. The production employs extensive cross-dressing, lavish costuming, and live music in the tradition of medieval German *minnesang* as well as contemporary electric guitar, all composed, played, and occasionally sung by pop star Rufus Wainwright. His *Sonnetten* received rousing ovations at its Berliner Ensemble premiere in 2009. "If I had studied theatre," Wilson has said, " I would never make the work I do."

Wilson's work is no longer considered performance art: his pieces have a theme, they are not improvised, and the performers usually (but not always) play characters other than themselves. But Wilson shares with performance art a disdain for logical language and plot construction and a corresponding preference for combining music, movement, sculpture, video, painting, lighting, poetry, and human expressiveness. "I hate ideas," Wilson has said, and in their place he presents visions, dreams, and impressions. Frequent collaborators such as nō and kabuki specialist Suzushi Hanayagi and the autistic poet Christopher

Knowles—a longtime Wilson friend—make non-Western and nontraditional contributions to most of Wilson's work, as do overscale props, ideographic and kinetic scenery, the free intermixing of humans and puppets, utterly nontraditional casting, and his decidedly unhurried stage movements—often appearing as if his characters are underwater. Every aspect-even the sheer duration—of Wilson's work has forced a reexamination of the nature of performance and the relationship of audience and art, meaning and aesthetics, raising questions about the very foundations of dramaturgy: Why do we watch theatre? What are we looking for? What do we care about?

## Julie Taymor

Julie Taymor, born in 1953, is clearly the junior member of this select grouping, and her record of achievement is consequently far slimmer than Brook's or Wilson's. Nonetheless, her contribution to theatre is no less than colossal.

The world knows Taymor for the gigantic commercial success of her Disney-produced *The Lion King,* which received Broadway's Tony Award for best

Julie Taymor's *The Lion King* forges a profound alliance between experimental theatre, African ritual, Asian dance and puppetry, and American mass-market entertainment (namely, the Disney Corporation and Broadway). Here, South African vocalist Tsidii Le Loka plays the role of Bafiki, the singer-narrator, amid leaping gazelles and a menagerie of other animals.

musical in 1998 and won Taymor an unprecedented *two* Tony Awards, for direction and costume design. Nearly ten years later, *The Lion King,* appealing equally to adults and children, was still running to packed houses in five countries (see the chapter on musical theatre). But what most of the world does not know is that Taymor's entire career up to this show was not in the commercial theatre at all but was buried deep in the core of the avant-garde.

Born in Newton, Massachusetts, Taymor spent many of her youthful years in global travel and study, learning traditional Asian culture and performance techniques in India, Sri Lanka, and Japan, learning from Balinese dancers and Indonesian *wayang kulit* (shadow-puppet) masters in Seattle, and studying with noted avant-garde masters Jacques Lecoq at the School of Mime in Paris and with the celebrated theorist/director Herbert Blau at Oberlin College in Ohio. Soon she was directing cutting-edge productions of classical plays (Shakespeare's *Titus Andronicus, The Tempest,* and *The*

*Taming of the Shrew,* Carlo Gozzi's eighteenth-century *King Stag*), primarily at off-Broadway's Theatre for a New Audience and the American Repertory Theatre in Cambridge, Massachusetts. For her first Broadway production in 1996, Taymor directed Horacio Quiroga's *Juan Darien,* a fantastical music-drama about a baby jaguar who becomes human; she also designed the production's masks and puppets, coauthored the script adaptation, and shared design credits for scenery and costume. She received a Tony nomination for directing and a nomination for scenic design for this debut, and clearly emerged as a leading director of provocative works.

The *Lion King,* however, with its budget of $20 million (an all-time Broadway record), far exceeded any scale on which Taymor (or any other American director) had previously operated. In its spectacular opening scene, 26-foot-tall giraffes lope soulfully across the vast African plain and a 13-foot-long elephant, more than 11 feet high, makes an astonishing entrance down the auditorium aisle: it might as well have been Julie Taymor sashaying down the theatre aisle. By play's end the audience had seen 53 performers and 232 puppets representing twenty-five different species of animals, birds, fish, and even insects; spectators gawked at gazelles leaping in staggered unison, birds courting wildly in midair, warthogs wobbling across the stage, wildebeests stampeding, flowered vines descending from the trees, and an enormous, latticed sun rising to reveal the radiant African dawn. But none of this was literal illusion: in a brilliant (but perfectly Asian) technique, Taymor had openly revealed the theatricality of the puppetry and the musicality of the production rather than hiding them to maintain a realistic illusion. Her puppets' heads were located well above the faces of the actors who wore them so that the audience was continually aware of the actors manipulating (and often speaking for) each animal; all of the strings, wheels, and sticks of the puppetry mechanics were in full sight.

Moreover, *The Lion King* is a global show for a global audience. Designing the costumes and codesigning the masks and puppets, Taymor ingeniously mixed Javanese rod puppetry and Balinese headdresses with African masks and stilts. The music (by the English Elton John and South African Lebo M) and lyrics (by Englishman Tim Rice, Lebo M, and Taymor herself) combined Western and African rhythms and languages, respectively, and were played by an orchestra not buried in a below-stage pit but rather extending into audience boxes on both sides of the stage, each box holding costumed African drummers and chanters playing the score. Taymor seemed, in this work, to put the entire world—and all of its species—on a single Broadway stage.

Taymor continues to create exciting and often brave spectacles, now on film as often as on a stage. Her 1999 film of *Titus,* adapted from her earlier stage production, is a remarkable though controversial version of one of Shakespeare's earliest, least-liked, and certainly most savage plays. Her 2002 film *Frida,* about the life of Mexican artist Frida Kalho, received six Academy Awards. For the Metropolitan Opera in New York she staged a lavish production of Mozart's *Magic Flute,* which she adapted into a shorter version staged in New York and carried nationally by satellite in 2007, and for the Los Angeles Opera she staged the world premiere of *Grendel,* composed by her longtime companion, Elliot Goldenthal, again receiving high plaudits. Taymor's 2009 film version of Shakespeare's *The Tempest* features the celebrated British

actress Helen Mirren as "Prospera" (a female version of Shakespeare's Prospero) and African actor Djimon Hounsou as Caliban. Scheduled to open in 2010 is *Spider-Man,* a Broadway musical Taymor is directing and coauthoring, with music by Bono and The Edge.

# THEATRE TODAY: WHERE CAN YOU FIND IT?

Theatre happens all over the world: in villages, campuses, prisons, resorts, and parks; at local and international festivals; on ocean liners and at suburban dinner theatres; on temporary stages in rural churchyards and within historic ruins; and, increasingly, at so-called site-specific venues, such as a Manhattan apartment, a worker's meeting hall, a parking lot, or, in a recent Romanian production, an interurban railway car. But mostly, current theatre is found in cities, and without question New York City is the primary locus of theatrical activity in the United States.

## New York City

Every year Manhattan is the site of more performances, more openings, more revivals, more tours, and more dramatic criticism than any half dozen other American cities put together. Theatrically, New York is the showcase of the nation. In the minds of many Americans, the Big Apple is simply the place to experience theatre. New York's hundred-plus playhouses are a prime tourist attraction and a major factor in the local economy. Moreover, in the minds of most theatre artists—actors, directors, playwrights, and designers—New York is the town where the standards are the highest, the challenges the greatest, and the rewards the most magnificent. "Will it play in Peoria?" may be the big question in the minds of film and television producers, but "Will it play in New York?" remains a cardinal concern in the rarefied world of American professional theatre. Therefore the reality of New York is surrounded by a fantasy of New York, and in a "business" as laced with fantasy as is the theatre, New York commands strategic importance of incomprehensible value. The professional New York theatre, however, comes in three different and quite distinct categories: Broadway, off-Broadway, and off-off-Broadway.

**Broadway** Mapmakers know Broadway as the longest street in Manhattan, slicing diagonally down the entire length of the island borough. Nearly everybody else knows Broadway as the historic and commercial

Great actors as well as great plays attract audiences, and an all-star cast of Marcia Gay Harden, Hope Davis, Jeff Daniels, and James Gandolfini was assembled—all are onstage almost the entire evening—for the Broadway production of *God of Carnage,* by French playwright Yasmina Aeza, which won the 2009 Tony for best play. Seeming at first a realistic drama—two couples politely trying to come to terms about a playground fight between their eleven-year-old sons—the play quickly becomes a riotous farce about social and gender differences in the contemporary urban upper-middle class. The distinguished actors excelled in every role. Harden received the Tony for her performance, and Gandolfini was nominated for one. The brilliantly paced direction was by Matthew Warchus, who also won the Tony; Mark Thompson designed the highly stylized contemporary apartment.

apex of the American theatre, the "Great White Way" (referring to its bright lights), where tourists from around the world head, sometimes on their first day of arrival, to catch a "Broadway play." What a Broadway play is today, however, is not always what it was in the past.

New York theatre has always been centered near Broadway, but at first that center was much farther downtown. Broadway's first theatre, the Park, was erected in 1798 at Broadway and the Bowery. The theatre district subsequently moved northward, as did the city's center, first to 14th Street, then to 23rd Street (where actor Edwin Booth built the magnificent Booth's Theatre in 1869), and eventually to Longacre (now Times) Square, at Broadway and 42nd Street, in 1893. The forty-four theatres that make up today's official Broadway Theatre District are almost all within the dozen blocks north from Times Square, making for a concentration of theatrical excitement unique in the world. The great growth of a truly American drama took place in the current Broadway district. This is where Eugene O'Neill, Arthur Miller, Tennessee Williams, William Inge, and Edward Albee saw their masterpieces produced; it is where George M. Cohan, Ethel Merman, Mary Martin, and Barbra Streisand sang and danced, and where John Barrymore, Marlon Brando, Helen Hayes, Henry Fonda, Alfred Lunt, Lynn Fontanne, and thousands of others acted their way into America's hearts and, subsequently, into Hollywood's films.

The TKTS Booth between Seventh Avenue and Broadway at 47th Street in midtown Manhattan was rebuilt and enlarged in 2009 to better serve theatergoers who wish to buy last-minute and reduced-price tickets to Broadway and off-Broadway shows. The booth is a two- to five-minute walk from all Broadway theatres, and a ten-to fifteen-minute walk or subway ride to most off-Broadway ones. The usual discount is 50 percent, less a nominal fee. Ticket-buyers usually have to wait ten to thirty minutes in line, but most find the conversations among fellow ticket-buyers—"What plays have you seen so far?" and "What did you like?"—part of the true New York theatergoing experience.

After falling victim to urban decay in the 1960s, when it became a haven for sex shops, drug addicts, and porn theatres, Broadway was restored to its former glory by city-sponsored redevelopment: 42nd Street was reclaimed from the drug dealers and prostitutes; new theatres were built and old ones refurbished. In 2009 Broadway completed its most commercially successful season in history, with box-office income of $943.3 million, twice what it had been fifteen years before.

The Broadway "Road"—the collection of Broadway productions that tour to major cities throughout North America—extends the "Broadway experience" to audiences almost as numerous as those attending the same shows in New York. Together with Broadway's annual Tony Awards, televised nationally since 1967, the theatre activity in the dozen-odd blocks of the theatre district in mid-Manhattan now sustains a vibrant international profile.

Yet Broadway is hardly the sum of American theatre. Broadway's lure is its dazzling visual and social excitement, its heady mix of bright lights and famed celebrities, its trend-setting fashions, big-buck entertainments, and high-toned Tony Awards. The Broadway stakes are higher than anywhere else in theatre ("If you can make it there, you'll make it anywhere"), and its energy is electric. And the TKTS Booth (Broadway at 47th Street) sells half-price tickets for most shows, making the experience affordable for almost everyone. But Broadway is no longer the place where new plays routinely originate, as it was in 1947 when Tennessee Williams's *A Streetcar Named Desire* and Arthur Miller's *All My Sons* debuted there.

Broadway today is primarily the staging ground for extravagantly produced musicals, both new (*Wicked, Next to Normal, Billy Elliot, Jersey Boys, Mary Poppins, In the Heights*) and revived (*Chicago, South Pacific, West Side Story, Hair*). Secondarily, Broadway is the showcase for the best (or at least the most commercially promising) new plays from America's off-Broadway (David Auburn's *Proof,* John Patrick Shanley's *Doubt,* Neil LaBute's *reasons to be pretty*); for new plays from abroad (from France, Yasmina Reza's Art and *God of Carnage;* from England, Conor McPherson's *The Seafarer,* Tom Stoppard's *The Coast of Utopia,* and Martin McDonagh's *The Lieutenant of Inishmore*); and for new works from America's top-ranking regional theatres—including 2008 Tony and Pulitzer Prize winner *August: Osage County* from Chicago's Steppenwolf, Seattle's Intiman Theatre production of *Light in the Piazza,* and Chicago's Goodman Theatre productions of *Desire Under the Elms, Long Day's Journey into Night,* and *Death of a Salesman,* all of which made it to Broadway in the first decade of the twenty-first century.

Finally, Broadway is the site of many major revivals from the international dramatic repertory, including recent star-heavy productions of ancient and modern classics such as *Waiting for Godot* with Nathan

Regional theatre produces much of America's greatest drama. Tracy Letts's *August: Osage County,* a large scale (thirteen actors, three-plus hours) realistic comedy about a wildly dysfunctional Oklahoma family, was created by Chicago's Steppenwolf Theatre Company, long famed for its ensemble acting. Following its Chicago premiere, the show went on to Broadway, where it was awarded the 2008 Pulitzer Prize for Drama, along with the Tony, New York Critics Circle, and Drama Desk Awards. Steppenwolf artistic director Anna D. Shapiro ingeniously staged the quarrelings and couplings—of the many characters shown here in the now-famous dinner scene in the second act—so that audience members felt they knew each one of the characters personally, and probably also felt they knew someone in their own lives exactly like them. Deanna Dunagan (*center, with pearl necklace*) plays the central role of Violet, the drug-addicted family matriarch, for which she received the Tony Award for best actress. Steppenwolf-based designers included Todd Rosenthal (scenery), Ana Kuzmanic (costumes), and Ann G. Wrightson (lighting).

Lane, John Goodman, and Bill Irwin, *Salome* with Al Pacino, *The Seagull* with Kristin Scott Thomas, *Hamlet* with Jude Law, *Our Town* with Paul Newman, *Cat on a Hot Tin Roof* with Ashley Judd and Jason Patric, *Moon for the Misbegotten* with Kevin Spacey, *King Lear* and *Inherit the Wind* with Christopher Plummer, *Mary Stuart* with Janet McTeer, and *The Caretaker* with Patrick Stewart.

Rarely does a new play premiere directly on Broadway today. The costs are usually far too high to risk on an untested product. Even new works by America's (and the world's) most successful playwright, Neil Simon, now ordinarily see their first productions off-Broadway or in a regional theatre. For despite high ticket prices, which in 2010 ascended to as much as $125 for straight plays and $135 for musicals (not to mention "premium" tickets at double these prices for patrons seeking front-and-center seats), the majority of Broadway productions fail to recoup their expenses. Increasingly, therefore, Broadway producers look for new plays whose worth has been "proven" in less-expensive off-Broadway, or in the subsidized European (chiefly English) theatre, or on a not-for-profit American regional stage. Only a star-studded revival or a new musical with Tony Award potential is otherwise likely to be "bankable" and offer sufficient opportunity for commercial success. Nonetheless, Broadway remains the primary showcase for the most fully realized theatrical entertainment—and often inspiration—that America has to offer.

**Off-Broadway and Off-Off-Broadway** Not all of New York theatre is performed in the forty-four theatres that, as defined by their contracts with Actors' Equity Association and other unions, constitute "official" Broadway. At least two hundred New York theatres are not in the "Broadway" category, many of them fully professional and most of the others semi-professional (that is, they engage professional actors and other artists who, by mutual agreement, are not paid minimum union salaries). The symbolic centrality of Broadway, however, is so strong that these theatres are named not for what they are but for what they are not: some are "off-Broadway" theatres, and others are "off-off-Broadway."

*Off-Broadway* is a term that came into theatrical parlance during the 1950s and now includes forty to sixty theatres found throughout New York neighborhoods—with concentrations on West 42nd Street, Greenwich Village, the SoHo area, Chelsea, Union Square, and Manhattan's Upper East and Upper West Sides. Several of the best off-Broadway houses, ironically, are in the Broadway geographic area itself (American Place Theatre, Manhattan Theatre Club, Playwrights Horizons) but operate in somewhat smaller theatres and therefore under off-Broadway contracts. Some of the best theatre in America—including eventual Tony and Pulitzer Prize winners—has come out of these companies in recent years.

*Off-off-Broadway,* a term dating from the 1960s, denotes semiprofessional or even amateur theatres located in the metropolitan area, often in church basements, YMCAs, coffeehouses, and converted studios or garages. The actors' union treats off-off productions under its "Showcase Code," for although actors and other artists are not paid salaries, they may enjoy exposure and press reviews that could lead to auditions for the off-Broadway and eventually Broadway roles to which most aspire. Other off-off habitués, however, find the anticommercialism, artistic excitement, experimental spirit, and cultural camaraderie of the off-off more appealing than the monetary benefits of its alternatives. The annual Obie Awards, given by the *Village Voice,* recognize outstanding work in both off- and off-off Broadway theatres and often are more accurate indicators of national theatre trends than are the more glamorous Tonys.

The non-Broadway New York theatre generates passionate and vigorous theatrical creativity. Leaner and less costly than their Broadway competitors, off and off-off attract audiences of their own, many of whom would never think of going to Times Square to see a play. And with their lower ticket prices (particularly in the off-off), and subscription seasons (particularly in the off), many companies have lured successive generations of audiences to new and exciting works before they reach the Broadway masses.

## Regional American Theatre: Not for Profit

Almost no professional theatre was produced on any sort of regular basis outside of New York City until 1950. That was the year in which Arena Stage was founded in Washington, D.C. In the next fifteen years other "regional" theatres opened: Houston's Alley Theatre, San Francisco's Actors' Workshop, and Minneapolis's Guthrie Theatre among them. In the following decade theatres opened almost weekly around the country, and now there are nearly *five hundred* such professional theatres, operating in almost every state.

These theatres, though professional to varying degrees, are nearly all not-for-profit (or nonprofit)—meaning that they are in business not to make money but to create art. Not-for-profit theatres receive box-office revenue, of course, but they supplement that income with government and foundation grants and from private donations that, if the theatre has been legally registered as a nonprofit corporation, provide tax deductions to the donors. Some of these theatres, such as the Public Theatre, the Manhattan Theatre Club, and Playwrights Horizons, operate as part of New York's off-Broadway. The vast majority, however, are scattered throughout the country and produce over two thousand productions each year, providing Americans in hundreds of cities and towns an opportunity to see professional theatre, often at its very best. An annual Tony Award for regional theatre cites the most distinguished of these groups, and thirty such theatres have been so honored.

Nonprofit theatres vary enormously in character. Some concentrate on classics, some on American classics, some on specific ethnic repertories, some on the European avant-garde, many on new plays and theatrical experiments. Some operate in ninety-nine-seat spaces with modest budgets; others operate multiple stages and are large-scale operations: the Guthrie Theatre in Minneapolis, for example, ran its 2008 season on a $33.9 million budget.

Many American regional theatres fill their houses with family audiences in December with productions of a Christmas play—nearly always an adaptation of Charles Dickens's novel *A Christmas Carol*. This production, with South Coast Repertory veteran Hal Landon front and center as Scrooge, is from the final scene of SCR's twenty-ninth annual production of the play, adapted by Jerry Patch, in 2008.

Most of America's best-known regional theatres are located in six cities that might be considered America's regional theatre centers—cities where people actually go for a week or a weekend simply to attend theatre. In the following discussion, the theatres marked with an asterisk have won a regional-theatre Tony.

Boston The *American Repertory Theatre, in Cambridge, was founded by critic/educator/director Robert Brustein in 1980. It has been one of America's most experimental companies since its founding and has been known particularly for giving free rein to many of the most creative directors working in the United States, including Andrei Serban, Peter Sellars, Adrian Hall, Jonathan Miller, Anne Bogart, Susan Sontag,

Des McAnuff, JoAnne Akalaitis, and Robert Wilson. Boston's Huntington Theatre is another major producer, now operating in the restored Boston Center for the Arts and earning praise for its new plays and its long-time devotion to the theatre of August Wilson.

Chicago With as many as two hundred theatre companies, the thriving "Loop" theatre district (six major theatres within five downtown blocks), fourteen hundred professional actors, and at least a score of nationally distinguished directors and playwrights, Chicago rightfully stands as America's "second city" for theatrical culture, and its many theatres have been the breeding ground for hundreds of bright and creative American actors, including Alan Arkin, Gilda Radner,

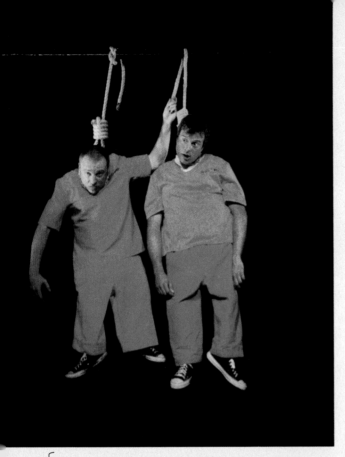

One of the highlights of the 2009 Fringe Festival in New York was *666*, a one-hour piece created and performed in pantomime by Madrid's self-styled "slapstick theater company" Yllana. The wordless play, raucously hysterical, treats four death-row inmates, the crimes they committed, and their attitudes about the death penalty they each face. The actors, said a *New York Times reviewer*, "pester the audience, laugh themselves silly killing one another and dedicate considerable creative resources to plumbing the comic possibilities of urine." This is exactly what one might expect from a performance at the American (or Spanish) theatre's "fringe."

Dan Aykroyd, Alan Alda, Joe Mantegna, David Schwimmer, John Mahoney, John Malkovich, Gary Sinese, and Joan Allen, as well as playwright David Mamet and directors Mike Nichols, Elaine May, Mary Zimmerman, and Frank Galati. Among the leading theatres in Chicago are the *Goodman, the city's oldest (originally founded in 1925) and largest; the *Steppenwolf, premier developer of what has been called the "Chicago style" of intensely realistic acting; and the *Victory Gardens, devoted entirely to new work.

**Los Angeles** Founded in 1965, the *Mark Taper Forum is distinguished for its production of new American plays, many of them subsequently receiving national recognition: Tony Kushner's *Angels* in America, Robert Schenkkan's *The Kentucky Cycle*, Mark Medoff's *Children of a Lesser God*, Luis Valdez's *Zoot Suit*, Marsha Norman's *Getting Out*, Michael Christopher's *The Shadow Box*, George C. Wolfe's *Jelly's Last Jam*, Daniel Berrigan's *The Trial of the Catonsville Nine*, and David Henry Hwang's *Yellow Face* had either their premieres or major developmental productions at the Taper. These works constitute a remarkable diversity of authorial interests and backgrounds. Forty-five miles south of Los Angeles, *South Coast Repertory vies for attention with its only slightly older rival, having premiered many outstanding new plays including David Henry Hwang's *Golden Child*, Craig Lucas's *Prelude to a Kiss*, Richard Greenberg's *Three Days of Rain*, Margaret Edson's *Wit*, Amy Freed's *Freedomland* and *The Beard of Avon*, and Lynn Nottage's *Intimate Apparel*, all of which have had "legs"—a theatre term for an extended life elsewhere, particularly in New York.

**Minneapolis** The *Guthrie Theatre was founded by the celebrated English director Tyrone Guthrie in 1963 and, with a continuing series of distinguished artistic directors, has maintained the highest artistic and creative standards in staging world theatre classics from all periods in the heart of America's Midwest.

**Seattle** With seven professional companies, Seattle is the most exciting theatre city in the great Northwest. Its major stages include the *Seattle Repertory Theatre, which premiered the Broadway-bound productions of Wendy Wasserstein's *The Heidi Chronicles* and *The Sisters Rosensweig*, as well as Herb Gardner's *Conversations with My Father;* and the *Intiman (its name derived from August Strindberg's theatre in Stockholm), which initially premiered Robert Schenkkan's *The Kentucky Cycle* and more recently the musical *The Light in the Piazza*, which subsequently moved to Broadway. Meanwhile ACT—A Contemporary Theatre—enlivens the city scene with its longtime devotion (forty-plus years) to strictly new plays.

**Washington, D.C.** *Arena Stage, founded in 1950, is one of America's oldest and most distinguished theatres (it received the first-ever Tony regional award, in 1976). It owes its name to the shape of the original stage—the audience surrounds the actors. Now several times removed from its original location, and with its "theatre-in-the-round" format augmented by more conventional staging configurations elsewhere on its campus, the Arena operates on behalf of a deliberately aggressive mission: "to produce huge plays of all that is passionate, exuberant, profound, deep and

Most American Shakespeare festivals make a point of being, indeed, festive—none more so than the Utah Shakespearean Festival, which each year performs *The Greenshow* before each evening performance. Staged beside the USF's replica of a Shakespearean-era theatre, and performed by interns selected from applicants around the country, the show is free to all comers—those attending the play and those just showing up to see a family-friendly show that mixes Elizabethan singing and dancing with comic skits reflecting early English entertainment. This bouncy 2008 USF *Greenshow* was directed by Kirsten Sham.

dangerous in the American spirit." The company is also dedicated to an American repertoire that echoes the racial and ethnic mix of its diverse city, emphasizing its "long-standing commitment to encourage participation by people of color in every aspect of the theatre's life." But Arena Stage is only one of twenty-nine major theatres in the nation's capital, including the distinguished Shakespeare Theatre Company, which often presents celebrated actors (Patrick Stewart, Stacy Keach, Kelly McGillis) in classic dramas, and the Woolly Mammoth, devoted to new plays.

There are dozens of theatre towns in the United States, and hundreds of theatres. What was simply a "movement" during the 1960s and 1970s has now become, quite simply, America's national theatre. For the regional theatre is where the vast majority of America's best-known plays have first been shaped and exposed since the 1970s. More and more, the American national press is attuned to major theatre happenings in the nonprofit sector. More and more, the Broadway audiences, while admiring the latest "hit," are aware that they are seeing that hit's second, third, or fourth production. National theatre prizes such as the Pulitzer, once awarded only for Broadway productions, are now claimed by off-Broadway theatres (Lynn Nottage's *Ruined*) and by regional companies (Steppenwolf's *August: Osage County*). World-renowned actors such as Al Pacino, John Mahoney, Dianne Wiest, Mary Louise Parker, Maggie Gyllenhaal, Matthew Broderick, and Brian Dennehy, once

seen live only on Broadway stages and on tour, now also appear in many of the country's nonprofits. For the first time in America's history, the vast majority of Americans can see first-class professional theatre created in or near their hometowns, and professional theatre artists can live in any major city in the country—not only in New York.

## Shakespeare Festivals

In Broadway's mid-twentieth-century heyday there was also *summer stock,* a network of theatres, mainly located in resort areas throughout the mountains of the Northeast, that provided summer entertainment for tourists and assorted local folks. This "straw-hat circuit," as it was called, produced recent and not-so-recent Broadway shows, mainly comedies, with a mix of professional theatre artists from New York and young theatrical hopefuls from around the country; it was America's vacation theatre and professional training ground.

Summer stock is mostly gone today, but in its place has arisen another phenomenon that, like summer stock, is unique to the United States. This is the vast array of Shakespeare festivals, begun during the Great Depression and now flourishing in almost every state. The Oregon Shakespeare Festival, in rural Ashland, is the much-heralded (and Tony Award-winning) grandparent of this movement. Founded by local drama teacher Angus Bowmer, whose three-night amateur production of *The Merchant of Venice* in 1935 was preceded by an afternoon boxing match "to draw the crowds," the Oregon festival, which immediately discovered that Shakespeare outdrew the pugilists, now produces—under artistic director Bill Rauch, who assumed the post in 2007—no less than eleven plays each year, plus a free, outdoor "Greenshow," attracting 350,000 spectators during a ten-month season in a town of less than 20,000 people!

There are now more than two hundred other North American Shakespeare festivals, many of them largely or partially professional. Particularly notable are the New York Shakespeare Festival, the Stratford Festival in Canada, the Utah Shakespearean Festival (also Tony Award-winning) in Cedar City, and well-known festivals in Alabama, New Jersey, California, Colorado, Illinois, and Idaho—all drawing audiences from broad regions. Characteristic of these operations is a core of two to four Shakespearean productions, normally performed outdoors, together with more contemporary plays that are often performed on adjacent indoor stages. This arrangement curiously resembles that of Shakespeare's original company, the King's Men, which by the end of Shakespeare's career was performing plays of many authors at both the outdoor Globe and the indoor Blackfriars. In addition to providing exciting classical and modern theatre to audiences around North America, often in rural areas and at reasonable prices, Shakespeare festivals provide a wonderful bridge for aspiring performers and designers segueing from college training to professional employment. And more than the old summer stock, the festivals offer opportunities to work with an ambitious classical theatre repertory as well.

## Summer and Dinner Theatres

There remain some notable professional summer theatres without the word *Shakespeare* in their names. The Williamstown Theatre Festival in Massachusetts is probably the best of these, employing many of New York's better-known actors, designers, and directors, eager to leave the stifling city in July and August to spend a month or two in this beautiful Berkshire village, where they may play Chekhov (for which the theatre is justly famous), Brecht, O'Neill, Williams, and newer plays in elegantly mounted productions. The Berkshire Theatre Festival in Stockbridge, Massachusetts, is also a highly accomplished professional summer theatre, located in a culturally rich

area just two hours north of New York, where, in the afternoons, visitors can also drop in at Tanglewood to see the Boston Symphony Orchestra rehearsing in shirtsleeves.

Dinner theatres were introduced to suburban America in the 1970s, offering a "night-on-the-town" package of dinner and a play in the same facility. Their novelty has worn thin, however, and only a few of them remain, generally offering light comedies, mystery melodramas, and pared-down productions of golden-age Broadway musicals.

## Amateur Theatre: Academic and Community

There is an active amateur theatre in the United States, some of it operating in conjunction with educational programs. More than a thousand U.S. colleges and universities have drama (or theatre) departments offering degrees in these fields, and another thousand collegiate institutions put on plays, or give classes in drama, without having a full curriculum of studies. Several thousand high schools, summer camps, and private schools also teach drama and mount plays. Much of this dramatic activity is directed toward general education. The staging of plays has been pursued at least since the Renaissance as a way to explore dramatic literature, human behavior, and cultural history—as well as to teach skills such as public speaking, self-presentation, and foreign languages. Practical instruction in drama has the virtue of making the world's greatest literature physical and emotional; it gets drama not only into the mind but into the muscles—and into the heart and loins as well. Some of the world's great theatre has emerged from just such academic activity. Four or five "University Wits" dominated Elizabethan playwriting before Shakespeare arrived on the scene, and Shakespeare's company competed with publicly presented school plays that had become popular in London during his career (such plays "are now the fashion," says a character in *Hamlet*). Several plays that changed theatre history-such as Alfred Jarry's *Ubu Roi* and Tom Stoppard's *Rosencrantz and Guildenstern Are Dead*—were first conceived as extracurricular college projects.

The founding of the Yale Drama Department (now the Yale School of Drama) in 1923 signaled an expanded commitment on the part of American higher education to assume not merely the role of theatre educator and producer but also that of theatre

Persons who do not live in major American theatre cities may find fine drama close to home at a local university. Many academic drama and theatre departments have professional theatre artists on their faculties who guide and occasionally participate in campus productions, some also engage outside professional directors-some of high distinction—to stage productions with their students The University of California—Irvine (where this book's author teaches) engaged the renowned Romanian director Mihai Maniutiu to direct this 2009 campus production of Euripides' *The Bacchae*. Scenery was designed by faculty artist Luke Canterella, costumes and lighting were by graduate students Jessica Mueller and Zac Law, respectively, and graduate actor Ryan Imhoff (*standing*) played Dionysus.

trainer. Today, the majority of American professional theatre artists receive their training in American college and university departments devoted, in whole or in part, to that purpose. As a result, academic and professional theatres have grown closer together and many artists are working as both theatre professionals and theatre professors. For this reason, performances at many university theatres may reach sophisticated levels of excellence and, on occasion, equal or surpass professional productions of the same dramatic material.

Community theatres are amateur groups that put on plays for their own enjoyment and for the entertainment or edification of their community. There are occasions when these theatres, too, reach levels of excellence. Some community theatres are gifted with substantial funding, handsome facilities, and large subscription audiences, and some (such as the Laguna Playhouse in California) become professional. One should always remember that many of the greatest companies in the theatre's history, including Konstantin Stanislavsky's Moscow Art Theatre and André Antoine's Parisian Théâtre Libre, began, essentially, as amateur community theatres. One should also remember that the word *amateur* means "lover" and that the artist who creates theatre out of love rather than commercial expedience may in fact be headed for the highest, not the lowest, levels of art. Community theatre has, then, a noble calling: it is the theatre a community makes out of and for itself, and it can tell us a lot about who we are and what we want.

## Beyond North America

Few spectator experiences are as challenging and fascinating as seeing plays from a culture—and a country—other than your own. Theatre from other countries—and continents—presents a variety of styles, techniques, and ideas that will make your eyes pop and your mind explode. The global theatre transcends local ideologies; it can make antagonists into partners and turn strangers into friends. As theatre once served to unite the ten tribes of ancient Attica, so it may serve in the coming era to unite a world too often fractured by prejudice and divided by ignorance. Nothing could be more vital in today's world than sharing popular "entertainment"—and being reminded of the original meaning of *entertain:* "to bring together."

A trip to an international drama festival, in the United States or abroad, is a superb way to sample the theatres of several countries within a short period of time. But nothing can quite match a theatre tour abroad, where an adventurous theatergoer can see the theatrical creativity of another culture in its own setting and with its own, intended audience. Seeing kabuki in Tokyo, with the audience shouting *kakegoe* (cries of approval) at climactic moments, or attending an Igbo *mmonwu* (masquerade) under the African sun, with the audience sitting and standing around the performers, cheering them on and swaying to the beat of their drums, is an experience that cannot be equaled.

Admittedly, few Americans are able or willing to devote the time and resources to travel to Asia or Africa solely for theatergoing, and those who do will find the theatrical attractions on those continents far apart, and hard to get to, one from the other. A theatre trip to Europe, however, where dozens of distinct and dazzling theatrical cultures are never more than a brief train ride away, is a venture upon which more and more Americans embark.

Literally millions of Americans each year find their way to England for this very reason. Indeed, Americans often account for up to one-third of the theatre audiences in London, where productions, in addition to revered classics and extravagant musicals, may in any given year feature new and provocative works by such celebrated current English dramatists as Tom Stoppard, Mark Ravenhill, Alan Ayckbourn, Charlotte Jones, Martin McDonagh, Howard Brenton, David Hare, and Caryl Churchill. Highlighting London's mainstream theatre scene are the government-subsidized Royal National Theatre (colloquially known as "the NT"), which houses three stages in a modern complex

Current Latin American theatre is usually experimental and often intensely political. Here, in the 1998 Teatro Ubu (San José, Costa Rica) premiere of Argentinian-Quebecois Luis Thenon's *Los Conquistadores,* Maria Bonilla (director-actor at Costa Rica's National Theatre) kneels in anguish at the plight of her son, whom she discovers listed among citizens who mysteriously "disappeared" but were generally known to have been tortured and killed by official goon squads.

Caryl Churchill has been one of England's most prominent avant-garde playwrights for more than three decades; her *Three More Sleepness Nights* (1980), which presents the convoluted conversations of two different couples, one young and the other not, was revived with great success in 2009 by England's Royal National Theatre. Paul Ready plays Pete and Hattie Morahan is Dawn in the production directed by Gareth Machin.

The Royal National Theatre complex, on the south bank of the Thames River in London and only a five-minute walk from that city's great museums and attractions, is arguably the English-speaking world's best site to see and experience outstanding dramatic productions. With its three separate theatres (the Olivier, the Lyttleton, and the Cottlesoe), and its extensive company of fine actors, directors, and designers, the NT, as it is generally known, produces a broad spectrum of exquisitely staged classics, modern revivals, and audacious new plays each season— often at very affordable prices for students. The multistory complex, now a treasured institution, also offers free admission to its public areas, exhibitions, bars, and restaurants during the day and presents free music concerts prior to most performances.

"Panto" is a traditional English Christmastime entertainment for both adults and children. (The word is short for "pantomime" but bears little relation to the American art of that name.) Here the distinguished classical actor Ian McKellen (*right*) plays Widow Twankey (cross-gender casting is essential to panto), and Roger Allam plays Abbanazar in a 2004-05 version staged at London's Old Vic. "Panto has everything theatrical—song, dance, verse, slapstick, soliloquy, audience participation, spectacle, cross-dressing and a good plot, strong on morality and romance—what more could you want from a family outing?" says McKellen. The outrageous canto costuming is by Mark Bouman.

Tourist literature portrays the island of Ireland as a peaceful and beautiful land, but unfortunately it has suffered fiercely contentious rule for most of its political history. Martin McDonagh, English-born but of Irish parents, writes about the island's notorious "troubles," as they are famously called there, and his 2002 *The Lieutenant of Inishmore,* a dark (and many say tasteless) comedy of violence, torture, and killings (of both humans and animals), both shocked and fascinated London audiences. Paul Lloyd (*hanging upside down*) and Peter McDonald are shown here in one of the play's grimmer scenes.

The Druid Theatre of Dublin has specialized in staging the classic works of Irish dramatist John Millington Synge, whom Garry Hynes, the Druid's artistic director, jocularly calls the company's "house playwright." *Playboy of the Western World,* which caused riots at its 1907 premiere, is Synge's masterpiece: a profoundly realistic portrayal of the language, customs, morality, and sense of humor of rural Ireland—specifically the Aran Islands, where Synge spent many summers and generally set his plays. Hynes first staged the play in 1975. This scene is from her 2008 reprise of that production as seen in Los Angeles. Scenery was by Francis O'Connor, and costumes were by Kathy Strachan.

on the south bank of the Thames; the nearby Globe Theater—a replica of Shakespeare's original outdoor playhouse that highlights Shakespearean-era drama during the summer months; and the West End theatre district on and around Shaftesbury Avenue and Covent Garden, which is comparable to New York's Broadway in its mix of musicals, new dramas, and classical revivals, sometimes playing long commercial runs after their initial premieres at the National. There is also a London "fringe" of smaller theatres, roughly comparable to off-Broadway, which is often where the most exciting action is, particularly at the always-adventurous Almeida, Cheek by Jowl, Complicite, Donmar Warehouse, and Royal Court theatres. And in Shakespeare's natal town of Stratford-upon-Avon, little more than an hour's train ride away, you can see productions by the Royal Shakespeare

Company, which produces their namesake's work (and much else) in three theatres in that town, as well as seasonally in London and on tours throughout the United Kingdom. Theatre ticket prices in England are less than in the United States, and an official half-price TKTS Booth, comparable to the one in New York, may be found in London's Leicester Square.

World travelers can explore other English-speaking dramatic centers as well. Ireland has provided a vast repertoire to the stage since the seventeenth century. Indeed, most of the great "English" dramatists of the eighteenth and nineteenth centuries—George Farquhar, Oliver Goldsmith, Richard Sheridan, Oscar Wilde, and George Bernard Shaw—were actually Irish by birth. In the twentieth century, a genuinely Irish drama became immensely popular in the hands of William Butler Yeats, Sean O'Casey, and Brendan

South African playwright Athol Fugard cowrote *The Island* with actors John Kani and Winston Ntshona, who played the two roles—of convicts at hard labor in South Africa's brutal Robben Island prison—in the play's 1973 Cape Town premiere and in London and Broadway showings the following year, which attracted international attention to the play and, in New York, earned Tony Awards for the two actors. Here Kani and Ntshona repeat their roles in a 2003 revival at the Brooklyn Academy of Music.

Behan. But possibly no period of Irish drama is as rich as the current one, which includes major established playwrights such as Brian Friel (*Philadelphia, Here I Come; Translations; Dancing at Lughnasa*) and newer ones such as Sebastian Barry (*The Steward of Christendom, Whistling Psyche*), Conor McPherson (*The Weir, The Seafarer*), and English-Irish Martin McDonagh (*The Beauty Queen of Leenane, The Cripple of Inishmaan, The Pillowman, A Behanding in Spokane*). Most of these plays make their way to the United States, but seeing them in their natural surroundings, as at the Abbey or Gate Theatres of Dublin and the Druid Theatre of Galway, is a special treat.

In Canada, theatre flourishes in every province. The city of Toronto boasts two hundred professional theatre companies and the status, after London and New York, of the largest professional theatre metropolis in the English-speaking world. With its celebrated dramatists David French (writing in English) and Michel Tremblay (in French), plus the internationally prominent playwright/director Robert Lepage, two major summer festivals in Ontario—one for Shakespeare in Stratford, the other for George Bernard Shaw in Niagara-on-the-Lake—and a strong network of repertory companies and avant-garde groups throughout the country, Canada today enjoys a virtual flood of new Canadian playwrights, directors, and theatre critics who are developing global reputations.

Australia also has a fine theatrical tradition and a lively contemporary scene. Veteran playwrights David Williamson (his *Scarlett O'Hara at the Crimson Parrot* opened in Melbourne in 2008) and Louis Nowra (*The Emperor of Sydney* in 2007) have long flooded that country's stages with provocative plays. They are now supplemented by a host of younger writers who flourish in both standard repertory and offbeat, alternative theatres in Melbourne, Sydney, and Brisbane—as well as at Australia's biennial Adelaide Arts Festival.

And South Africa has given the world one of its most prominent living playwrights, Athol Fugard, whose *Sizwe Banzi Is Dead, The Island, Master Harold ... and the Boys, A Lesson from Aloes, Valley Song, My Children! My Africa!*, and *Playland*, mostly premiered at the Market Theatre of Johannesburg. Both Fugard and the Market Theatre have won their reputations not only for the outstanding quality of their work but for their courageous and effective confrontation of that country's now-concluded policy of apartheid. In the postapartheid era, Fugard has written new plays, often autobiographical, dealing with his continuing struggles to reconcile contemporary Africa with both its roots and its future; these include the notable *Valley Song* (1996) and its sequel, *Coming Home* (2009).

For travelers willing to manage a foreign language, France and Germany—the countries that spawned the theatre of the absurd and the theatre of alienation, respectively—are immensely rewarding theatre destinations. Each country provides an outstanding mix of traditional and original theatre. French and German theatre, like that of most European countries, enjoys strong government support, which keeps ticket prices at a fraction of what they are in the United States and England.

France has five fully supported national theatres. Four of them are in Paris—including the historic Comédie-Française, founded in 1680 out of the remains of Molière's company shortly after his death; the historic Odéon, now a "Theatre of Europe," presenting home-based plays as well as productions from around the continent; and the Théâtre du Chaillot, which focuses on new plays and dance pieces and whose Web site includes outstanding video clips of current productions.

In Germany, where major dramatic activity is spread more broadly throughout the country (there is no recognized German cultural "capital" remotely comparable to London or Paris), federal and city governments support more than 150 theatres, and about sixty theatre festivals, in just about every large city on the map. The modern German theatre, often called "post-Brechtian" because the brash, experimental style of most productions takes off from the influence of Bertolt Brecht (his Berliner Ensemble remains one of the leading theatres in that country today), is considered revolutionary in its breaking of theatrical stage conventions. German directors Peter Stein, Matthais Langhoff, Claus Peymann, and Frank Castorf have pioneered in theatrical innovations that have influenced theatres around the world. In addition to the Berliner Ensemble, currently headed by Peymann, Berlin boasts Castorf's super-radical Volksbühne and each May mounts an annual *Theatertreffen* (Theatre Meeting), bringing what a jury of critics selects as the ten best German-language theatre productions (out of the four hundred they evaluate) from Germany, Austria, and Switzerland. Theatertreffen productions are chosen almost entirely for their innovative direction and design, and for their contribution to the future of theatre in the German-speaking world. Attending such events puts the audience in contact with the most adventurous theatre in western Europe.

Other western European countries—particularly Spain, Italy, Sweden, Denmark, Finland, Switzerland, Belgium, and the Netherlands—also have extremely active theatre communities and their own legendary actors and directors. And they too are wonderful places to engage in the theatre of the present and see a glimpse of the theatre of the future. The most exciting theatre in Europe today, however, according to many observers (including your author), is in Eastern Europe.

Because the theatres of eastern European countries faced strict government censorship during the postwar Soviet era (from 1945 until the early 1990s), their playwrights were relatively muffled in comparison to western European counterparts, and it was directors who took the lead in creating both the "new theatre" that all audiences crave and the "dangerous theatre" discussed earlier in this chapter that expresses subversive political ideas in artistically flamboyant styles. And they did this by mounting radical reconstructions of classical plays—for what Communist party official would dare complain about a director who wanted to stage a two-thousand-year-old Greek tragedy, even one that treated the overthrow of a despotic government? Thus, eastern European theatre (including the theatre of what was then East Germany and some of the German directors discussed above who began there), became a "director's theatre." The art of directing—and the acting and design that emanated from it-created a theatre of ancient plays produced "in code," with their hidden contemporary meanings—often subversive-clear to intelligent audiences but opaque to Soviet censors. Indeed, the eastern European theatre played a major role in the sweeping away of Communist rule in the Soviet bloc, particularly in Czechoslovakia, where in 1989 the "Velvet Revolution" led by Václav Havel, a prominent dissident Czech playwright, brought about the overthrow of the Communist government and the election of Havel as president of Czechoslovakia.

Within eastern Europe, the country of Romania deserves special recognition, because, with a population smaller than that of Texas, it has produced an extraordinary collection of world-famous directors. Andre Serban, Mihai Maniutiu, Gábor Tompa, Silviu Purcarete, and Liviu Ciulei have international reputations for innovative brilliance and creativity. "In the

Much of eastern European theatre, even in these early decades of the twenty-first century, remains focused on World War II and its aftermath. This Russian production of *Life and Fate,* adapted from a long-suppressed novel of that name by Vasily Grossman and directed at St. Petersburg's Maly Theatre by the company's artistic director, Lev Dodin, concerns oppression in European countries that suffered under equally brutal Nazi and Soviet regimes between the 1930s and 1980s. In this scene, prisoners in a Nazi concentration camp have been ordered to form a marching band and perform naked while standing outdoors in a snowfall. Behind them is a steel "fence," which in happier scenes represents a volleyball net. The four-hour production was rewarded by a rousing, tearful, fifteen-minute standing ovation following its closing performance at a 2009 Lincoln Center Theatre Festival engagement in New York.

field of directing, it is not Romania but America that needs to catch up," said Senior Editor Randy Gener in a 2007 cover story on Romanian theatre for *American Theatre,* the country's most distinguished publication in that field.

Each of those Romanian directors seeks not only to produce plays but to reinvent the theatre itself: the way it works, the way it thinks, the way it projects ideas and images to its audiences. Each has worked frequently in Europe, Asia, and the United States. Ciulei headed the Guthrie Theatre in Minneapolis for many years. Serban directs regularly at the American Repertory Theatre in Cambridge, Massachusetts,

and teaches at Columbia University in New York. Purcarete's *Les Danaïdes* (with a cast of more than one hundred) was the sensation of New York's 1997 Lincoln Center Theatre Festival. Tompa and Maniutiu (respectively) head the Hungarian-language and Romanian-language national theatres of Cluj—in Transylvania, where both of those languages are spoken—and have taught and directed at University of California campuses at (respectively) San Diego and Irvine. Except for the retired Ciulei, they all continue to direct in their home country, and they now face competition from many younger Romanian disciples who are building on their discoveries.

Romanian theatre is intellectually bold, stylistically innovative, physically demanding of its performers, and emotionally demanding of its audiences. There is no doubt that Randy Gener's estimate of Romania's importance to the theatre's future is accurate; the entire Spring 2009 issue of Yale University's *Theater* journal was also devoted to Romanian theatre today.

And for those readers—the vast majority, of course—who aren't making foreign theatre tours this year, the Internet provides a wonderful way to catch a glimpse of and a feeling for the works described in these pages. A quick Web search—beginning with the theatre companies or the directors named—quickly leads to photos and in many cases videos of their latest work, plus archival photos of many of the productions mentioned.

## CONCLUSIONS ABOUT THEATRE TODAY?

Can we draw any conclusions about theatre today? No, we cannot, because what is current is never concluded. The current theatre is in process; it is *current*, a river that is continually running, continually replenished with fresh rainwater and snowmelt. What is hot today may be cold tomorrow. But the theatre of today is our theatre and it is your theatre: there to apprehend, to enjoy, to appreciate, and to respond to. It is not just a series of plays, or a spectrum of performances, but a communication between individuals and peoples that raises levels of human discourse and artistic appreciation. It responds to individual impulses of creativity and collective demands for human contact and understanding. It synthesizes the impulses of artists and audiences, and it fosters a focused interaction that incorporates our human experience, aspirations, and values. Like a river, theatre began long before the advent of recorded history and "keeps on rolling."

And it is always new. As Heraclitus said twenty-five hundred years ago, "We cannot step twice in the same river; for when I step in the river for a second time, neither I nor the river are the same."

# The Critic and the Dramaturg

I T IS 10:30 P.M. The lights fade a final time, the curtain falls, the audience applauds, and the play is over. The actors go back to their dressing rooms, take off their makeup, and depart. The audience disperses into the night. But the theatrical experience is not over; in important ways, it is just beginning.

A play does not begin and end its life on a stage. A play begins in the mind of its creator, and its final repository is the minds and memories of its audiences. The stage is simply a focal point where communication in the form of theatrical performance takes place. After the performance is over, the play's impact remains. It is something to think about, talk about, fantasize about, and live with for hours, days, and years to come. Some plays we remember all our lives: plays whose characters are as indelible in our memories as the ' people in our personal lives, plays whose settings are more deeply experienced than were many of our childhood locales, and plays whose themes abide as major object lessons behind our decision making. Should we take up arms against a sea of troubles? Can we depend on the kindness of strangers? What's in a name? Shall we be as defiant as Prometheus? as determined as

Oedipus? as passionate as Romeo? as accepting as Winnie? as noble as Hecuba? What is Hecuba to us, or we to Hecuba? We talk about these matters with our friends.

We also talk about the production—about the acting, the costumes, the scenery, the sound effects. Were we convinced? impressed? moved? transported? changed? Did the production hold our attention throughout? Did our involvement with the action increase during the play, or did we feel a letdown after the intermission? Did we accept the actors as the characters they were playing, or were we uncomfortably aware that they were simply "acting" their parts rather than embodying their roles?

The printed text of a play is another focal point where communication takes place. That play the teacher or director asked you to read yesterday: Did it "get to" you? Could you follow the story? Were you interested in the characters? Did it move you emotionally or stimulate you intellectually? Did it make you want to take action politically? Why? Why not? Could you visualize its actions, its settings, its impact on a theatre audience? Could you imagine casting it with actors you have seen on stage or screen? Were there aspects of the play that you thought could be changed for the better?

When you address any of those sorts of questions about a performance or a play text, you are engaging in *dramatic analysis*. Some people do this for a living. A person who does so publicly, explaining to readers or listeners his or her reactions to a play or a play performance, is a creator of *dramatic criticism* and is called a *drama critic* or a *play reviewer*. A person who engages in dramatic analysis from within the theatre itself, as a coparticipant in what might eventually become a production, is called a *dramaturg*, and his or her analysis is known as *dramaturgy*.

Dramatic analysis can take numerous forms: production reviews in newspapers, blogs, or periodicals or on television; feature newspaper or magazine articles about individual theatre artists or companies; scholarly books about dramatic literature, history, or theory. More commonly, dramaturgy results in close collaboration with individual playwrights seeking to improve the theatrical potential of their plays, and in background notes in theatre programs and advertising. Dramatic analysis is the informed, articulate, and communicative response of the critic or reviewer to what he or she has seen in the theatre, or of the dramaturg to what he or she has read in the plays submitted to a theatre company or producer for possible production.

# CRITICAL AND DRAMATURGICAL PERSPECTIVES

What makes a play particularly successful? What gives a theatrical production significance and impact, and what makes it unforgettable? What should we be looking for when we read a play or see a dramatic production?

We have, of course, complete freedom in making up our minds, for the price of theatrical admission carries with it the privilege of thinking what we wish and responding as we will. But five perspectives can be particularly useful in helping us focus our response to any individual theatrical event: the play's social significance, its human or personal significance, its artistic quality, its theatrical expression, and its capacity to entertain.

## Social Significance

Theatre, as we have seen throughout this book, is always tied to its culture. Many theatres have been directly created or sustained by governments and ruling elites: the Greek theatre of the fifth century B.C. was a creation of the state; the medieval theatre was generated by the church, the township, and the municipal craft guilds; and the Royal theatre was a direct extension of a monarchy. Even in modern times, government often serves as sponsor or cosponsor or silent benefactor of the theatre. But the intellectual ties between a theatre and its culture extend well beyond merely political concerns: thematically, the theatre has at one time or another served as an arena for the discussion of every social issue imaginable. In modern times, the theatre has approached from different perspectives such issues as alcoholism, homosexuality, venereal disease, prostitution, public education, racial prejudice, capital punishment, thought control, prison reform, character assassination, civil equality, political corruption, and military excess. The best of these productions have presented the issues in all of their complexity and have proffered solutions not as dogma but as food for thought—for great theatre has never sought to purvey pure propaganda.

The playwright is not necessarily brighter than the audience or even better informed. The playwright and his or her collaborators, however, may be able to focus public debate, stimulate dialogue, and turn public attention and compassion toward social injustices,

Directors often work very closely with dramaturgs, as when Romanian director Gábor Tompa collaborated with dramaturg Visky András in adapting Nobel Prize—winner Imre Kertész's introspective Hungarian novel about a Holocaust survivor, *Kaddish for an Unborn Child,* into a production that won critics' awards in Romania in 2008 and at France's Avignon Theatre Festival in 2009 Titled *Long Friday* (Naître à jamais in French), the play is a meditation on the survivor's refusal to have children since, as he says repeatedly, "Children were born at Auschwitz." Tompa's performers tackled the deeply provocative work with astounding athleticism, continually crashing to the floor and bouncing back again amid the singing of baleful dirges in Hebrew, Hungarian, Romanian, Greek, Italian, French, English, Spanish, and German The design was by Carmencita Brojboiu.

inconsistencies, and irregularities. The theatre artist traditionally is something of a nonconformist; the artist's point of view is generally to the left or right of the social mainstream, and her or his perspective is of necessity somewhat unusual. Therefore, the theatre is in a strong position to force and focus public confrontation with social issues, and at its best it succeeds in bringing members of the audience into touch with their own thoughts and feelings about those issues.

## Human Significance

The theatre is a highly personal art, in part because it stems from the unique (and often oblique) perspectives of the playwrights who initiate it and the theatre artists who execute it and in part because its audiences all through history have decreed that it be so. The greatest plays transcend the social and political to confront the hopes, concerns, and conflicts faced by all humankind: personal identity, courage, compassion, fantasy versus practicality, kindness versus self-interest, love versus exploitation, and the inescapable problems of growing up and growing old, of wasting and dying. These are some of the basic themes of the finest plays and of our own stray thoughts as well; the best plays simply link up with our deepest musings and help us put our random ideas into some sort of order or philosophy. The theatre is a medium in which we invariably see reflections of ourselves, and in the theatre's best achievements those reflections lead to certain discoveries and evaluations concerning our own individual personalities and perplexities.

## Artistic Quality

The theatre is an art of such distinctive form that even with the briefest exposure we can begin to develop certain aesthetic notions as to what that form should be. We quickly come to know—or think we

Political street theatre is an open interaction between actor-activists and audiences in which the elements of theatre—acting, costumes, playwriting, and directing—are all subservient to the goal of reforming society and the theatre artists are fully engaged in this goal. Here members of a Filipino troupe—with one actor masked as President Gloria Arroyo—protest what they consider government abuses of human rights in a political street drama in Manila.

know—honesty onstage, for without being experts we feel we can recognize false notes in acting, in playwriting, and even in design.

Beyond that, we can ask a number of questions of ourselves. Does the play excite our emotions? Does it stimulate the intellect? Does it surprise us? Does it thrill us? Does it seem complete and all of a piece? Are the characters credible? Are the actors convincing? enchanting? electrifying? Does the play seem alive or dead? Does it seem in any way original? Is it logically sound? Is the action purposeful, or is it gratuitous? Are we transported, or are we simply waiting for the final curtain? In the last analysis, does the play fit our idea of what a play should be—or, even better, does it force us, by its sheer luster and power, to rewrite our standards of theatre?

Aesthetic judgments of this sort are necessarily comparative, and they are subjective as well. What seems original to one member of the audience may be old hat to another; what seems an obvious gimmick to a veteran theatergoer can seem brilliantly innovative to a less jaded patron. None of this should intimidate us. An audience does not bring absolute standards into the theatre—and certainly such standards as it brings are not shared absolutely. The theatrical response is a composite of many individual reactions. But each of us has an aesthetic sensibility and an aesthetic response. We appreciate colors, sights, sounds, words, actions, behaviors, and people that please us. We appreciate constructions that seem to us balanced, harmonic, expressive, and assured. We appreciate designs, ideas, and performances that exceed our expectations, that reveal patterns and viewpoints we didn't know existed. We take great pleasure in sensing underlying structure: a symphony of ideas, a sturdy architecture of integrated style and action.

## Relationship to the Theatre Itself

As we've already discussed, plays are not simply things that happen in the theatre; they are theatre—which is to say that each play or play production redefines

In early 2009, American theatre fans were dismayed to hear that Gerard Alessandrini's *Forbidden Broadway,* which since 1982 had been spoofing Broadway shows in New York, was going to close forever—but were relieved not long afterward when it reopened in London and later began a tour throughout the United States. Shown here at the London reopening in 2009 is Anna-Jane Casey in a parody of the hit musical *Wicked.* A classic piece of metatheatre, *Forbidden Broadway* makes clear that the theatre is able to poke fun at itself—which it has done for many, many years, in plays by Aristophanes (*The Frogs*), Molière (*The Versailles Rehearsals*), Shakespeare (*A Midsummer Night's Dream*), and Chekhov (*The Seagull*), among numerous others.

the theatre itself and makes us reconsider, at least to a certain extent, the value and possibilities of the theatre itself. In some cases the playwright makes this reconsideration mandatory, by dealing with theatrical matters in the play itself. Some plays are set in theatres where plays are going on (Luigi Pirandello's *Six Characters in Search of an Author,* Michael Frayn's *Noises Off,* Mel Brooks's *The Producers*); other plays are about actors Qean-Paul Sartre's *Kean*) or about dramatic characters (Tom Stoppard's *Rosencrantz and Guildenstern Are Dead*); still other plays contain plays within themselves (Anton Chekhov's *The Seagull,* William Shakespeare's *Hamlet*) or the rehearsals of such plays (Shakespeare's *A Midsummer Night's Dream,* Molière's *The Versailles Rehearsal,* Jean Anouilh's The Rehearsal).

We use the term *metatheatre,* or *metadrama,* to describe those plays that specifically refer back to themselves in this manner, but in fact all plays and play productions can be analyzed and evaluated on the way they use the theatrical format to best advantage and the way they make us rethink the nature of theatrical production, for all plays stand within the spectrum of a history of theatre and a history of theatrical convention (see the chapter titled "What Is a Play?"). All plays and productions can be studied, often with illuminating results, from the perspective of how they adopt or reject prevailing theatrical conventions, how they fit into or deviate from prevailing dramatic genres, and how they echo various elements of past plays or productions—and what theatrical effects, good and bad, such historical resonances may have.

## Entertainment Value

Finally, we look upon all theatre as entertainment. Great theatre is never less than pleasing. Even tragedy delights. People go to see *Hamlet* not for the purpose of self-flagellation or to wallow in despair but, rather, to revel in the tragic form and to experience the liberating catharsis of the play's murderous finale. Hamlet himself knows the thrill of staged tragedy:

HAMLET: What players are they?

ROSENCRANTZ: Even those you were wont to take such

delight in, the tragedians ...

What is this entertainment value that all plays possess? Most obviously the word *entertainment* suggests "amusement," and so we think immediately of the hilarity of comedy and farce; indeed, most of the literature regarding theatrical entertainment concentrates on the pratfalls and gags that have been part of the comic theatre throughout its history. But entertainment goes far beyond humor. Another definition for *entertainment* is "that which holds the attention" (from the French *entre* [between] and *tenir* [to hold], thus "to hold together" or "to bring together"). This definition casts more light on our question. It means that entertainment includes the enchantment of romance; the dazzle of brilliant debate, witty epigram, and biting repartee; the exotic appeal of the foreign and the grotesque; the beauty and grandeur of spectacle; and the nuance and crescendo of a musical or rhythmic line. It accommodates suspense and adventure, the magic of sex appeal, and the splendor of sheer talent. Finally, of course, it includes any form of drama that profoundly stirs our feelings and heightens our awareness of the human condition. It is no wonder that Hamlet delights in the performance of tragedians—and that we delight in *Hamlet*—for the mixture of ideas, language, poetry, feelings, and

Pierre Corneille's remarkable *L'Illusion Comique* (*The Comic Illusion*), first staged in 1636, is often considered the first truly metatheatrical play as its actors play characters who are also acting in the play that their "characters" are watching. This 2009 production by Bulgarian director Galin Stoev at the Comédie-Française in Paris emphasizes Corneille's baroque conflation of illusion and reality by employing a series of windows that at times are transparent and at times are smeared to the point of obscurity. Scenery and costumes were designed by Saskia Louwaard and Katrijn Baeten; lighting was by Bruno Marsol.

actions that constitute great tragedy confers one of life's sublime entertainment experiences.

Indeed, the theatre is a storehouse of pleasures, not only for the emotional, intellectual, spiritual, and aesthetic stimulation it provides but also for its intrinsic social excitement. Theatre is a favored public meeting place for people who care about each other. "Two on the aisle" implies more than a choice seating location; it implies companionship in the best theatrical experience, for the theatre is a place to commune in an especially satisfying way with strangers. When in the course of a dramatic performance we are gripped by a staging of romantic passion or stunned by a brilliantly articulated argument or moved by a touching denouement, the thrill is enhanced a hundredfold by the certainty that we are not alone in these feelings, that possibly every member of the audience has been stirred to the same response. Theatre, in its essence, serves to rescue humankind from an intellectual

and emotional aloneness, and therein lies its most profound "entertainment" value.

## CRITICAL AND DRAMATURGICAL FOCUS

Those five perspectives on the theatre experience-on its social, personal, artistic, theatrical, and entertainment values—are all implicit in the responses of any audience, regardless of its training or theatrical sophistication. Those are the five angles from which we view and judge plays—and judge them we do, for our involvement with a play naturally generates a series of comparisons: the play vis-à-vis other plays, the play vis-à-vis our personal experiences, the play vis-à-vis other things we might have done that evening. Judging plays and performances, which has been done formally since ancient Greek times and continues today

Of course a great deal of theatre is created mainly, if not solely, to provide sheer audience entertainment Although it deals with appalling subject matter, Mel Brooks's farcically satirical *The Producers* was designed purely for pleasure—as if to allow its audience to shake off, once and for all, the horrors of Adolf Hitler's regime Matthew Broderick is here shown surrounded by a bevy of beautiful chorus girls

through the well-publicized Tony and Obie awards, Pulitzer Prizes, and Critics Circle citations, is one of the fundamental aspects of theatrical participation—and it is participation open to amateur and professional alike.

## Professional Criticism

Professional criticism takes the basic form of production reviews and scholarly books and articles written, for the most part, by persons who specialize in this activity, often for an entire career.

Newspaper reviews of play productions remain common throughout the theatre world; indeed, the box-office success of most theatres depends on favorable press coverage. In the commercial Broadway theatre, favorable newspaper reviews—particularly from the extremely influential *New York Times*—are almost essential to guarantee a successful run, and sternly unfavorable reviews may mean a closing within a week or two. Although newspaper theatre coverage has diminished somewhat (indeed, newspapers themselves have been diminishing in the twenty-first century), any decline in press reviews has been more than made up for by an explosion of theatre Web sites and blog reviews. If you type "`Henry V review 2009" into an online search engine, you will come up with hundreds of reviews—from both newspapers and theatre blogs—for productions of *Henry V* around the world in that year. If you add the name of a city or theatre where such a production was staged, you will find the full complement of critical response the work has so far engendered.

In New York (and most theatre capitals around the world), newspaper reviews generally appear the morning after the opening performance, which usually takes place in late afternoon rather than evening to meet the paper's press deadline. Customarily, after that performance, actors and producers and their fans gather at Sardi's restaurant in Broadway's Theatre District, where they pretend to eat dinner while awaiting the first TV reviews, generally appearing on the eleven o'clock news program, and advance copies of the following morning's *Times,* published just blocks away. This is "instant criticism," and the television reporters or journalists who tackle such assignments must be very fluid at articulating their impressions immediately. Outside New York, newspaper critics and blogsters usually take from two days to a week to review a production, allowing themselves the luxury of considered opinions and more polished essays.

Still, the journalist's or blogger's review must be limited to a brief, unstudied reaction rather than being a detailed or exhaustive study. It provides a firsthand, audience-oriented response to the production, often vigorously and wittily expressed, and may serve as a useful consumer guide for the local theater-going public. Writing skill rather than dramatic expertise is often the newspaper critic's principal job qualification, and at many smaller papers, staff reporters with little dramatic background are assigned to the theatre desk. But many fine newspaper critics throughout the years—New York's Ben Brantley and Los Angeles's Charles McNulty, for example—have proven extremely subtle and skillful at transcending the limitations of their particular profession and have written highly intelligent dramatic criticism that remains pertinent long after its consumer-oriented function has run its course.

More scholarly critics, writing without the deadlines or strict space restrictions of journalists, are able to analyze plays and productions within detailed, comprehensive, and rigorously researched critical contexts. They are therefore able to understand and evaluate, in a more complex way, the achievements of playwrights and theatre artists within any or all of the five perspectives we have discussed. Scholarly critics (and by *scholarly* we mean only "one who studies") seek to uncover hidden aspects of a play's structure, to analyze its deep relationships to social or philosophical issues, to probe its various meanings and dramatic possibilities, to define its place in cultural history, to amplify its resonance of earlier works of art, to shape its future theatrical presentations, and to theorize about larger issues of dramaturgy, art, and human understanding. Such criticism is itself a literary art, and the great examples of dramatic criticism have

included brilliantly styled essays that have outlasted the theatrical works that were their presumed subjects: Aristotle, Goethe, Shaw, and Nietzsche are among the drama critics who, simply through their analyses of drama, have helped shape our vision of life itself.

The scholarly critic, ordinarily distinguished by her or his broad intellectual background and exhaustive research, writes with a comprehensive knowledge of the specific subject—a knowledge that includes the work of all important previous scholars who have studied the same materials. The professional scholar is not content to repeat the opinions or discoveries of others but seeks to make fresh insights from the body of literature (play texts and productions, production records, previous scholarship) that constitutes the field of study.

Scholarly critics tend to work within accepted methodologies, which develop and change rapidly in contemporary academic life. Traditional methodologies include historical and biographical approaches ("the man and his work"), thematic and rhetorical analyses, studies of character and plot, examinations of staging and theatrical styles, and detailed exegeses of meaning, or *explication du texte.* More contemporary methodologies include systems and theories developed since the 1970s, particularly structuralist, semiotic, and deconstructive approaches; these bypass traditional questions of history, biography, character, theme, and meaning and focus instead on the internal relationships of various dramatic ingredients and their particular combination in a self-referential dramaturgic system. Contemporary methodologies, which draw heavily from the fields of philosophy, linguistics, anthropology, and critical theory, are intellectually demanding and difficult to master; they provide, however, stunning insights to those properly initiated.

## Professional Dramaturgy

The dramaturg (sometimes spelled "dramaturge") is now a fixture in many professional theatres, particularly those that have large repertoires, regularly produce new plays, or stage plays from past eras for which historical or production research may prove useful. The duties of a dramaturg can be quite varied, depending on the needs of the theatre company, its individual directors, and the dramaturg's particular strengths and interests.

The dramaturg first took a prominent place in the theatre during the German Enlightenment, in the person of the poet, playwright, philosopher, librarian, and scholar Gotthold Lessing (1729-1781). Several of his own plays became German classics—particularly *Nathan the Wise* and *Emilia Galotti*—but Lessing's major contribution to world theatre was his appointment as in-house critic for the German National Theatre in Hamburg in 1767; indeed, that date is considered the dramaturg's Year Number One. In that role, Lessing promoted Aristotle's theories and Shakespeare's repertoire to the German stage and in 1769 published his Hamburg Dramaturgy (*Hamburgische Dramaturgie*), in which he reviewed more than fifty theatre productions and compiled 104 short essays on what he considered essential theatre principles. From that time forward, the dramaturg became a well-established position in Europe, as both in-house critic and literary adviser. A century later, Vladimir Nemirovich-Dantchenko played that role for Artistic Director Konstantin Stanislavsky when they jointly founded the Moscow Art Theatre. In the United States, the dramaturg position did not gain wide currency—certainly not by that name—until the 1960s and after.

Dramaturgs occasionally freelance but usually work for theatre companies on annual contracts. They research background information on plays the company produces (their historical sources, production history, and both common and new critical approaches). They advise company directors on possible script adaptations of plays currently in preparation or under consideration (available translations, differing published versions and the advantages of each, potential editorial cuts or additions). They work with playwrights whose scripts have been selected for development. In doing so, they may suggest structural revisions, ask for clarification of plot points (which may lead to content revisions), and help playwrights bring their visions into line with what the theatre company hopes the production can achieve for its intended audience. When a theatre company solicits new plays—most American companies do this—the dramaturg often plays the largest role in reading what comes in (sometimes delegating the first reading to an assistant) and evaluating each manuscript's potential for the company. Sometimes a dramaturg is called upon to help assemble a script, as by providing a translation or adapting a novel (such as Dickens's ever-popular *A Christmas Carol*) into dramatic form.

In addition, the dramaturg often serves as a director's assistant in researching a play's period and its social contexts, the precise meanings of any historical references, words in foreign, archaic, or regional languages, the music and art of the play's era, and, if there is no speech coach, the dialects of the play's region. A producer may tap the dramaturg to provide program essays about the play, its background, and perhaps the playwright's background, to give the audience a context in which to better enjoy the play—particularly one that has significant historical, political, philosophical, or literary interest.

Finally, a dramaturg—when the theatre director wishes—may serve the company as Lessing did the Hamburg National Theatre, as an in-house critic: attending rehearsals, asking questions, making suggestions, and providing (when asked) his or her opinion about which of a play's points are coming across powerfully, which ones are puzzling or flat, and where the production is not maximizing the potential of its script. Obviously, tact is a requirement for this role, but the more important need is for a clear understanding of dramatic structure and what will motivate the anticipated audience to think, feel, laugh, and exult—and then buy tickets to the next production.

## Student Criticism and Dramaturgy

Serving as a dramaturg or writing dramatic criticism for a school paper is a wonderful way for college and even high school students to affect—and become a part of—the theatre. Writing a play review, in fact, is a common class assignment, and a relatively easy way to "get published," particularly on a blog site. Choosing one or more (but not all!) of the five perspectives cited earlier in this chapter can provide a good starting point for writing an analysis of a production. Some simple but effective methodologies for writing both class essays and production reviews for local or school newspapers are provided in the Online Learning Center for *Theatre* at www.mhhe.com/cohen9e and in *Enjoy the Play!*, accompanying this text.

# WE ARE THE CRITICS

Whether we are professional writers, students, or just plain theatergoers, we are all critics of the theatre. As audience members, we are a party to the theatrical experience, not passive receptacles for its contrived effects. The theatre is a forum of communication, and communication demands mutual and active participation.

To be an *observant* critic, we need only go to the theatre with an open mind and sharply tuned senses. Unfettered thinking should be a part of every theatrical experience, and provocative discussion should be its aftermath.

# Spotlight

## Dramaturg Jerry Patch

One of America's leading and longtime dramaturgs, Jerry Patch has played a dramaturgical role in the development of four Pulitzer Prize—winning plays (David Lindsay Abaire's *Rabbit Hole*, Donald Margulies's *Dinner with Friends*, Margaret Edson's *Wit*, and Lynn Nottage's *Ruined*), four other Pulitzer-nominated ones (Amy Freed's *Freedomland*, Richard Greenberg's *Three Days of Rain*, and Donald Margulies's *Sight Unseen* and *Collected Stories*), and about 150 other plays.

Most of this work took place in his three-plus decades as head dramaturg at South Coast Repertory in Southern California, but he also spent eight seasons as artistic director of the Sundance Theatre Program in Utah, which includes the noted Sundance Playwrights Laboratory and he was coartistic director of San Diego's Old Globe Theatre for three years until, in 2008, he was invited to New York to assume the post of director of artistic development at the distinguished Manhattan Theatre Club, where your author interviewed him for this profile.

One of Patch's greatest successes was discovering Margaret Edson's *Wit* in the mid-1990s. It was one of the hundreds of plays submitted annually "over the transom" (unsolicited, unrepresented by an agent, and written by a beginning playwright unknown to the theatre's management) to South Coast Repertory.

"When we got it," Patch said, "its core was there, but elements in the first draft showed the playwright's inexperience. I knew there was an intelligence there, and the story that moved me was very human, and I was impressed that for all of Vivian Bering's [the lead character's] intelligence, she was most comforted by the nurse giving her a Popsicle. For a woman in her twenties to write this work was pretty amazing, so even though it wasn't seaworthy at that time, it was full of potential. So we took a couple of years—maybe three—working with Maggie to get the play to where it made sense for us to produce it. During that time we gave her regular dramaturgical feedback, we gave it a public reading, and finally we put it into rehearsal, during which we encouraged her to trim it from two acts and over' yvo hours to a ninety-minute one-act—a very different structure. It was absolutely amazing, and she's an amazing woman."

*Wit* won the Pulitzer Prize in 1990. You can see an excerpt of the script in the chapter titled "The Playwright."

Patch acknowledges that today's New York theatre is at least as much about star actors as it is about new plays. He says that it was difficult to get Lynn Nottage's *Ruined*

---

To be an *informed critic*, we need sufficient background to provide a context for opinion and evaluation. A play may be moving, but is it as moving as The Three Sisters? as passionate as *Prometheus*? as romantic as *Romeo and Juliet*? as funny as *The Bourgeois Gentleman*? as intriguing as *Happy Days*? An actor's voice may be thrillingly resonant, but how does it compare with the voice of Patrick Stewart? If our opinions are to have weight and distinction, they may do so only against a background of knowledge and experience. If we are going to place a performance on a scale ranging from one to ten, our friends (or readers) must know what is our "one" and what is our "ten."

To be a *sensitive* critic, we must be receptive to life and to artistic experience. The most sensitive criticism comes from a compassionate approach to life, to humankind, and to artistic expression; this approach elicits and provokes a personalized response to dramatic works. Sensitive criticism admits the critic's needs: it begins from the view that life is difficult and problematical and that relationships are demanding. Sensitive critics are questing, not smug; humane, not self-absorbed; eternally eager for personal discovery and the opportunity to share it. They recognize that we are all groping in the dark, hoping to encounter

helping hands along the way in the adventure of life—that this indeed is the hope of theatre artists too.

To be a *demanding* critic is to hold the theatre to the highest standards of which it is capable, for, paradoxically, in the theatre's capacity to entertain, to supply immediate gratification, lies the seed of its own destruction. As we have seen so often in the preceding pages, the theatre wants to be liked. It has tried from its very beginning to assimilate what is likable in the other arts. Almost scavenger-like, it has appropriated for itself in every era the most popular music and dance forms, the most trendy arguments, vocabularies, philosophies, technologies, and fashions in dress. In the process, alas, it often panders to tastelessness and propagates the meanest and most shallow values of its time. And here the drama critic in each of us can play a crucial role. The very need of the theatre to please its patrons tends to beget crass insecurity: to resort to simple sensationalism in exchange for immediate approval. Cogent, fair-minded, penetrating criticism keeps the theatre mindful of its own artistic ideals and its essential responsibility to communicate. It prevents the theatre from either selling out completely to the current whim or bolting the other way into a hopelessly abstract and arcane self-absorption.

produced in New York, because it had "no stars, and, with eleven actors and understudies and a couple of musicians, it was not a cheap show to put on. And what's it about? A woman who gets raped in the Congo! So at first we had to paper the hell out of the house [give away free tickets] to get audiences. But once people saw it, they became its advocates. The play became a grand event and we extended it several times; nearly everyone who saw it recommended it."

Patch had worked with Nottage before, at Sunclance on her earlier Crumbs from the *Table of Joy*, and then at South Coast for the copremiere (in a coproduction with Baltimore's Centerstage) of her *Intimate Apparel*. The latter won "every critics' prize that year *except* the Pulitzer;" Patch says wistfully.

*Ruined* first opened at Chicago's Goodman Theatre, where it remained in development until its New York debut at Manhattan Theatre Club. Before its MTC opening, Patch—along with his MTC colleague Mandy Greenfield—"mostly just went to the rehearsals and gave notes. We just asked questions, such as 'This is what I'm getting—is it what you want?' and 'Could this be shorter?' Lynn took it from there, and the play went all the way." In all, *Ruined* received thirteen best-play awards—including the Drama Desk, New York Critics, Outer Critics, and Obie awards, as well as the 2009 Pulitzer Prize.

Patch well remembers being told at the start of his career, "No kid ever dreamed of growing up to be a dramaturg." With the enormous contribution dramaturgs now make to the American theatre—and, indeed, to American culture—it is not surprising that students around the country are now contradicting that observation.

Director of Artistic Development Jerry Patch sits in his Manhattan Theatre Club office, surrounded, as always, by dozens of new play manuscripts.

To be an *articulate* critic is to express our thoughts with precision, clarity, and grace. "I loved it" or "I hated it" is not criticism but rather a crude expression of opinion and a wholly general opinion at that. Articulation means the careful building of ideas through a presentation of evidence, logical argument, the use of helpful analogy and example, and a style of expression neither pedantically turgid nor idiosyncratically anarchic. Good criticism should be a pleasure to write, a pleasure to read; it should make us want to go deeper into the mysteries of the theatre and not suffocate us with the prejudices or egotistical displays of the critic.

In sum, the presence of a critical focus in the audience—observant, informed, sensitive, demanding, and articulate—keeps the theatre honest. It inspires the theatre to reach its highest goals. It ascribes importance to the theatrical act. It telegraphs the expectations of the audience to producer, playwright, director, and actor alike, saying, "We are out here, we are watching, we are listening, we are hoping, we care: we want your best-and then we want you to be better yet." The

theatre needs such demands from its audience. The theatre and its audience need to be worthy coparticipants in a collective experience that enlarges life as well as art.

If we are to be critics of the theatre, then, we must be knowledgeable, fair, and open-minded; receptive to stimulation and excitement; open to wisdom and love. We must also admit that we have human needs.

In exchange, the theatre must enable us to see ourselves in the characters of the drama and in the performers of the theatre. We must see our situations in the situations of plays and our hopes and possibilities in the behavior staged before us. We must be drawn to understand the theatre from the *inside* and to participate in thought and emotion in a play's performance.

Thus do we become critics, audience, and participants in one. The theatre is then no longer simply a remote subject encountered in a book, in a class, or in the entertainment columns of the world press; the theatre is part of us.

It is *our* theatre.

# Glossary

Within the definitions, terms that are defined in this glossary appear in *italic*.

**absurd** The notion that the world is meaningless, derived from an essay, "The Myth of Sisyphus," by Albert Camus, which suggests that human beings have an unquenchable desire to understand but that the world is eternally unknowable. The resulting conflict puts individuals in an "absurd" position, like Sisyphus, who, according to Greek myth, was condemned for eternity to push a rock up a mountain, only to have it always roll back down before it reached the top. The philosophical term gave the name to a principal postwar dramatic *genre: theatre of the absurd.*

**act** (*verb*) To perform in a play. (*noun*) A division within a play. Acts in modern plays are separated by an *intermission.* Full-length modern plays are customarily divided into two acts, sometimes three. Roman, Elizabethan, and neoclassic plays were usually printed in five acts, but the actual stage productions were not necessarily divided by intermissions, only stage clearings.

**ad-lib** A line improvised by an actor during a performance, usually because the actor has forgotten his or her line or because something unscripted has occurred onstage. Sometimes an author directs actors to ad-lib, as in crowd scenes during which individual words cannot be distinguished by the audience.

**aesthetic distance** The theoretical separation between the created artifice of a play and the "real life" the play appears to represent.

**agon** "Action," in Greek; the root word for "agony." Agon refers to the major struggles and interactions of Greek *tragedy.*

**alienation effect** A technique, developed by German playwright Bertolt Brecht, by which the actor deliberately presents rather than represents his or her character and "illustrates" the character without trying to embody the role fully, as *naturalistic* acting technique demands. This effect may be accomplished by "stepping out of character"—as to sing a song or to address the audience directly—and by developing a highly objective and didactic mode of expression. The actor is alienated from the role ("estranged" and "distanced" are perhaps better terms—all translations of the German word *Verfremdung*) in order to make the audience more directly aware of current political issues. This technique is highly influential, particularly in Europe.

**amphitheatre** In Rome, a large elliptical outdoor theatre, originally used for gladiatorial contests. Today the term is often used to designate a large outdoor theatre of any type.

**anagnorisis** "Recognition," in Greek. Aristotle claimed that every fine *tragedy* has a recognition scene, in which the *protagonist* discovers either some fact unknown to her or him or some moral flaw in her or his character. Scholars disagree as to which of these precise meanings Aristotle had in mind. See also *hamartia.*

**angle wing** A flat wing to which is hinged a second flat wing at an angle—usually between 90 and 115 degrees. Used extensively in seventeenth-century scenery, where it was painted to represent, among other things, diagonal walls on either side of the stage or exterior corners of buildings. See *flat; wings.*

**antagonist** In Greek *tragedy*, the "opposer of the action"; the opponent of the *protagonist.*

**Apollonian** That which is beautiful, wise, and serene, in the theories of Friedrich Nietzsche, who believed *drama* sprang from the junction of Apollonian and *Dionysian* impulses in Greek culture.

**apron** The part of the stage located in front of the *proscenium;* the forwardmost portion of the stage. The apron was used extensively in the English *Restoration* period, from whence the term comes. Today, it is usually called the *forestage.*

**aragoto** The flamboyant and exaggerated masculine style of acting employed in certain *kabuki* roles.

**arena stage** A stage surrounded by the audience; also known as "theatre-in-the-round." *Arena* is a Latin term meaning "sand," and it originally referred to the dirt circle in the midst of an *amphitheatre.*

**aside** A short line in a play delivered directly to the audience; by dramatic convention, the other characters onstage are presumed not to hear it. Popular in the works of William Shakespeare and of the *Restoration* period, the aside has made a comeback and is used to good effect, in conjunction with the longer *direct address,* by contemporary American playwrights such as Margaret Edson and Neil LaBute.

**audition** The process whereby an actor seeks a role by presenting to a director or casting director a prepared reading or by "reading cold" from the text of the play being presented.

**avant-garde** Artists who abandon conventional models and create works that are in the forefront of new movements and styles.

**backstage** The offstage area hidden from the audience that is used for *scenery* storage, for actors preparing to make entrances, and for stage technicians running the show. "Backstage plays," such as *The Torchbearers* and *Noises Off*, "turn the set around" and exploit the furious activity that takes place backstage during a play production.

**biomechanics** An experimental acting system, characterized by expressive physicalization and bold gesticulation, developed by the Russian director Vsevolod Meyerhold in the 1920s.

**black musical** See *black theatre*.

**black theatre** In America, theatre that is generally by, with, and about African Americans.

**black-box theatre** A rectangular room with no fixed seating or stage area; this theatre design allows for a variety of configurations in staging plays.

**blocking** The specific staging of a play's movements, ordinarily by the director. "Blocking" refers to the precise indications of where actors are to move, moment by moment, during the performance. Often this is worked out ("blocked out") on paper by the director beforehand.

**book** In a *musical,* the *dialogue* text, apart from the music and song lyrics.

**border** A piece of flat *scenery,* often black velour but sometimes a *flat,* which is placed horizontally above the set, usually to *mask* the lighting instruments. Borders are often used with side *wings,* in a scenery system known as "wing and border."

**box set** A stage set consisting of hard scenic pieces representing the walls and sometimes the ceiling of a room, with one wall left out for the audience to peer into. This set design was developed in the nineteenth century and remains in use today in *realistic* plays.

**Broadway** The major commercial theatre district in New York, roughly bordered by Broadway, Eighth Avenue, 42nd Street, and 52nd Street.

**bunraku** A Japanese puppet-theatre, founded in the sixteenth century and still performed today.

**burlesque** Literally, a *parody* or mockery, from an Italian amusement form. Today the term implies broad, coarse humor in *farce,* particularly in parodies and *vaudeville*-type presentations.

**business** The minute physical behavior of the actor—fiddling with a tie, sipping a drink, drumming the fingers, lighting a cigarette, and so forth. Sometimes this is controlled to a high degree by the actor or the director for precise dramatic effect; at other times the business is *improvised* to convey *verisimilitude.*

**call** An oral command, normally whispered over an intercom by the stage manager to the appropriate operator, to execute a specific lighting, sound, or scene-shift cue as, for example, "Sound cue number 121—go!" See also *cue sheet; tech run-through.*

**callback** After the initial *audition,* the director or casting director will "call back" for additional—sometimes many—readings by the actors who seem most promising. Rules of the actors' unions require that actors be paid for callbacks exceeding a certain minimum number.

**caricature** A character portrayed very broadly and in a stereotypical fashion, ordinarily objectionable in realistic dramas. See also *character.*

**catharsis** In Aristotle's *Poetics,* the "purging" or "cleansing" of the terror and pity that the audience feels during the *climax* of a *tragedy.*

**character** A "person" in a play, as performed by an actor. Hamlet, Oedipus, Juliet, and Willy Loman are characters. Characters may or may not be based on real people.

**chiton** The full-length gown worn by Greek tragic actors.

**choral ode** See *ode.*

**chorus** (1) In classic Greek plays, an ensemble of characters representing the general public of the play, such as the women of Argos or the elders of Thebes. Originally, the chorus numbered fifty; Aeschylus is said to have reduced it to twelve and Sophocles to have increased it to fifteen. More recent playwrights, including Shakespeare and Jean Anouilh, have occasionally employed a single actor (or a small group of actors) as "Chorus," to provide narration between *scenes.* (2) In *musicals,* an ensemble of characters who sing or dance together (in contrast to soloists, who sing or dance independently).

**chou** In *xiqu,* clown characters and the actors who play them.

**classic drama** Technically, plays from classical Greece or Rome. Now used frequently (if incorrectly) to refer to Elizabethan, Jacobean, and French *neoclassical,* masterpieces. See also *modern classic.*

**climax** The point of highest tension, when the conflicts of the play are at their fullest expression.

**comedy** Popularly, a funny play; classically, a play that ends happily; metaphorically, a play with some humor that celebrates the eternal ironies of human existence ("divine comedy").

**comic relief** In a *tragedy,* a short comic scene that releases some of the built-up tension of the play—giving the audience momentary "relief" before the tension mounts higher. The porter scene in Shakespeare's *Macbeth* is an often-cited example; after the murder of Duncan, a porter jocularly addresses the audience as to the effect of drinking on sexual behavior. In the best tragedies, comic relief also provides an ironic counterpoint to the tragic action.

**commedia dell'arte** A form of largely improvised, masked street theatre that began in northern Italy in the late sixteenth century and still can be seen today. The principal characters—Arlecchino, Pantalone, Columbina, Dottore, and Scapino among them—appear over and over in thousands of commedia stories.

**company** A group of theatre artists gathered together to create a play production or a series of such productions. See also *troupe.*

**convention** A theatrical custom that the audience accepts without thinking, such as "when the curtain comes down, the play is over." Each period and culture develops its own dramatic conventions, which playwrights may either accept or violate.

**cue** The last word of one speech that then becomes the "signal" for the following speech. Actors are frequently admonished to speak "on cue" or to "pick up their cues," both of which mean to begin speaking precisely at the moment the other actor finishes.

**cue sheet** A numbered list of lighting, sound, or scene-shift changes coordinated with precise moments marked in the stage manager's prompt book. See also *call.*

**curtain call** The last staged element, in which the actors, after the play ends and the audience has begun to applaud, come forward to graciously accept the applause by bowing.

**cycle plays** In medieval England, a series of *mystery plays* that, performed in sequence, relate the story of the Judeo-Christian Bible, from the Creation of the Universe to Adam and Eve to the Crucifixion to Doomsday. The York Cycle includes forty-eight such plays.

**cyclorama** In a *proscenium theatre,* a large piece of curved *scenery* that wraps around the rear of the stage and is illuminated to resemble the sky or to serve as an abstract neutral background. It is usually made of fabric stretched between curved pipes but is sometimes a permanent structure made of concrete and plaster.

**dada** A provocative and playful European art movement that followed World War I and is characterized by seemingly random, unstructured, and "anti-aesthetic" creativity. It was briefly but deeply influential in poetry, painting, and theatre.

**dan** In *xiqu,* the female roles and the actors who play them.

**denouement** The final scene or scenes in a play devoted to tying up the loose ends after the *climax* (although the word originally meant "the untying").

**deus ex machina** In Greek *tragedy,* the resolution of the *plot* by the device of a god ("deus") arriving onstage by means of a crane ("machina") and solving all the characters' problems. Today, this term encompasses any contrived play ending, such as the discovery of a will. This theatrical element was considered clumsy by Aristotle and nearly all succeeding critics; it is occasionally used ironically in the modern theatre, as by Bertolt Brecht in *The Threepenny Opera.*

**dialogue** The speeches—delivered to one another—of the *characters* in a play. Contrast with monologue.

**diction** One of the six important components of *drama,* according to Aristotle, who meant by the term the intelligence and appropriateness of the play's speeches. Today,

the term refers primarily to the actor's need for articulate speech and clear pronunciation.

**didactic** drama Drama dedicated to teaching lessons or provoking intellectual debate beyond the confines of the play; a dramatic form espoused by Bertolt Brecht. See also *alienation effect.*

**dim out** To fade the lights gradually to blackness.

**dimmer** In lighting, the electrical device (technically known as a "potentiometer") that regulates the current passing through the bulb filaments and, thereby, the amount of light emitted from the lighting instruments.

**Dionysia** The weeklong Athenian springtime festival in honor of Dionysus; after 534 B.C., it was the major play-producing festival of the ancient Greek year. Also called "Great Dionysia" and "City Dionysia."

**Dionysian** Characterized by passionate revelry, uninhibited pleasure-seeking; the opposite of *Apollonian,* according to Friedrich Nietzsche, who considered *drama* a merger of these two primary impulses in Greek culture.

**Dionysus** The Greek god of *drama* as well as the god of drinking and fertility. Dionysus was known as Bacchus in Rome.

**direct address** A character's speech delivered directly to the audience, common in Greek *Old Comedy* (see *parabasis*), in Shakespeare's work (see *soliloquy*), in *epic theatre,* and in some otherwise realistic modern plays (such as Tennessee Williams' *The Glass Menagerie*).

**discovery** A *character* who appears onstage without making an entrance, as when a curtain opens. Ferdinand and Miranda are "discovered" playing chess in Shakespeare's *The Tempest* when Prospero pulls away the curtain that was hiding them from view.

**dithyramb** A Greek religious rite in which a *chorus* of fifty men, dressed in goatskins, chanted and danced; the precursor, according to Aristotle, of Greek *tragedy.*

**divertissement** A French term, now accepted in English, for a frothy entertainment, intended to "divert" the audience from more serious matters.

**documentary** drama Drama that presents historical facts in a nonfictionalized, or slightly fictionalized, manner.

**doggerel** Coarse, unsophisticated poetry, usually with short lines and overly obvious rhymes, often used comically by Shakespeare to indicate simplistic verse written or performed by characters in his plays, such as Orlando's amateur love poems to Rosalind in *As You Like It* or the play of "Pyramus and Thisbe" presented by inexperienced performers in the last act of *A Midsummer Night's Dream.*

**domestic tragedy** A *tragedy* about ordinary people at home.

**double** (*verb*) To play more than one role. An actor who plays two or more roles is said to "double" in the second and following roles. Ordinarily the actor will seek, through a costume change, to disguise the fact of the doubling; occasionally, however, a production with a *theatricalist* staging may make it clear that the actor doubles in many roles. (*noun*) To Antonin Artaud, the life that drama reflects, as discussed in his book *The Theatre and Its Double*. See also *theatre of cruelty*.

**downstage** The part of the stage closest to the audience. The term dates back to the eighteenth century, when the stage was *raked* so that the front part was literally lower than the back (or *upstage*) portion.

**drama** The art of the theatre; plays, playmaking, and the whole body of literature of and for the stage.

**dramatic** Plays, scenes, and events that are high in conflict and believability and that would command attention if staged in the theatre.

**dramatic criticism** A general term that refers to writings on drama, ranging from journalistic play reviews to scholarly analyses of dramatic *genres*, periods, *styles*, and theories.

**dramatic irony** The device of letting the audience know something the characters don't, as in Shakespeare's Macbeth, when King Duncan remarks on his inability to judge character—while warmly greeting the man (Macbeth) who we already know plans to assassinate him.

**dramaturg (also spelled "dramaturge")** A specialist in play construction and the body of dramatic literature, dramaturgs are frequently engaged by professional and academic theatres to assist in choosing and analyzing plays, to develop production concepts, to research topics pertinent to historic period or play production *style*, and to write program essays. The dramaturg has been a mainstay of the German theatre since the eighteenth century and is becoming increasingly popular in the English-speaking world.

**dramaturgy** The art of play construction; sometimes used to refer to play structure itself.

**drapery** Fabric—often black—mainly used as neutral *scenery to mask* (hide) actors when they leave the lit (active) area of the stage. Also refers to a front curtain (a "main drape"), which is often red.

**dress rehearsal** A *rehearsal* in full costume; usually also with full *scenery, properties,* lighting, sound, and technical effects. Such rehearsals are ordinarily the last ones prior to the first performance before an audience.

**drop** A flat piece of *scenery* hung from the *fly gallery,* which can "drop" into place by a flying system.

**emotion memory** A technique in which an actor stimulates emotion by remembering the feelings he or she experienced during a previous, real-life event. Employed since ancient times, it was developed and named by Konstantin Stanislavsky (who, however, subsequently disowned it) and was promoted in America by Lee Strasberg. Also called "affective memory."

**empathy** Audience members' identification with dramatic characters and their consequent shared feelings with the plights and fortunes of those characters. Empathy is one of the principal effects of good drama.

**ensemble** Literally, the group of actors (and sometimes directors and designers) who put a play together; metaphorically, the rapport and shared sense of purpose that bind such a group into a unified artistic entity.

**environmental theatre** Plays produced not on a conventional stage but in an area where the actors and the audience are intermixed in the same "environment" and there is no precise line distinguishing stage space from audience space.

**epic theatre** As popularized by Bertolt Brecht, a style of theatre in which the play presents a series of semiisolated episodes intermixed with songs and other forms of *direct address,* all leading to a general moral conclusion or set of integrated moral questions. Brecht's *Mother Courage* is a celebrated example. See also *alienation effect*.

**epilogue** In Greek *tragedy,* a short concluding *scene* of certain plays, generally involving a substantial shift of tone or a *deus ex machina*. Today, the epilogue is a concluding scene set substantially beyond the time frame of the rest of the play, in which characters, now somewhat older, reflect on the preceding events.

**episode** In Greek *tragedy,* a scene between characters and between choral *odes*. The word literally means "between odes."

**existential drama** A play based on the philosophical notions of existentialism, particularly as developed by Jean-Paul Sartre. Existentialism, basically, preaches that "you are your acts, and nothing else" and that people must be held fully accountable for their own behavior. *No Exit* contains Sartre's most concise expression of this idea.

**exodos** In Greek *tragedy,* the departure ode of the chorus at the end of the play.

**exposition** In play construction, the conveyance, through *dialogue,* of story events that occurred before the play begins.

**expressionism** An artistic *style* that greatly exaggerates perceived reality in order to express inner truths directly. Popular mainly in Germany between the world wars, expressionism in the theatre is notable for its gutsy dialogue, piercing sounds, bright lighting and coloring, bold scenery, and shocking, vivid imagery.

**farce** Highly comic, lighthearted, gleefully contrived drama, usually involving *stock situations* (such as mistaken identity or discovered lovers' trysts), punctuated with broad physical stunts and pratfalls.

**flat** A wooden frame covered by fabric or by a hard surface and then painted, often to resemble a wall or portion of a wall. The flat is a traditional staple of stage *scenery,* particularly in the realistic theatre, because it is exceptionally lightweight, can be combined with other flats in various ways, and can be repainted and reused many times over several years.

**fly** (*verb*) To raise a piece of *scenery* (or an actor) out of sight by a system of ropes or wires. This theatre practice dates back at least to ancient Greek times. See also *deus ex machina*.

**fly gallery** The operating area for flying scenery, where fly ropes are tied off (on a pinrail) or where ropes in a counterweight system are clamped in a fixed position.

**follow-spot** A swivel-mounted spotlight that can be pointed in any direction by an operator.

**footlights** In a *proscenium theatre,* a row of lights across the front of the stage, used to light the actors' faces from below and to add light and color to the setting. Footlights were used universally in previous centuries but are employed only on special occasions today.

**forestage** See *apron.*

**found object** In scene or costume design (and art in general), an item that is found (rather than created) and is incorporated into the finished design.

**full house** Audience seating filled to capacity. See also *house.*

**genre** A French noun meaning "kind"; a term used in dramatic theory to signify a distinctive class or category of play—*tragedy, comedy, farce,* and so on.

**geza** The *stage right,* semienclosed musicians' box in *kabuki* theatre. This term also refers to the music that is played in this box.

**gidayu** The traditional style of chanting in kabuki and *bunraku* theatre.

**greenroom** A room near the stage where actors may sit comfortably before and after the show or during scenes in which they do not appear. This room is traditionally painted green; the custom arose in England, where the color was thought to be soothing.

**ground plan** A schematic drawing of the stage setting, as seen from above, indicating the location of stage-scenery pieces and furniture on (and sometimes above) the floor. A vital working document for directors in *rehearsal,* as well as for technicians in the installation of *scenery.*

**hamartia** In Aristotle's *Poetics,* the "tragic flaw" of the *protagonist.* Scholars differ as to whether Aristotle was referring primarily to a character's ignorance of certain facts or to a character's moral defect.

**hanamichi** In the *kabuki* theatre, a long narrow runway leading from the stage to a door at the back of the auditorium that is used for highly theatrical entrances and exits right through the audience. For some plays, a second hanamichi may be added.

**Hellenistic theatre** Ancient Greek theatre during the fourth and third centuries B.C. The surviving stone theatres of Athens and Epidaurus date from the Hellenistic period, which began well after the great fifth-century tragedies and comedies were written. The Hellenistic period did produce an important form of comedy (*New Comedy*), however, and Alexandrian scholars during this period collected, edited, and preserved the masterpieces of the golden age.

**high comedy** A comedy of verbal wit and visual elegance, usually peopled with upper-class characters. The *Restoration* comedies of William Congreve (1670-1729) and the Victorian comedies of Oscar Wilde (1854-1900) are often cited as examples.

**hikimaku** The traditional striped curtain of the *kabuki* theatre.

**himation** The gownlike basic costume of the Greek tragic actor.

**house** The audience portion of the theatre building.

**hubris** In Greek, "an excess of pride"; the most common *character* defect (one interpretation of the Greek *hamartia*) of the *protagonist* in Greek *tragedy.* "Pride goeth before a fall" is a Biblical expression of this foundation of tragedy.

**improvisation** *Dialogue* or stage *business* invented by the actor, often during the performance itself. Some plays are wholly improvised, even to the extent that the audience may suggest situations that the actors must then create. More often, improvisation is used to "fill in the gaps" between more traditionally memorized and rehearsed scenes.

**inciting action** In play construction, the single action that initiates the major conflict of the play.

**ingenue** The young, pretty, and innocent girl role in certain plays; also used to denote an actress capable of playing such roles.

**interlude** A *scene* or staged event in a play not specifically tied to the *plot;* in medieval England, a short moral play, usually comic, that could be presented at a court banquet amid other activities.

**intermission** A pause in the action, marked by a fall of the curtain or a fade-out of the stage lights, during which the audience may leave their seats for a short time, usually ten or fifteen minutes. Intermissions divide the play into separate *acts.* In England, known as "the interval."

**jing** In *xiqu,* the "painted-face" roles, often of gods, nobles, or villains.

**jingju** "Capital theatre" in Chinese; the Beijing (Peking) opera, the most famous form of *xiqu.*

**kabuki** One of the national theatres of Japan. Dating from the seventeenth century, kabuki features magnificent flowing costumes; highly stylized *scenery,* acting, and makeup; and elaborately styled choreography.

**kakegoe** Traditional shouts that *kabuki* enthusiasts in the audience cry out to their favorite actors during the play.

**kathakali** Literally, "story play"; a traditional dance-drama of India.

**kōken** Black-garbed and veiled actors' assistants who perform various functions onstage in *kabuki* theatre.

**kunqu** (sometimes kunju) The oldest form of Chinese *xiqu* still performed, dating from the sixteenth century.

**kyōgen** A comic, often farcical, counterpoint to Japanese *nō* drama, to which it is, surprisingly, historically related.

**lazzo** A physical joke, refined into traditional *business* and inserted into a play, in the *commedia dell'arte.* "Eating the fly" is a famous lazzo.

**Lenaea** The winter dramatic festival in ancient Athens. Because there were fewer foreigners in town in the winter, comedies that might embarrass the Athenians were often performed at this festival rather than at the springtime *Dionysia*.

**light plot** The layout—on paper—showing the positions where stage lights are to be hung and how they are wired (connected) into the numbered electrical circuits of the theatre facility.

**liturgical drama** *Dramatic* material that was written into the official Catholic Church liturgy and staged as part of regular church services in the medieval period, mainly in the tenth through twelfth centuries. See also *mystery play*.

**low comedy** Comic actions based on broad physical humor, scatology, crude punning, and the argumentative behavior of ignorant and lower-class *characters*. Despite the pejorative connotation of its name, low comedy can be inspired, as in the "mechanicals" scenes of Shakespeare's *A Midsummer Night's Dream*. Good plays, such as this one, can mix low comedy with *high comedy* in a highly sophisticated pattern.

**mask** (*noun*) A covering of the face, used conventionally by actors in many periods, including Greek, Roman, and *commedia dell'arte*. The mask was also used in other sorts of plays for certain occasions, such as the masked balls in Shakespeare's *Romeo and Juliet* and *Much Ado About Nothing*. The mask is a symbol of the theatre, particularly the two classic masks of Comedy and Tragedy. (*verb*) To hide backstage storage or activity by placing in front of it neutrally colored *flats* or drapery (which then become "masking pieces").

**masque** A minor dramatic form combining dance, music, a short allegorical text, and elegant *scenery* and costuming; often presented at court, as in the royal masques written by Ben Jonson, with scenery designed by Inigo Jones, during the Stuart era (early seventeenth century).

**melodrama** Originally a term for *musical* theatre, by the nineteenth century this became the designation of a suspenseful, plot-oriented *drama* featuring all-good heroes, all-bad villains, simplistic *dialogue*, soaring moral conclusions, and bravura acting.

**metaphor** A literary term designating a figure of speech that implies a comparison or identity of one thing with something else. It permits concise communication of a complex idea by use of associative imagery, as with Shakespeare's "morn in russet mantle clad."

**metatheatre** Literally, "beyond theatre"; plays or theatrical acts that are self-consciously theatrical, that refer back to the art of the theatre and call attention to their own *theatricality*. Developed by many authors, including Shakespeare (in plays-within-plays in *Hamlet and A Midsummer Night's Dream*) and particularly the twentieth-century Italian playwright Luigi Pirandello (*Six Characters in Search of an Author, Tonight We Improvise*), thus leading to the term "Pirandellian" (meaning "metatheatrical"). See also *play-within-the-play*.

**mie** A "moment" in *kabuki* theatre in which the actor (usually in an aragoto role) suddenly "freezes" in a tense and symbolic pose.

**mime** A stylized art of acting without words. Probably derived from the *commedia dell'arte*, mime was revived in France during the mid-twentieth century and is now popular again in the theatre and in street performances in Europe and the United States. Mime performers traditionally employ whiteface makeup to stylize and exaggerate their features and expressions.

**modern** A difficult term to pin down because it literally refers to work of "the present"—which, however, is always changing. The term popularly means "up-to-date," but arts scholars employ it mainly in reference to works created between, approximately, 1890 and 1945, which were called modern in their own time (e.g., "Modern art") and now—in contrast to *postmodern* works—can be roughly categorized into identified artistic styles (e.g., realism, naturalism, expressionism, absurdism, epic theatre) of those years.

**modern classic** A term used to designate a play of the *modern* era that has nonetheless passed the test of time and seems as if it will last into the century or centuries beyond, such as the major works of Anton Chekhov, George Bernard Shaw, and Samuel Beckett. Contrast with *classic drama*.

**monologue** A long unbroken speech in a play, often delivered directly to the audience (in which case it is more accurately called a *soliloquy*).

**morality play** An allegorical medieval play in which the characters represent abstractions (Good Deeds, Death, and so on) and the overall impact of the play is moral instruction. The most famous in English is the anonymous *Everyman* (fifteenth century).

**motivation** That which can be construed to have determined a person's (or a *character's*) behavior. Since Konstantin Stanislavsky, actors have been encouraged to study the possible motivations of their characters' actions. See also *objective*.

**music theatre** A dramatic *genre* that employs, normally in addition to spoken dialogue (but see *sung-through*), a musical score with a dozen or more songs and dances. Also called "musical theatre."

**musical** (*noun*) A single work of *music theatre*—such as *Oklahoma!* or *The Producers*.

**musical comedy** A *musical* intended mainly as light comic entertainment, emphasizing comedy and youthful romance as well as singing.

**mystery play** The most common term referring to medieval plays developed from liturgical drama that treated Biblical stories and themes. (They were also known as "pageant plays" in England, as "passion plays" when dealing with the Crucifixion of Jesus, and as "Corpus

Christi plays" when performed in conjunction with that particular festival.) Unlike *liturgical dramas,* which were in Latin, mystery plays were written in the vernacular (English, French, German, Italian, Spanish, and Russian versions exist) and were staged outside the church.

**naturalism** A version of *realism* advancing the notion that the natural and social environment, more than individual willpower, controlled human behavior. Its proponents, active in the late nineteenth and early twentieth centuries, sought to dispense with all theatrical convention in the search for *verisimilitude*—or, as the naturalists would say, *a slice of life.*

**neoclassicism** Literally, "new classicism." A renewed interest in the literary and artistic theories of ancient Greece and Rome and an attempt to reformulate them for the current day. A dominant force in seventeenth-century France, neoclassicism promoted restrained passion, balance, artistic consistency, and formalism in all art forms; it reached its dramatic pinnacle in the tragedies of jean Racine.

**New Comedy** Greek comic dramas—almost all of which are now lost—of the late fourth to the second centuries B.C. Considerably more realistic than the *Old Comedy* of Aristophanes, New Comedy employed *stock characters* and domestic scenes; it strongly influenced Roman author Plautus and, through him, Renaissance comedy.

**nō** The classical dance-drama of Japan. Performed on a bare wooden stage of fixed construction and dimensions and accompanied by traditional music, nō is the aristocratic forebear of the more popular *kabuki* and has remained generally unchanged since its fourteenth-century beginnings.

**objective** The basic "goal" of a *character.* Also called "intention," "goal,"or "victory." Since Konstantin Stanislavsky, the actor has been urged to discover his or her character's objectives and, by way of "living the life of the character," to pursue that character's objective during the course of the play.

**ode** In Greek *tragedy,* a song chanted or sung by the chorus and often accompanied by dance. Also called "choral ode."

**off-Broadway** The New York professional theatre located outside the *Broadway* district; principally in Greenwich Village and around the Upper East and West Sides. Developed in the 1950s, when it was considered *avant-garde,* the off-Broadway theatre is now more of a scaled-down version of the Broadway theatre, featuring *musicals* and commercial *revivals* as much as (or more than) original works.

**off-off-Broadway** A term designating certain theatre activity in New York City, usually nonprofessional (although with professional artists involved) and usually experimental and *avant-garde.* Off-off-Broadway developed in the 1970s as a supplement to the commercialism of both Broadway and, increasingly, off-Broadway.

**Old Comedy** Ancient Greek comedy of the fifth century B.C., mainly known to us through the bawdy, satirical, and even slapstick comedies of Aristophanes.

**onnagata** "Women-type" roles in *kabuki,* which, like all the roles, are played by men.

**"open the house"** A direction to admit the audience. See also *house.*

**orchestra** (1) In the ancient Greek or Roman theatre, the circular (in Rome, semicircular) ground-level acting area in front of the stagehouse, or *skene.* It was used primarily by the *chorus.* (2) In modern U.S. theatre buildings, the ground-level section of the audience, which usually slopes upward at the rear. Distinct from the mezzanine and balconies and ordinarily containing the more expensive seats. In England, known as "the stalls."

**parabasis** The "coming-forward" of a *character* in Greek *Old Comedy* who then gives a *direct address* to the audience in the middle of the play. In Aristophanes' plays, the parabasis is often given in the author's name and may have been spoken by Aristophanes himself. The parabasis was often unrelated to the *plot* and dealt with the author's immediate political or social concerns.

**parados** (1) The *ode* sung by the chorus entering the orchestra in a *Greek tragedy.* (2) The space between the stage-house (skene) and audience seating area (*theatron*) through which the chorus entered the orchestra.

**parody** Dramatic material that makes fun of a dramatic genre or mode or of specific literary works; a form of theatre that is often highly entertaining but rarely has lasting value.

**passion play** A medieval play about Jesus and his trial and crucifixion, still performed in many towns and villages around the world during Easter week.

**pathos** "Passion," in Greek; also "suffering." The word refers to the depths of feeling evoked by *tragedy;* it is at the root of our words "sympathy" and "empathy," which also describe the effect of drama on audience emotions. See also *empathy.*

**peripeteia** The change of course in the protagonist's fortunes that, according to Aristotle, is part of the *climax of a tragedy.*

**pièce bien faite** See *well-made play.*

**platform** A tablelike construction of any height, built to be stood upon, that creates raised flooring for a designated portion of the stage.

**play-within-the-play** A play "presented" by characters who are already in a play, like "The Murder of Gonzago," which is presented by "players" in *Hamlet.* Many plays are in part about actors and plays and contain such plays-within-plays; these include Anton Chekhov's *The Seagull,* Jean Anouilh's The Rehearsal, and Shakespeare's *A Midsummer Night's Dream* and *The Taming of the Shrew.*

**plot** The events of the play, expressed as a series of linked dramatic actions; in common terms, the story of the play. Plot is the most important component of a play, according to Aristotle.

**postmodern** A wide-ranging term describing certain post-World War II artistic works characterized by non-linearity, self-referentiality if not self-parody, and multiple/ simultaneous sensory impressions.

**practical** A *property* that works onstage the way it does in life. For example, a "practical" stove, in a stage setting, is one on which the characters can actually cook. A "nonpractical" stove, by contrast, is something that only looks like a stove (and may in fact be a stove without insides).

**preview** A performance prior to a production's formal opening, primarily intended to allow the director and cast to make final changes in response to audience reactions. There may be one preview or many; Broadway productions often have several weeks of previews.

**problem play** A realistic play that deals, often narrowly, with a specific social problem. George Bernard Shaw's *Mrs. Warren's Profession,* for example, is virtually a dramatic tract on prostitution. The term was most popular around the beginning of the twentieth century.

**producer** (1) In America, the person responsible for assembling the ingredients of a play production: financing, staff, theatre, publicity, and management. Not ordinarily involved in the day-to-day artistic direction of the production, the American producer nonetheless controls the artistic process through her or his authority over personnel selection and budgeting. (2) Until recently in the English theatre, the theatre artist whom Americans refer to as the director.

**prologue** In Greek *tragedy,* a speech or brief scene preceding the entrance of the *chorus* and the main action of the play, usually spoken by a god or gods. Subsequently, the term has referred to a speech or brief scene that introduces the play, as by an actor in certain Elizabethan plays (often called the chorus) and in the *Restoration.* The prologue is rarely used in the modern theatre.

**properties** Or "props"; the furniture and handheld objects (hand props) used in play productions. These are often real items (chairs, telephones, books, etc.) that can be purchased, rented, borrowed, or brought up from theatre storage; they may also, particularly in period or stylized plays, be designed and built in a property shop.

**proscenium arch** The arch separating the audience area from the main stage area. The term derives from the Roman playhouse, in which the proscenium (literally, *pro skene,* or "in front of the stage") was the facing wall of the stage. Modern *thrust* and *arena stages* have no proscenium.

**proscenium theatre** A rectangular-roomed theatre with a *proscenium arch* separating the audience on one end from the stage at the other. The proscenium theatre was first popular in the late seventeenth century and reached its apogee in the late nineteenth and early twentieth centuries. Still the basic theatre architecture of America's Broadway and of major European theatre companies.

**protagonist** In Greek *tragedy,* the "carrier of the action"; in any drama, the principal *character,* often opposed by an antagonist.

**raked stage** A sloped stage, angled so that the rear (*upstage*) area is higher than the forward (*downstage*) area. A raked stage was standard theatre architecture in the seventeenth century and is often used today in scene design but rarely in a theatre's permanent architecture.

**realism** The general principle that the stage should portray, in a reasonable facsimile, ordinary people in ordinary circumstances and that actors should behave, as much as possible, as real people do in life. Although the roots of realism go back to Euripides, it developed as a deliberate contrast to the florid *romanticism* that swept the European theatre in the mid-nineteenth century. See also *naturalism,* which is an extreme version of realism.

**recognition** See *anagnorisis.*

**rehearsal** The gathering of actors and director to put a play into production; the period in which the director stages the play and the actors develop and repeat their *dialogue* and actions; etymologically, a "reharrowing," or repeated digging into. In French, the comparable term is *répétition.*

**repertory** The plays a theatre company produces. A company's current repertory consists of those plays available for production at any time.

**Restoration** In England, the period following the restoration of the monarchy in 1660. In the theatre, the period is particularly noted for witty and salacious comedies, through to William Congreve's brilliant *The Way of the World* in 1700.

**revival** The remounting of a play production after its initial closing.

**rising action** In play construction, the escalating conflict; events and actions that follow the *inciting action.*

**ritual** A traditional cultural practice, usually religious, involving precise movements, music, spoken text, or gestures, that serves to communicate with deities. Ritual is often incorporated into plays, either as *conventions* of the theatre or as specific dramatized actions.

**romanticism** A nineteenth-century European movement away from *neoclassic* formalism and restraint and toward out-sized passions, exotic and grotesque stories, florid writing, and all-encompassing worldviews. Supplanted late in the century by *realism,* romanticism survives today primarily in grand opera and nineteenth-century-based *musicals.*

**rotating repertory** The scheduling of a series of plays in nightly rotation. This is customary in most European theatres and in many American Shakespeare festivals; it is otherwise rare in America. See also *repertory.*

**samisen** The three-stringed banjolike instrument used in *kabuki* and *bunraku.*

**satire** A play or other literary work that ridicules social follies, beliefs, religions, or human vices, almost always in a lighthearted vein. Satire is not usually a lasting theatre form, as summed up by dramatist George S. Kaufman's classic definition: "Satire is what closes on Saturday night."

**satyr** A mythological Greek creature, half man and half goat, who attended *Dionysus* and represented male sexuality and drunken revelry; goatskin-clad followers of Dionysus who served as the *chorus of the satyr play.*

**satyr play** The fourth play in a Greek *tetralogy.* Satyr plays were short bawdy *farces* that parodied the events of the *trilogies* that preceded them.

**scansion** The study of verse for patterns of accented and unaccented syllables; also known as "metrics."

**scene** (1) The period of stage time representing a single space over a continuous period of time, now usually marked by a stage clearing and a noticeable change in the lighting; the subdivision of an act. (2) The locale where the events of the play are presumed to take place, as represented by *scenery* (as in "the scene is the Parson's living room"). (3) Of scenery, as "scene design."

**scenery** Physical constructions that provide the specific acting environment for a play and that often indicate, by representation, the locale where a scene is set; the physical *setting* for a scene or play.

**scenography** *Scene* design, particularly as it fits into the moving pattern of a play or series of plays. Scene design is four-dimensional, comprising three physical dimensions plus time.

**scrim** A theatrical fabric woven so finely that when lit from the front it appears opaque and when lit from behind it becomes transparent. A scrim is often used for surprise effects or to create a mysterious mood.

**script** The written version of a play.

**semiotics** The study of signs, as they may be perceived in literary works, including plays. Semiotics is a contemporary tool of *dramaturgical* analysis that offers the possibility of identifying all the ingredients of *drama* (staging as well as language) and determining the precise conjunctions between them.

**set piece** A single piece of *scenery* that represents a fixed object, such as a tree or a bathtub.

**setting** Or "set"; the fixed (stable) stage *scenery.*

**sheng** In *xiqu,* the male roles and the actors who play them.

**shite** The principal *character* (the "doer") in *nō.*

**skene** The Greek stagehouse (and root word of *scene*). The skene evolved from a small changing room behind the *orchestra* to a larger structure with a raised stage and a back wall during the Greek period.

**slapstick** Literally, a prop bat made up of two hinged sticks that slap sharply together when the bat is used to hit someone; a staple gag of the *commedia dell'arte.* More generally, slapstick is any sort of very broad physical stage humor.

**slice of life** Pure *naturalism:* stage action that realistically represents an ordinary and arbitrary "slice" of the daily activity of the people portrayed.

**soliloquy** A *monologue* delivered by a single actor with no one else onstage; sometimes played as the *character* "thinking aloud" and sometimes as a seeming *dialogue* with the (silent) audience.

**sound effects** A term referring to single sounds, normally played from offstage and often prerecorded, that represent specific (and usually realistic) sounds, such as a telephone ringing, a car braking, or a cannon firing. Today, such effects are mostly incorporated into a play's overall sound design.

**stage business** See *business.*

**stage directions** Scene descriptions, *blocking* instructions, and general directorial comments written, usually by the playwright, in the *script.*

**stage left** Left, from the actor's point of view.

**stage machinery** A variety of mechanical devices, including hoists, cranes, rolling carts, and turntables, used to move or change actors or *scenery.* Many, though now electrified, date from ancient Greek times.

**stage right** Right, from the actor's point of view.

**stasimon** A choral *ode* between scenes (*episodes*) in a Greek *tragedy.*

**stock character** A *character* recognizable mainly for his or her conformity to a standard ("stock") dramatic stereotype: the wily servant, the braggart soldier, the innocent virgin, and so on. Most date from at least Roman times.

**stock situation** One of a number of basic *plot* situations—the lover hiding in the closet, twins mistaken for each other, and so on—that, like *stock characters,* have been used in the theatre since Plautus and before.

**storyboard** A series of rough preliminary drawings that, when looked at in sequence, visually illustrate an imagined order of stage moments—the sequencing of the *scenery* and the flow of the action—in a play being prepared for production.

**style** The specific manner in which a play is shaped, as determined by its *genre,* its historical period, the sort of impact the director wishes to convey to the audience, and the skill of the artists involved. The term generally refers to these aspects inasmuch as they differ from *naturalism,* although it could be said that naturalism is a style.

**stylize** To deliberately shape a play (or a setting, a costume, etc.) in a specifically non-naturalistic manner.

**subplot** A secondary *plot,* usually related to the main plot by play's end. The Gloucester plot in *King Lear* and the Laertes plot in *Hamlet* are examples.

**subtext** According to Konstantin Stanislavsky, the deeper and usually unexpressed "real" meanings of a *character's* spoken lines. Of particular importance in the acting of realistic plays, such as those of Anton Chekhov, where the action is often as much between the lines as in them.

**summer stock** Theatre companies, located mostly in vacation areas of the American Northeast, that produce a season of plays (often one per week) during the summer months. Particularly popular in the three decades following World War II, when they mainly offered light, Broadway-styled comedies and provided pleasant entertainment for vacationers, salaries for unemployed New York actors, and break-in opportunities for student apprentices. The surviving companies, such as the Williamstown Theatre Festival in Massachusetts, have since become much more artistically ambitious.

**sung-through** (*noun*) A *musical* that has no spoken *dialogue*.

**surrealism** An art movement of the early twentieth century, in which the artist sought to go beyond *realism* into superrealism.

**symbolism** The first major antirealistic movement in the arts and in the theatre. Symbolism, which emphasizes the symbolic nature of theatrical presentation and the abstract possibilities of drama, flourished as a significant movement from the late nineteenth century to the early twentieth century, when it broke into various sub-movements: *expressionism, surrealism, theatricalism,* and many others.

**tableau** A "frozen moment" onstage, with the actors immobile, usually employed at the end of a *scene,* as the curtain falls or the lights dim.

**technical rehearsal** A stop-and-start *rehearsal,* in which a play's technical elements—mainly scene shifts, lighting, and sound cues—are precisely timed and integrated with the acting. See also *cue sheet.*

**tech run-through** A nonstop *rehearsal* of the play with all technical elements called by the stage manager and executed. See also *call; cue sheet.*

**tetralogy** Four plays performed together in sequence. In ancient Greek theatre, this was the basic pattern for the tragic playwrights, who presented a *trilogy* of tragedies, followed by a *satyr play.*

**text** A play *script.* This term is sometimes used to indicate the spoken words of the play only, as apart from the stage directions and other material in the script.

**theatre—and drama** These words are often used interchangeably, yet they also have distinct meanings. "Theatre" is the broader term and can denote all of the elements of theatrical production (plays, scenery, staging, acting). "Drama" mainly focuses on plays performed in a theatrical environment. This difference in meaning reflects the words' separate etymologies: theatre is that which "is seen," and drama is that which "is done." So "theatre" can mean a building, but "drama" cannot. And "dramatic" suggests actions, in both plays and life, that are compelling; but "theatrical," when referring to real-life behavior, implies overly showy or sensationalistic.

**theatre-and theater** Theatre is the French (and British) spelling; *theater* the German. Both spellings are common in the United States.

**theatre of alienation** See alienation *effect; epic theatre.*

**theatre of cruelty** A notion of theatre developed by the French theorist Antonin Artaud (1896-1948). Artaud's goal was to employ language more for its sound than for its meaning and to create a shocking stream of sensations rather than a coherent *plot* and cast of *characters.* Although Artaud's practical achievement was slight, his theories have proven extraordinarily influential.

**theatre of the absurd** A theatrical style, named by Martin Esslin in his 1961 book of that title, that has been applied to the post-World War II plays of Samuel Beckett, Eugène Ionesco, jean Genet, and others, mostly Europeans. Esslin employed the term, derived from an essay by Albert Camus (see *absurd*), to describe plays with unrealistic and illogical plots, repetitious and disconnected language, and unclear themes, reflecting a world in which humans "absurdly" seek meaning but never find it.

**theatre-in-the-round** See *arena stage.*

**theatricalist** A contemporary style that boldly exploits the theatre itself and calls attention to the theatrical contexts of the play being performed. This term is often used to describe plays about the theatre that employ a *play-within-the-play.*

**theatron** From the Greek for "seeing place"; the original Greek theatre.

**thespian** Actor; after Thespis, the first Greek actor.

**thrust stage** A stage that projects into the seating area and is surrounded by the audience on three sides.

**tragedy** From the Greek for "goat song"; originally meant a serious play. Tragedy was refined by Greek playwrights (Thespis, sixth century B.C., being the first) and subsequently the philosopher Aristotle (384-322 B.C.) into the most celebrated of dramatic *genres:* a play that treats, at the most uncompromising level, human suffering. The reason for the name is unclear; a goat may have been the prize, or the *chorus* may have worn goatskins.

**tragic flaw** See *hamartia.*

**tragicomedy** A play that begins as a *tragedy* but includes comic elements and ends happily. Tragicomedy was a popular genre in the eighteenth century but is rarely employed, at least under that name, in the modern theatre.

**traveler** A curtain that, instead of flying out (see *fly*), moves horizontally and is usually opened by dividing from the center outward.

**trilogy** Three plays performed in sequence; the basic pattern of ancient Greek tragedies, of which one—Aeschylus's *The Oresteia* (*Agamemnon, The Libation Bearers, and The Eumenides*)—is still extant.

**trope** A written text, usually in dialogue form, incorporated into the Christian worship service. In the tenth century A.D. tropes became the first *liturgical dramas.*

**troupe** A group of actors who perform together, often on tour. See also *company.*

**unit set** A set that, by the moving on or off of a few simple pieces and perhaps with a change of lights, can represent all the scenes from a play. The unit set is a fluid and economical staging device, particularly useful for Shakespeare productions.

**unities** The unity of place, unity of time, unity of action, and unity of tone were the four "unities" that *neoclassic* critics of the seventeenth century claimed to derive from Aristotle; plays said to "observe the unities" were required to take place in one locale, to have a duration of no more than one day (in an extreme interpretation, in no more time than the duration of the play itself), and to concern themselves with no more than one single action. Aristotle made no such demands on playwrights, however, and very few authors have ever succeeded in satisfying these restrictive conventions.

**upstage** (*noun*) In a *proscenium theatre,* the part of the stage farthest from the audience; the rear of the stage, so called because it was in fact raised ("up") in the days of the *raked stage.* (*verb*) To stand upstage of another actor. Upstaging is often considered rude, inasmuch as it forces the *downstage* actor to face upstage (and away from the audience) in order to look at the actor to whom she or he is supposed to be speaking. Figuratively, the term may be used to describe any sort of acting behavior that calls unwarranted attention to the "upstaging" actor and away from the "upstaged" one.

**vaudeville** A stage variety show, with singing, dancing, comedy skits, and animal acts; highly popular in America from the late 1880s to the 1930s, when it lost out to movies, radio, and subsequently television.

**verisimilitude** Lifelikeness; the appearance of actual reality (as in a stage *setting*).

**wagoto** In *kabuki,* "soft-style" acting performed by certain male romantic characters.

**waki** The secondary character in *nō.*

**well-made play** *Pièce bien falte* in French; in the nineteenth century, a superbly plotted play, particularly by such gifted French playwrights as Eugène Scribe (1791-1861) and Victorien Sardou (1831-1908); today, generally used pejoratively, as to describe a play that has a workable *plot* but shallow characterization and trivial ideas.

**West End** The commercial theatre district of London, England.

**wings** In a *proscenium theatre,* vertical pieces of *scenery* to the left and right of the stage, usually parallel with the *footlights.*

**working drawings** Designer's drawings that show how a prop or a piece of *scenery* looks, and indicate how it should be constructed. See also *properties.*

**xiqu** Chinese for "tuneful theatre"; the general term for all varieties of traditional Chinese theatre, often called "Chinese opera."

**zadacha** Russian for "task" (though commonly translated as "objective"); according to Konstantin Stanislavsky, a character's (fictional) tasks (or goals), which the actor must pursue during the play.

# Credits

## PHOTO CREDITS

**Chapter 10** Pages 262, 264, Sara Krulwich/*The New York Times*/Redux; p. 267, © Geraint Lewis; p. 268, m Paul Kolnik; p. 269, © Joan Marcus; p. 270, © Geraint Lewis (2); pp. 271, 272L, Sara Krulwich/*The New York Times*/ Redux; p. 272R, © Craig Schwartz; p. 273, Sara Krulwich/ *The New York Times*/Redux; p. 274, Photo by Henry DiRocco/SCR; p. 275, Photos by Robert Cohen; p. 278, m Martine Franck/Magnum Photos; p. 279, © Geraint Lewis; p. 280, Sara Krulwich/*The New York Times*/Redux; p. 281, © Geraint Lewis; p. 283T, © Anne-Christine Poujoulat/Agence France-Presse/ Getty Images; p. 283B, © Geraint Lewis; p. 284T, © Fritz Curzon/ArenaPAL/ The Image Works; p. 284B, © Geraint Lewis; p. 285, © Richard Termine; p. 287, © Geraint Lewis (2); p. 288, Henry DiRocco/SCR; p. 289L, Sara Krulwich/*The New York Times*/ Redux; p. 289R, m Paul Kolnik; p. 290, © Bill Cooper/ArenaPAL/The Image Works; p. 292, © Kevin Berne/kevinberne.com; p. 293, m Geraint Lewis; p. 294, © Laurencine Lot/Photo Lot; p. 296, © Marc Enguerand; pp. 297, 299, © Joan Marcus; p. 300, Photo by Robert Cohen; p. 301, Sara Krulwich/*The New York Times*/ Redux; p. 303, Photo by Henry DiRocco/SCR; p. 304, Mabel Cainzos/yllana.com; p. 305, Karl Hugh/© Utah Shakespearean Festival; p. 307, © Paul Kennedy; p. 308, Courtesy Maria Bonilla, University of Costa Rica; p. 309T, © Geraint Lewis; p. 309B, Photo by Robert Cohen; p. 310, © Geraint Lewis (2); p. 311, m Nick Burchell, Courtesy of the Druid Theatre Company; p. 312, © Richard Termine; p. 314, © Ken Reynolds.

**Chapter 11** Page 316, © Geraint Lewis; p. 319, © István Biró, Courtesy of the Hungarian Theatre of Cluj; p. 320, m Reuters/Corbís; p. 321, © Geraint Lewis; p. 322, ©Laurencine Lot/Photo Lot; p. 323, © Paul Kolnik; p. 327, Photo by Robert Cohen.

# Brief Bibliography

The following brief bibliography lists selected sources for further research, with an emphasis on recent works. For a fuller bibliography, go to the Online Learning Center at www.mhhe.com/cohen9e.

## Broad Surveys of Drama and Theatre

Auslander, Philip. *From Acting to Performance.* New York: Routledge, 1997.

Banham, Martin, ed. *The Cambridge Guide to Theatre.* Cambridge: Cambridge University Press, 1995.

Beckerman, Bernard. *Dynamics of Drama: Theory and Method of Analysis.* New York: Knopf, 1970.

Bentley, Eric. *The Life of the Drama.* New York. Atheneum, 1964.

Boardman, Gerald, and Thomas S. Hischak. *The Oxford Companion to American Theatre.* Oxford University Press, 2004. Brockett, Oscar G. *History of the Theatre.* 9th edition. Boston: Allyn & Bacon, 2003.

Esslin, Martin. *An Anatomy of Drama.* New York: Hill & Wang, 1976.

Kennedy, Dennis. *The Oxford Encyclopedia of Theatre and Performance.* Oxford: Oxford University Press, 2003.

Pavis, Patrice. *Dictionary of the Theatre: Terms, Concepts, and Analysis.* Toronto: University of Toronto Press, 1998.

Pottlitzer, Joanne. *Hispanic Theater* in the United States and Puerto Rico. New York: Ford Foundation, 1988.

Sanders, Leslie C. *The Development of Black Theatre in America.* Baton Rouge: Louisiana State University Press, 1998. Styan, J. L. Drama, Stage and Audience. Cambridge: Cambridge University Press, 1960.

## Specialized Studies

### The Ancients

Ashby, Clifford. *Classical Greek Theatre:* New Views of *an Old Subject.* Iowa City: University of Iowa Press, 1999.

Beacham, Richard C. *The Roman Theatre and Its Audience.* Cambridge, MA: Harvard University Press, 1992.

Rehm, Rush. *The Play of Space: Spatial Transformation in Greek Tragedy.* Princeton, NJ: Princeton University Press, 2002.

———. *Radical Theatre: Greek Tragedy and the Modern World.* London: Duckworth, 2003.

Taplin, Oliver. Greek Tragedy in Action. London: Routledge, 1985.

———. *The Stagecraft of Aeschylus.* Oxford: Clarendon Press, 1977.

Wiles, David. *Greek Theatre Performance.* Cambridge: Cambridge University Press, 2000.

Zimmerman, Bernhard. Greek Tragedy: An Introduction. Translated by Thomas Marier. Baltimore: Johns Hopkins University Press, 1991.

### The Middle Ages

Chambers, E. K. *The Medieval Stage.* 2 vols. Oxford: Clarendon Press, 1903.

Clopper, Lawrence M. Drama, Play and Game: *English Festive Culture in the Medieval and Early Modern Period.* Chicago: University of Chicago Press, 2001.

Gusick, Barbara L, and Edelgard E. DuBruck. *New Approaches to European Theatre of the Middle Ages.* New York: Peter Lang, 2004.

Ogden, Dunbar H. *The Staging of Drama in the Medieval Church.* Newark: University of Delaware Press, 2002.

### The Renaissance

Bloom, Harold. Shakespeare: *The Invention of the Human.* New York: Riverhead Books, 1998.

Chambers, E. K. *The Elizabethan Stage.* 4 vols. London: Oxford University Press, 1923.

Kiernan, Pauline. *Staging Shakespeare in the New Globe.* NewYork: St. Martin's Press, 1999.

Mann, David. *The Elizabethan Player.* New York: Routledge, 1991.

Worthen, W. B. *Shakespeare and the Force of Modern Performance.* Cambridge: Cambridge University Press, 2003.

### Asian Theatre

Brandon, James R., ed. *Nō and Kyōgen in the Contemporary World.* Honolulu: University of Hawai'i Press, 1997.

Gunji, Masakatsu. *Kabuki.* Tokyo: Kodansha International, 1988.

Richmond, Farley P., Darius L. Swann, and Phillip B. Zarilli, eds. *Indian Theatre: Traditions of Performance.* Honolulu: University of Hawai'i Press, 1990.

Van Erven, Eugène. *The Playful Revolution: Theatre and Liberation in Asia.* Bloomington: Indiana University Press, 1992.

Wang-ngai, Siu, with Peter Lovrick. *Chinese Opera.* Vancouver: University of British Columbia Press, 1997.

### Royal Theatre

Holland, Peter. *The Ornament of Action: Text and Performance in Restoration Comedy.* New York: Cambridge University Press, 1979.

Lawrenson, T. E. *The French Stage in the XVIIth Century.* Manchester, England: Manchester University Press, 1957.

McBride, Robert. *Aspects of 17th Century French Drama and Thought.* Totowa, NJ: Rowman & Littlefield, 1980.

## Modern and Postmodern Theatre

Artaud, Antonin. *The Theatre and Its Double.* Translated by Mary C. Richards. New York: Grove Press, 1958.

Bigsby, C. W. E. *A Critical Introduction to Twentieth-Century American Drama.* 3 vols. Cambridge: Cambridge University Press, 1985.

Birringer, Johannes H. *Theatre, Theory, Postmodernism.* Bloomington: Indiana University Press, 1991.

Brecht, Bertolt. *Brecht on Theatre.* Translated by John Willett. New York: Hill & Wang, 1965.

Brook, Peter. *The Empty Space.* New York: Atheneum, 1968.
Esslin, Martin. *Brecht: The Man and His Work.* New York: Doubleday, 1960.

. *The Theatre of the Absurd.* Rev, ed. New York: Doubleday, 1969.

Majumdar, Ramendu, and Mofidul Hoque, eds. *The World of Theatre: 2008 Edition.* Dhaka, Bangladesh: Bangladesh Centre of ITI, 2008.

Marranca, Bonnie, and Gautam Dasgupta, eds. *Interculturalism and Performance.* New York: PAJ Publications, 1991.

Natalle, Elizabeth J. *Feminist Theatre: A Study in Persuasion.* Metuchen, NJ: Scarecrow Press, 1985.

Shaw, George Bernard. *The Quintessence of Ibsenism.* London: Constable, 1913.

## Music Theatre

Everett, William A., and Paul R. Laird. *The Cambridge Companion to the Musical.* Cambridge: Cambridge University Press, 2002.

Hischack, Thomas S. *Boy Loses Girl: Broadway's Librettists.* Lanham, MD: Scarecrow Press, 2002.

Most, Andrea. Making Americans: *Jews and the Broadway Musical.* Cambridge, MA: Harvard University Press, 2004.

## Practical Theatre Arts

Aronson, Arnold. *American Set Design.* New York: Theatre Communications Group, 1985.

Benedetti, Jean. *Stanislavsky.* London: Methuen, 1988.

Carnicke, Sharon Marie. *Stanislavsky in Focus.* Amsterdam: Harwood Press, 1998.

Chaikin, Joseph. *The Presence of the Actor.* New York: Atheneum, 1972.

Cohen, Robert. *Acting Power.* Palo Alto, CA: Mayfield, 1978.

Izenour, George. *Theatre Design.* 2d ed. New Haven, CT: Yale University Press, 1996.

Pecktal, Lynn. *Costume Design.* New York: Back Stage Books, 1993.

Reid, Francis, *Designing for the Theatre.* New York: Routledge, 1996.

. *The Stage Lighting Handbook.* Sth ed. New York: Routledge, 1996.

Roach, Joseph R. *The Player's Passion: Studies in the Science of Acting.* Newark: University of Delaware Press, 1985.

Sofer, Andrew. *The Stage Life of Props.* Ann Arbor: University of Michigan Press, 2003.

Stanislavski, Konstantin. *An Actor's Work.* Translated by Jean Benedetti. London: Routledge, 2008.

Svoboda, Joseph, *The Secret of Theatrical Space.* New York: Applause Theatre Books, 1993.

Walne, Graham, ed. *Effects for the Theatre.* New York: Drama Book Publishers, 1995.

# Index

Dean, James, 71, 77
*Dearest Enemy* (Rodgers & Hart), 250
*Death of a Salesman* (Miller), 24-25, *25*, 35, 77, 89, 267, 300
Delacorte Theatre (New York), 69, 166
Dembélé, Habib, *293*
Demodocos company, *14*
demonstration, 129
Dench, Judi, *91*
Denis, Maurice, 228
Dennehy, Brian, *25*, 305
denouement, 36, G-3. *See also* plot
*The Deputy*, 265
*Le Dernier Caravansérnil (The Last Carnival)* (Mnouchkine), *278*
dervishes, 197
design, 11, 135-138
    digital technologies, 185-186
    and directors, 108, 109, 120-121, 136, 152
    goals of, 137-138
    photo essay, 108-109
    process, 136-137
    projection, 181-183, *181, 182,* 240
    sound, 29-30, *112,* 147, 177-181, *177*
    special effects, 183-184
    technical production, 186-187, 190-191
    *See also* costume; lighting; makeup; scenery; theatre architecture
*Desire under the Elms* (O'Neill), 300
deus ex machina, G-3
dialectics, 241, 242
dialogue, G-3. *See also* language; playwrights/playwriting; *specific plays*
Dickens, Charles, 291, 303
diction, 29, G-3. *See also* language
didactic drama, 52, 156, 240, G-3. *See also* Brechtian theatre
Diderot, Denis, 14, 71
differently-abled people, 279
digital technologies, 185-186
dimmers, G-3
dimming out, G-3
*Dinner at Eight,* 168
dinner theatre, 306
*Dinner with Friends* (Margulies), 326
Dionysia, 2, 4, 52, 200, 202-203, G-3
Dionysian impluse, 264-265, G-3
Dionysius, 200, 213, G-3
Diphilos, 193
direct address, G-3. *See also* soliloquies
directors/directing, 11, 93-107, 120-133
    actor-coaching, 127-129
    and blocking, 109, 125-126
    and casting, 121-124
    conception phase, 102-103, 105-107, 108, 120
    and convention, 32
    coordination, 131-132
    and costume, 167
    and design, 108, 109, 120-121, 136, 152
    and dramaturgs, 325
    Eastern Europe, 105, 126, 313
    and first reading, 109
    history, 94-97

and lighting, 160
musical theatre, 252-253
pacing, 129-131
and performance, 132
photo essay, 98-100
play selection, 101-102
and playwrights, 41, 94
and producers, 97, 101
and realism, 95
and rehearsal, 88-89
and sound design, 180
staging, 125-127
symbolist theatre, 229
and technical production, 186
training, 132-133
women, 271
*Dirty Linen* (Stoppard), 47
*Dirty Rotten Scoundrels* (Yazbek), 258
discipline, 87, 96-97
discovery, G-3
Disney Corporation, 257-258, 296-297
*The Distance from Here* (LaBute), 59, 60, 285
*Distracted* (Loomer), 183
dithyramb, 139, 172, 200, 202, G-3
divertissement, G-3
Dizzia, Maria, *44*
documentary drama, 26, G-3
Dodd, Jon, 176 Dodin, Lev, 139, 314 doggerel, G-3
Dogon ritual (Mali), *196,* 199
*A Doll's House* (Ibsen), 124, 224, *225*
domestic tragedy, G-3
*Don Giovanni* (Mozart), 99
Donmar Warehouse (London), 311
Donmar Warehouse Theatre (London), 223
Doran, Gregory, 84
Dostoevsky, Fyodor, 145
doubling, G-3-4
*Doubt* (Shanley), 169, 300
Dowling, Eddie, 181-182
downstage, G-4
Doyle, Richard, *27*
*Dr. Faustus* (Mamet), 55
*Dracula, the Musical,* 169
drama, G-4, G-10
dramatic criticism, 317-327
    and antirealism, 239-240
    and dramaturgy, 37
    inclusiveness of, 325-327
    and pacing, 129
    perspectives of, 318-322
    professional, 323-324
    Royal theatre, 210
dramatis personae, 201
dramaturgs, 318, 319, 324-325, G-4
    dramaturgy, 28-37
    characters, 28-29
    climax, 36 conflict, 34-36
    conventions, 30-32
    defined, G-4
    denouement, 36
    diction, 29

exposition, 33-34, 37
music, 29-30
and playwriting process, 53-54
plot, 28, 33-36
and postmodernism, 54
postplay, 36-37
preplay, 32-33
spectacle, 30
temporal structure, 32
theme, 29
*See also* dramaturgs; *specific elements*
drapers, *110,* 187, 190
drapery, 144-145, G-4
*A Dream Play* (Strindberg), 229, 236
dream states, 31
*Dreamgirls,* 256
Dresher, Paul, 184
dress rehearsal, *116, 118,* 131, G-4
dressers, *116, 118,* 190
*Drinking in America* (Bogosian), 291
*Driving Miss Daisy* (Uhry), *226*
drops, 141, G-4
*The Drowsy Chaperone,* 267
Druid Theatre (Dublin), 311
Druid Theatre (Galway), 312
*Drunk Enough to Say I Love You* (Churchill), 188
Du Liniang, *215*
Du Prez, John, 257
*DuBarry was a Lady* (Porter), 249
Duke Theatre (New York), 271
Dunagan, Deanna, *301*
Duncan, Lindsay, *157*
Dungate, Ron, 270
Duphly, Jacques, 112
Durang, Christopher, 282
Durante, Jimmy, 251
duration, 22
Dürrenmatt, Friedrich, 238
Duse, Eleanora, 276
*Dutchman* (Baraka), 272-273
dyers, 187

*East of Eden,* 77
Eastern Europe, 105, 126, 139, 313-315
*Eastern Standard* (Greenberg), 160
Easton, Richard, *268*
Ebb, Fred, 98-99
economy, 51-52
Edgar, David, 277
*The Edge,* 298
Edinburgh International Festival (Scotland), 54, 128, 225, 287
Edson, Margaret, 48, 50, 271, 304, 326
Egoyan, Atom, 73
Egypt. *See* ancient Egypt
*Eli Joe* (Beckett), 73
Ehle, Jennifer, *166*
Einstein, Albert, 222
Elder, Lonne, 111, 273
Eldridge, David, 188
*Electra* (Euripides), 38, *85*
electricians, 190
Eliot, T. S., 256
*Elisabeth* (Kunze & Levay), 257